Napoleon at War

Napoleon Bonaparte

Napoleon at War
The Military Career of Napoleon Bonaparte
from Toulon to Waterloo

Montgomery B. Gibbs

Napoleon at War
The Military Career of Napoleon Bonaparte from Toulon to Waterloo
by Montgomery B. Gibbs

First published under the title
Military Career of Napoleon the Great

Leonaur is an imprint of Oakpast Ltd
Copyright in this form © 2012 Oakpast Ltd

ISBN: 978-1-78282-050-5 (hardcover)
ISBN: 978-1-78282-051-2 (softcover)

http://www.leonaur.com

Publisher's Notes

The views expressed in this book are not necessarily those of the publisher.

Contents

Preface	9
Boyhood Days and Early Career	13
Bonaparte's Campaign in Italy, 1796-7	39
Expedition to Egypt	88
Passage of the Alps, and Battle of Marengo	114
Ulm and Austerlitz	140
The Battle of Jena	168
The Battle of Eylau	182
Friedland and Peace of Tilsit	191
War With Spain	200
War With Austria, 1809	216
The Battle of Wagram	227
Campaign of Russia	240
The Campaign of 1813	273
The Invasion of France	292
Exile To Elba	320
The Hundred Days. Waterloo	340
Conclusion	380

To
My Friend
John L. Stoddard
This Volume is
Affectionately
Dedicated.

He fought a thousand glorious wars,
And more than half the world was his;
And somewhere, now, in yonder stars,
Can tell, mayhap, what greatness is.
—Thackeray

Preface

As the closing chapters of this volume were being written, a "Napoleonic wave" seemed to be passing over the country, an echo, no doubt, of the furore which Napoleon's name has excited in France during the past three years. One writer wittily says:

Where'er I turn, I'm forced to learn,
Some detail of his life,
I read about his sword and hats,
And how he beat his wife.

It seems but fair, therefore, for the author of this volume to declare that the revival of interest in the career of the man who for fifteen years had been the glory of France, has in no way caused the hasty writing, or publication, of this anecdotal military history. It is the result of years of study, and represents, not only a careful reading of those authorities which all must have access to who would write intelligently of the subject, but also of the more recent volumes which have appeared from time to time, each having something new to reveal concerning the seemingly inexhaustible fund of information pertaining to son of a poor Corsican gentleman, who as his greatest biographer has said of him, "played in the world the parts of Alexander, Hannibal, Cæsar and Charlemagne."

There has never been a time, during the last fifty years at least, when the public was not eager to learn something new concerning the wonderful career of the man who once held all Europe prisoner in the folds of the French flag. The world regards Napoleon Bonaparte as a *military genius* at least, whatever it may think of the political or social side of his life, and its relation to France. The writer does not believe that they are inseparably connected, and in offering this work it is his desire to better acquaint the admirers, as well as the enemies of the "Little Corporal," with his military career, not technically, but to picture him as his marshals, generals and soldiers knew him on the battlefield and around the campfire.

Many of these famous marshals and generals, who shared day by day all the glories and perils of their chief, and who vied with him in their activity and daring, have lately given to the world their "Memoirs," published many years after their death, for obvious reasons. From them one gets a much clearer insight into the true characteristics of their heroic leader. Being men of slight education their writings are confined largely to the gossip of the campaigns in which they were active participants, and in reading them one is often tempted to believe that Napoleon was in command of both belligerent armies, so accurately did this giant among warriors forecast the movements of the enemy on the battlefield; and after victory had favoured his bold strokes, finding himself in a position to reshape, at will, the map of Europe; for he conducted his campaigns with a degree of skill which, it is conceded by all military authorities, has never been excelled.

No man ever understood how to excite emulation, by distributing praise or blame, as did Napoleon. Chaboulon well says that the ascendancy possessed by the emperor over the minds and courage of the soldiery was truly incomprehensible. A word, a gesture, was sufficient to inspire them with enthusiasm, and make them face the most terrible ordeals. If ordered to rush to a point, although the extreme danger of the manoeuvre might at first strike the good sense of the soldiers, they immediately reflected that their general would not have issued such a command without a motive, or have exposed them wantonly. "He knows what he is about," they would say, and immediately rush on to death, uttering shouts of "Long live the emperor!"

No attempt is here made to give a history of France from the time Bonaparte first made his entrance into the drama of which he was so soon to be the leading actor. The successive periods of the Revolution, the Directory, the Consulate and the Empire are only introduced when found necessary to explain the rapidly advancing steps of this wonderful character in history, the worshiped idol of an entire nation, that his military career may be the better understood; hence it has been thought advisable to refer briefly, at times, to the relations of France with other countries, and the cause of his spending, during the ten years of his reign as emperor, exactly fifty-four days less in camp, and under the enemy's fire, so to speak, than he did in his royal residences!

This, then, is the story of the man who personally commanded in 600 skirmishes, and 85 pitched battles, resigning at last his leadership on the field of Waterloo, a victim of treachery and incompetency exceeding even his own well-grounded fears; but even after these years of constant warfare and conquest, after maintaining huge armies in almost all parts of the world, he left France the richest nation in the universe, and in possession of a larger amount of specie than the rest of Europe; and notwithstanding the fact that in 1796, when he was given command of the Army of Italy, he found his government not only incapable of paying its ragged and weary troops, but unable, even, to feed them!

M. B. G.

Chicago, Ill. December 31, 1894.

An Account of the Remarkable Campaigns of
the "Man of Destiny"

1
Boyhood Days and Early Career

When Napoleon was a pupil of the Military School at Brienne, as a pensioner of the king, he wrote to his mother in Corsica:

"With Homer in my pocket, and my sword by my side, I hope to carve my way through the world!"

Bonaparte was then a youth of but ten years of age. For nearly thirty-five years from this time his life was a series of achievements, the success of which has rarely been equalled,—from a military standpoint, never.

His infancy was only different from that of most other boys in that he showed great animation of temper, and an impatience of inactivity, by which children of quick perception and lively sensibility are usually distinguished.

It has been said that the name "Napoleon" was given to the newborn infant of Madame Bonaparte, according to a common custom among Catholics, of naming the child after the saint on whose festival it is baptized, and that the 16th of August, the day of young Bonaparte's baptism, was the festival of St. Napoleon, (Napoleone), a saint then peculiar to Corsica.

On the confirmation of young Bonaparte at the Paris Military School the archbishop who officiated, manifesting some astonishment at the name "Napoleon," said he did not know of any such saint, and that there was no such name in the calendar.

"That should be no rule," replied Napoleon quickly, "since there are an immense number of saints, but only three hundred and sixty-five days!"

While an exile at St. Helena Napoleon said to O'Meara, his surgeon, "Saint Napoleon ought to be much obliged to me, and place all his credit in the other world to my account. The poor devil! No one knew him once, he had not even a day in the calendar. I procured him one, and persuaded the pope to assign to him the 15th of August, my birthday."

It has frequently been said of Napoleon that he was born to command. From his earliest youth he chose arms for his profession, and in every study likely to be of service to the future soldier he distinguished himself above his contemporaries. With the mathematical tutors he was always a great favourite. His ardour for the abstract sciences amounted to a passion, and was combined with a singular aptitude for applying them to the purposes of war, while his attention to pursuits so interesting in themselves was stimulated by his natural ambition and desire of distinction in this science.

Even before Napoleon began his systematic training for a military career, and while but nine years of age, he developed a fondness for mimic warfare that frequently astonished his older companions, many of whom were his superiors both in strength and endurance; but none of whom were able to cope with him in strategy, or whose resources, when put to test, were so versatile. At Ajaccio, the place of his birth, the city boys were often engaged in personal encounters with the youths from the country. At first these contests were but the natural outcome of a jealousy which is so often found to exist between city and country boys, who meet upon the same playground. At length this feeling of rivalry became more bitter, and on some occasions, especially on holidays, when the country lads were in the habit of "coming to town," as many as a score of them were often to be found on each side engaged in pitched battles with sticks and stones.

The country youths had for a time been eminently successful in these encounters, and were disposed to *braggadocio* manners. They went about the streets with their heads lifted high, and as a result, the older folks soon began to take an interest in the outcome of the assaults. On several occasions, too, the parents of the youths were interested spectators of the contests, and although the flying missiles were extremely likely to injure the onlooker, no suggestion of putting an end to the battles was ever proposed by the older heads.

Young Bonaparte was much chagrined at these defeats, and sought to find reasons for them. When not an active participant he would often withdraw to some secluded spot, and there watch the movements of either side, hoping, no doubt, to detect some flaw in their manner of fighting that he might take advantage of it at a later date, and thus recover the good name of his city comrades. It could not be

Bonaparte at the Siege of Toulon

in numbers that defeat lay for they were almost always equally divided, and besides, there seemed to be an unwritten law between them that "Man against man" must in common honour be observed.

Finally Bonaparte hastily gathered about him a few of his chosen friends, in whom he had the most confidence, and laid before them a plan, which, if followed, he assured them would not only humiliate their hated rivals, but would also result in their complete overthrow. With shouts of approval his plan was at once declared "a tip-top one" and his lieutenants proceeded to carry out his orders. He directed that a certain number of boys be formed into a company, whose duty it should be to supply ammunition. A *"defi"* was then sent to the conquerors who promptly replied that they had nothing to fear. It soon became noised about among the inhabitants of Ajaccio that a "final contest" was to be fought on a certain day, and hours before the time set, hundreds of spectators were on hand to witness the contest which was destined to re-establish the prestige of the city boys. At length the fated hour arrived and the country boys made their appearance on the battlefield, armed with short sticks,—their usual weapons,—and full of confidence. For a short time Napoleon and his followers maintained their position against these sturdy warriors, although, as heretofore, they found themselves overmatched by mere force of brute strength.

Napoleon now gave the signal agreed upon to retreat. Slowly his forces gave way, endeavouring at the same time to keep up an appearance of fighting to the best of their ability. To reassure the country chaps that they were overpowering their contestants purely on their fighting merits, an occasional rally was ordered by the city leader; but this show of resistance was always followed by him with another retreat more pronounced than that which preceded it. At length Napoleon found himself with his followers on the shore of the sandy beach and the country lads believed themselves conquerors once more. "Victory!" "Victory!" they cried, as they came rushing up, expecting a complete surrender. In their haste to make a final assault the pursuers had not noticed that each of the city boys had laid down his stick and had his hand upon the ground. In it was grasped tightly a stone which was still partially covered by the sands of the beach.

"Ready! Fire!" shouted Napoleon, and immediately the air was filled with swift-flying stones, each of which was followed by a second and that by a third missile, all landing with terrific force on the unprotected heads and shoulders of the over-confident country lads.

They had cried victory before the battle was won.

In another moment they found themselves disorganized and the victims of shouts of derision that came from the spectators who had followed the retreating forces to see the final outcome of the battle. Sticks at a distance of 20 or 30 feet were no match for the new weapons of the city lads, and reluctantly they turned and fled, having themselves no stones to throw.

Now it was Napoleon's forces who were the pursuers; but the ranks of the sturdy country lads were sadly depleted and their resistance was brief.

That night Napoleon was a hero in Ajaccio. With the older folks gathered about him he told and retold how he and his followers had spent the preceding night burying stones in the sand, that they might have them for weapons on the morrow when Napoleon's plan, which included retreat to this point on the beach, might be turned into the victory they had been assured would follow their arrival there.

The student of Napoleon's military campaigns will detect in this manoeuvre a striking similarity to more sanguine contests on the battlefield where human lives were at stake.

Throughout his life Napoleon's stronghold was strategy, and never was it more clearly illustrated than in this harmless contest of his youth, and to which he often recurred when passing an hour or two with his marshals and generals while preparing for contests on which the fate of France depended.

Up to a few years ago,—it may to this present time,—an interesting relic of Napoleon's childhood was preserved in his native place. It was a small brass cannon, weighing about thirty pounds, and it is said he would leave all other amusements for the pleasure of firing off this dangerous plaything. His favourite retreat was a solitary summer house, among the rocks on the sea shore, about a mile from Ajaccio, where his mother's brother had a villa. The place is now in ruins; it afterwards came to be known as "Napoleon's Grotto." Nothing interested him more during these early years, than to hear his mother tell the story of her exciting hardships as she fled from one part of the island to another before the conquering French. Thus, unconsciously, she no doubt nurtured in her second son that warlike spirit which was manifested in him to such a marked degree in after years.

During the time Napoleon attended school, young men were taught that the only fame worth striving for was that won by military achievements. Napoleon's parents, herefore, exerted all the influence they could command to gain scholarships for the education of their two oldest sons,—Joseph and Napoleon. Their prayers were at last granted owing to the invaluable aid of Monsieur de Marboeuf, Bishop of Autun and nephew of the governor of Corsica. Joseph was to take orders and to be placed in the college of Autun; Napoleon, intended for the navy, was to go to the school at Brienne, having previously gone through a course at Autun so as to learn sufficient French to be able to follow the lectures. They started on this journey, which was to have so much influence on their future lives, on December 15, 1778. After a halt at Florence to procure papers showing the ancient nobility of the Bonaparte family, and which were necessary to Napoleon before entering the school at Brienne, they proceeded to Autun. The herald declared that, "Young Napoleon Bonaparte possessed the nobility necessary for admission into the ranks of the gentlemen who are educated by His Majesty in the royal schools." Charles Bonaparte had been able to satisfy the authorities that his patent of nobility was authentic and privileged him to sign his name "de Bonaparte."

Napoleon arrived at Brienne, on the 23rd of April, 1779, having in three months at Autun "learned sufficient French to enable him to converse easily and to write small essays and translations."

At Brienne Bourrienne, whose friendship for him commenced thus early, describes him as follows:

> Bonaparte was noticeable at Brienne for his Italian complexion, the keenness of his look, and the tone of his conversation with masters and comrades. There was almost always a dash of bitterness in what he said. He had very little of the disposition that leads to attachments; which I can only attribute to the misfortunes of his family ever since his birth and the impression that the conquest of his country had made on his early years.

The fact that he was a brave, manly boy, all biographers agree in recording. His poverty subjected him to mortification among his comrades, who also ridiculed him on account of his country and twitted him with the obsolete saint whose name he bore. These taunts he allowed himself to settle with the offenders openly and never descended to report them to his tutors. On one occasion, with Bourrienne, who became his private secretary in later years, he suffered several days' imprisonment rather than reveal the names of the real offenders who had neglected their duties.

Napoleon's promptitude of reply was displayed on many occasions during his attendance at this school. One day as he was undergoing an examination by a general officer, he answered all the questions proposed with so much precision, and accompanied by such a depth of penetration, that the general, the professors and the students, were astonished. At length, in order to bring the interrogatories to a close, Napoleon was asked the following question:

"What line of conduct would you adopt in case you were besieged in a fortified place and was destitute of provisions?"

"So long as there were any in the camp of the enemy, I should never be at a great loss for a supply," came the answer quickly, amid the applause of the pupils.

One of the most delightful winters of Napoleon's early life was that of 1782, spent at this military school. He was just at that age when a boy most keenly enjoys new scenes and new excitements. It was the thirteenth winter of his life. He was older than most boys are at thirteen. His mind and his muscles were better developed. But, nevertheless, he was still a boy.

It happened that this winter was one of the coldest and most severe in the history of France, so memorable by the quantity of snow that fell and which accumulated upon the roads in great quantities. The snow came early and stayed late, and the students could find but little amusement without doors. Napoleon was the first to suggest that it be used to develop their practical knowledge, and at the same time to beguile the weary hours they would otherwise be compelled to spend within doors. He said one day:

"Let us divide into two hostile forces and battle, while the snow lasts, for the possession of the play ground."

The proposition was received with favour and was unanimously accepted. By common consent Napoleon, whose authority no one questioned, was chosen to command the projected mimic war, the school being divided into two equal armies. Extensive fortifications of snow were at once erected by busy hands who then armed themselves for the coming fray. So complete were the arrangements that even the inhabitants of the village gave up all other pursuits to witness the battles. For fifteen days, while the snow lasted, they built forts and counter-forts, dug trenches, constructed bastions and made or met sallies with snowball battles, neglecting for the nonce their less interesting studies.

It is related that Napoleon was greatly enraged one day to find that the other side had tried to get the best of his men by putting a round stone into each snowball, but when someone advised him to imitate the tactics of the foe he indignantly refused, saying that he would win without doing so or be beaten.

The fort of the enemy was at last captured after Napoleon had gone through the formalities of a siege, in which he displayed much of the quickness of combination for which he was noted on the battlefield in after years. His soldierly methods electrified his fellow students and astonished the professors as well. Bourrienne says:

> This little sham war was carried on for the space of a fortnight, and did not cease until a quantity of gravel and small stones having got mixed with the snow of which we made our bullets, many of the combatants, besiegers as well as besieged, were seriously wounded. I well remember that I was one of the worst sufferers from this sort of grape-shot fire.

In 1783 Bonaparte, on the recommendation of the inspector of the twelve military schools, was sent from Brienne to the Royal Military School at Paris to have his education completed in the general school,—an extraordinary compliment to the genius and proficiency of a boy of fifteen. He was one of three to receive that honour, a tribute paid to the precocity of his extraordinary mathematical talent, and the steadiness of his application. The entry made at that time in the military records says:

> Monsieur de Bonaparte (Napoleon) born August 15th, 1769; in height four feet, ten inches, ten lines; of good constitution, health excellent, character mild, honest and grateful; conduct exemplary; has distinguished himself by application to mathematics; understands history and geography tolerably well; is indifferently skilled in merely ornamental studies, as well as in Latin; would make an excellent sailor; deserves to be passed to the Military School at Paris.

The young student did not arrive in Paris in the guise of the future conqueror of the world. On the contrary, he looked like a "newcomer;" he gaped at everything he saw, and gazed about in a dazed sort of way. As a Corsican compatriot who met him as he was getting out of the coach has said:

> His appearance was that of a youth whom any scoundrel would try to rob after seeing him, if indeed he had anything worth taking!

However, it should not be forgotten that he was but a youth of fifteen, felt his poverty keenly, and was about to enter into the noise and extravagant life of the rich students of this royal military school. As he himself said in 1811:

> All these cares spoiled my early years; they influenced my temper and made me grave before my time.

At the Paris school Napoleon laboured hard, as he had done at Brienne for five years, being especially proficient, as before, in mathematics. Everything was very luxurious here, and Bonaparte complained in a memorial, which he presented to the superintendent of the establishment, that the mode of life was too expensive and delicate for "poor gentlemen" and could not properly prepare them either for returning to their "modest homes," or for the hardships they would encounter in war. He proposed that instead of a regular dinner of two courses daily, the students should have ammunition bread and soldiers' rations, and be compelled to mend and clean their own stockings and shoes. "If I were king of France," he said one day to a companion, "I would change this state of things very quickly!" This memorial is said to have done him no service, for every third boy that looked on him was a duke from his cradle, while the young Corsican was still a "pensioner of the king;" but the schools established by him after he became emperor were on that severe plan. Meneval, his second private secretary, says:

"Although believing in the necessity of show and magnificence in public life, Napoleon remained true to these principles, while lavishing wealth on his ministers and marshals: 'In your private life' said he, 'be economical and even parsimonious; in public be magnificent.'"

On being reproved one day by an uncle of the Duchess d'Abrantes for ingratitude as a "pensioner of the king," he broke out furiously with an expression of indignation. "Silence!" said the gentleman at whose table he was sitting; "It ill becomes you, who are educated by the king's bounty, to speak as you do."

"I am not educated at the *king's* expense," replied Bonaparte, his face flushed with rage, "but at the expense of the *nation!*"

Young Napoleon made but poor advancement in the German language while at this school, and by reason of it offended M. Bauer his tutor. One day, not being in his place, M. Bauer inquired where he was, and was told that he was attending his examination in the class of artillery.

"Oh! so he does learn something," said the professor ironically.

"Why, sire, he is the best mathematician in the school," was the reply.

"Ah, I have always heard it remarked and I have always believed, that none but a fool could learn mathematics!"

"It would be curious," said Napoleon, who related this anecdote when he was emperor, "to know whether M. Bauer lived long enough to ascertain my real character, and to enjoy the confirmation of his own judgment."

Napoleon had not been in the Military School of Paris a year,—during which time his father had died,—and had barely completed his sixteenth year, when he successfully passed the examination, in August 1785,—for a commission in a regiment of artillery.

On September 1st the decree was signed which assigned Bonaparte as Second-Lieutenant in the company of bombardiers of the regiment of La Fere garrisoned at Valence. At the time of the examination there were thirty-six vacant places. M. de Feralio, one of the professors of the military school charged with this examination, is said to have inscribed on the margin, opposite to the signature of Napoleon, the following

> A Corsican by character and by birth. If favoured by circumstances this young man will rise high.

This professor was very fond of his young pupil, and when at school is said to have occasionally supplied him with pocket money. After his death Napoleon granted a handsome pension to his widow.

Napoleon's corps was at Valence when he joined it. Arriving there he was an occasional frequenter of the drawing room of Madame du Colombier, and it is said he made love to her daughter; but when not so engaged, he was devoted to his military studies, and read frequently from the *Lives of Plutarch*, a volume of which he generally carried about him. He also occupied himself in writing a *History of Corsica* which, when completed, the Abbe Raynal and other friends praised very highly; but he was unable to find a publisher for it.

At Valence Napoleon found the officers of his regiment divided, as all the world then was, into two parties; the lovers of the French monarchy, and those who desired its overthrow. Napoleon openly sided with the latter. "Had I been a general," said he, in the evening of his life, "I might have adhered to the king; being a subaltern I joined the patriots."

In the beginning of 1792 Napoleon became captain of artillery, unattached, and happening to be in Paris, witnessed the lamentable scenes of the 20th of June, when the revolutionary mob stormed the Tuileries, and Louis XVI. and his family, after undergoing innumerable insults and degradations, with the utmost difficulty preserved their lives. As he was strolling about with Bourrienne he saw the mob, numbering between five and six thousand, ragged and ridiculously armed, coming from the outskirts and making for the Tuileries. "Let us follow these scoundrels," he said. They went with the crowd into the garden before the palace, and when the king appeared at one of the windows on the balcony, surrounded by revolutionists, and with the red cap of liberty, the emblem of the Jacobins, on his head, Napoleon could no longer suppress his contempt and indignation. "Poor driveller!" said he, loud enough to be heard by those near him; "how could he suffer this rabble to enter? If he had swept away five or six hundred with his cannon, *the rest would be running yet!*" Napoleon always abhorred anarchy. He said there was no remedy for mobs but grape-shot, and believed thoroughly in the theory of shooting first and listening to peace negotiations afterwards.

He was also a witness of the still more terrible 10th of August, in the same year, when the palace being once more invested, the National Guard assigned for its defence took part with the assailants. This time the royal family were obliged to take refuge in the National Assembly, and the brave Swiss Guards were massacred almost to a man.

Bonaparte was a firm friend of the Assembly, to the charge of a part of which, at least, these excesses must be laid; but the spectacle disgusted him. The yells, screams, and pikes with bloody heads upon them, formed a scene which he afterwards described as "hideous and revolting." But with what a different feeling of interest would he have looked on that infuriated populace, those still resisting though overpowered Swiss, and that burning palace, had any seer whispered to him: "Emperor that shall be, all this blood and massacre is but to prepare your future empire!"

He mingled little in society; but he saw much of the people and took sides irrevocably with the cause of the nation. At this time he was without employment and very poor, wandering idly about Paris, and living chiefly at cheap restaurants. As yet he had been but a spectator of the Revolution, destined to pave his own path to sovereign power; but it was not long before circumstances called him to play a part in this tragic drama which was then attracting the attention of the civilized world.

It was shortly after these stirring scenes in Paris, that Bonaparte visited his mother in Corsica, arriving there with his sister Eliza on September 17th, 1792. For the first time in thirteen years the family was reunited, and their joy would have been complete had their circumstances not been so sad. Their resources were diminishing day by day and the recovery of what was due them became constantly more difficult, owing to civil discords. The only fund upon which they could rely seems to have been Napoleon's pay as an artillery officer.

The following year, while Bonaparte was still enjoying the leave of absence from his regiment, an expedition arrived from France to deprive General Paoli, governor of Corsica, of his control, he having denounced the National Assembly as the enemy of France. Paoli endeavoured to enlist Napoleon in his cause; among other flatteries he patted him on the back and said: "You were cast in an antique mould; you are one of Plutarch's men. The whole world will talk of you," but the young Corsican was loyal to France, and was not to be deceived by either entreaties or flattery. He declared his belief that Corsica was too weak to maintain independence, that she must fall under the rule either of France or England, and that her interests would be best served by adhering to the former. Napoleon then tendered his sword to Salicetti, one of the Corsican deputies to the Convention, and was appointed provisionally to the command of a battalion of National Guards.

The first military service on which he was employed for his native country was the reduction of a small fortress, called the Torre di Capitello, near Ajaccio. He took it, but was soon besieged in it, and he and his garrison, after a gallant defence, and living for some time on horseflesh, were glad to evacuate the tower, and escape to the sea. Paoli was soon reinforced by England, and the Bonapartes were among those who were banished from the country. During this Corsican revolution the inhabitants were much divided as to the rights of England and France in the island. An officer in the French troops, who sided with England, was much scandalized at the position taken by the Bonapartes,—Joseph, Napoleon and Lucien. One day, in the hearing of Napoleon, the officer made use of some very harsh language towards them, and was especially bitter against Napoleon. At this a friend defended him with much warmth and finished by saying to the officer: "Sir, you are not worth a pair of Napoleon's old boots!"

In the year 1800, Napoleon then being First Consul of France, the officer who had defended him, and who had for some time followed his standard, and had been raised to distinction by him, happening to meet Bonaparte among a large party at dinner at the house of the First Consul's mother, was drawn aside before the company placed themselves at the table, and with his finger over his mouth, Napoleon said in a half-joking, half-serious manner: "My dear sir, not a word, I entreat you, about the old boots!"

As a result of the insurrection in Corsica Napoleon saw Ajaccio in ashes, and the home of his childhood pillaged and burned ere he took his departure. His mother and sisters took refuge first at Nice, and afterwards at Marseilles, where for some time they suffered all the inconveniences of poverty and exile. At that period nothing was more deplorable than Bonaparte's prospects; nothing more uncertain than the future. But he believed that fortune would not always abandon him. France was in the hands of men who acted largely from self-interest, and here he apparently saw a chance to carve his way to fame by getting in the vortex of the Revolution. It was probably on this occasion that he repeated the well-known words:

> In a revolution a soldier should never despair if he possesses courage and genius.

Napoleon now resolved to rejoin his regiment; he had chosen France for his country, and ever afterwards it was his home until exiled to St. Helena.

During the night of August 27th, 1793, Toulon was delivered to the English, and its subsequent siege and retaking was destined to be the first incident of importance which enabled Bonaparte to distinguish himself in the eyes of the French Government, and of the world at large. The head of Louis XVI had rolled from the block, and a month afterwards the Convention had declared war against England.

Early in September France was attacked on every side, and a third of her provinces had rebelled against the government established at Paris, which enforced its supremacy by a regime carried on under a Reign of Terror. Among the provinces in open insurrection were all those of the south. An army corps invested Lyons, while another, after subduing Marseilles, marched against Toulon, the great arsenal and seaport, and delivered by the Bourbons into the hands of England. Adjutant Cervoni was at once dispatched to Marseilles to ascertain if he could find in that town some artillery officer of distinction to whom might be intrusted the chief command of the siege batteries before Toulon.

While strolling through the streets Cervoni met with a captain of artillery who was, like himself, perambulating the thoroughfares. This captain was a Corsican and a compatriot; his name was Napoleon Bonaparte. He was covered with the dust of the road along which he had been walking; for he had just arrived from Avignon, whither he had escorted a convoy of ammunition, and was on his way to Nice. Cervoni thought that Bonaparte would be just the man to watch over the movements of the army before Toulon: he appeared very young,—he was only twenty-four years of age—but it was stated that a month before the Republican army was on the point of beating a retreat in front of Avignon when he, with two field-pieces and eighty men, bombarded the town in the rear so effectively that the inhabitants and federal troops were overcome with fright and, convinced that they had been betrayed, abandoned the place to the Republicans who entered victorious, thanks to the boldness and foresight of Captain Bonaparte.

Cervoni invited him to enter a *café*; Bonaparte accepted, and the two men had a chat over a bowl of punch. The young captain doffed his hat, so that his features were lighted up by the blue flame of the liquor; his complexion was sallow and his head large, measuring as it did twenty-three inches round. If the size of his skull was large, the space between the two cheek-bones was enormous. The hair grew low on his forehead; the well-arched brows disclosed large eyes, sharp as steel, cold, clear and piercing; the aquiline nose was of the most delicate shape, the lower lip strong and receding, while the chin and the jaws were as well developed as the skull.

After a conference Napoleon departed for Toulon where he was promoted to the rank of Brigadier-General of Artillery, with the command of the artillery during the siege. The arsenal was filled with military stores, and twenty-five English and Spanish battleships were then riding in the harbour to protect it. Three months had passed, during which time no apparent progress had been made towards the recapture of the town, and when Napoleon arrived he was invested with the command of the artillery train.

A strong fort commanded the harbour, and after a careful examination Napoleon said the only way to retake Toulon was to neglect the body of the town, carry "Little Gibraltar," and the city would surrender in two days. Napoleon's brother Lucien visited him about this time. They went together one morning to a place where a fruitless assault had been made, and two hundred Frenchmen were dead upon the ground. On beholding them Napoleon exclaimed: "If I had commanded here all these brave men would still be alive!" A moment later he added: "Learn from this example, young man, how indispensable and imperatively necessary it is for those to possess knowledge who aspire to the command of others."

Napoleon's own account of his experiences here is extremely interesting, and was thus related by him during his exile at St. Helena:

> I reported, as I had been ordered to do to General Cartaux, (a portrait painter of Paris) who was in charge of the revolutionary forces. He was a tall man, all covered with gilt decorations, and a type of the militia officer. I saw at once that he was utterly incompetent to the task that had been laid out for him. I said: 'I have been directed to assist, under your order, in the taking of Toulon.' He replied: 'We need no assistance in taking Toulon; but since they have sent you here you may enjoy yourself as best you can and see the siege.' Then he gave orders to have me treated with courtesy.
>
> Well, the next morning I went out with the general to look at the preparations for bombarding the stronghold. He called an *aide-de-camp* and asked in a business-like manner: 'Are the red-hot shot ready?' I was surprised, but said nothing. The subordinate replied: 'Oh, yes, the men have been busy all night heating them.' I was now more surprised than ever, but still kept silent. What followed would have made me believe they were trying to guy me if their manner had not been so serious. General Cartaux asked how they were going to get the red-hot shot over to the guns. That seemed to puzzle the *aide-de-camp*. The general himself didn't know what to do. After a great deal of speculation, and some swearing, he asked me what I would do under the circumstances. I said:
>
> 'You will find it an excellent idea to try the range of your guns with cold shot first. If the range isn't right the hot-shot will be of no service.'
>
> He laughed merrily and agreed with me. The order was given to try the range. The result was that the cold shot didn't carry more than a third of the distance. The bombarding of the fort was put off another day.
>
> Luckily Gasparin, the direct representative of the people with

plenary powers, came riding up that night, and I told him what I had seen and heard. He agreed that the man in command was incompetent, and put me in charge. You all know the rest. I began the attack on the outlet of Toulon and was successful. Gasparin consoled Cartaux by telling him that I was only a subordinate, and that all the glory would go to him anyhow.

During this siege of the "Little Gibraltar Castle" Bonaparte showed his extensive knowledge of mankind, and which enabled him to discover and attach to him those men whose talents were most distinguished, and most capable of rendering him service. Several who afterwards became marshals and generals under the empire, first made Napoleon's acquaintance at Toulon. Among these were Duroc and Junot. During one of the days of this long siege Napoleon, in passing one of the trenches, called for someone to write an order from his dictation, and in obedience to this request a young and handsome soldier stepped out of the ranks, and resting his paper on the breastwork, began to write as directed. Scarcely had he done so when a cannon ball fell at his feet and covered both commander and private with dirt. The soldier laughingly held up his paper and said: "Thank you, now I shall need no sand."

Napoleon was so pleased with his bravery, and ready wit, that he immediately promoted him. The name of this fortunate man was General Junot; he subsequently became Duke of Abrantes and was one of the most distinguished generals of the empire under Napoleon. An apparent total insensibility to fatigue was observed in the young Corsican officer at this time. He worked through daylight, and slept nights wrapped in a blanket under his guns till his batteries were ready to begin operations.

During the siege Paris was very restless, and after a few weeks had passed it became almost the sole topic of conversation at the capital; the newspapers contained innumerable suggestions for the ending of the siege, and hundreds of letters were addressed to the officers at Toulon, telling them how to drive the English from the shores of France. One day fifteen carriages arrived at Toulon containing sixty young men who had journeyed thither from the capital; they were gorgeously arrayed and asked to be presented to the commander-in-chief.

Bonaparte received the party courteously and asked what he could do for them. "Citizen Bonaparte," said the spokesman, "we come from Paris. The patriots there are indignant at your indecision and delay.

The soil of the Republic has been violated. She trembles to think that the insult still remains unavenged. She asks, 'Why is Toulon not yet taken? Why is the English fleet not yet destroyed?' In her indignation she has appealed to her brave sons. We have obeyed her summons and burn with impatience to fulfil her expectations. We are volunteer gunners from Paris. Furnish us with arms. Tomorrow we will march against the enemy!"

Early on the following day Napoleon conducted the "volunteers" to the seashore. During the night he had ordered a number of cannon placed in position and as he pointed to the black hull out at sea he said: "Sink that ship!"

At some distance from the shore lay an English frigate, upon whose deck were to be seen a formidable array of cannon, all pointed shorewards.

"But there is no shelter here!" said the volunteers in chorus. At this moment a broadside was fired by the gunners on the frigate and the brilliantly decorated patriots from the capital fled in every direction, amid the smiles of the commander-in-chief who at once gave orders for his own gunners to return the fire of the enemy.

Toulon was at last retaken on December 17th, the siege having lasted four months.

When Bonaparte at last raised the French emblem over the city, and as it floated with the breezes over a scene of desolation long remembered by those who witnessed it, he said to Dugommier: "Go to sleep; we have taken Toulon!"

It was here that Napoleon was first severely wounded. When his body was being prepared for burial at St. Helena there was found upon his left thigh so deep a scar that it was nearly possible to place one's finger in it. This had been caused by a bayonet thrust received during this engagement, and in consequence of which he nearly lost his leg. In addition to the wound he had a number of horses shot under him. Another of the dangers which he incurred was of a singular character. An artilleryman being shot at the gun which he was serving, while Napoleon was visiting a battery, the commander took up the dead man's rammer, and to give encouragement to the soldiers, charged the gun with his own hands. The gunner had been afflicted with a skin disease which Napoleon contracted from the weapon, and for a number of years afterward he suffered from its ravages.

Soon after the retaking of Toulon Bonaparte accompanied General Dugommier to Marseilles. Someone struck with his appearance asked the general *who that little bit of an officer was, and where he picked him up?*

"That officer's name," replied the general, "is Bonaparte: I picked him up at the siege of Toulon, to the successful termination of which he eminently contributed; and you will probably see, one day, *that this little bit of an officer* is a greater man than any of us!"

Napoleon was now rapidly rising in reputation. His science as an artillery officer and his valour had saved France from humiliation—taught her enemies to respect her—had suppressed the spirit of insurrection in the southern provinces, and had given the government of the Convention control of the whole army.

It has been said that Napoleon's fame first came to the knowledge of Barras, a member of the Directory, through a letter taken by his young *protegé* to Paris not long after this siege. It was a commendatory letter addressed to Carnot in which Barras thus expressed himself: "I send you a young man who has distinguished himself very much during the siege, and earnestly recommend you to advance him speedily: *If you do not, he will most assuredly advance himself!*"

Bonaparte's name was on the list of those whom the veteran Dugommier recommended for promotion, and he was accordingly confirmed in his provisional situation of chief of battalion and appointed to hold that rank in Italy. He therefore proceeded to join the headquarters of the French army then lying at Nice. Here he suggested a plan by which the Sardinians were driven from the Coe di Tendi. Saorgio, with all its stores, soon surrendered, and the French obtained possession of the maritime Alps, so that the difficulties of advancing into Italy were greatly diminished. Of these movements, however, Napoleon's superior officers reaped as yet the honour. While directing the means of attaining these successes Bonaparte acquired a complete acquaintance with that Alpine country in which he was shortly to obtain victories in his own name, not in that of others who were now rapidly acquiring reputation by acting on his timely suggestions.

One of his favourite methods of planning manoeuvres he originated at this time while studying his maps and plans of the Alpine country. He had so familiarized himself with the locality that no point of importance was unknown to him. With this data before him, Bonaparte would sit for hours, intent on studying the maps of the country, and upon which he had stuck pins, the heads of which he had covered with wax of various shades. One colour was used to designate the French, another the enemy, and by changing the location of the pins on the map he formed various intricate plans of attack and retreat that some years later were most valuable to him. This ingenious scheme is often used at the present day by large wholesale houses to designate the territory of their salesmen while travelling about the country.

While in Nice Napoleon was suddenly arrested and thrown into prison on an order sent from Paris by the Committee of Public Safety. He had been sent there with secret instructions from the government "to collect facts that would throw light upon the intentions of the Genoese government respecting coalition, etc.," and although he acquitted himself with all the care necessary to success, his excess of zeal came nearly ending fatally to him, for it was a time when it was safe to have secrets from no one. It was a time, too, when revolutionists owed it to themselves to arrest their predecessors, and as there had been a change in the government, Napoleon's secret journey was unknown to Salicetti and Albitte, who had succeeded Ricord.

Young Robespierre, who received the order of arrest, was much astounded at it. The document added that the prisoner was to be at once brought under a strong escort to Fort Carré near Antibes and there imprisoned and tried "for treason against the Republic." Robespierre asked Napoleon to come into his room, and showed him the document, which might mean death. Then he said: "You must not go away yet. I will put you under arrest, and then I will write to my brother, who has some influence with the committee. He may be able to get the order rescinded."

Napoleon refused to get agitated over his arrest. Junot, Sebastiani and Marmont, his young *aides-de-camp*, had formed a plan of escape and advised him to choke the guard, steal a small boat, and flee to the Corsican coast, where he could hide himself in the mountains. Bonaparte, knowing his innocence, refused to try to escape, but addressed the following letter to Junot, *et al*:

> I fully recognize your friendship, my dear Junot, in the proposition you make me: you have long known the sincerity of mine for you, and I hope that you trust in it. Men may be unjust towards me, my dear Junot, but for me my innocence is sufficient. My conscience is the tribunal before which I summon my conduct. This conscience is calm when I question it. Do nothing, therefore; all friendly greetings.   Bonaparte.
> *Under arrest at Fort Carré, Antibes.*

It was only when told that he was dismissed from the army, and declared unworthy of public confidence, that he addressed a spirited letter to Albitte and Salicetti, the committee that ordered his arrest, and which caused them to reconsider their resolution.

In his dramatic communication to this committee, Bonaparte said in part:

> You have suspended me from my functions, arrested and declared me suspected. Therein you have branded me without judging,—or rather judged without hearing. . . . . Hear me; destroy the oppression that environs me, and restore me in the estimation of patriotic men. An hour after, if villains desire my life, I shall esteem it but little; I have despised it often.

In a few days the influence of the great Robespierre had made itself felt; a message was consequently received rescinding the order and Napoleon was honourably discharged from custody. His papers had been examined, and as nothing was found in them to implicate him, he was set at liberty at once. In those stormy times more than one innocent man had been sent to the guillotine on a less flimsy accusation than this, and Napoleon had, therefore, good reason to be thankful for the interposition of Robespierre.

At this time the young warrior was most studious, and is said to have thus early acquired the habit of taking short snatches of sleep, which seemed to refresh him fully as much as the longer periods required by others. While at Nice one of his friends, on a particular occasion, went to Napoleon's apartments long before daybreak, and not doubting that he was still in bed, knocked gently at the door, fearful of disturbing him too abruptly. Upon entering his chamber he was not a little astonished at finding Bonaparte dressed as during the day, with plans, maps and various books scattered around him.

"What!" exclaimed the visitor, "not yet in bed?"

"In bed," replied Napoleon, "I am already risen."

"Indeed, and why so early?"

"Oh, two or three hours are enough for any man to sleep!" was the general's reply.

Some years later, when Bonaparte was forming the "*Code Napoleon*," he astonished the Council of State by the readiness with which he illustrated any point in discussion by quoting the Roman Civil Law, a subject which might seem entirely foreign to him, since the greater part of his life had been passed on the battlefield. On being asked how he had acquired so familiar a knowledge of law affairs he replied:

When I was lieutenant I was put under arrest, unjustly, it is true, but that is nothing to the point. The little room which was assigned for my prison contained no furniture but an old chair and an old cupboard: in the cupboard was a ponderous volume, older and more worm-eaten than all the rest. It proved to be a digest of the Roman law. As I had neither paper, pens, ink or pencil, you may easily imagine that this book was a valuable prize to me. It was so voluminous and the leaves were so covered with marginal notes in manuscript that, had I been confined one hundred years I could never have been idle. I was only deprived of my liberty ten days; but, on recovering it, I was saturated with Justinian and the decisions of the Roman legislators. *Thus, I picked up my knowledge of the Civil Law.*

Bonaparte did not resume his functions at Nice, after his release from imprisonment, but repaired to Marseilles where his mother was living in distressed circumstances. Before the end of the year he again came to Paris to solicit employment. At first he met with nothing but repulses. Aubry, president of the military committee, objected to his youth, at which Bonaparte replied rather sharply: "One ages quickly on battlefields, and I have just left one." The president, who had not seen much actual service himself, thought he was insulted, and treated Napoleon very coldly in consequence.

Shortly afterwards Bonaparte was offered the command of a brigade of infantry which he refused, declaring that nothing could induce him to leave the artillery. Writing to Sucy, a friend, on this subject, Napoleon said:

> I have been ordered to serve as a general of the line in La Vendée. I will not accept. Many soldiers could direct a brigade better than I, and few have commanded artillery with greater success.

His refusal was followed by the erasure of his name from the list of general officers in employment. Sometime later he asked for a commission to Turkey to form a barrier against the encroachments of Russia and England, but it was not granted. No answer was returned to his memorial, over which he conversed for some weeks with great enthusiasm. "How strange it would be," he said to his friends, "if a little Corsican should become king of Jerusalem." Already he was contemplating greatness, and firmly believed in his "Star of Destiny."

At length he was nominated to the command of a brigade of artillery in Holland. The long-deferred appointment was, no doubt, very welcome; but in the meantime his services were called for in a more important field. When the National Guard sided with the enemies of the convention, and took up arms against the government, a man of force and decision was needed to defend them from the insurgents. A collision had taken place on October 3rd, 1795, when the troops of the convention were withdrawn by that body. The insurgents, who represented the forty-eight sections of Paris, were prepared to attack the Palace of the Tuileries next morning with upwards of 40,000 men, and take the government in their own hands. The nation, and especially the superior classes, aided by the Royalists, were indignant at the conduct of the members of the convention,—who schemed to perpetuate themselves in office,—and formed a most formidable opposition to the measures of the existing government.

General Bonaparte was at the theatre when informed of the events that were passing. He at once hastened to the Assembly where he found the members in the heat of debate and greatly exercised over their approaching danger.

Deliberating with Tallien and Carnot, Barras, who had been present at Toulon during the siege, said: "There is but one man who can save us. I have the man whom you want; *it is a little Corsican officer who will not stand upon ceremony!*" Napoleon was sent for and notified that he had been chosen to defend the government as second in command under Barras. Unknown to the Assembly, he had been present at their meeting, and heard all that had been said of him. He deliberated on the best course to pursue for more than half an hour, and at last decided to take up their cause, if allowed to do so in his own way. When Barras presented Napoleon to the convention as a fit man to be intrusted with the command, the President asked:

"Are you willing to undertake the defence of the convention?"

"Yes," was the reply.

"Are you aware of the magnitude of the undertaking?"

"Perfectly; and I am in the habit of accomplishing that which I undertake. I accept, but I warn you that, once my sword is out of the scabbard, I shall not replace it until I have established order."

He refused, however, to accept the appointment unless he received it free from all interference. The trembling convention quickly yielded, and although Barras enjoyed the title of "Commander-in-chief," Bonaparte was actually in control of the troops.

Upon consultation with Menou, who was then in prison, and

whom he succeeded, Napoleon quickly obtained the information desired. He learned that the available defence consisted of but 5,000 soldiers of all descriptions, with 40 pieces of cannon then at Sablons and guarded by only one hundred and fifty men. Without the loss of a moment Napoleon began his preparations for the morrow which was to decide whether the mob was to triumph, and France lose all the fruits of her Revolution, or law and order be established. His first act was to dispatch Murat, then a major of *chasseurs*, to Sablons, five miles off, where the cannon were posted. The sectionaries sent a stronger detachment to seize these cannon immediately afterwards; and Murat, who passed them in the dark, would have gone in vain had he received his orders but a few moments later, or had he been less active.

When the reveille sounded on the morning of October 4th, over 32,000 National Guards advanced by different streets to the siege of the palace; but its defence was in firmer hands than those of Louis XVI.—the hero of Toulon was now at the helm.

At the Church St. Roche the column which was advancing along the Rue St. Honoré, found a detachment of Napoleon's troops drawn up in line with two cannon to dispute their passage. It is unknown which side began the firing, but in an instant Napoleon's artillery swept the streets and lanes, scattering grape-shot among the National Guards, and producing such confusion that they were soon compelled to give way. The first shot was a signal for opening all the batteries which Bonaparte had established, the quays of the Seine opposite the Tuileries being commanded by his guns below the palace and on the bridges.

In less than an hour the action was over. The insurgents fled in all directions, leaving the streets covered with the dead and wounded. The troops of the convention then marched into the various sections, disarmed the terrified inhabitants, and before nightfall everything was quiet. The sun went down as calmly over the helpless city as though nothing had happened. That same evening the theatres were opened and illuminated, and there were general rejoicings on almost every hand.

Napoleon's star rose that night above the horizon; all Paris rushed to catch a glimpse of the young commander, and for many years afterwards France continued to look to him for protection,—and not in vain.

On the night of the 13th *Vendemiaire* Napoleon wrote to his brother Joseph, saying:

At last all is finished and I hasten to send you news of myself. The Royalists, formed into sections, were becoming daily more threatening. The convention gave orders for the disarmament of the Lepelletier Section which resisted the troops. Menou, who commanded, was, it is said, a traitor, and was immediately disgraced. The convention appointed Barras to command the armed forces; the committee named me to command them under him. We placed our troops; the enemy came to attack us at the Tuileries. We killed many of them, and lost thirty killed and sixty wounded of our men. We have disarmed the Sections, and all is peace again. As usual I am unhurt.

P.S. Fortune is on my side.

Love to Eugenie and Julie.

Within five days from the defeat of the sections Napoleon was named second in command of the Army of the Interior, and shortly afterwards Barras, finding his duties as director sufficient to occupy his time, gave up the command to his "little Corsican officer."

After his inauguration as general of the armed force of Paris, Bonaparte waited on each of the five directors. While on a visit to Carnot a celebrated writer was there by invitation,—it being presentation day,—and as the young commander entered, was singing at the *piano forte* accompanied by a young lady. The entrance of Napoleon, then a short, well-made, olive-complexioned youth, amidst five or six tall young men who seemed to pay him the greatest attention, was a very surprising contrast, and made something of a stir.

On Bonaparte's entrance Carnot bowed with an air of perfect ease and self-possession, and as he passed by the author the latter inquired of the host who the gentlemen were.

The director answered: "The general of the armed force of Paris and his *aides-de-camp*."

"What is his name?" said the author.

"Bonaparte."

"Has he any military skill?"

"So it is said."

"What has he ever done to render himself conspicuous?"

"He is the officer who commanded the troops of the Convention on the Thirteenth *Vendemiaire*." (Day of the defeat of the Sections).

A shade passed over the visage of the inquirer, who happened to be one of the electors of the *Vendemiaire*, and he retired to one of the dark corners to observe the new visitor in thoughtfulness and in silence. Carnot then took occasion to predict that the young general would soon take another step to fame and glory.

It was about this time that a lady asked Napoleon: "How could you fire thus mercilessly upon your countrymen?"

"A soldier," he replied calmly, "is only a machine to obey orders!"

A few years before, while at a party given in the drawing rooms of M. Neckar, a celebrated financier, the Bishop of Autun commended Fox and Sheridan for having asserted that the French army, by refusing to obey the orders of their superiors to fire upon the populace, had set a glorious example to all the armies of Europe; because, by so doing, they had shown themselves that men, by becoming soldiers, did not cease to be citizens. Napoleon said quickly,:

> Excuse me, if I venture to interrupt you, but as I am an officer, I must claim the privilege of expressing my sentiments. I sincerely believe that a strict discipline in the army is absolutely necessary for the safety of our constitutional government and for the maintenance of order. Nay, if our troops are not compelled unhesitatingly to obey the commands of the executive, we shall be exposed to the blind fury of democratic passions which will render France the most miserable country on the globe!

The action of the Assembly in placing Napoleon in command of the troops in Paris had caused his name to appear frequently in the newspapers, and thenceforth it emerged from obscurity. As commander his first act was to intercede for and gain the acquittal of Menou, his predecessor, who was then in prison, principally because of his failure to put down the rioters.

Bonaparte now began to hold military levees, at one of which an incident occurred which gave at once a new turn in his mode of life, and a fresh impetus to the advance of his fortunes. A beautiful boy about twelve years old appeared before Napoleon and said: "My name is Eugene Beauharnais. My father, Viscount, and a general of the Republican armies, has died on the guillotine, and I am come to pray you, sir, to give me his sword." Bonaparte caused the request to be complied with, and the tears of the boy, as he received and kissed the relic, excited the commander's interest.

The next day the youth's mother, Josephine Beauharnais, came to thank Napoleon for his kind treatment of her son, and her beauty and singular gracefulness of address made a strong impression upon him.

Sometime later he offered Josephine[1] his hand; she, after some hesitation, accepted it, and the young general by his marriage, which was celebrated on March 5th, 1796, thus cemented his favourable connection with the society of the Luxembourg, and in particular, with Tallien and Barras, at that time the most powerful men in France.

The first meeting with Eugene, and its influence upon Napoleon's marriage with Josephine, has been sometimes questioned by historians, many of whom have seemingly neglected the exile's own verification of the story at St. Helena, in which, after relating the incident of Josephine's visit, he said to Dr. O'Meara:

> I was much struck with her appearance (Josephine's), and still more with her *esprit*. This first impression was daily strengthened, and marriage was not long in following.

Tranquillity was now restored in Paris, and the Directors had leisure to turn their attention to the affairs of the Army of Italy, which was then in a most confused and unsatisfactory condition. They determined to place it under it a new general, and Bonaparte, then but twenty-six years of age, was appointed to the command of the Army of Italy. It is said that when the command was given Napoleon by Carnot (grandfather of the late Sadi-Carnot, president of the present French Republic), the latter told him it was to the command of men alone that he could be appointed, the troops being destitute of everything but arms. Bonaparte replied, that provided he would let him have men enough, that it was all he wanted; he would answer for the rest, a promise that was soon fulfilled, for instead of an army wanting everything, it became, at the enemy's expense, one of the best appointed in Europe.

It was afterwards a matter of dispute between Carnot and Barras as to which of them had first proposed his appointment to this command. It is admitted in one of Josephine's letters that Barras had promised to procure the position for Bonaparte before his marriage took place.

One of the directors hesitated and said to Napoleon, "You are too young."

"In a year," he answered, "I shall be either old or dead!"

---

1. *Napoleon's Letters to Josephine* by Henry Foljambe Hall also published by Leonaur.

2

Bonaparte's Campaign in Italy, 1796-7

When Napoleon set out from Paris on the 21st of March 1796, to take command of the Army of Italy, after a honeymoon of but three days, he traversed France with the swiftness of a courier, turning aside but a few hours at Marseilles with his mother and family, whom he was now able to provide for in an adequate manner. His letters to Josephine were full of passionate expressions of tenderness, and regret at their separation. But after paying his tribute to the affections, his heart was speedily filled with exultation and triumph. For the first time he was chief in command; the power within him was now free to direct his actions, unhampered by the restraint he had so long felt in the capital. He was extremely anxious to commence the career to which Fate called him, by placing himself at the head of the Army of Italy at once.

It would not be difficult to imagine with what delight this young general—then scarcely twenty-six years old—advanced to an independent field of glory and conquest, confident in his own powers, and in the perfect knowledge of the country which he had previously acquired. He had under his command such men, already distinguished in war by success and bravery as: Augereau, Massena, Serrurier, Joubert, Lannes, Murat, La Harpe, Stengel and Kilmaine, all of whom were astonished at the youthful appearance of their new commander.

It was not without some discontent that the old generals beheld a young man, lately their inferior, taking the command over their heads,—to which each supposed he had a prior claim, and reaping the benefits of a plan of operations they did not imagine to have originated with himself. As he rode along the ranks the soldiers observed that he did not sit well on horseback, and complained that a "mere boy" had been sent to command them. The young general, however, soon obtained that respect for his character, which had been denied to his physical constitution. The firmness he exhibited, soon put a stop to the insubordination which had prevailed in the army; and, even before they had conquered under him, the troops became as submissive as at any subsequent period, when his character was fully established.

Some years before, when Bonaparte was conversing at Toulon with M. de Volney, the well-known Corsican traveller and literary man, at a dinner given to the two friends by Turreau, then in command of the military force at Nice, a campaign in Italy was suggested. After the dessert was brought in Napoleon said to Turreau: "Don't you think it's altogether too bad to have 10,000 men lying idle here at Nice when the Republic could make such excellent use of them in Italy?"

"Possibly," replied Turreau, "but we can do nothing; we have no order to move from the Committee of Public Safety."

"Then," said Napoleon, "it is your duty to make the committee ashamed of its inactivity."

"What would you do if you could act as you pleased?" asked Turreau. Napoleon promised to give a reply the next evening. At the time fixed he came prepared with a complete plan of campaign written out and classified under seventeen heads. It involved the invasion and conquest of Italy on almost the same lines that he was now about to undertake, and the outgrowth partially of that meeting, for Turreau forwarded the plan to the Committee of Public Safety at Paris on condition that it be put in the hands of Carnot, in whose judgment Napoleon had confidence. Carnot looked over the plan and was delighted. He was unable to secure immediate action, but two years later, when the invasion of Italy was determined upon, he had sufficient influence to see that Napoleon was put in charge of it.

Bonaparte arrived at the headquarters of the army at Nice on the 27th of March, 1796. The French Army of Italy, which amounted to 31,000 available men, had endured great hardships and privations, were destitute of shoes, clothing, and almost everything which their comfort demanded. The cavalry was wretchedly mounted and they were very deficient in artillery. To silence their complaints, and reconcile them to their situation, as well as to endear them to himself, Napoleon lived familiarly with his soldiers, participated in their hardships and privations, and redressed many of their grievances. "My brave fellows," he said to them on one occasion, while endeavouring to revive their spirits; "although you suffer great privations, you have no reason to be dissatisfied; everything yields to power; if we are victorious, the provisions and the supplies of the enemy become ours; *if we are vanquished, we have already too much to lose."*

The allies, Austrian and Sardinian, were a greatly superior force, numbering as they did 80,000 men, were well equipped with supplies, and occupied in their own, or a friendly country, all the heights and passes of the Alps. Berthier, then on Napoleon's staff as major-general, took great pleasure in showing as a curiosity in after years a general order by which three *louis-d'or* were granted as a great supply for an outfit to each general of division, and dated on the very day of the victory at Albinga.

On the 8th of April Napoleon wrote to the Directory:

I found this army, not only destitute, but without discipline; their insubordination and discontent were such that the malcontents had formed a party for the *dauphin*, and were singing songs opposed to the tenets of the Revolution. You may, however, rest assured that peace and order will be re-established; by the time you receive this letter, we shall have come to an engagement.

It was under such circumstances that Bonaparte proposed forcing a passage to Italy and converting the richest territory of the enemy into the theatre of war. He said to his destitute and disheartened men:

Soldiers, you are naked and ill-fed; the Republic owes you much, but she has nothing with which to pay her debts. Your endurance and patience amidst these barren rocks deserves admiration; but it brings you no glory. I come to lead you into the most fertile plains the sun shines upon. Rich provinces, and great cities will soon be in your power; there you will reap riches and glory—they will be at your disposal. Soldiers of Italy! with such a prospect before you, can you fail in courage and perseverance?

This was the commander's first address to the army, and the words of encouragement which he gave them shot martial enthusiasm through their veins like electric fire. Under the incompetent management of Scherer the army, which had obtained some success against the Austrian general, De Vins, had been without glory, although their battalions were headed by valiant officers whose leader had neglected to improve his good fortune. The French soldiers were thirsting for a commander capable of leading them on to fame and glory, the conquest of Italy, therefore, seemed reserved for General Bonaparte.

Napoleon's system of tactics, although then unknown even to his officers, were a fixity with him. They appear to have been grounded on the principle that "the commander will be victorious who assembles the greatest number of forces upon the same point at the same moment, notwithstanding an inferiority of numbers to the enemy when the general force is computed on both sides." He eminently possessed the power of calculation and combination necessary to exercise these decisive manoeuvres.

Napoleon's career of victory began, as it continued, in defiance of the established rules of warfare, and what distinguished him above all his contemporaries was his ability to convert the most unfavourable circumstances into the means of success. He perceived that the time was come for turning a new leaf in the history of war. With such numbers of troops as the impoverished Republic could afford him, he soon saw that no considerable advantages could be obtained against the vast and highly-disciplined armies of Austria and her allies unless the established rules of etiquette and strategy were abandoned. It was only by such rapidity of motion as should utterly surprise the superior numbers of his adversaries that he could hope to concentrate the entire energy of a small force, such as he commanded, upon some point of a much greater force, and thus defeat them. He knew he would have to deal with veteran soldiers and experienced generals—men who had learned the art of war before he was born. He therefore resolved that every movement should be made with celerity, and every blow be levelled where it was least expected.

To effect such rapid marches as he had determined upon, it was necessary that the soldiery should make up their minds to consider tents and baggage as idle luxuries; and that instead of a long and complicated chain of reserves and stores, they should dare to rely wholly for the means of sustenance on the countries into which their venturesome leader might conduct them.

The objects of Napoleon's expedition were to compel the king of Sardinia, who maintained a powerful army in the field, to abandon the alliance of Austria; to compel Austria to concentrate her forces in her Italian provinces, thus obliging her to withdraw them from the bank of the Rhine where they had long hovered. It was hoped, also, to humble the power of the Vatican and break the prestige of its Jesuitical diplomacy forever. He had as yet achieved no fame in the field and not a general in Europe would have blamed him if he had only succeeded in holding the territory of Nice and Savoy, which France had already won.

Napoleon's plan of reaching the fair regions of Italy differed from that of all former conquerors; they had uniformly penetrated the Alps at some point of access in that mighty range of mountains; he judged that the same end might be accomplished more easily by advancing along the narrow strip of comparatively level country that intervenes between those enormous barriers and the shores of the Mediterranean Sea, and forcing a passage at the point where the last or southern extremity of the Alps melt, as it were, into the first and lowest of the Appenine range.

No sooner did he begin to concentrate his troops towards this region than Beaulieu, the Austrian general, took measures for protecting Genoa and the entrance of Italy with a powerful, disciplined and well-appointed army. He posted himself with one column at Voltri, a town on the sea some ten miles west of Genoa; D'Argenteau, with another column occupied the heights of Montenotte, while the Sardinians, led by General Colli, formed the right of the line at Ceva. This disposition was made in compliance with the old system of tactics; but it was powerless before new strategy. The French could not advance towards Genoa but by confronting some one of the three armies and these Beaulieu supposed were too strongly posted to be dislodged.

On the morning of the 12th of April, 1796, when D'Argenteau advanced from Montenotte to attack the column of Rampon, he found that by skilful manoeuvres during the night Napoleon had completely surrounded him—a man who had fancied there was nothing new to be done in warfare.

On the previous day the Austrians had driven in all the outposts of the French and appeared before the redoubt of Montenotte. This redoubt, the last of the intrenchments, was defended by 1,500 men commanded by Rampon who made his soldiers take an oath, during the heat of the attack, to defend it or perish in the intrenchments, to the last man. The repeated assaults of the French were without avail, their advancement was checked and they were kept the whole night at the distance of a pistol shot, 400 men being killed by the fire of their musketry alone.

At daybreak, the following morning, Bonaparte then being at the head of the French forces, and having introduced two pieces of cannon into the redoubt during the night, the action was recommenced with great vigour and with varying success. The contest had continued for some time, when Bonaparte, with Berthier and Massena appearing suddenly with the centre and left wing of the army upon the rear and flank of the enemy, at once commenced a furious attack, filled them with terror and confusion, and decided the fate of the day. D'Argenteau, who commanded the rear, had fought gallantly, but seeing that to continue the battle would only end in total destruction, he fled, leaving his colours and cannon, a thousand killed and two thousand prisoners.

Thus was the centre of the great Austrian army completely routed before either its commander-in-chief at the left, or General Colli at the right, knew that a battle had begun. It was from this battle, the first of Napoleon's victories, that the French emperor told the Emperor of Austria, some years later, that he dated his nobility. "Ancestors?" said Napoleon, "I, sir, am an ancestor myself; my title of nobility dates from Montenotte!"

This victory enabled the French, under La Harpe, to advance to Cairo, and placed them on that side of the Alps which slopes toward Lombardy.

Beaulieu now fell back on Dego, where he could open his communication with Colli, who had retreated to Millessimo, a small town about nine miles from Dego. Here the two commanders hoped to unite their forces. They were soon strongly posted, and dispatching couriers to Milan for reinforcements, intended to await their arrival before risking another battle. It was their object to keep fast in these positions until succour could come from Lombardy; but Napoleon had no intention of giving them such a respite; his tactics were not those of other generals.

The morning after the victory of Montenotte Bonaparte dispatched Augereau to attack Millessimo; Massena to fall on Dego, and La Harpe to turn the flank of Beaulieu.

Massena carried the heights of Biestro at the point of the bayonet, while La Harpe dislodged the Austrian general from his position, which separated him hopelessly from the Sardinian commander and put him to precipitate flight. By these movements Bonaparte was in such a position, that, though they had not traversed, his army had at all events scaled the Alps.

Meanwhile Augereau had seized the outposts of Millessimo and cut off Provera, with 2,000 Austrians who occupied an eminence upon the mountain of Cossaria, from the main body of Colli's army. Provera took refuge in a ruined castle which he defended with great bravery, hoping to receive assistance from Colli.

The next morning Napoleon, who had arrived in the night, forced Colli to battle and compelled him to retreat Ceva. Provera imitated the gallant example of Colonel Rampon in his defence, but not with the same success. He was compelled to surrender his sword to Bonaparte at discretion, after a loss of 10,000 in killed and prisoners, twenty-two cannon and fifteen standards. The French found on the summit of the Alps every species of ammunition and other necessities which the celerity of their march had prevented them from carrying.

Dego, situated at the summit of the Alps, secured the entrance of the French into Italy, cut off the communications between the Austrian and Sardinian armies, and placed the conqueror in a situation to crush them in succession one after the other. Beaulieu, fully sensible of the danger of his situation, collected the best troops in his army, and at break of day on the 15th of April, retook Dego at the head of 7,000 men.

The Austrians stood two attacks headed by Napoleon, but at the third Causse rushed forward, holding his plumed hat on the point of his sword, and Dego was soon again in possession of the French. For this piece of gallantry he immediately received the rank of brigadier-general. Here also, Lannes, who lived to be a Marshal of the Empire, first attracted the notice of Napoleon, and was promoted from lieutenant-colonel to colonel. The triumph, however, was purchased with the life of the brave General Causse. He was carried out of the *mêlée* mortally wounded. Napoleon passed near him as he lay.

"Is Dego retaken?" asked the dying officer. "It is ours," replied Napoleon.

"Then long live the Republic!" cried Causse, "I die content."

Hotly pursued by the victors, Colli rallied his fugitives at Mondovi, where they again yielded to the irresistible onset of the French, the Sardinian commander leaving his best troops, baggage and cannon on the field. The action was a most severe one in which, among others, the French general, Stengel, a brave and excellent officer, was killed, and the cavalry would have been overpowered but for the desperate valour of Murat.

The Sardinians lost ten stands of colours and fifteen hundred prisoners, among whom were three generals. The Sardinian army had now ceased to exist, and the Austrians were flying to the frontiers of

Lombardy.

Napoleon, following up his advantage, entered Cherasco, a strong place about ten miles from Turin, as a conqueror. Here he dictated the terms by which the Sardinian king could still wear a crown. From the castle where he stood, and looking off on the garden-fields of Lombardy—which had gladdened the eyes of so many conquerors—with the Alps behind him, glittering in their perennial snows, Napoleon said to his officers: "Hannibal forced the Alps—we have turned them." To his soldiers, whom he addressed in a proclamation, he said:

> In fifteen days you have gained six victories, taken twenty-one stands of colours, fifty-five pieces of cannon, several fortresses, and conquered the richest part of Piedmont: you have made 15,000 prisoners, killed or wounded upwards of 10,000 men. Hitherto you have fought for barren rocks, rendered famous by your valour, but useless to your country. Your services now equal those of the victorious army of Holland and the Rhine. You have provided yourselves with everything of which you were destitute. You have gained battles without cannon! passed rivers without bridges! made forced marches without shoes! bivouacked without strong liquors and often without bread! Republican *phalanxes*, Soldiers of Liberty, only, could have endured all this. Thanks for your perseverance! If your conquest of Toulon presaged the immortal campaign of 1793, your present victories presage a still nobler. But, soldiers, you have done nothing while so much remains to be done; neither Turin or Milan are yours. The ashes of the Conquerors of the Tarquins are still trampled by the assassins of Basseville.

To the Italians Napoleon said:

> People of Italy! The French Army comes to break your chains. The people of France are the friends of all nations—confide in them. Your property, your religion and your customs shall be respected. We make war with those tyrants alone who enslave you.

The French soldiers, flushed with victory, were eager to continue their march, and the people of Italy hailed Napoleon as their deliverer. The Sardinian king did not long survive the humiliation of the loss of his crown—he died of a broken heart within a few days after signing the treaty of Cherasco.

In the meantime the couriers of Napoleon were almost every hour riding into Paris with the news of his victories, and five times in six days the Representatives of France had decreed that the Army of Italy deserved well of their country.

Murat was sent to Paris bearing the news of the capitulation of the king of Sardinia, and twenty-one stands of colours. His arrival caused great joy in the capital.

The consummate genius of this brief campaign could not be disputed, and the modest language of the young general's dispatches to the Directory lent additional grace to his fame. All the eyes of Europe were fixed in admiration on his career.

In less than a month's campaign Napoleon laid the gates of Italy open before him; reduced the Austrians to inaction; utterly destroyed the Sardinian king's army, and took two great fortresses called "the keys to the Alps!"

To effect the rapid movements required for such results, everything was sacrificed that came in the way, not only on this occasion, but on every other. Baggage, stragglers, the wounded, the artillery—all were left behind, rather than the column should fail to reach the destined place at the destined time. Napoleon made no allowance for accidents or impediments. Things until now reckoned essential to an army were dispensed with; and, for the first time, troops were seen to take the field without tents, camp equipage, magazines of provisions, and military hospitals. Such a system naturally aggravated the horrors of war. The soldiers were, necessarily, marauders, and committed terrible excesses at this first stage of the campaign; but every effort was made, and with much success, to prevent this evil after conquest had put the means of regular supply within the power of the commander-in-chief. The wounded were frequently left behind for want of the means of conveyance. According to one authority, the loss by the disorders inseparable from this means of war was four times as great as by the fire or the sword of the enemy.

The army, nevertheless, adored its fortunate general, and it still doted upon him even when undeceived respecting his providence for it.

"To be able to solve this enigma," says General Foy, "it was requisite to have known Napoleon, the life of camp and of glory, and, above all, one must have a French head and heart."

With the sufferings of the army, he never failed to show an active sympathy when it did not tend to the compromise of his plans. The hours, too, spent by Napoleon on the field after a battle, endeared him to his followers. He visited the hospitals in person and made his officers, after his example, take the utmost interest in this duty. His hand was applied to the wounds; his voice cheered the sick. All who recovered could relate individual acts of kindness experienced from him by themselves or their comrades.

It was at this period that a medal of Napoleon was struck at Paris as conqueror of Montenotte. The face is extremely thin, with long, straight hair. On the reverse, a figure of Victory is represented flying over the Alps, bearing a palm branch, a wreath of laurel and a drawn sword. It was the first of the splendid series designed by Denon to record the victories and honours of France's great warrior.

Napoleon determined to advance without delay, giving Tuscany, Venice, and the other Italian States no time to take up a hostile attitude. After accomplishing so much, a general of less enterprise might have thought it right to rest awhile and wait for reinforcements before attempting further conquest, but not so with Napoleon. The French Army, to which recruits were now flocking from every hospital and depot within reach, was ordered to prepare for instant motion.

It was after one of the successful movements of this period that an old Hungarian officer was brought prisoner to Bonaparte, who entered into conversation with him, and among other matters asked what he thought of the state of the war. "Nothing," replied the prisoner, who did not know he was addressing the commander-in-chief, "nothing can be worse. Here is a young man who knows absolutely nothing of the regular rules of war; today he is in our rear, tomorrow on our flank, the next day again in our front. Such violations of the principles of the art of war are intolerable sir, and we do not know how to proceed!"

To secure the route to Milan it was necessary to drive the Austrians from the banks of the Adda, behind which they had retired after a heavy loss at Fombio. Lannes upon that occasion gave proofs of his astonishing intrepidity; at the head of a single battalion, he attacked between seven and eight thousand Austrians, and not content in causing their flight, he pursued them ten miles, following the trot of their cavalry on foot.

Having collected an immense quantity of artillery and the main division of his army at a narrow wooden bridge erected across this stream at the town of Lodi, General Beaulieu awaited the arrival of the French, confident of defending the passage of the Adda and arresting their progress. Beaulieu had placed a battery of thirty cannon

Bonaparte at the Battle of Rivoli

so as to completely sweep every plank of the bridge. Had he removed the structure, which was about 500 feet in length, when he changed his headquarters to the east bank of the river, he might have made the passage much more formidable than even his cannon made it.

Well aware that his conquest would never be consolidated till the Austrian army was totally vanquished, and deprived of all its Italian possessions, Bonaparte hastened to pursue the enemy to Lodi. Coming up on the 10th of May, he easily drove the rearguard of the Austrian army before him into the town, but found his further progress threatened by the tremendous fire of thirty cannon stationed at the opposite end of the bridge so as to sweep it completely. The whole body of the enemy's infantry drawn up in a dense line, supported this appalling disposition of the artillery.

Bonaparte's first care was to place as many guns as he could get in direct opposition to the Austrian battery. He was determined that no obstacle should oppose his victorious career, and at once resolved to pass the bridge.

Exposed to a shower of grape-shot from the enemy's batteries, Napoleon at last succeeded in planting two pieces of cannon at the head of the bridge on the French side, and to prevent the enemy from destroying it a column was immediately formed from the troops that at once appeared, determined to carry the pass. The French now commenced a fearful cannonading. Bonaparte himself appeared in the midst of the fire, pointing with his own hand two guns in such a manner as to cut off the Austrians from the only path by which they could have advanced to undermine the bridge.

Observing, meanwhile, that Beaulieu had removed his infantry to a considerable distance backwards, to keep them out of the range of the French battery, Napoleon instantly detached General Beaumont and his cavalry, with orders to gallop out of sight, ford the river, and coming suddenly upon the enemy, attack them in the rear. When that took place Napoleon instantly drew up a body of 3,000 grenadiers in close column under the shelter of the houses, and bade them prepare for the desperate attempt of forcing a passage across the narrow bridge, in the face of the enemy's thickly-planted artillery.

A sudden movement in the flanks of the enemy now convinced Napoleon that his cavalry had arrived and charged the enemy's flank, and he instantly gave the word. In a moment the brave grenadiers wheeled to the left and were at once upon the bridge, rushing forward at a charge step, and shouting: "*Vive la République!*;" but the storm of grape-shot from the enemy's guns checked them for a moment. It was a very sepulchre of death and a burning furnace of destruction pouring out its broadsides of fire in defence of its position; a hundred brave men fell dead. The advancing column faltered under the redoubled roar of the guns and the rattle of grape-shot.

Lannes, Napoleon, Berthier and L'Allemand now hurried to the front, rallied and cheered the men, and as the column dashed across and over the dead bodies of the slain which covered the passageway, and in the face of a tempest of fire that thinned their ranks at every step, the leaders shouted: "Follow your generals, my brave fellows!"

Lannes was the first to reach the other side, Napoleon himself being second.

The Austrian artillerymen were bayoneted at their guns before the other troops, whom Beaulieu had removed too far back in his anxiety to avoid the French battery, could come to their assistance. Beaumont pressing gallantly with his horse upon the flank, and Napoleon's infantry forming rapidly as they passed the bridge, and charging on the instant, the Austrian line at once became involved in inextricable confusion. The contest was almost instantly decided; the whole line of Austrian artillery was carried; their order of battle broken; their troops routed and put to flight.

The slaughter of Austrians amounted to vast numbers, while the French lost but 200 men. Thus did Bonaparte execute with such rapidity and consequently with so little loss "the terrible passage," as he himself called it, "of the bridge of Lodi." It is justly called one of the most daring achievements on record.

The victory of Lodi had a great influence on Napoleon's mind. He declared subsequently that neither his success in quelling the "Sections," nor his victory at Montenotte, made him regard himself as anything superior; but that after Lodi, for the first time the idea dawned upon him that he would one day be "a decisive actor," as he himself put it, on the stage of the military and political world. That he was a fatalist is well-known, it being a frequent expression with him that "*every bullet is marked.*"

On this occasion the soldiers conferred on him the nick-name of "Little Corporal." The original cause of the appellation, as applied to Bonaparte, has been related by Napoleon himself. He says that when he commanded near the Col di Tende the army was obliged to traverse a narrow bridge, on which occasion he gave directions that no women should be allowed to accompany it, as the service was particularly difficult, and required that the troops should be continually on the alert; to enforce such an order he placed two captains on the bridge with instructions, on pain of death, not to permit a woman to pass. He subsequently repaired to the bridge himself, for the purpose of ascertaining whether his orders were being scrupulously obeyed, when he found a crowd of women assembled, who, as soon as they saw him, began to revile him, exclaiming: "Oh, then, *petit corporal*, it is you who have given orders not to let us pass!"

Some miles in advance Napoleon was surprised to see a considerable number of women with the troops. He immediately ordered the two captains to be put under arrest and brought before him, intending to have them tried immediately. They protested their innocence, asserting that no women had crossed the bridge. Bonaparte caused some of the females to be brought before him, and learned with astonishment, from their own confession, that they had emptied some casks of provisions and concealed themselves therein, by which means they had passed over unperceived.

After every battle the oldest soldiers convened a council in order to confer a new rank on their young general, who, on making his appearance, was saluted by his latest title. Bonaparte, therefore, was nominated *corporal* at Lodi, and *sergeant* at Castiglione. It was "Little Corporal," however, that the soldiery constantly applied to him ever afterwards.

The fruits of this splendid victory at Lodi were twenty pieces of cannon, and between two and three thousand killed, wounded and prisoners, and the loss by the enemy of an excellent line of defence.

When Europe heard of the battle they named the conqueror "The Hero of Lodi."

Beaulieu contrived to withdraw a part of his troops, and gathering the scattered fragment of his force together, soon threw the line of the Mincio, a tributary of the Po, between himself and his enemy. The great object, however, he had attained,—he was still free to defend Mantua.

The French following up their advantages at Lodi, pursued the Austrians with great celerity. They advanced to Pizzighitone, which immediately surrendered. Pushing on to Cremona they met with like success, and the vanguard, having taken the route to Milan, entered this city on the 14th of May, having on their march received the submission of Pavia, where they found most of the magazines of the Austrian army. The tri-coloured flag now waved in triumph from the extremity of the Lake of Como and the frontiers of the country to the gates of Parma.

The Austrians having evacuated Milan, when the French prepared to enter it, a deputation of the inhabitants laid the keys of its gates at their feet. A few days later, although the archduke had fled from his capital, overwhelmed with sorrow and mortification, the people collected in vast multitudes to witness the entry of the French, whom they hailed as their deliverers. The imperial arms were taken down from the public buildings and at the ducal palace this humorous advertisement was posted up:

> A House to Rent.
>   Inquire for the keys at
>   Citizen Salicetti's,
>   The French Commissioner.

The entry of Bonaparte into Milan under a triumphal arch and surrounded by the grenadiers of Lodi, among whom some generals were conspicuous, was eminently brilliant. The splendid carriages of the nobility and aristocracy of the capital went out to meet and salute him as the "Deliverer of Italy," and returned in an immense cavalcade, amidst the shouts and acclamations of an innumerable multitude, and accompanied by several bands playing patriotic marches, the procession stopping at the palace of the archduke, where Bonaparte was to take up his headquarters. The ceremonies of the day were concluded by a splendid ball at which the ladies showed their Republican feeling by wearing the French national colours in every part of their dress. On the same day Bonaparte entered Milan the treaty with the king of Sardinia and the Directory was signed at Paris.

Napoleon now addressed himself again to his soldiers, reminding them of their victories and responsibilities yet to come:

> To you, soldiers, will belong the immortal honour of redeeming the fairest portion of Europe. The French people, free and respected by the whole world, shall give to Europe a glorious peace, which shall indemnify it for all the sacrifices it has borne the last six years. Then by your own firesides you shall repose, and your fellow-citizens, when they point out any one of you, shall say: 'He belonged to the Army of Italy!'

From that period the Army of Italy was no longer a tax upon France, but on the contrary was a great source of revenue to her, and assisted in paying her other armies. Six weeks after the opening of the campaign, independent of ten million of *francs* placed at the disposal of the Directory, Bonaparte sent upwards of two hundred thousand *francs* to the Army of the Alps, and a million to the Army of the Rhine, thereby paving the way to his future greatness.

Bonaparte remained but six days in Milan; he then proceeded to pursue Beaulieu, who had planted the remains of his army behind the Mincio. The Austrian general had placed his left on the great and strong city of Mantua, which had been termed "the citadel of Italy," and his right at Peschiera, a well-known Venetian fortress. The Austrian veteran occupied one of the strongest positions that it is possible to imagine, and Bonaparte hastened once more to dislodge him.

The French Directory, meanwhile, had begun to entertain suspicion as to the ultimate designs of their young general, whose success and rising fame had already reached so astonishing a height. That they were exceedingly jealous of him there seems to be no doubt, and they determined to check, if they could, the career of a man of whom they seemed to be in fear. Bonaparte was therefore ordered to take half his army and lead it against the pope and the king of Naples, and leave the other half to terminate the conquest with Beaulieu at Mantua, under the orders of Kellerman. He answered by offering to resign his command:

> One half of the Army of Italy cannot suffice to finish the matter with the Austrians. It is only by keeping my force entire that I have been able to gain so many battles and to be now in Milan. You had better have one bad general than two good ones!

The Directory did not dare to persist in displacing the chief whose name was considered as the pledge of victory, and he continued to assume the entire command of the Army of Italy.

Another unlooked-for occurrence delayed for a few days the march upon Mantua. The success of the French and their exactions where victorious, had fostered the ire of a portion of the populace throughout Lombardy. Reports of new Austrian levies being poured down the passes of Tyrol were spread and believed. Insurrections against the conqueror now took place in various districts, placing thirty thousand men in arms. At Pavia the insurgents were entirely triumphant; they seized the town and compelled the French garrison to surrender. This flame, had it been suffered to spread, threatened immeasurable evil to the French cause.

Lannes instantly marched to Binasco, stormed the place, burnt it and put many of the insurgents to the sword. Napoleon appeared before Pavia, blew the gates open, took possession and later caused the leaders to be executed. At Lugo, where another insurrection took place, the leaders were tried by court martial and condemned.

These examples quelled the insurrectionists, and the French advanced on the Mincio. Bonaparte made such disposition of his troops that Beaulieu believed he meant to cross that river, if he could, at Peschiera. Meanwhile the French had been preparing to cross at another point, and on the 30th of May actually forced the passage of the Mincio, not at Peschiera, but further down at Borghetto. The Austrian garrison at this point in vain destroyed one arch of the bridge. Bonaparte quickly supplied the breach with planks, and his men, flushed with so many victories, charged with a fury not to be resisted. While the French were labouring to repair the bridge, under the fire of the enemy's batteries, impatient of delay, fifty grenadiers threw themselves into the river, holding their muskets over their heads with the water up to their chins, General Gardanne, a grenadier in courage as well as in stature, being at their head. The Austrians who were nearest, recollecting the terrible column at Lodi, fled. When the bridge was repaired the French entered Vallegio, where Beaulieu's headquarters had been stationed a short time previous. The latter was obliged to abandon the Mincio as he had the Adda and the Po, and to take up the new line of the Adige.

The left line of the Austrian force, learning from the cannonade that the French were at Borghetto, hastened to ascend the Mincio with a view of assisting in the defence of the division engaged with the enemy. They arrived too late, however, to be of assistance, as the commander at Borghetto had retreated before they arrived. They came, however, unexpectedly, and at a moment when Bonaparte and a few friends, believing the work of the day to be over and the village safe from the enemy, were about to sit down to dinner, as they thought, in security. Sebetendorff, who commanded the division, came up rapidly into the village, but with no idea what a prize was within his grasp. Bonaparte's attendants had barely time to shut the gates of the inn, and alarm their chief by the cry, "To arms!" They defended the house with obstinate courage while Bonaparte threw himself on horseback and galloping out by a back passage, effected the narrowest of escapes, proceeding at full speed to join Massena's forces.

It was shortly after this that Bonaparte met with an experience that gave him the idea of the "Imperial Guard of Napoleon" and which throughout his military career he ever afterwards maintained as a personal guard. It was the duty of this body, consisting of veterans who should number at least ten years of active service, to remain always near the person of the commander-in-chief, and who were only brought into action when important movements or desperate emergencies required their utmost energies. They were placed under the command of Bessieres at this time, and were known as "*Le Corps de Guides.*"

During the same campaign Bonaparte again narrowly escaped being taken a prisoner. Wurmser, who had been compelled to throw himself into Mantua, having suddenly debouched on an open plain, learned from an old woman that not many minutes before the French general, with only a few followers, had stopped at her door and fled at the sight of the Austrians. Wurmser immediately dispatched parties of cavalry in all directions to whom he gave orders that if they came up with Napoleon he should not be killed or harmed; fortunately, however, for the French commander, destiny and the swiftness of his horse saved him.

In their different engagements, the grenadiers had learned to laugh and sport at death; they despised the Austrian cavalry and nothing could equal their intrepidity but the gaiety with which they performed their forced marches, singing alternately songs in praise of their country and of love. Instead of sleeping they amused themselves during most of the night, each telling a tale, or forming his own plans of operation for the following day.

Sebetendorff was soon assaulted by a French column and retreated, after Beaulieu's example, on the line of the Adige. The Austrian commander had, in effect, abandoned for a time the open country of Italy. He now lay on the frontier, between the vast tract of rich province, which Napoleon had conquered, and the Tyrol. Mantua, which possessed immense natural advantages, and into which the retreating general had flung a garrison of full fourteen thousand men, was, in truth, the last and only Italian possession of the imperial crown, which, as it seemed, there might be a possibility of saving.

Beaulieu anxiously awaited the approach of new troops from Germany, to attempt the relief of this great city; and Bonaparte, eager to anticipate the efforts of the imperial government, sat down immediately before it.

Mantua lies on an island, being cut off on all sides from the main land by the branches of the Mincio, and approachable only by five narrow causeways of which three were now defended by strong and regular fortresses or intrenched camps; the other two by gates, drawbridge and batteries. The garrison was prepared to maintain the position, was well-nigh impregnable and the occupants awaited the hour to discover whether Napoleon possessed any new system of attack capable of shortening the usual operations of a siege as effectually as he had already done by the march and the battle.

It was a matter of high importance that Napoleon should reduce this place quickly, for a large army under Field-Marshal Wurmser, one of the most able and experienced of the Austrian generals, was about to enter Italy. His commencement gave cause for much alarm to those within the fortress. Of the five causeways, by sudden and overwhelming assaults, he obtained four; the garrison was cut off from the main land except at the fifth causeway, the strongest of them all, named from a palace near it, "La Favorita." It seemed necessary, however, in order that this blockade might be complete, that the Venetian territory, lying immediately behind Mantua, should be occupied by the French, and the claim of neutrality was not allowed to interfere with Napoleon's plans.

"You are too weak," said Bonaparte, when a Venetian envoy reached his headquarters, "to enforce neutrality on hostile nations such as France and Austria. Beaulieu did not respect your territory when his interest bade him violate it; nor shall I hesitate to occupy whatever falls within the line of the Adige."

Garrisons were placed forthwith in Verona and all the strong places of that domain. Napoleon now returned to Milan to transact important business, leaving Serrurier and Vaubois to blockade Mantua.

The king of Naples, utterly confounded by the success of the French, was now anxious to secure peace on whatever terms proposed, and Bonaparte, knowing that it would result in a withdrawal of some valuable divisions from the army of Beaulieu, arranged an armistice which was soon followed by a formal peace, and the Neapolitan troops, abandoning the Austrian general, began their march to the south of Italy. This was followed by peace arrangements with the Pope of whom Napoleon demanded, and obtained, as a price of the brief respite from invasion, a million sterling, one hundred of the finest pictures and statues in the papal gallery, a large supply of military stores and the cession of Ancona, Ferrara and Bologna, with their respective domains. The siege of the citadel of Milan, rigorously pressed, was at length successful. The garrison capitulated on the 29th of June, and by the 18th of July, one hundred and forty pieces of cannon were before Mantua.

The French general had stripped Austria of all her Italian possessions except Mantua, and the tri-colour was waving from the Tyrol to the Mediterranean. Napoleon was now, in effect, master of Italy. Future success seemed to him to be assured, although the French Directory was with difficulty persuaded to let him follow the course he had adopted for himself.

The cabinet of Vienna at last resolved upon sending stronger reinforcements to the Italian frontier, and Bonaparte was now recalled from Milan to the seat of war to defend himself against them. What the Austrian court now feared was that Napoleon, who had already annihilated her Italian army, and had wrested from her the Italian domains, would soon march into the heart of her empire and dictate a peace under the walls of her capital. All Italy was now subdued or in alliance with the French Republic except Mantua.

Beaulieu, who had been so thoroughly routed by Napoleon, was to be no longer trusted. Finding himself incompetent to withstand a general "whose mistress was glory and whose companion was Plutarch" while traversing the Tyrol with the wrecks of his army, forwarded a letter to Vienna which fully displayed the irritated feelings of the veteran commander at this time. He said:

> I hereby make known to you that I have only 20,000 men remaining, while the enemy's forces exceed 60,000. I further apprise you, that it is my intention to retreat tomorrow,—the next day—the day following—nay, every day,—even to Siberia, should they pursue me so far. My age accords me liberty to be thus explicit. Hasten to ratify peace, be the conditions what they may!

Wurmser, whose reputation was of the best, and who was older than Beaulieu but not less obstinate, was sent to replace him, and 30,000 men were drafted from the armies on the Rhine charged with restoring the fortunes of Austria beyond the Alps. Wurmser's orders, too, were to strengthen himself, on his march, by whatever recruits he could raise among the warlike and loyal population of the Tyrol.

When he fixed his headquarters at Trent, Wurmser mustered in all 80,000 men, while Napoleon had but 30,000—not 60,000 as Beaulieu had stated—to hold a wide country in which abhorrence of the French cause was now prevalent, to keep the blockade of Mantua, and to oppose this fearful odds of numbers in the field. The French commander was now, moreover, to act on the defensive, while his adversary assumed the more inspiriting character of the invader.

Wurmser was unwise enough to divide his magnificent army into three separate columns, which, united, Napoleon never could have met; but each of which was soon successively broken and captured. Melas with the left wing was to march down the Adige and expel the French from Verona; Quasdonowich with the right wing followed the valley of the Chiese towards Brescia, to cut off Napoleon's retreat on Milan; Wurmser himself led the centre down the left shore of Lake Guarda towards the besieged castle of Mantua.

The eye of Napoleon, who had hitherto been watching with the intensity of an eagle's gaze all the movements of his antagonist, now saw the division of Quasdonowich separated from the centre and left wing, and he flew to the encounter, although he was obliged to draw off his army from the siege of Mantua, something which very few generals would have done. On the night of July 31st, he buried his cannon in the trenches and intentionally marked his retreat with every sign of precipitation and alarm. Before morning the whole French Army had disappeared from Mantua and by a forced march regained possession of Brescia. Napoleon was hurrying forward to attack the right wing of the Austrian army before it could effect a junction with the central body of Wurmser.

A courier could hardly have borne to Quasdonowich the news of his raising the siege of Mantua before Napoleon had attacked and overwhelmed him, and he was glad to save his shattered forces by falling back on the Tyrol.

This ill-omened beginning aroused the ire, and quickened the evolutions of Wurmser, and falling on the rearguard of Massena under Pigeon, and Augereau under Vallette, the one abandoned Castiglione and the other retired on Lonato. These inconsiderable Austrian successes were obtained by good generalship, and Wurmser now attempted to open a communication with his defeated lieutenant. His columns were weakened by extending the line, and Massena at once hurled two strong columns on Lonato, retaking it, and throwing the Austrian forces into utter confusion.

The Battle of Lonato occurred on the 3rd of August (1796). At daybreak the whole of the French army was in motion, Augereau moving with the right wing towards Castiglione. General Pigeon, who commanded the French advance guard, was taken prisoner with three pieces of cannon; when, at the moment the Austrians were extending their line, Napoleon sent forward in close columns the 18th and 32nd demi-brigades, which being supported by a strong reserve, broke the enemy's line of battle. The artillery and prisoners made under General Pigeon, were thus retaken, and the French entered Lonato.

At Castiglione a firm stand was again taken by the fleeing Austrians, but Augereau forced the position against a defence double in numbers and for which he was afterward created Duke of Castiglione in memory of his exploit.

On that day the Austrians lost twenty pieces of cannon, from three to four thousand men killed and wounded, and four thousand prisoners, among whom were three generals. Before this engagement Napoleon suddenly found himself placed between two armies each of which was more numerous than his own. In this situation of affairs, no one of his generals entertained the least hope; but what was the astonishment of the soldiers, when they first assembled in presence of their chief, to observe no alteration in his countenance. "Fear nothing," said the commander to them, "show that you remain unchanged; preserve your valour, your just pride, and the remembrance of your triumphs; in three days we shall retake all that we have lost. Rely on me! You know whether or not I am in the habit of keeping my word."

In this memorable battle Napoleon raised himself to an equality with the greatest generals. Although the position in which he was placed was critical to an eminent degree, he contrived to turn all the success gained by Wurmser to the advantage of the French Army, and that by the mere strength of his genius alone. Junot distinguished himself by extraordinary efforts of courage in these actions. He was thus mentioned in the dispatch sent by Napoleon to the Directory after the victory:

> I ordered my *aide-de-camp*, General-of-Brigade Junot, to put himself at the head of my company of Guides to pursue the enemy and overtake him by great speed at Dezenzano. He encountered Colonel Bender with a party of his regiment of hussars, whom he charged; but Junot, not wishing to waste his time by charging the rear, made a detour on the right, took the regiment in front,—wounded the colonel whom he attempted to take prisoner when he was himself surrounded,—and after having killed six of the enemy with his own hand, was cut down and thrown into a ditch.

Bonaparte and the Sleeping Sentinel

The Austrians, still able to collect 25,000 men and a numerous cavalry, now fled again in all directions upon the Mincio where Wurmser himself, meanwhile, had been employed in revictualling Mantua. When Wurmser reached this point he was utterly astounded to find the trenches abandoned and no enemy to oppose. One of the defeated Austrian divisions wandering about without method in anxiety to find their commander or any part of his army that was still in the field, came suddenly on Lonato, the scene of the recent battle, and at a moment when Napoleon was there with only his staff and Guard about him. He was not aware that any considerable body of the enemy remained in the neighbourhood, and but for his great presence of mind must have been taken prisoner.

As it was, he turned his critical position into an advantage. The officer who had been sent to demand the surrender of the town was brought blindfolded, according to custom on such occasions, to his headquarters. Bonaparte, by a secret sign, caused his whole staff to draw up around him, and when the bandage was removed from the messenger's eyes, exclaimed to him: "What means this insolence? Do you beard the French general in the very centre of his army? Go and tell your general that I give him eight minutes to lay down his arms; he is in the midst of the French Army, and if a single gun is fired, I will cause every man to be shot." The officer, appalled at discovering in whose presence he stood, returned to his comrades with Napoleon's message.

The general of the enemy's column now made his appearance, stating his willingness to surrender and capitulate. "No" replied Bonaparte with energy, "you are all prisoners of war." Seeing the Austrian officers consulting together Napoleon instantly gave orders that the artillery should advance and commence the attack.

On observing this the general of the enemy's forces exclaimed, "We all surrender at discretion!" The shortness of time allowed prevented the truth from being discovered, and they gave in to a force about one-fourth of their own. They believed that Lonato was occupied by the French in numbers that made resistance impossible. When the four thousand men had laid down their arms they discovered that if they had used them nothing could have prevented Napoleon from being taken as their prize!

Wurmser, whose fine army was thus being destroyed in detail, now collected together the whole of his remaining force, and advanced to meet the conqueror. He had determined on an assault and was hastening to the encounter. They met between Lonato and Castiglione, and Wurmser was totally defeated, besides narrowly escaping being himself taken a prisoner. He was pursued into Trent and Roveredo, the positions from which he had so lately issued confident of victory. In this disastrous campaign he had now lost forty thousand soldiers—half his army—and all his artillery and stores, while Bonaparte placed his own loss at seven thousand. The French soldiers have called this succession of victories "the campaign of five days." The rapid marches and incessant fighting had exhausted the troops, and they now absolutely required rest.

During the exciting days while the campaign with Wurmser lasted, Napoleon never took off his clothes, nor did he take the time to sleep except at brief intervals of less than an hour. His exertions, which were followed by such signal triumphs, were such as to demand some repose, yet he did not pause until he saw Mantua once more completely invested. The reinforcement and revictualling of the garrison were all that Wurmser could show in requital of his lost artillery, stores and forty thousand men.

While Napoleon was giving some respite to his wearied army and rendering the subjugation of Italy complete, Austria was hurrying a new army to the relief of its aged but not disheartened marshal. The reinforcements of twenty thousand fresh troops at last arrived, and Wurmser was again in the field with fifty thousand men—an army vastly larger than Napoleon's. But once more he divided his forces and again each division was to be cut to pieces. He marched thirty thousand men to the relief of Mantua, and left Davidowich at Roveredo with twenty thousand men to protect the passes of the Tyrol. The two Austrian divisions were now separated and their fate was sealed.

On September 4, by the most rapid marches Europe had ever seen, Napoleon, having penetrated the designs of the Austrian general, reached Roveredo where Davidowich was intrenched in a strong position before the city, covered by the guns of the Calliano castle overhanging the town.

The camp was yielded on the same day before the terrific charge of General Dubois and his hussars. The latter, though mortally wounded, cheered his men on with his dying words, and as he fell pressing the hand of the general-in-chief, said: "Let me hear the shout of victory for the Republic before I die." These words fired his troops with deep ardour, and they drove the Austrians through the town and carried the frowning heights of the castle at the point of the bayonet, as they had carried the batteries of Lodi. The French pursued the fleeing Austrians throughout the night and Wurmser was cut off from the Tyrol.

Scarcely had the Austrian commander recovered from his surprise at hearing of the overthrow of his lieutenant at Roveredo before Napoleon, by a march of sixty miles in two days, descended in front of his vanguard at Primolano and cut it to pieces, taking four thousand prisoners. The same night Napoleon's army advanced on Bassano where on Sept. 8 Wurmser made his last stand with the main body of his army.

While Augereau penetrated the town on his left, Massena entered it on his right, seizing the cannon that defended the bridge on the Bretna and overthrowing the old grenadiers who attempted to cover the retreat of their general. Five thousand prisoners, five standards, thirty-five pieces of cannon with their caissons fell into the hands of the French, and Wurmser himself narrowly escaped being taken. Lannes seized one of the standards with his own hands; and, in consequence, Bonaparte demanded for him the rank of general of brigade. "He was," he said, "the first who put the enemy to rout at Dego, who passed the Po at Plaisance, the Adda at Lodi, and the first to enter Bassano."

The number of the dead near the latter place was considerable. Curious to ascertain the loss of the enemy, Bonaparte in the evening rode over the field with his staff, when his notice was attracted by the howlings of a dog that seemed to increase as they approached the spot whence the yells proceeded. Napoleon said some years later:

> Amidst the deep silence of a beautiful moonlight night a dog, leaping suddenly from beneath the clothes of his dead master, rushed upon us, and then immediately returned to his hiding-place, howling piteously. He alternately licked his master's hand, and ran toward us, as if at once soliciting aid and seeking revenge. Whether, owing to my own particular turn of mind at the moment, the time, the place, or the action itself, I know not, but, certainly, no incident, on any field of battle, ever produced so deep an impression on me. I involuntarily stopped to contemplate the scene. This man, thought I, has friends in the camp, or in his company, and here he lies forsaken by all except his dog. What a lesson Nature presents here, through the medium of an animal. What a strange being is man! And how mysterious are his impressions! I had, without emotion, ordered battles

Bonaparte Escapes Capture at Lonato

which were to decide the fate of the army; I beheld, with tearless eyes, the execution of those operations by which numbers of my countrymen were sacrificed; and here my feelings were roused by the howlings of a dog! Certainly, at that moment, I should have been easily moved by a suppliant enemy. I could very well imagine Achilles surrendering up the body of Hector at the sight of Priam's tears.

In these terrible marches Napoleon endured the same privations as his men;—baggage and staff appointments were unable to keep up with such rapid movements. He shared his bread with one of his privates who lived to remind him of this night when the Republican general had become the Emperor of France. It was during Napoleon's progress through Belgium in 1804, while reviewing a division of the army that he was visited in one of the towns by a soldier of the fourth regiment of infantry who stepped forward and thus addressed him:

> General, in the year Five of the French Revolution, being in the valley of Bassano, I shared with you my ration of bread when you were very hungry. You cannot have forgotten the circumstance. I request, in return, that you provide bread for my father who is worn with age and infirmity. I have received five wounds in the service and was made corporal and sergeant on the field of battle. I hope to be made a lieutenant on the first vacancy.

Napoleon recollected the soldier and immediately acknowledged the reasonableness of both his demands, which were speedily complied with.

After the most heroic resistance Wurmser again fled. Six thousand Austrians laid down their arms, and the commander with his fleeing forces took refuge about the middle of September in Mantua, whither they were pursued by Napoleon's cavalry.

Wurmser was now strictly blockaded within the citadel of Mantua with sixteen thousand men. These, with ten thousand dispersed in the Tyrol, were all that remained of his army of 60,000 men with which he was to reconquer Italy. He had also lost seventy-five pieces of cannon, thirty generals and twenty-two stands of colours. Marmont, one of Napoleon's *aides-de-camp*, was sent with these latter trophies to the Directory at Paris. Perceiving that Wurmser now intended to avoid a general action Napoleon returned to Milan, leaving General Kilmaine to conduct the blockade.

While at Milan, Napoleon had just mounted his horse one morning, when a dragoon, bearing important dispatches, presented himself.

The commander gave a verbal answer, and ordered the courier to take it back with all speed.

"I have no horse," the man answered; "I rode mine so hard that it fell dead at your palace gates."

Napoleon alighted. "Take mine," he said.

The man hesitated.

"You think him too magnificently caparisoned and too fine an animal;" said Napoleon. "Nothing is too good for a French soldier!"

Again a call was made on Vienna to send a new army and a greater general to restore the Hapsburg dominion in Italy. In reply another powerful armament was dispatched to the Italian frontier and this, the fourth campaign against Napoleon, was intrusted to the supreme command of Alvinzi, an officer of high reputation.

Field-Marshal Alvinzi was placed at the head of an army of forty-five thousand men to which he joined eighteen thousand under Davidowich in the Tyrol. His object was to raise the blockade of Mantua, release Wurmser and, with a force which would by the accession of the garrison of the latter amount to an army of eighty thousand men with which to oppose only thirty thousand. With these he expected to reconquer Lombardy.

Three large armies, advancing with similar prospects, had already been destroyed by Napoleon; a fourth now prepared to pour down upon him, under still more terrible circumstances. The Battle of St. George and the strict blockade of Wurmser in Mantua took place in the middle of September. Alvinzi's army commenced its march in the beginning of October.

Napoleon instantly ordered Vaubois and Massena to advance to the attack of Davidowich, whose forces were collected in the Tyrol, before he could form a junction with Alvinzi. Both failed. Vaubois, after two days' fighting was conquered; lost Trent and Calliano, and was forced to retreat. Massena in consequence had to effect a retreat without attempting an engagement, and Alvinzi approaching fast gained possession of all the country between the Brenta and the Adige and the command of the Tyrol. The two Austrian generals might now have effected a junction, but they neglected their opportunity. Napoleon hastened to Verona, Alvinzi having taken the same route.

It seemed likely that Austria, in this new campaign, was destined to recover her immense losses. Napoleon was now contending against an enemy vastly superior in numbers and most completely appointed. But twelve battalions had been sent to him from France to recruit his exhausted regiments, and nothing but the employment of the highest military skill could now save him from destruction.

He said, in writing to the Directory:

> The army so inferior in numbers, has been more weakened by the late engagements, while the promised reinforcements have not arrived. The heroes of Millessimo, Lodi, Castiglione, and Bassano, are dead or in the hospitals. Joubert, Lanusse, Victor, Lannes, Charlot, Murat, Dupuis, Rampon, Menard, Chabrand, and Pigeon are wounded; we are abandoned at the extremity of Italy. Had I received the 103rd, three thousand five hundred strong, I would have answered for everything. Whereas, in a few days, 40,000 men, perhaps, will not be sufficient to enable us to make head against the enemy.

His men too, were becoming dispirited at the failure of the government to send reinforcements, and no longer fought with their accustomed vigour and enthusiasm. The retreating forces came before him with dejected looks. But the genius of Napoleon was not yet exhausted; with him discouragement was not despair. He ordered Vaubois' division—which had abandoned Calliano—drawn up on the plain of Rivoli, and thus addressed them:

> Soldiers, I am not satisfied with you: you have shown neither bravery, discipline, nor perseverance. No position could rally you: you abandoned yourselves to a panic terror; you suffered yourselves to be driven from situations where a handful of brave men might have stopped an army. Soldiers of the 29th and 85th, you are not French soldiers. Quartermaster-general, let it be inscribed on their colours: 'They no longer belong to the Army of Italy!'

The effect of these words was electric. The veteran grenadiers who had braved the terrific charges at Lodi sobbed like children and broke their ranks to cluster round their commander to plead for one more trial. Several of the veteran grenadiers, who had deserved and obtained badges of distinction, called out from the ranks: "General! we have been misrepresented; place us in the van of the army and you shall then judge whether we do not belong to the Army of Italy."

They were at last forgiven by their indignant commander, and when they were again arrayed against the enemy they quickly redeemed their lost reputation and gained new laurels. But a spirit of discontent pervaded the French Army. "We cannot work miracles," said the soldiers. "We destroyed Beaulieu's great army, and then came Wurmser with a greater. We conquered and broke him to pieces, and then came Alvinzi more powerful than ever. When we have conquered him Austria will pour down on us a hundred thousand fresh soldiers and we shall leave our bones in Italy."

Although much dispirited, Napoleon was by no means disposed to abandon his campaign; to his soldiers he said by way of encouragement:

> We have but one more effort to make and Italy is ours. The enemy is no doubt superior to us in numbers, but not in valour. When he is beaten Mantua must fall, and we shall be masters of all; our labours will be at an end, for not only Italy but a general peace is in Mantua. You talk of returning to the Alps, but you are no longer capable of doing so. From the dry and frozen bivouacs of those sterile rocks you could very well conquer the delicious plains of Lombardy; but from the smiling flowery bivouacs of Italy you cannot return to Alpine snows. Only beat Alvinzi and I will answer for your future welfare.

Ere long the French forces were once more ready for battle. Alvinzi had occupied the heights of Caldiero and by the middle of November threatened Verona. Massena attacked the heights but found them impregnable. The French were repulsed with considerable loss. Napoleon found it necessary to attempt taking the heights by other means in order to prevent the junction of Davidowich and Alvinzi. Pretending, therefore, to retreat on Mantua after his discomfiture, he returned in the night and placed himself in the rear of Alvinzi's army. When his columns advanced on Arcola the enemy thought at first it was only a skirmish and that the main army of the French was in Verona. The position of Arcola rendered any attack upon it so extremely hazardous that scarcely anyone would have conceived the idea of making the attempt. The village is surrounded by marshes intersected by small streams, by ditches and by three causeways or bridges, across which alone the marshes are passable.

Arcola and the bridge leading to it were defended by two battalions of Alvinzi's army, and two pieces of cannon which commanded

Bonaparte at the Bridge of Arcola

the bridge. The other two causeways were unprotected.

Napoleon ordered a division to charge the bridge of Arcola at daybreak. The attempt seemed even to the intrepid Augereau to be courting death, but he was a true soldier and obeyed orders.

On November 15 a column advanced on each of the three causeways. Augereau's division occupied the bridge of Arcola which was swept by the enemy's cannon and assailed in flank by their battalions. Even the chosen grenadiers, led by Augereau with a standard in his hand, faltered and fell back under the destructive fire, fleeing over the corpses of nearly half their comrades. It was a most critical situation, and one in which a false step or the loss of a few moments meant ruin. Napoleon, who knew that the moment was decisive, dashed at the head of the column, snatched a standard, and hurrying onwards planted the colours with his own hands on the bridge amidst a hail of balls from the enemy's artillery and musketry. As he did so he cried out: "Soldiers! are you no longer the brave warriors of Lodi? Follow your general!"

His soldiers rallied and rushed with him till they grappled with the Austrian division, but the sudden arrival of a fresh column of the enemy made it an impossibility to maintain their ground. The French fell back, and Napoleon, being in the very midst of the fight, was himself seized by his faithful grenadiers who bore him away in their arms through smoke, the dead and dying, as they were driven backwards inch by inch with dreadful carnage. Mounting a horse the commander once more prepared to make a charge at the head of his heroic troops, when his steed became unmanageable and plunged headlong throwing its rider into a morass up to his waist.

The Austrians were now between Napoleon and his baffled column. As the smoke rolled away the army at once perceived the critical position of their general. During this crisis Lannes pressed forward through the marsh and reached his commander as also did the gallant Muiron, the friend and *aide-de-camp* of Napoleon. Almost at the same moment a shot was fired at Napoleon. It was received by Muiron, who had interposed himself, and he died covering Napoleon's body with his own. But still the person of the commander remained in the utmost peril.

The grenadiers now formed in an instant, and with the cry, "Forward, soldiers, to save your general!" threw themselves upon the enemy, rescued their "Little Corporal" from his critical position and overthrew the Austrian columns that defended the bridge. Napoleon was quickly at their head again, rallied the column, struck terror through the ranks of the enemy, and Arcola was soon taken. Two other engagements followed at this point, in each of which the French were victorious, Massena pursuing the enemy until darkness compelled him to desist. The Austrians lost twelve thousand men killed, six thousand prisoners, eighteen pieces of cannon and four stands of colours. The loss of the French was less considerable in numbers than in the importance of the prominent individuals who fell during those three days, when the generals acted as soldiers, continually fighting at the heads of their columns. The great art of Napoleon, on that occasion, he having but 13,000 to oppose 40,000 men, was to maintain the combat in the midst of a morass where the enemy could not deploy. Upon such a field of battle, only the heads of the columns could engage; whereas, on a plain, the French army would in all probability have been surrounded.

Napoleon said at St. Helena that he considered himself in the greatest danger at Arcola.

When too late Davidowich made an advance upon Verona, but retreated quickly on hearing of Alvinzi's defeat at Arcola. Wurmser, too, made a desperate sally and was repulsed. He still held out, however. The horses of the garrison had long since been killed and salted for use; the men were reduced to half rations, and their numbers were being rapidly reduced by disease.

This fourth attempt of Austria to conquer Napoleon ended, therefore, as did the previous ones, in failure. It was one of the most memorable campaigns in history, in the course of which all the resources of skilled warriors were exhibited, not in a contest of a few hours but a succession of memorable battles. As yet, however, the young commander was but a temporary victor; the weakness of the Army of Italy did not permit him to draw all the advantages he had promised himself from Arcola. Alvinzi was now thoroughly beaten, his losses were very great, and like his predecessors he sent to Vienna for reinforcements to continue his contest against Bonaparte, who had repaired to Verona which he fixed upon as the central point of operations.

Once more the Austrian general's preparations were completed for a fresh campaign, and on January 7, 1797, at the head of sixty thousand soldiers, consisting of volunteers from the best families in Vienna and battalions from the Army of the Rhine, Croats, Hungarians, Tyroleans, etc., Alvinzi descended from the northern barriers of Italy to release the brave Wurmser from his prison at Mantua, and again attempt to "overwhelm the French invaders." A messenger dispatched to Wurmser from the imperial court was captured by the French, and dispatches concealed in wax balls recovered. From these Napoleon learned the present designs, signed by the emperor's own hand, of the Austrian Government:—Alvinzi was once more placed at the head of sixty thousand men, and was again to march into Lombardy and to raise the siege of Mantua: Wurmser was directed to hold out to the last extremity: If the army of Alvinzi could be reunited with the garrison, the destruction of the French seemed undoubted; if not, and if, in the course of hostilities, he found it best to abandon Mantua, he was directed to cut his way into Romagna and to take command of the papal troops, the pope having broken the treaty of Bologna, and raised an army of seven thousand men to act in concert with Wurmser, when he should be released from Mantua.

Again the Austrian Army,—the fifth—was divided, one column under Alvinzi for the line of the Adige; the other for the Bretna under General Provera, who was to join the marshal under the walls of Mantua.

When Napoleon learned this at his headquarters at Verona he posted Joubert at Rivoli to dispute Alvinzi's passage, and Augereau to watch the movements of Provera, knowing that within a few hours he could concentrate his own forces on either column.

At sunset on the 13th of January Joubert's messenger brought the news that he had met Alvinzi and with difficulty held him in check through the day. Napoleon examined with the utmost attention the maps and descriptions of the places, the reports of the generals, and those of his spies and light troops and passed a part of the night in a state of uncertainty and indecision. At length on receiving fresh reports he exclaimed: "It is clear—it is clear: to Rivoli!" and, quickly giving his orders to his aides assigning the troops to their different routes, he left a garrison at Verona and with General Massena and all the disposable troops he repaired to General Joubert. By one of his lightning marches he reached the heights of Rivoli two hours after midnight. Below in the valley five separate encampments of the Austrian army were visible in the moonlight. Napoleon quickly decided to force Alvinzi to battle before he was ready. Joubert, confounded by the display of Alvinzi's gigantic force was in the very act of abandoning his position when the French commander checked his movement, and, bringing up more battalions, forced the enemy from a position they had seized on the first symptoms of the French retreat.

From the eminence on which he stood Napoleon's keen eye soon penetrated the secret of Alvinzi's weakness,—that his artillery had not yet arrived. To force him to accept battle, Napoleon took every possible means to conceal his own arrival and prolonged, by a series of petty manoeuvres, the enemy's belief that they had to do with a mere outpost of the French. Alvinzi was fully deceived, and instead of advancing on some great and well-arranged system, suffered his several columns to endeavour to force the heights by insulated movements which the real strength of Napoleon easily enabled him to baffle. Two field-pieces had been abandoned by their drivers and which were seized by the enemy, when an officer whose name is not recorded, advancing, cried out: "Fourteenth, will you let them take your artillery?" Berthier, who had purposely suffered the enemy to approach, then opened a terrible fire, which levelled men and horses round the guns, and upon which the Austrians immediately fell back.

A moment later the bravery of the enemy resulted in their nearly overthrowing the French on a point of pre-eminent importance, but Napoleon himself, galloping to the spot, roused by his voice and action the division of Massena who, having marched all night, had laid down to rest in the extreme of weariness. They started up at the commander's voice and the Austrian column was speedily repulsed.

The French artillery was soon in position, while that of the Austrians, as Napoleon had guessed, had not yet come up, and this circumstance decided the fortune of the day. The batteries of the French made havoc of the broken columns; the cavalry made repeated charges; four out of the five divisions were thus broken and utterly routed. The fifth now made its appearance in the rear of the French. It had been sent round to outflank Napoleon and take higher ground in his rear according to the orders of the Austrian general before the action. When Lusignan's division achieved its destined object it did so,—not to complete the misery of a routed, but to swell the prey of a victorious, enemy. Instead of cutting off the retreat of Joubert, Lusignan found himself insulated from Alvinzi and forced to lay down his arms to Bonaparte. Had this movement been made a little sooner it might have turned the fortune of the day: as it was, the French soldiers only exclaimed: "Here come further supplies to our market!" and very soon the Austrians, exposed to a heavy fire from the artillery, were forced to surrender.

"Here was a good plan," said Napoleon, "but these Austrians are not apt to calculate the value of minutes."

Bonaparte at the Battle of St. George

Had Lusignan gained the rear of the French an hour earlier, while the contest was still hot in front of the heights of Rivoli, he might have aided in the complete overthrow of Napoleon instead of being defeated on one of the brightest days in the young commander's career.

In the course of the day Bonaparte had remained in the hottest of the fight, which lasted during twelve hours, and had three horses shot under him, and although much fatigued, hardly waited to see Lusignan surrender ere he set off with reinforcements to the Lower Adige to prevent Wurmser from either housing Provera or joining him in the open field and so effect the escape of his own formidable garrison. The flying troops of Alvinzi were left to the care of Massena, Murat and Joubert.

Marching all day and the next night Napoleon reached the vicinity of Mantua late on the 15th. He found the enemy strongly posted and Serrurier's position highly critical. A regiment of Provera's hussars had but a few hours before established themselves in the suburb of St. George. This Austrian corps had been clothed in white cloaks resembling those of a well-known French regiment of hussars, and advancing towards the gate would certainly have been admitted as friends but for the sagacity of an old sergeant, who could not help fancying that the white cloaks had too much of the gloss of novelty about them to have stood the wear and tear of three Bonapartean campaigns. He instantly closed the barriers and warned a drummer who was near him of the danger. These two gave the alarm and the guns of the blockading force were instantly turned upon their pretended friends who were forced to retire.

Napoleon himself passed the night in walking the outposts, so great was his anxiety. At one of these he found a grenadier sentinel asleep from exhaustion and taking his gun, without waking him, performed a sentinel's duty in his place for about half an hour. When the man, starting from his slumbers, perceived with terror and despair the countenance and occupation of his general, he fell on his knees before him. "My friend," said Napoleon mildly, "here is your musket. You had fought hard and marched long and your exhaustion is excusable; but a moment's inattention might at present ruin the whole army. I happened to be awake and have held your post for you. You will be more careful another time!"

Such acts of magnanimity endeared Napoleon to his soldiers, and, while he rarely relaxed in his military discipline, he early acquired the devotion of his men who told and retold anecdotes of his doings in camp and on the battlefield, and as the stories spread from column to column his followers came to regard him with a veneration that few older commanders have been able to instil in their men. Another anecdote is related of Bonaparte, when upon the point of commencing one of his great battles in Italy. As he was disposing his troops in order of attack, a light dragoon stepping from the ranks, requested of the commander a few minutes private conversation to which Napoleon acquiesced, when the soldier thus addressed him: "General, if you will proceed to adopt such and such measures, the enemy must be defeated."

"Wretched man," exclaimed the commander, "hold your tongue; you will surely not betray my secret" at the same time placing his hand before the mouth of the dragoon.

The soldier in question was possessed of an inherent military capacity and appreciated every arrangement necessary to insure victory. The battle terminating in favour of Napoleon, he issued orders that the poor fellow should be conducted to his presence; but all search for him proved fruitless, he was nowhere to be found: a bullet had no doubt terminated his military career.

The next morning there ensued a hot skirmish, recorded as the Battle of St. George. The tumult and slaughter were dreadful and Provera with his whole force were compelled to lay down their arms. Wurmser, who had hazarded a sortie from Mantua to join his countrymen, was glad to make his way back again, and retire within the old walls, in consequence of a desperate assault headed by Napoleon in person, who threw himself between Wurmser and Provera and beat them completely one after the other. Provera now found himself cut off hopelessly from Alvinzi and surrounded by the French; he was disheartened and defeated. He and his five thousand men laid down their arms on the 16th of January, and various bodies of the Austrian force scattered over the country followed their example. This latter engagement was called the battle of La Favorita from the name of a country house near which it was fought. The 75th at this battle refused cartridges: "With such enemies as we have before us," said they, "we must only use the bayonet."

The Battles of Rivoli and La Favorita had disabled Alvinzi from continuing the campaign. Thus had the magnificent army of Austria ceased to exist in three days.

Such was the prevailing terror of the enemy at this time that in one instance René, a young officer keeping guard of a position with about one hundred and fifty men, suddenly encountered and took prisoners a small body of Austrians. On advancing to reconnoitre, he found himself in front of a body of eighteen hundred more, whom a turn in the road had concealed from his sight. "Lay down your arms!" said the Austrian commandant. René answered with boldness, "Do you lay down your arms! I have destroyed your advance guard;—ground your arms, or no quarter!" The French soldiers joined in the cry, and the whole body of the astonished Austrians absolutely laid down their arms to a party, which they found to their exasperation when too late, was in numbers one twelfth of their own.

Wurmser was now thoroughly disheartened in not receiving relief, and as his provisions were by this time exhausted, found himself at length in dire straits. Napoleon sent him word of the rout and dispersion of the Austrian army and summoned him to surrender. The old soldier proudly replied that "he had provisions for a year," but a few days later he sent his *aide-de-camp*, Klenau to the headquarters of Serrurier with an offer of capitulation. General Serrurier, as commander of the blockade, received the bearer of Wurmser's message in which he stated that he was "still in a condition to hold out considerably longer, unless honourable terms were granted."

Napoleon, who had been seated in a corner of his tent wrapped in his cloak, now came forward and addressed himself to the Austrian envoy, who had no suspicion in whose presence he had been speaking, and taking his pen, wrote down marginal answers to the conditions proposed by Wurmser. He granted terms more favourable than might have been exacted in the extremity to which the veteran was reduced:

> These are the conditions to which your general's bravery entitles him if he opens his gates tomorrow. He may have them today; a week, a month hence, he shall have no worse: he may hold out to his last morsel of bread. Meantime tell him that General Bonaparte is about to set out for Rome.

The envoy now recognized Napoleon, and on reading the paper perceived that the proposed terms were more liberal than he had dared to hope for; he then owned that only three days' provisions remained in Mantua.

The capitulation was forthwith signed and on the 2nd of February, 1797, Wurmser and his garrison of 13,000 men marched out of Mantua: 7,000 were lying in the hospitals. When the aged chief was by the fortunes of war to surrender his sword, he found only Serrurier ready to receive it. Napoleon was unwilling to be a witness to the humiliation of the distinguished veteran, and had left the place before the surrender, thus sparing the conquered veteran the mortification of giving up his sword to so youthful a commander. This delicate generosity on the part of the French general was never forgotten by Wurmser.

The terms of surrender agreed to by Bonaparte were not readily accepted by the French Directory, who urged him to far different conduct. He wrote in reply:

> I have granted the Austrian such terms as were, in my judgment, due to a brave and honourable foe, and to the dignity of the French nation.

The loss of the Austrians at Mantua amounted altogether to not less than 30,000 men, besides innumerable military stores and upwards of 500 brass cannon.

The conqueror sent Augereau to Paris with the sixty captured standards of Austria, and his arrival at the capital was celebrated as a national festival. Thus it was that Napoleon, with a total force at the utmost, of 65,000 men, conquered, in their own country, and under the eye and succouring hand of their own government, five successive armies, amounting, in all, to *upwards of 300,000 well-appointed well-provisioned soldiers*, under old and experienced commanders of approved courage. Such was the conquest of Lombardy.

Sometime later Wurmser sent Napoleon a letter by special messenger acknowledging the generosity and delicacy of conduct of the French commander at Mantua, and at the same time apprising him by his *aide-de-camp* of a conspiracy to poison him in the dominions of the pope, with whom he was about to wage war.

A few brief engagements with papal troops followed the capitulation of Wurmser, the pope fearing that the conqueror would enter the "Eternal City;" but Napoleon, by a rapid movement, threw his infantry across the River Senio, where the enemy was encamped, and met with but a brief resistance. Shortly afterwards the pope entered into negotiations with the French commander, and the treaty of Tolentino followed on the 13th of February, 1797, conceding to the French one hundred of the finest works of art, several castles and legations, and about two millions of dollars.

Napoleon was now master of all Northern Italy with the exception of the territories of Venice, which announced that it had no desire but to preserve a perfect neutrality.

More than a month had now elapsed since Alvinzi's defeat at Rivoli; in nine days the war with the pope had reached its close; and, having left some garrisons in the town on the Adige to watch the neutrality of Venice, Napoleon hastened to carry the war into the hereditary dominions of the Austrian emperor. Twenty thousand fresh troops had joined his victorious standard from France, and at the head of perhaps a larger force than he had ever before mustered, he proceeded towards the Tyrol where, according to his information, the main army of Austria, recruited once more to its original strength, was preparing to open a sixth campaign under the orders,—not of Alvinzi, but of a general young like himself, and hitherto eminently successful, the Archduke Charles, who had defeated the courage and skill of Jourdan and Moreau on the Rhine, and was now to be opposed to Napoleon.

The story of this sixth campaign is but a repetition of the five that preceded it. The archduke, a young prince of high talents, and upon whom the last hopes of the Austrian Empire reposed, compelled by the council of Vienna to execute a plan he had the discrimination to condemn, was destined to lead but a short campaign, although he had the best army Austria could enrol. This army once more proceeded to begin operations on a double basis, and Napoleon permitted him to assume the offensive.

On the 9th of March, 1797, the French commander's headquarters were fixed at Bassano, and he proceeded vigorously on his career of conquest. He issued one of his stirring proclamations, in which he told his soldiers that a grand destiny was still reserved for them, and then advanced to attack the archduke. He found the latter posted upon the plains bordering on the banks of the River Tagliamento in front of the rugged Carinthian mountains which guard the passage in that quarter from Italy to Germany. Detaching Massena with a division of cavalry to effect the passage of the Piave where the Austrian division of Lusignan was posted, Napoleon determined to charge the archduke in front. Massena was successful in driving Lusignan before him as far as Belluno, where he, with a rear guard of 500, surrendered, and thus turned the Austrian flank.

On the 16th of March, the two armies headed by Napoleon, and the Archduke Charles in person, were drawn up on opposite sides of the Tagliamento, face to face. Bonaparte then attempted to effect the passage of the river, but after a formal display of his forces, which was met by similar demonstrations on the Austrian side of the river, he suddenly broke up his line, retreated, and took up his bivouac. The archduke concluded that, as the French had been marching all the night before, their leader wished to defer the battle until another day, and in like manner withdrew to his encampment. About two hours later Napoleon rushed with his whole army, who had merely laid down in ranks, upon the margin of the Tagliamento,—no longer adequately guarded,—and had forded the stream ere the Austrian line of battle could be formed. In the passage of the Tagliamento Napoleon was so nearly drowned, by the submersion of his carriage, that he for some moments gave up all thoughts of being rescued.

This affair was the first in which the division of Bernadotte had borne a part. He arrived upon the borders of the Tagliamento at the very moment of the combat: throwing himself into the river he exclaimed to his followers, "Think that you are the Army of the Rhine, and that the Army of Italy is looking on you!"

In the action which followed the troops of the archduke displayed much gallantry, and charged the French repeatedly with the greatest courage, but every effort to dislodge Napoleon failed; at length retreat was deemed necessary, and eight pieces of cannon and some provisions were left behind, the French following in close pursuit.

Adjutant General Kellerman distinguished himself at the head of the French cavalry and received many wounds in executing the manoeuvres that decided the success of the day; he was subsequently charged with carrying the trophies taken from the enemy to France.

The pursuers stormed Gradisca, where they made 6,000 prisoners; and the archduke continuing his retreat, occupied in the course of a few days Trieste, Fiume and every stronghold in Carinthia. In the course of a campaign of twenty days the Austrians fought Bonaparte ten times; but the overthrow on the Tagliamento was never recovered. Their army was melting away like the snows of the Tyrol.

At last the Austrian leader decided to reach Vienna by forced marches, there to gather round him whatever force the loyalty of his nation could muster, and make a last stand beneath the walls of the capital. The archduke expected to reap great advantage from enticing the French army into the heart of Austria, where, divided by many wide provinces and mighty mountains and rivers from France, and with Italy once more in arms behind them, he hoped to cut off their source of supplies and compel them to retreat from a greatly reinforced imperial army.

From the period of the opening of the campaign the archduke had lost nearly 20,000 men made prisoners, so that the Austrians could make no stand except upon the mountains in the neighbourhood of the Capital.

Vienna, however, was terror-stricken on hearing that Napoleon who was only sixty leagues distant, had stormed the passes of the Julian Alps. The imperial family—embracing little Marie Louise, then scarcely six years old, afterwards Napoleon's wife—fled with their crown jewels and treasures into Hungary; the middle classes became clamorous for a termination of the six years' war, and the archduke was ordered to avail himself of the first pretence which circumstances might afford for the opening of a negotiation. Napoleon wrote to the archduke suggesting peace:

> While brave soldiers carry on war they wish for peace; Has not the war already lasted six years? Have we not killed men enough, and inflicted sufficient sufferings on the human race? Europe has laid down the arms she took up against the French Republic. Your nation alone perseveres; yet blood is to flow more copiously than ever. Whatever be the issue, we shall kill some thousands of men on both sides, and after all we must come to an understanding, since all things have an end, not excepting vindictive passions. . . . . For my part, general, if the overture I have the honour to make to you should only save the life of a single man, I should feel more proud of the civic crown, I should think I thereby merited, than of all the melancholy glory that the most distinguished military successes can afford.

The archduke replied within two hours after the receipt of the letter and a series of negotiations followed, which with Napoleon's rapid advance on Vienna, finally brought about the provisional treaty of Leoben, signed April 18, 1797. Napoleon, without waiting for full power from the Directory to complete the treaty, took the responsibility upon himself and signed it on the part of France on the 19th of April. The Austrian plenipotentiaries had set down as a primary concession that "the Emperor acknowledged the French Republic."

"Strike that out!" said Napoleon; "the Republic is like the sun that shines by its own light; none but the blind can fail to see it. We are our own masters and shall establish any government we prefer." "If the French people should one day wish to create a monarchy," he afterwards remarked, "the emperor might object that he had recognized a Republic."

This treaty was followed by a complete surrender on the part of the Venetian Senate which had violated its pledges of neutrality, and a democratic government was formed, provisionally, on the model of France. Venice consented to surrender to the victor large territories on the mainland of Italy; five ships of war, $600,000 in gold and as much more in naval stores, twenty of her best works of art and 500 ancient manuscripts. Napoleon took possession of the city, and the history of the Venetian Republic was ended. In their last agony the Venetian Senate made a vain attempt to bribe Napoleon with a purse of seven millions of *francs* for more favourable terms, reminding him of the proverbial ingratitude of all popular governments and of the slight attention which the French Directory had hitherto paid to his personal interests. "That is all true enough," he replied, "but I will not place myself in the power of this duke." To a larger tender on the part of Austria he replied: "If greatness or richness is to be mine, it must come from France."

Among the works of art sent by Napoleon to Paris was the celebrated picture of St. Jerome from the Duke of Parma's gallery. The duke, to save this treasure, offered Napoleon two hundred thousand dollars, which the conqueror refused to take, saying: "The sum which he offers us will soon be spent; but the possession of such a masterpiece at Paris will adorn that capital for ages, and give birth to similar exertions of genius."

The fall of Venice gave Napoleon the means of bringing his treaty with Austria to a more satisfactory conclusion than had been indicated in the preliminaries of Leoben. After settling the affairs of Venice and establishing the new Ligurian Republic he took up his residence at the palace of Montibello, near Milan, with Josephine, whom he had not seen since his departure from France a year before. The final settlement with Austria's commissioners was purposely delayed by that empire, it being the universal belief that the government of France was approaching a new crisis, and Austria hoped from such an event to derive considerable advantage.

Napoleon was becoming weary of the protracted negotiations and threats of the Austrian ambassadors. One day in the latter's chamber, he suddenly changed his demeanour. "You refuse to accept our ultimatum," said he, taking in his hands a beautiful vase of porcelain, which stood on the mantelpiece near him. The Austrian bowed. "It is well," said Napoleon, "the truce is broken, war is declared, but mark me,—within three months I shall shatter Austria as I now shatter this brittle affair!" So saying he dashed the fragile piece furiously to the floor, breaking it into a thousand pieces, and left the room. The ambassador followed him, and finding him preparing to march on Vienna, made submissions which induced him to once more resume negotiations, the result of which was the treaty of Campo-Formio, so called from the humble village at which it was signed on the 17th of October, 1797.

Bourrienne relates that while Napoleon was occupied with the organization of Venice, Genoa and Milan, he used to complain of the want of *men*. "Good God!" said he, "how rare *men* are! There are eighteen millions in Italy and I have with difficulty found two real ones,—Dandolo and Lelzi." These two actual "men" were immediately employed in important services, and justified his estimation of them.

It was from the palace of Montibello, five leagues from Milan, that Napoleon wrote to the Directory:

> From these different points (the islands of the Mediterranean, which he proposed to seize) we can command that sea, keep an eye on the Ottoman Empire, which is crumbling to pieces, and we can render the supremacy of the ocean almost useless to Great Britain. *Let us take possession of Egypt*, which lies on the road to India, and there we can found one of the mightiest colonies in the world. It is in Egypt we must make war on England.

To perfect the treaty with Austria Napoleon received orders from the French Directory to appear at a congress at Rastadt, all the German powers being summoned to meet there for that purpose. He took an affecting leave of his soldiers, in which he said in closing: "Soldiers, when you talk of the princes you have conquered, of the nations you have set free, and the battles you have fought in two campaigns, say: 'In the next two we shall do still more.'" He then proceeded by way of Switzerland, carrying with him the unbounded love and devotion of one of the finest armies that the world had ever seen.

A person who saw Napoleon at this time described his impressions of him in the following letter, which appeared in one of the Paris journals in December 1797:

> With lively interest and extreme attention, I have observed this extraordinary man, who has performed such great deeds, and

about whom there is something which seems to indicate that his career is not yet closed. I found him very like his portraits—little, thin, pale, with an air of fatigue, but not of ill-health, as has been reported of him. He appears to me to listen with more abstraction than interest, and that he was more occupied with what he was thinking of than with what was said to him. There is a great intelligence in his countenance, along with which may be marked an air of habitual meditation which reveals nothing of what is passing within. In that thinking head, in that bold mind, it is impossible not to believe that some daring designs are engendering *which will have their influence on the destinies of Europe!*

Napoleon remarked afterwards:

My extreme youth when I took command of the Army of Italy," "made it necessary for me to evince great reserve of manners and the utmost severity of morals. This was indispensable to enable me to sustain authority over men so greatly superior in age and experience. I pursued a line of conduct in the highest degree irreproachable and exemplary. In spotless morality I was a Cato and must have appeared such to all. My supremacy could be retained only by proving myself a better man than any other man in the army. Had I yielded to human weakness I should have lost my power.

At the first interview between Napoleon and the veteran generals whom he was to command, Rampon undertook to give the young commander some advice. Napoleon who was impatient of advice, exclaimed:

Gentlemen, the art of war is in its infancy. The time has passed in which enemies are mutually to appoint the place of combat, advance hat in hand and say: '*Gentlemen will you have the goodness to fire!*' We must cut the enemy to pieces, precipitate ourselves like a torrent upon their battalions and grind them to powder. Experienced generals conduct the troops opposed to us. So much the better! Their experience will not avail them against me. Mark my words, they will soon burn their books on tactics and know not what to do.

Arriving at Rastadt Napoleon found that the multiplicity of details to be arranged was likely to require a long stay, and as his personal relations with the Directory were of a doubtful kind, he abandoned the conduct of the diplomatic business to his colleagues and reached Paris after a triumphal march, on the 20th of November, 1797. During his absence he had been the salvation of France, and his arrival created a great sensation in the capital. He was hailed with the most rapturous applause by the people, the streets through which he was expected to pass were thronged, and wherever he was seen the air was filled with shouts of, "Long live the general of the Army of Italy!"

BONAPARTE AT THE SIEGE OF MANTUA

3

Expedition to Egypt

On the 2nd of October, 1797, during Napoleon's absence in Italy, the Directory announced to the French people its intention of carrying the war with England into England itself. The immediate organization of a great invading army was therefore ordered, and "Citizen General Bonaparte," the Conqueror of Italy, was designated to command the forces.

It was some months before this decision was acted upon, however, and in the meantime Napoleon lived quietly in a small, modest house in the Rue Chantereine, which he had occupied before he set out for Italy. Shortly after his return, on going home one evening, he was surprised to find workmen engaged in changing the sign bearing the name of the street to "*Rue de la Victoire,*" in commemoration of his Italian campaign. He seemed to avoid as much as possible at this time the honors of popular distinction and applause that the people heaped upon him. One morning he sent his secretary to a theatre manager to ask him to give that evening two very popular pieces, "if such a thing were possible."

"Nothing is impossible for General Bonaparte," replied the courtly manager; "the Conqueror of Italy has long ago erased that word from the dictionary!"

This flattering answer afforded Napoleon a hearty laugh. He went to the performance and although endeavouring to maintain his usual privacy, was discovered and loudly called upon to come forward. The honour which he esteemed most was his nomination as a member of the Institute. He frequently attended its meetings and was also fond of appearing in the costume worn by the members.

When congratulated by Bourrienne on some noisy demonstration of popular favour, he answered in the words of Cromwell; "Bah!

they would crowd as eagerly about me if I were on my way to the scaffold!"

Wherever he went he was still the Bonaparte of Lodi, Arcola and Rivoli.

Meanwhile the government gave him no adequate reward for his important services in Italy. He had not when he returned to France, three hundred thousand *francs* in his possession, though he had transmitted fifty millions to the State. "I might easily," he said to Las Casas, "have brought back ten or twelve millions; I never made out any accounts, nor was I ever asked for any." On the eve of his departure for Egypt he became possessed of Malmaison and there deposited nearly all his property. He purchased it in the name of his wife, older than himself, and consequently, in case of his surviving her, he must have forfeited all right to the same. The fact, as stated by himself, was, that he never had a taste or desire for the acquirement of riches.

He willingly accepted the new appointment now pressed upon him by the government, who seemed anxious that he should not remain in Paris to take part in the civil business of the State. In this latter direction he had no desire for continued service. In Napoleon's own language, "the pear was not yet ripe," and, like Cæsar, he would have preferred being first in a village to being second in Rome. The first scheme of the French Directory was to make a descent upon England and to place Napoleon at the head of the invading army, but their counsels continually fluctuated between this project and the Egyptian expedition. Napoleon said to Bourrienne on the 29th of January:

> Bourrienne, I shall remain here no longer; they (the Directory) do not want me; there is no good to be done; they will not listen to me. I see, if I loiter here, I am done for quickly. Here everything grows flat; my glory is already on the wane. This little Europe of yours cannot supply the demand. We must move to the East. All great reputations come from that quarter. But I will first take a turn round the coast to assure myself what can be done. If the success of a descent upon England appears doubtful, as I fear, the army of England shall become the army of the East, and I am off for Egypt.

He at length resolved to bring the question of the invasion to a decision by a personal survey of the coast opposite England. While there he busied himself for a time in suggesting improvements in fortifications and in selecting the best points for embarking an invading force. Many local improvements of great importance, long afterwards effected, were first suggested by him at this period; but the time had not come for invading England.

Napoleon had suggested to Talleyrand, minister of foreign affairs, some months before, the propriety of making an effort against England in another quarter of the globe; i. e., of seizing Malta, proceeding to Egypt, and therein gaining at once a territory capable of supplying to France the loss of her West Indian colonies, and the means of annoying Great Britain in her Indian trade and empire.

The East presented to him a field of conquest and glory, and to this he now again recurred. "Europe is but a mole hill," he said; "All the great glories have come from Asia where there are six hundred millions of men." He soon returned to Paris and made his views known to the Directory, declaring that an invasion of England was a wild chimera. To Bourrienne, his school companion, who asked him concerning his contemplated invasion after he had been on the coast a week he said: "The risk is too great; I sha'n't venture it. I don't want to trifle with the fate of France."

The temptation of the Directory was great, and as it would find employment for Napoleon at a distance from France, the Egyptian expedition was finally determined upon; but kept a great secret.

While the attention of Great Britain was now riveted on the coast, it was on the borders of the Mediterranean that his ships and the troops really destined for action, were assembling. Everyone wished to accompany Napoleon to the East—civilians, scholars, engineers, artists, all wished to make the journey. Napoleon selected and equipped the army, raised money and collected ships. He was employed night and day in the organization of the armament which was to be under his command absolutely.

In April and May 1798 the various squadrons of the French fleet were assembled at Toulon, and everything was soon in readiness. The main body was assembled at Toulon but the embarkment was to take place at Civita Vecchia. When asked if he should remain long in Egypt, Napoleon replied: "A few months, or six years; it all depends upon circumstances."

When all was in readiness Bonaparte called his vast army together and in sight of the ships which were to carry them from the shores of France, said to his followers:

"Rome fought Carthage on sea as well as on the land; England is the Carthage of France. I have come to lead you, in the name of the Divinity of Liberty, across mighty seas, and into distant regions, where your valour may achieve such life and glory as will never await you beneath the cold skies of the West. Prepare yourselves, soldiers, to embark under the tri-colour for achievements far more glorious than you have won for your country on the blushing plains of Italy."

He agreed to give each soldier seven acres of land, and as his promises had not hitherto been violated, the soldiers heard him with joy, and prepared to obey him with alacrity. They answered his address with loud cheers and cries of, "Long live the Republic!" The English government vigilantly observed the preparations that were going on, and kept a fleet in the Mediterranean under the command of Nelson. It was highly important that the French squadron should sail without delay, in order to avoid the risk of being discovered by the English cruisers, but contrary winds detained it for ten days. This interval was employed by Napoleon in attention to the minutest details connected with the finely appointed force under his command.

On the evening of the 19th of May, 1798, fortune favoured him, and the troops were all embarked, while the English fleet, under Nelson, "the Neptune of the Seas," was compelled to go into port to repair ships disabled in a violent gale. The French fleet, which was supplied with water for a month, and with food for two months, carried about 40,000 men of all sorts, and ten thousand sailors. In the army were many veteran soldiers, selected from the Army of Italy and commanded by the first generals of France. Kléber, Desaix, Berthier, Regnier, Murat, Lannes, Andreossi, Junot, Menou, and Belliard all served in this campaign.

Josephine had accompanied her husband to Toulon, and remained with him to the last moment; their farewell was most affecting. As the last of the French troops stepped on board, the sun rose with great brilliancy on the mighty armament—one of those dazzling suns which the soldiers often referred to with delight as "the suns of Napoleon," and sails were immediately set for the East.

On the 8th of June the convoys from Italy joined the squadron out at sea; on the 10th the whole fleet was assembled before Malta. The first object of Napoleon was to take possession of that island. He had already secured a secret party among the knights, and a very slight demonstration of hostilities spread consternation among them and they opened their gates to the French without delay. Nearly all the knights entered the ranks of the French Army. As the French troops passed through the almost impregnable fortifications General Caffarelli dryly remarked to Napoleon that it was fortunate there was someone to open the gates for them; had there been no garrison at all, it would have been terrible hard work.

Leaving a sufficient garrison in Malta the French squadron was again under sail on the 16th. While the officers and savants devoted much time to the discussion of military and scientific topics the great object of excitement and solicitude was to elude the English fleet. The French vessels were encumbered with civil and military baggage, provisions, stores, etc., and densely crowded with troops. Napoleon was anxious to avoid such an encounter: "God grant that we may pass the English without meeting them," he remarked to Admiral Brueyes.

Nelson was now in full pursuit. At Naples he heard of their landing at Malta and that their destination was Egypt. He arrived at Malta just after they had left the island and missed overtaking them by an accident. During a hazy night, on which they lay off Candia, the French were alarmed by the report of guns on their starboard, and it afterwards proved that those were signals between the ships of Nelson's fleet, so close were the two hostile squadrons to each other without being aware of it. Napoleon received positive information of this proximity the following morning and ordered Brueyes to steer at once for Cape Aza, about twenty-five leagues distant from Alexandria. This precaution foiled Nelson who crowded sail for Alexandria.

Napoleon finally reached his destination on the first of July undisturbed, the tops of the minarets of Alexandria announcing that his point was gained. As he was reconnoitring the coast at the very moment that danger seemed over a strange sail appeared on the verge of the horizon: "Fortune!" exclaimed he, "I ask but six hours more,—wilt thou refuse them?" The vessel proved not to be English, but French and the disembarkation, near a structure called the tower of Marabout, three leagues to the eastward of Alexandria, immediately took place in spite of a violent gale and a tremendous surf. Egypt was then nominally a province of the Porte, and governed by a Turkish *pasha* who was at peace with France.

Bonaparte met with no opposition in landing, and by 3 o'clock in the morning commenced his march upon Alexandria with three divisions of his army. He had little difficulty in entering Alexandria, although he met with resistance and General Kléber, who commanded the attack, was wounded. The French lost about two hundred men.

Bonaparte exacted of his troops, under penalty of death, consideration of all the laws and religion of the country, and to the people of

Egypt he addressed a proclamation in which he said:

> They will tell you that I come to destroy your religion; believe them not: I come to restore your rights, to punish the usurpers, and I respect, more than the Mamelukes ever did, God, his Prophet and the *Koran*. . . . . . Thrice happy they who shall be with us! Woe unto them that take up arms for the Mamelukes!—they shall perish.

The Mamelukes were considered by Napoleon to be, individually, the finest cavalry in the world. They rode the noblest horses of Arabia, and were armed with the best weapons which the world could produce: carbines, pistols, etc., from England, and sabres of the steel of Damascus. Their skill in horsemanship was equal to their fiery valour. With that cavalry and the French infantry, Bonaparte said it would be easy to conquer the world.

Napoleon himself remained some days in Alexandria and left on the 7th of July, leaving Kléber in command, being anxious to force the Mamelukes to an encounter with the least possible delay. General Desaix was sent forward with 4500 men to Beda. The commission of learned men remained at Alexandria, until Napoleon should reach Cairo, with the exception of Monge and Berthollett who accompanied the commander.

The march over the burning sands of the desert brought extreme misery and unheard-of sufferings to the troops; the air was full of pestiferous insects, the glare of the sand weakened the men's eyes, and water was scarce and bad. Even the gallant spirits of Murat and Lannes could not sustain themselves, and they trampled their brilliant cockades in the sand in a fit of rage in the presence of the troops. The common soldiers asked, with sarcastic or angry murmurs, if it was here the general designed to give them their "seven acres of land." "The rogue" said they, "he might, with safety, have promised us as much as we pleased; we should not abuse his good nature." They, however, bore a grudge against Caffarelli, who they thought had advised the expedition, and used to say, as he hobbled past with his wooden leg, "He does not care what happens; he is sure to have one foot at least in France."

Napoleon alone was superior to all these evils. It required, however, more than his example of endurance and the general influence of his firm character to prevent the army from breaking into open mutiny. He said at St Helena:

> Once I threw myself amidst a group of generals, and, address-

ing myself to the tallest of their number with vehemence, said, 'You have been talking sedition; take care lest I fulfil my duty; your five feet ten inches would not hinder you from being shot within two hours.'

On the 10th of July, 1798, the army reached the Nile at Rahmanié:

Savary says in his memoirs:

We no sooner saw the river than soldiers, officers and all rushed into it; each, regardless whether it was sufficiently shallow to afford security from danger, only sought to quench his burning thirst, and stooped to drink from the stream, the whole army presenting the appearance of a flock of sheep.

Napoleon says:

We encamped on immense quantities of wheat, but there was neither mill nor oven in the country.

The men bruised the grain between stones and baked it in the ashes or parched and boiled it.

The army soon moved on towards Cairo, but the men were unable to leave the ranks for a single instant without certain death from the spears or scimitars of those matchless Mameluke horsemen; and, therefore, although so near the Nile, several fell dead from thirst. But the worriment of their minds was their worst evil. They began to say there was no great city of Cairo; that they believed it would prove only a collection of wretched huts. In this state they came up, on the 13th, with the Mamelukes at Chebreis. They were drawn up in battle array under Mourad Bey, one of their most powerful chiefs, and were a magnificent body of cavalry, glittering with gold and silver and mounted on splendid horses.

The battle commenced without a moment's hesitation on either side. Each Mameluke, feeling in himself the valour of a host, rushed in the singleness of his purpose, as if alone against the opposing mass; and with repeated charges, endeavoured, by every means of unbridled fury or consummate skill, to break the solid squares of the French Army. They were at length beaten back with the loss of about three hundred.

After the action at Chebreis the French army continued to advance during eight days without opposition of any enemy except the hovering Arabs who lay in wait for every straggler from the main column.

The order of march towards Cairo was systematically arranged; each division of the army moved forward in squares six men deep on each side; the artillery was at the angles; and in the centre the ammunition, the baggage, and the small body of cavalry still remaining. Napoleon himself when he rode always made use of a dromedary, though he at first suffered a sensation resembling seasickness from its peculiar motion, said he sometime later:

> I never passed the desert without experiencing very painful emotions. It was the image of immensity to my thoughts. It showed no limits. It had neither beginning nor end. It was an ocean for the foot of man.

On the 19th of July the soldiers' eyes were gladdened by the sight of the grand pyramids on the horizon. Still advancing towards Cairo, the distant monuments swelling upon the eye at every step, the army reached Embabé on the 21st and found the Mamelukes in battle array to dispute their further progress.

While every eye was fixed on these hoary monuments of the past, Napoleon sighted with his glass a vast army of the *Beys* spread out before him, the right posted on an intrenched camp by the Nile, its centre and left composed of that brilliant cavalry with which they were by this time acquainted. Napoleon perceived, too, and what had escaped the observation of all his staff, that the 40 pieces of cannon on the intrenched camp of the enemy were without carriages, and consequently could be levelled in but one direction. He instantly decided on his plan of attack by preparing to throw his forces on the left, where the guns could not be available. Mourad Bey, who commanded the Mamelukes, penetrated the French commander's design, and his followers at once advanced gallantly to the encounter.

"Soldiers, you are about to fight the rulers of Egypt," said Napoleon, as he raised his hands high in the air and formed his troops into separate squares to meet the assault; "from the summits of yonder pyramids forty centuries behold you." These imposing and mysterious witnesses were not appealed to in vain, and the great battle began at once at the foot of the ancient and gigantic monuments, the French advancing in five grand squares, Napoleon heading the centre square. In an instant the Mamelukes came charging up with impetuous speed and loud cries. They rushed on the line of bayonets, backed their horses upon them, and at last, maddened by the firmness which they could not shake, dashed their pistols and carbines into the faces of the French troops.

The first manoeuvre of the French Army disconcerted the plans of the Mamelukes; still they continued to charge. The places of the dead and dying were instantly supplied by new warriors, who fell in their turn. They daringly penetrated even between the spaces occupied by the squares commanded by Regnier and Desaix, so that the desperate horsemen were exposed to the incessant fire of both faces of the divisions at the distance of fifty paces. Many of the French fell from each other's fire in the resistance to this act of desperation.

Those who had fallen wounded from their seats crawled along the sand and hewed at the legs of their enemies with their scimitars; but nothing could move the intrepid French. Bayonets and the continued roll of musketry by degrees thinned the host around them. When Bonaparte at last advanced with his battalions upon the main body, and divided one part from the other, such was the confusion and terror of the Mamelukes that they abandoned their works and flung themselves by hundreds into the Nile. The carnage was prodigious, thousands were left bleeding on the sands, and multitudes more were drowned. It was the custom of the Mamelukes to carry their treasures with them on their bodies when they went to battle, and every one that fell made a French soldier rich for life, as the bodies of the slain were all rifled. In his report of the engagement, Bonaparte said:

> After the great number of battles in which the troops I command have been opposed to superior strength, I cannot but praise their discipline and coolness on this occasion; for this novel species of warfare has made them display a patience contrasting oddly with French impetuosity. If they had given way to their ardour, they would not have gained the victory, which was only to be obtained by great calmness and patience. The cavalry of the Mamelukes evinced great bravery. They defended their fortunes; for there was not one of them upon whom our soldiers did not find three, four or five hundred gold pieces.

Savary, who fought in Desaix's division, which had to stand the first attack of the Mamelukes, has given a striking description of the impression produced by their furious onset.

> Although the troops that were in Egypt had been long inured to danger, every one present at the battle of the Pyramids must acknowledge, if he be sincere, that the charge of the Mamelukes was most awful, and that there was reason, at one moment,

to apprehend their breaking through our formidable squares, rushing upon them, as they did, with a confidence which enforced silence in our ranks, interrupted only by the word of command. It seemed as if we must inevitably be trampled in an instant under the feet of this cavalry of Mamelukes, who were all mounted upon splendid chargers, richly caparisoned with gold and silver trappings, covered with draperies of all colours and waving scarves, and who were bearing down upon us at full gallop, rending the air with their cries. The whole character of this imposing sight filled the breasts of our soldiers with sensations to which they had hitherto been strangers, and made them vividly attentive to the word of command. The order to fire was executed with a quickness and precision far exceeding what is exhibited in an exercise or upon parade.

More than fifty pieces of cannon and four hundred loaded camels became the spoil of the conquerors.

Mourad and a remnant of 2000 of his Mamelukes retreated on Upper Egypt. These were all that escaped with life out of the matchless body of men who in such superb array had bid scornful defiance to the European invaders only a few hours before. Cairo surrendered; Lower Egypt was entirely conquered. Such were the immediate consequences of the "Battle of the Pyramids."

Many of the promiscuous rabble of infantry reached Cairo in advance of the French and there they spread realistic accounts of the dreadful power of Napoleon and his army.

The name of Bonaparte now spread panic through the East, and the victor was considered invincible. The inhabitants called him "King of Fire," from the deadly effect of the musketry in the engagement at the Pyramids which decided the conquest of the country. By the earliest dawn the victor prepared to take possession of the conquest he had made, but was spared all difficulties by its unconditional surrender. A deputation of the *shieks* and chief inhabitants waited upon him at his headquarters in the country house of Mourad Bey, to implore his clemency and submit to his power. He received them with the greatest kindness and informed them of his friendly intentions towards them and that his hostility was entirely confined to the Mamelukes.

Cairo and its citadel were immediately occupied by the French troops, and on the 24th of July Napoleon made his public entry into the capital, amidst a great concourse of people.

The savants who accompanied Bonaparte on the expedition lost no time in taking advantage of their opportunities, and at once began to ransack the monuments of antiquity, and founded collections which reflected much honour on their zeal and skill. Napoleon himself, accompanied by many officers of his staff, visited the interior of the Great Pyramid of Cheops, attended by many *muftis* and *imans*, and on entering the secret chamber in which, three thousand years before, some Pharaoh had been interred, repeated once more his confession of faith: "There is no God but God, and Mohammed is his Prophet."

The learned Orientals who accompanied him responded with sarcastic solemnity: "Thou hast spoken like the most learned of the prophets; but God is merciful."

Ten days after the battle at the pyramids had been fought and won, Nelson, who had scoured the Mediterranean in quest of Napoleon, discovered the French fleet, commanded by Admiral Brueyes, at anchor in the Bay of Aboukir. A terrific engagement ensued, lasting twenty-four hours, including a whole night. A solitary pause occurred at midnight when the French ship *Orient*, a superb vessel of 120 guns, took fire and blew up in the heart of the conflicting squadrons, with an explosion that for a moment silenced rage in awe. Admiral Brueyes himself perished. The next morning two shattered ships, out of all the French fleet, with difficulty made their escape to the sea. The rest of the magnificent fleet was utterly destroyed or remained in the hands of the English, who have since called the engagement "The Battle of the Nile."

The ships were arranged in a semi-circular compact line of battle, and so close to the shore that Brueyes had supposed it was impossible to get between them and the land; but his daring enemy, who well knew all the surroundings, soon convinced him of his mistake. The van of the English fleet, six in number, successfully rounded the French line, dropping anchor between it and the shore, and opened their fire, while Nelson, with his other ships, ranged along it on the outer side and so placed the French fleet between two tremendous fires. Admiral Brueyes was wounded early in the action, but continued to command with the utmost energy. When he fell mortally wounded he would not suffer himself to be carried below. "A French admiral ought to die on his quarter-deck," he replied to the entreaties of his friend Gantheaume who succeeded him.

It was on his return from Salahié to Cairo, whither Napoleon had pursued the Mameluke chief, Ibrahim Bey, and defeated him, that he

BONAPARTE AS GENERAL-IN-CHIEF OF THE
ARMY OF ITALY

was met by a messenger, with information of the destruction of the French fleet by Nelson in the roads of Aboukir. It was a terrible blow to Napoleon, who was thus shut off from all intercourse with France; his soldiers were thus completely isolated, hundreds of miles from home, and compelled to rely on their own arms and the resources of Egypt. He had been so anxious about the fleet as to write twice to Admiral Brueyes to repeat the order that he should enter harbour of Alexandria, or sail for Corfu; he had also, previously to leaving Cairo, dispatched Julien, his *aide-de-camp*, to enforce the order; but this unfortunate officer was surrounded and killed, with his escort, at a village on the Nile, where he had landed to obtain provisions.

A solitary sigh escaped Napoleon when he heard the news. "To the army of France," said he, "the fates have decreed the empire of the land—to England the sovereignty of the seas." Some years later, on learning of the results of the terrible naval battle at Trafalgar, in which Nelson was again victorious, but which cost him his life, Napoleon repeated this remark, adding, "Well, I cannot be everywhere." The seamen who had landed at Alexandria were now formed into a marine brigade, and made a valuable addition to the army. Very soon afterwards the Porte declared war against France.

Public improvements of various kinds were now begun at Cairo and Alexandria under Bonaparte's direction, and many continue to this day. In all quarters the highest discipline was preserved; and Napoleon exerted all the energy of his nature to increase the resources which remained to him, and to preserve and organize Egypt as a French province.

Savary says:

> At each step of his advance General Bonaparte quickly foresaw everything that was to be done to render available the resources of the most fertile country in the world and give them a suitable application.

So quickly had his mind recovered its tone that, on the 21st of August (only a week after he had learned of the destruction of his fleet at Aboukir), he founded an Institute at Cairo exactly on the model of that learned society in France. Monge was president; Napoleon himself, vice-president.

At Cairo a terrible insurrection occurred on the 21st of October, but it was soon put down by the French troops, after a bitter struggle in which many soldiers lost their lives. Napoleon was in the thickest of the conflict on horseback in the centre of thirty Guides and soon restored confidence among his soldiers. Tranquillity was restored in three days, after which many of the leaders were put to death. The others were pardoned.

Napoleon now proceeded to explore the Isthmus of Suez, where a narrow neck of land divides the Red Sea from the Mediterranean. He visited the Maronite Monks of Mount Sinai, and, as Mohammed had done before him, affixed his name to their charter of privileges; he examined, also, the Fountains of Moses, and on the 28th of December, 1798, nearly lost his life in exploring, during low water, the sands of the Red Sea, where Pharaoh is supposed to have perished while in pursuit of the Hebrews. Savary says:

"The night overtook us, the waters began to rise around us; the Guard in advance exclaimed that their horses were swimming. Bonaparte saved us all by one of those simple expedients which occur to an imperturbable mind. Placing himself in the centre he bade all the rest circle around him, and then ride out, each man in a separate direction, and each to halt as soon as he found his horse swimming. The man whose horse continued to march the last, was sure, he said, to be in the right direction; then accordingly we all followed, and reached Suez at two in the morning in safety, though so rapidly had the tide advanced that the water was at the breastplate of our horses ere we made the land."

In referring to this narrow escape from sharing the fate of Pharaoh, Napoleon remarked to Las Casas: "This would have furnished all the preachers in Christendom with a splendid text against me."

On his return to Cairo Bonaparte dispatched a trusty messenger into India, inviting Tippoo Saib to inform him of the condition of the English army in that section, and declaring that Egypt was only the first port in a march destined to surpass that of Alexander. According to his secretary, "he spent whole days in lying flat on the ground stretched on maps of Asia."

After having passed the balance of the year at Cairo the commander declared the time for action had now arrived. Leaving 15,000 men in and about Cairo, the division of Desaix in Upper Egypt, and garrisons in the chief towns, Bonaparte, on the 11th of February, 1799, marched for Syria at the head of 10,000 picked men, with the intention of crushing the Turkish armaments in that quarter before their chief force, which he learned was assembling at Rhodes, should have time to reach Egypt by sea.

The hostility of the Porte, which would of course be encouraged and assisted by England, implied impending danger on two points,— the approach of a Turkish army *via* Syria and the landing of another on the coast of the Mediterranean, under the protection of British ships. The necessity of forestalling their designs by an expedition to Syria was therefore apparent. In January, 1799, two Turkish armies were assembled; one at Rhodes; the other in Syria. The former was intended to make a descent upon the coast of Egypt at Aboukir, the latter had already pushed forward its advance guard to El-Arisch, a fort within the Egyptian territory, had established large magazines at Gaza and landed at Jaffa a train of artillery of forty guns.

Traversing the desert, seventy-five leagues across, which divides Egypt from Syria, with about twelve thousand men, one regiment being mounted on dromedaries, Napoleon took possession of the fortress El-Arisch on February 17th, after a vigorous assault. The march was made rapidly and in good order. Having resolved upon an immediate expedition into Syria, he did not wait to be attacked on both sides at the same time; but, according to his usual custom, determined to push forward and encounter one division of his enemies at a time. He addressed two letters to the Pasha of Syria, surnamed Djezzar or "the Butcher," from his horrible cruelties, offering him friendship and alliance, but the pasha observed a contemptuous silence as to the first communication, and replied to the second in his favourite fashion— seized the messenger and cut off his head. There was, consequently, nothing to be done with Djezzar but to fight him with such generals as Kléber, Bessieres, Caffarelli, Murat, Lannes, Junot and Berthier.

Pursuing his march, Napoleon took Gaza, the ancient city of the Philistines, without serious opposition, although three or four thousand of Djezzar's horse were drawn up to oppose them. At Jaffa, the Joppa of Holy Writ, the Moslems made a resolute defence, on March 6th, but at length the walls were carried by storm. Three thousand Turks died with arms in their hands in defence of the city, and the town was given up for three hours to pillage more savage than Napoleon had ever before permitted. This was followed by a massacre of hundreds of the barbarians who were marched out of Jaffa some distance from the town, in the centre of a battalion under General Bon, divided into small parties and shot or bayoneted to a man. Like true fatalists they submitted in silence, and their bodies were gathered into a pyramid where for half a century their bones were still visible in the whitening sand.

Napoleon, while admitting that the act was one of the darkest stains on his name that he had to acknowledge, still justified himself on the double plea that he could not afford soldiers to guard so many prisoners—estimated variously from 1200 to 3,000—and that he could not grant them the benefit of parole because they were the very men who had already been set free by him on such terms at El-Arisch after they had given their word not to serve against him for a year. Napoleon said at St. Helena:

> Now if I had spared them again and sent them away on their parole, they would directly have gone to St. Jean d'Acre, where they would have played me over again the same trick that they had done at Jaffa. In justice to the lives of my soldiers, since every general ought to consider himself as their father, and them as his children, I could not allow this. To leave as a guard a portion of my army, already small and reduced in number, in consequence of the breach of faith of those wretches, was impossible. I therefore .... ordered that the prisoners should be singled out and shot...... I would do the same thing tomorrow and so would any general commanding an army under such circumstances.

Napoleon now ascertained that the Pasha of Syria was at St. Jean d'Acre, so renowned in the history of the Crusades, and determined to defend that place to extremity with the force which had already been assembled for the invasion of Egypt. Sir Sidney Smith, with two ships of war, was cruising before the port and the garrison was assisted by European science.

The French Army moved on Acre, eager for revenge, while the necessary apparatus of a siege was ordered to be sent round by sea from Alexandria. Sir Sidney Smith was informed by Djezzar, of the approaching storm, and hastened to support him in the defence of Acre. Napoleon's vessels, conveying guns and stores from Egypt, fell into his hands and he appeared off the town two days before the French army came in view of it. He was permitted to regulate the plan of defence, turning Napoleon's own cannon against him from the walls.

Napoleon commenced the siege on the 18th of March and opened his trenches immediately on his arrival. "On that little town," he said to one of his generals, as they were standing together on an eminence, "On yonder little town depends the fate of the East: behold the key of Constantinople or of India."

He said about the same time to Bourrienne:

> The moment Acre falls all the Druses of Mount Lebanon will join me; the Syrians, weary of Djezzar's oppressions, will crowd to my standard: I shall march upon Constantinople with an army to which the Turks can offer no effectual resistance, and it is not unlikely that I may return to France by the route of Adrianople and Vienna, destroying the house of Austria on my way.

For ten days the French laboured hard in their trenches, being exposed to the fire of extensive batteries, formed chiefly of Bonaparte's own artillery. On March 28th, however, a breach was at last effected and the French mounted with such fiery zeal that the garrison gave way. Shortly afterwards Djezzar himself appeared on the battlements, and flinging his pistols at the head of his flying men, urged and compelled them to renew the defence, which they finally did, causing the French to retreat with great loss.

In the meantime Junot, having marched with his division to encounter a large Mussulman army that had been gathered among the mountains of Samaria, and was preparing to descend upon Acre, Napoleon was compelled to follow him to Nazareth, where he was rescued on April 8th. Here, as usual, the splendid cavalry of the Orientals were unable to resist the solid squares and well-directed musketry of the French. General Kléber, with another division, was in like manner rescued by the general-in-chief at Mount Thabor on April 15th, after the former had fought against fearful odds from six in the morning till one in the afternoon.

Napoleon now returned to the siege of Acre with all possible dispatch, pressed it on with desperate assaults day after day, losing many of his best soldiers. Accustomed to the easy victories which he had obtained on every encounter with the Turkish forces in Syria, he was not prepared to expect the determined resistance by which his progress was now arrested. Acre is surrounded by a wall flanked with towers, and was further defended by a broad and deep ditch with strong works. At one time the French succeeded in forcing their way into the great tower and in establishing themselves in one part of it for a time despite all opposition; but they were finally dislodged; each advantage ended with itself and no progress was made towards subduing the place. At another time a break was made in the walls in a distant part of the town, and a French party entered Acre at the opening. Djezzar then threw such a crowd of Turks upon them that all discipline was lost and nearly every French soldier met death. The brave Lannes, who headed the party, was with difficulty rescued after being desperately wounded.

During this siege Napoleon sent an officer with an order to the most exposed position; he was killed. He sent another, who was also killed; and so with a third. The order was imperative and Bonaparte had but two aides with him, Eugene Beauharnais and Lavalette. He signalled to the latter to come forward, and said to him in a low voice, so that Eugene could not hear: "Take this order, Lavalette, I don't want to send this boy and have him killed so young; his mother (Josephine) has intrusted him to me. You know what life is. Go!" The *aide* returned in safety.

On another occasion during the siege a piece of shell struck Eugene on the head: he fell, and lay for a long time under the ruins of a wall which the shell had knocked down. Bonaparte thought he was killed, and uttered a cry of grief. The youth was only wounded, however, and at the end of nineteen days asked leave to return to his post, in order to take part in the other assaults, which failed like the first, in spite of Bonaparte's obstinacy. "This wretched hole," said he, "has cost me a good deal of time and a great many men, but things have gone too far; I must try one last assault."

An instance of the enthusiastic attachment which Napoleon was capable of inspiring occurred during this memorable siege. One day, when the commander was in the trenches, a shell thrown by Sir Sidney Smith, fell at his feet. Two grenadiers immediately rushed towards him,—placed him between them, and raised their arms above his head so as to completely cover every part of his body. The shell burst without injuring one of the group, although they were covered with sand. Both these grenadiers were made officers immediately; one of them, subsequently, was the General Dumesnil, so much talked of 1814, for his resolute defence of Vincennes against the Russians. He had lost a leg in the campaign of Moscow; and to the summons to surrender he replied, "Give me back my leg and I will give up the fortress!" The fate of his heroic companion is not recorded.

The siege had now continued for sixty days. Napoleon once more commanded an assault on the 8th of May, and his officers and soldiers obeyed him with devoted but fruitless gallantry. "That Sidney Smith," he said later, "made me miss my fortune." The loss his army had by this time undergone was very great, and the hearts of all the men were quickly sinking.

Among the officers and men who fell on this memorable 8th of May was Croisier, the *aide-de-camp,* who had incurred the commander's displeasure at Jaffa. Napoleon had once before been violently irritated against him for some seeming neglect at Cairo, and the word "coward" had escaped him. The feelings of Croisier, then deeply affected had become insupportable since the event at Jaffa, and he sought death at every opportunity. On this day Napoleon observed the tall figure of his unfortunate *aide-de-camp* mounted on a battery, exposed to the thickest of the enemy's fire, and called loudly and imperatively, "Croisier, come down! you have no business there." Croisier neither replied nor moved; the next instant he received his death wound.

A Turkish fleet had now arrived to reinforce Djezzar, and upon the utter failure of the attack of the 21st of May, the eleventh different attempt to carry the place by assault, Napoleon yielded to stern necessity, raised the siege, and began his retreat upon Jaffa. On leaving this latter place six days after, a number of plague patients in the hospitals were found to be in a state that held out no hope of their recovery, and the commander, unwilling to leave them to the cruel practices of the Turks, suggested that opium be administered by one of the medical staff as a speedy death.

The various accounts of this incident in no way agree in detail. Bonaparte denied at St. Helena that the opium was given, but said that the patients, seven in number were abandoned. He declared also, that if his own son had been among the number he would have advised that it be done rather than to leave them to suffer the tortures of the Turks. Sir Sidney Smith found seven alive in the hospitals when he came up. A rearguard had been left to protect them and they probably galloped off before the English entered the place. Bourrienne, who acted as secretary to Napoleon at this time, gives a different account, while others assert that 500 men were thus disposed of. The real facts will probably never be known although both Hazlitt and Sir Walter Scott acquit Napoleon of all blame after a careful investigation of all the facts. That Bonaparte's motives were good his enemies generally admit, as he seems to have designed, by shortening these men's lives, to do them the best service in his power.

The retreating march was a continued scene of misery; the wounded and sick were many, the heat oppressive, and the burdens almost intolerable. Dejected by the sight of so much suffering Napoleon issued an order that every horse, mule and camel should be given up to the sick, wounded and infected. Shortly afterwards one of his attendants came to ask which horse he wished to reserve for himself. "Scoundrel!" the commander cried, "do you not know the order? Let everyone march on foot—I the first! Begone!" He accordingly, during the rest of the march, walked by the side of the sick, cheering them to hope for recovery, and exhibiting to all the soldiery the example at once of endurance and compassion. As he had done in Italy, Napoleon always shared the privations and fatigue of the army and their extremities were sometimes so great that the troops were compelled to contend with each other for the smallest comforts. Upon one occasion in the desert, the soldiers would scarcely allow their general to dip his hands in a muddy pool of water; and when passing the ruins of Pelusium, almost suffocated by heat, a soldier yielded him the ruins of an ancient doorway beneath which he contrived to shade his head for a few minutes and which Napoleon observed, "was no trifling favour."

On the march between Cesarea and Jaffa, Napoleon very narrowly escaped death. Many of the men had by this time regained their horses, owing to the continual death of the wretched objects who had been mounted upon them. The commander was so exhausted that he had fallen asleep on his horse. A little before daybreak, a native, concealed among the bushes close to the roadside, took aim at his head, and fired. The ball missed: the man was pursued, caught and ordered to be instantly shot. Four Guides drew their triggers, but all their carbines hung fire, owing to the extreme humidity of the night. The Syrian leaped into the sea, which was close to the road; swam to a ledge of rocks, which he mounted and there stood, undaunted and untouched by the shots of the whole troop, who fired at him as they pleased. Napoleon left Bourrienne behind to wait for Kléber, who formed the rear guard and to order him "not to forget the Naplousian." It is not certain that he was shot at last.

On his return to Cairo on the 14th of June, 1799, after a march of twenty-five days, Napoleon once more re-established himself in his former headquarters; but he had not long occupied himself with the establishment of a new government for Egypt which was then in a state of perfect tranquillity, when word came to him of a probable uprising at Alexandria. The commander therefore decided to go there at once. He arrived on the 24th of July and found his army posted in the neighbourhood of Aboukir, prepared to anticipate an attack of the Turks which had appeared off Aboukir under the protection of two British ships commanded by Sir Sidney Smith, on the morrow. Surveying their intrenched camp from the heights above, the commander said to Murat; "Go how it may, the battle of tomorrow will decide the fate of the world."

"Of this army at least," answered Murat; "but the Turks have no cavalry, and if ever infantry were charged to the teeth by horse, they shall be so by mine," a promise which the brave cavalry leader made good.

Next morning the Turkish outposts were attacked and the enemy driven in with great slaughter. The retreat might have ended in a rout but for the eagerness of the enemy who engaged in the task of spoiling and maiming those who fell before them. This gave to Murat the opportunity of charging the main body,—which had been drawn up in battle array on the field,—in flank with his cavalry. From that moment the engagement was no longer a battle but a massacre. The French infantry, under the rallying eye of Napoleon, forced a passage to the intrenchments, and attacking the Turks on all sides, caused them to throw themselves headlong into the waves, rather than await the fury of the French cavalry and the steady fire of the artillery. The sea at first appeared literally covered with turbans. It was only when weary with slaughter that quarter was given to about 6,000 men—the rest of the Turkish army, consisting of 18,000 having perished on the field or in the sea. Six thousand were taken prisoners.

The defeat of the Turks at Aboukir filled the French soldiers at Cairo with extreme rapture; Murat was promoted to the rank of a general of division and Napoleon ordered his name and that of Roize and the numbers of the regiments of cavalry present at the battle, engraved upon pieces of brass cannon. Mustapha Pasha, the commanding general of the Turks, on being brought into the presence of his victor, was saluted with these words: "It has been your fate to lose this day; but I will take care to inform the *sultan* of the courage with which you have contested it."

"Spare thyself that trouble," answered the proud *pasha*, "my master knows me better than thou."

On the evening after the battle, General Kléber embraced Bonaparte and said to him, "General, you are as great as the world!"

"It is not written on high that I am to perish by the hands of the Arabs," replied Napoleon.

This splendid and most decisive victory at Aboukir concluded Bonaparte's career in the East. It was imperiously necessary, ere he could have ventured to quit the command of the army, that he should have to his credit some such glory after the retreat from Syria. It preserved his credit with the public and enabled him to state that he left Egypt for the time in absolute security. After the engagement Napoleon sent a flag of truce to Sir Sidney Smith, and an interchange of civilities commenced between the English and the French. This circumstance, trifling in itself, led to important consequences. Among other things, a copy of a French journal, dated the 10th of June 1799 was sent ashore by Sir Sidney Smith. No news from France had reached Egypt for ten months. Napoleon seized the paper with eagerness and its contents verified his worst fears; he had said some time before while at Acre that he feared France was in trouble.

As he opened the paper he exclaimed: "My God! My presentiment is realized; the imbeciles have lost Italy! All the fruits of our victories are gone! I must leave Egypt." He then spent the whole night in his tent reading a file of the English newspapers which had been furnished him. From these he learned of Suwarrow's victories over the French in Italy and of the disastrous internal state of France. In the morning Admiral Gantheaume received hasty orders to prepare the two frigates *Muiron* and *Carrère* and two *corvettes*, for sea, with the utmost secrecy and dispatch, furnishing them with two months provisions for five hundred men.

Napoleon returned to Cairo on the 9th of August, but it was only to make some parting arrangements as to the administration of affairs there, for he had resolved to intrust Egypt to other hands, and at once set out for France. He reached Alexandria once more, and was there met by those whom he had decided should make the return voyage with him. He selected Berthier, Lannes, Murat, Marmont and Andréossy with five hundred picked men to accompany him: these with Monge and Denon proceeded to depart from Alexandria without delay. On the 18th a courier from Gantheaume brought information that Sir Sidney Smith had left the coast to take water at Cyprus. This was the signal for Napoleon's instant departure.

On the morning of August 23rd, 1799, Bonaparte and his chosen followers embarked at Rosetta on two frigates and two smaller vessels, which had been saved in the harbour of Alexandria. A lack of water, and an accident to one of the English ships had compelled the enemy to raise the blockade and so favoured his departure. In writing to the Divan and announcing his departure he said:

Remind the Musselmen frequently of my love for them. Acquaint them that I have two great means to conduct men—persuasion and force; with the one I gain friends, and with the other I destroy my enemies.

General Kléber was now placed in command of the Army of Egypt by Napoleon who informed his successor of the reasons of his departure for France, and his intention of sending recruits and munitions at the earliest possible moment. He said to Kléber, "The army which I confide to you is composed of my children; in all times, even in the midst of the greatest sufferings I have received the mark of their attachment; keep alive in them these sentiments. You owe this to the particular esteem and true attachment which I bear myself towards you."

The French frigates had hardly passed from sight of land when they were reconnoitred by an English *corvette*, a circumstance which seemed of evil augury. Bonaparte assured his companions by his usual allusions to his own "destiny" which he declared would protect him on sea as well as land. "We will arrive safe," said he, "fortune will never abandon us—we will arrive safe despite the enemy."

Napoleon left no responsibility upon the admiral to whom the various manoeuvres have been ascribed: "As if," says Bourrienne, "anyone could command when Bonaparte was present!"

By express directions of Napoleon, the squadron, instead of taking the ordinary course, kept close to the African coast, in the direction of the southern point of Sardinia; his intention being to take a northerly course along the northern coast of that island. He had irrevocably determined, that should the English fleet appear, he would run ashore; make his way, with the little army under his command, to Orin, Tunis, or some other port; and thence find another opportunity of getting to France.

The entire voyage was one of constant peril, for the Mediterranean was traversed in all directions by English ships of war. For twenty-one days, adverse winds, blowing from west or northwest, continually drove the squadron on the Syrian coast, or back towards Alexandria. It was once proposed that they should again put into that port, but Napoleon would not hear of it, declaring that he would brave any danger. On the 30th of September he reached Ajaccio, and was received with enthusiasm at the place of his birth; but according to his own phrase, "*it rained cousins*" and he was wearied with solicitations. "What will become of me," he said, "if the English, who are cruising hereabouts,

BATTLE OF THE PYRAMIDS

should learn that I have landed in Corsica? I shall be forced to stay here. That I could never endure. I have a torrent of relations pouring upon me."

Bourrienne says:

> His brilliant reputation had prodigiously augmented his family connections, and from the great number of his pretended god-children it might have been thought that he had held one-fourth of the children of Ajaccio at the baptismal font.

It was during his stay in Corsica that Napoleon first heard of the loss of the Battle of Novi by the French Army and of the death of Joubert, he exclaimed:

> But for that confounded quarantine I would hasten ashore, and place myself at the head of the Army of Italy. All is not over; and I am sure that there is not a general who would refuse me the command. The news of the victory gained by me, would reach Paris as soon as the Battle of Aboukir; that, indeed, would be excellent!

On the 7th of October the voyage was at last resumed, the winds being again favourable, and on the morning of the 9th, after a narrow escape from the English, he moored in safety in the bay of Fréjus.

The story he brought of the victory of Aboukir, gave new fuel to the flame of universal enthusiasm, and Napoleon's return to Paris bore all the appearance of a triumphal procession. The shouts of welcome with which he was hailed were echoed by the whole population of France. He returned from Egypt as a "conqueror," although almost alone; yet Providence designed in this apparently deserted condition that he should be the instrument of more astonishing changes than the greatest efforts of the greatest conquerors had ever before been able to effect upon the civilized world. Napoleon was regarded as the champion of liberty, as well as the successful military leader; and none of his actions, or expressed opinions had as yet contradicted such an estimation of his principles.

The campaign in Egypt was of little service to France, but to Napoleon it was most useful. Of the *aides-de-camp* whom he took with him four perished there, Croisier, Sulkowski, Guibert and Julian; two, Duroc and Eugene Beauharnais were wounded; Lavalette and Merlin alone returned safe and sound. Bonaparte had the highest regard for Josephine's son Eugene. He was brave and manly, and although a youth of seventeen soon won Bonaparte's lasting affection. If there was a dangerous duty,—to ride into the desert and reconnoitre the bands of Arabs or Mamelukes, Eugene was always the first to volunteer. One day when he was hastening forward with his usual eagerness, Bonaparte called him back, saying: "Young man, remember that in our business we must never *seek* danger; we must be satisfied with doing our duty, doing it well, and leaving the rest to God!"

At the capital Napoleon was received with every demonstration of joy by the French people, who now looked upon him as their liberator. All parties seemed to be weary of the Directory, and to demand the decisive interference of the unrivalled soldier. On his return he was much surprised to learn of the real condition of France, and to an emissary of Barras he said with some degree of feeling:

> What have you done with that land of France which I left to your care in so magnificent a condition? I bequeathed you peace, and on my return find war. I left you the memory of victories, and now I have come back to face defeats. I left with you the millions I had gathered in Italy, and today I see nothing in every direction but laws despoiling the people, coupled with distress. What have you done with the one hundred thousand of French citizens, my companions in glory, all of whom I knew? You have sent them to their death. This state of things cannot last; for it would lead us to despotism, and we require liberty reposing on a basis of equality.

The Directory offered him the choice of any army he would command. He did not refuse, but pleaded the necessity of a short interval of leisure for the recovery of his health and speedily withdrew from the conference in order to avoid any more such embarrassing offers. He had by this time, evidently, a very clear perception of the course before him, and had made up his mind to place himself in circumstances to confer high offices and commands, instead of accepting them.

In talking afterwards to Madame de Rémusat about this period in his career, Napoleon said:

> The Directory was not uneasy at my return; I was extremely on my guard, and never in my life have I displayed more skill. Everyone ran into my traps, and when I became the head of the State there was not a party in France that did not base its hopes on my success.

4

Passage of the Alps, and Battle of Marengo

At the time of Napoleon's return from the Egyptian expedition the legislative bodies of Paris were divided into two parties, the Moderates, headed by Sieyes, and the Democrats, by Barras. Finding it impossible to remain neutral, Bonaparte took sides with the former. Lucien, his brother, had just been elected president of the Council of Five Hundred; the subtle and able Talleyrand and the accomplished Sieyes were his confidants, and he determined to overwhelm the imbecile government and take the reins in his own hands. He had measured his strength, established his purpose, and, as France stood in need of a more energetic and regenerated government, he now went calmly to its execution.

During his absence in Egypt France had cause to deplore the loss of his military genius, and had hailed his return with rapturous acclamations. Napoleon's intentions were no sooner suspected than he was surrounded by all those who were discontented with the established government, and who found in him such a leader as they had long looked for in vain.

He soon opened negotiations with Sieyes who commanded a majority in the Council of Ancients, and had no sooner convinced him that the project of overturning the Directorial government was his object, than he was regarded as the instrument destined to give France that "systematic" constitution he had so long deliberated on and desired. Napoleon's overtures were therefore cordially met, and Sieyes gave all the weight of his influence to the impending revolution. Two men whose names have since been known all over Europe, were also added to the number of his adherents, Talleyrand, who had been recently deposed from a place in the ministry; and Fouché, minister of police. The talents of both were actively employed in his service and materially promoted his success. He had no faith in Fouché and used him without giving him his confidence. Lucien Bonaparte held the important post of president of the Council of Five Hundred; a circumstance highly advantageous to his brother at this juncture. It was there that the greatest opposition would be made to any attempt which was hostile to the Constitution of the Year Three.

A large portion of the army was certain to side with Napoleon. His house was now the resort of all the generals and men of note who had served under him in his campaigns in Italy and Egypt, Bernadotte alone standing aloof.

A meeting took place between Napoleon and Sieyes on the 6th of November 1799, in which it was finally determined that the revolution should be attempted on the 9th. This date, called in the history of the period, the 18th *Brumaire*, was exactly one month from the day of Napoleon's landing at Fréjus on his return from Egypt. The measures resolved upon were as follows: The Council of Ancients, taking advantage of an article in the constitution, which authorized the measure, were to decree the removal of the legislative bodies to St. Cloud, beyond the walls of the city. They were next to appoint Napoleon commander-in-chief of their own guard, of the troops of the military division of Paris, and of the National Guard. These decrees were to be passed at seven in the morning; at eight Napoleon was to go to the Tuileries, where the troops should be assembled, and there assume the command of the capital.

The Council of Ancients at length gathered in the Tuileries at an early hour, every arrangement having been made in accordance with these resolutions, declared that the salvation of the State demanded vigorous measures, and proposed through its president, (one of Napoleon's confidants)—the passage of the decrees already agreed upon. The decrees were at once adopted without debate and Napoleon notified. All had occurred as had been prearranged. Early on the morning of the 18th *Brumaire*, the house of Napoleon in the Rue de la Victoire was crowded with a large assemblage of officers. It was too small to hold them all and many were in the courtyard and entrances. Numbers of these were devoted to him; a few were in the secret, and all began to suspect that something extraordinary was soon to happen. Everyone was in uniform except Bernadotte who appeared in plain clothes. Displeased at this mark of separation from the rest Napoleon said hastily: "How is this? You are not in uniform!"

"I never am on a morning when I am not on duty," replied Bernadotte.

"You will be on duty presently," rejoined Napoleon.

"I have not heard of it; I should have received my orders sooner," came the answer quickly.

Napoleon now drew him aside, disclosed his plans and invited him to take part with the new movement against a detested government. Bernadotte's only answer was that "he would not take part in a rebellion," and with some reluctance made a half promise of neutrality.

The moment the decrees of the Council of Ancients arrived Napoleon came forward to the steps of his house, read the documents, and invited them all to follow him to the Tuileries. The enthusiasm of those present was now at the highest pitch and all the officers drew their swords, promising their services and fidelity. Napoleon instantly mounted, and placed himself at the head of the generals and officers. Attended by one thousand five hundred horse, he halted on the boulevard at the corner of the street Mont Blanc; he then dispatched some confidential troops under Moreau to guard the Luxembourg, and the Directory ceased to exist, although Barras entered a mild protest and then retired to his country residence to live upon the great spoils of his office.

The Council of Five Hundred, an hour or two afterwards, assembled to learn its fate. Resistance would have been idle, and adjourning for their next session at St. Cloud, they mingled with the enthusiastic people shouting, "*Vive la République!*" When they assembled at St. Cloud the next morning they found that beautiful *château* completely invested by the brilliant battalions under the orders of Murat.

At about one o'clock on the 19th *Brumaire* Napoleon appeared at St. Cloud attended by Berthier, Lefebvre, Lannes and all the generals in his confidence. Upon his arrival he learned that a heated debate had commenced in the Council of Ancients on the subject of the resignation of the directors and the immediate election of others. Napoleon hastily entered the hall accompanied only by Berthier and Bourrienne who attended as his secretary. He addressed the body with much difficulty and after many dramatic interruptions, told them that it was upon them he relied, declaring his belief that the Council of Five Hundred—corresponding in part with the lower house of Congress—would restore the convention, popular tumults, the scaffold, the Reign of Terror. He said:

I will save you from all these horrors, I and my brave comrades, whose swords and caps I see at the door of this hall; and if any hireling traitor talks of outlawry, to those swords will I appeal. You stand over a volcano. Let a soldier tell the truth frankly. I was quiet in my home when this Council summoned me to action. I obeyed: I collected my brave comrades, and placed the arms of my country at the service of you who are its head. We are repaid with calumnies—they talk of Cromwell—of Caesar. Had I aspired to power the opportunity was mine ere now. I swear that France holds no more devoted patriot. Dangers surround us. Let us not hazard the advantages for which we have paid so dearly—Liberty and Equality!

Rallying at the uproar which pursued him to the door, Napoleon turned round and called upon the council to assist him in saving the country; and with the words, "Let those who love me follow," he passed quickly out, reached the courtyard where he showed the soldiers the order naming him commander-in-chief, and then leaped upon his horse, shouts of "*Vive Bonaparte!*" resounding on all sides.

In the meantime the hostile Council of Five Hundred had assembled, and there a far different scene was passing. With the same steadiness of purpose and calmness of manner, Bonaparte walked into the chamber with two grenadiers on either side, who halted at the doors that were left open, while the general advanced towards the centre of the chamber.

At the sight of drawn swords at the passageway, and the presence of armed men at the doors of that deliberative body, loud cries of "Down with the traitor!" "Long live the Constitution!" etc., broke forth. Several of the members rushed upon Napoleon, some seized him by the collar and one is said to have attempted his life with a dagger. In an instant the grenadiers rushed forward exclaiming, "Let us save our general," and bore their commander from the hall.

Napoleon was quickly in the midst of his soldiers and found ready ears and enthusiastic spirits to listen to his excited words. "Soldiers," he said, "I offered them victory and fame—they have answered me with daggers."

It was at this moment that Augereau, whose faith in his former general's fortune began to waver, is said to have addressed him with the words, "A fine situation you have brought yourself into!" Upon which Napoleon answered, "Augereau, things were worse at Arcola;

take my advice, remain quiet; in a short time all this will change."

Meanwhile the commotion in the Council of Five Hundred rose to the highest pitch, a scene of the wildest confusion was taking place in the Assembly, and the grenadiers sent by Napoleon once more entered and bore Lucien, the president, from his colleagues. They had charged him with conspiracy and were about to vent their fury upon him, when he flung off the insignia of his office and was rescued.

Lucien found the soldiery without in a high state of excitement. He mounted a horse quickly that he might be seen and heard the better, and dramatically addressed the assembled troops:

> General Bonaparte, and you, soldiers of France, the President of the Council of Five Hundred announces to you that factious men with daggers interrupt the deliberations of the Senate. He authorizes you to employ force. The Assembly of Five Hundred is dissolved.

The soldiers received his harangue with shouts of,"*Vive Bonaparte!*" Still there was an appearance of hesitation, and it did not seem certain that they were ready to act against the representatives of the people, till Lucien drew his sword, and vehemently exclaimed, "I swear that I will stab my own brother to the heart, if he ever attempts anything against the liberty of Frenchmen."

This statement roused the soldiers to action and they were now ready to obey any order from Napoleon. At a signal from him, Murat, at the head of a body of grenadiers, at once started to execute the order of the president. With a roll of drums and levelled pieces, Lucien followed the detachment, mounted the tribune, and dispersed the Council of Five Hundred. The deputies were debating in a state of wild indecision and anxiety when the troops slowly entered. Murat, as they moved forward, announced to the council that it should disperse. A few of the members instantly retired; but the majority remained firm. A reinforcement now entered in close column headed by General Leclerc, the commanding officer, who said loudly, "In the name of General Bonaparte, the Legislative Corps is dissolved; let all good citizens retire. Grenadiers, forward!" The latter advanced, levelling their muskets with fixed bayonets and occupying the width of the hall. Most of the members at once made their escape by the windows with undignified rapidity; in a few minutes not one remained.

Lucien immediately assembled the "Moderate" members of the council who resumed its session, and in conjunction with that of the Ancients, a decree was passed investing the entire authority of the State in a Provisional Consulate of three—Napoleon, Sieyes and Roger-Ducos who were known as "Consuls of the French Republic." Thus ended the 18th and 19th *Brumaire*, (November 10th and 11th, 1799) one of the most decisive revolutions of which history has preserved any record; and, so admirable had been the arrangements of Napoleon, that it had not cost France a drop of blood. "During the greater part of this eventful day," says Bourrienne, "he was as calm as at the opening of a great battle."

The next day the three consuls met at Paris, and France once more began to make progress. At this meeting, Sieyes, who had up to this moment conceived himself to be the head, and the others but the arms of the new constitution, asked, as a form of politeness, "Which of us is to preside?"

"Do you not see," answered Ducos, "that the general presides?"

Sieyes had expected that Napoleon would content himself with the supreme command of all the armies, and had no idea that he was conversant with, or wished to interfere in profound and extensive political affairs and projects. He was, however, so astonished at the knowledge displayed by Napoleon in questions of administration, even to the minutest details, and in every department, that when their first conference was concluded, he hurried to Talleyrand, Cabanis, and other counsellors, assembled at St. Cloud, exclaiming, "Gentlemen, you have now a master. He knows everything, arranges everything, and can accomplish everything."

Those persons must know the character of Napoleon very imperfectly, who consider him great only at the head of armies; for he was able to acquit himself of the various functions of government with glory, shining equally as conspicuous in the cabinet as in the field.

Napoleon guided and controlled everything; humane laws were enacted; Christianity was again restored, and upwards of 20,000 French citizens now came forth from the prisons to bless his name. Many who had been exiled because they did not approve of the Reign of Terror and the despotism of the directory were recalled, and many other salutary reforms at once stamped the new government with the seal of public approbation and the confidence of Europe. In everything that was done the genius of Napoleon was visible. A great man was at the helm, and the world saw that his creative genius was regenerating France. The new constitution met the approval of the people, and in February 1800 the First Consul took up his residence in the Tuileries, the old home of the monarchs of France. Shortly afterwards Napoleon reviewed the Army of Paris, amounting to 100,000 men. When the 96th, 43rd and 50th demi-brigades defiled before him he was observed to take off his hat and incline his head, in token of respect at the sight of their colours torn to shreds with balls, and blackened with smoke and powder.

For the first time in modern history the world saw the greatest general of the age the civil chief of the most brilliant state in Europe. The First Consul now held frequent and splendid reviews of the troops. He traversed the ranks, now on horseback, now on foot; entered into the minutest details concerning the wants of the men and the service, and dispensing in the name of the nation, distinctions and rewards. A hundred soldiers who had signalized themselves in action, received from his hand the present of a handsome sabre each, on one of these occasions.

The Parisians received the new constitution with delight. The inhabitants also viewed the pomp and splendour of the Consular government with surprise and self-complacency. They reasoned little and hoped much. Napoleon was their idol, and from him alone they expected everything. The constitution continued the executive power in the hands of three consuls, who were to be elected for the space of ten years, and were then eligible to re-election. The First Consul held powers far superior to his colleagues. He alone had the right of nominating all offices, civil and military, and of appointing nearly all functionaries whatsoever. Napoleon assumed the place of First Consul without question or debate. He then named Cambacérès and LeBrun as Second and Third Consuls respectively.

It was about this time that Napoleon learned of the death of Washington. He forthwith issued a general order commanding the French army to wrap their banners in crape during ten days in honour of "a great man who fought against tyranny, and consolidated the liberties of his country." He then celebrated a grand funeral service to the memory of Washington in the council-hall of the Invalides. The last standards taken in Egypt were presented on the same occasion; all the ministers, the counsellors of state and generals, were present. The pillars and roof were hung with the trophies of the campaign of Italy and the bust of Washington was placed under the trophy composed of the flags of Aboukir.

Lockhart says:

From this day a new epoch was to date. Submit to that government, and no man need fear that his former acts, far less opinions, should prove any obstacle to his security—nay, to his advancement.

In truth the secret of Bonaparte's whole scheme is unfolded in his own memorable words to Sieyes:

> We are creating a new era—of the past we must forget the bad, and remember only the good.

During the absence of Bonaparte in Egypt the tri-colour which he had left floating on the castles along the Rhine, and from the Julian Alps to the Mediterranean, had been humbled, and England and Austria, with the allies they could bring into the coalition, were preparing once more to compel the French to retire to their ancient boundaries, and ultimately offer the crown to the exiled Bourbons.

But Napoleon knew that France needed internal repose, and he desired universal peace in Europe. He even went so far, in order to bring this about, as to address a letter to George III. in which he said:

> Your Majesty will see in this overture only my sincere desire to contribute effectually, for a second time, to a general pacification—by a prompt step taken in confidence, and freed from those forms, which, however necessary to disguise the feeble apprehensions of feeble states, only serve to discover in the powerful a mutual wish to deceive. France and England, abusing their strength, may long defer the period of its utter exhaustion; but I will venture to say that the fate of civilized nations is concerned in the termination of a war, the flames of which are raging throughout the whole world. I have the honour, etc., etc., Bonaparte.

If the king himself had had an opportunity to reply to this letter, as he afterwards admitted, it would have saved England millions of money, and Europe millions of lives; but in a very short-sighted letter, Lord Grenville, then Secretary of State, replied to Talleyrand, France's minister of Foreign Affairs, in which he said:

> The war must continue until the causes which gave it birth cease to exist. The restoration of the exiled royal family will be the easiest means of giving confidence to the other powers of Europe.

The refusal of England to treat with the Consular Government of France was to be expected, being perfectly in accord with the principles which guided the rulers of England at that period. They had joined the other governments of Europe in commencing war against France, in order to restore its legitimate sovereign, contrary to the will of the French people.

When Napoleon read the letter he said: "I will answer that from Italy!" and immediately called his generals together and ordered them to get ready for another campaign beyond the Alps. It is said that on receiving the reply from England Napoleon exclaimed to Talleyrand, "It could not have been more favourable," but this is credited by but few historians as it appears that his sincere convictions were that peace was best for France.

Three days after the Grenville letter, the First Consul electrified France by an edict for an army of reserve embracing all the veterans then unemployed, who had ever served the country, and a new levy of 30,000 recruits or conscripts as they were termed; and the most active preparations were rapidly made. At this time four great armies were already in the field—one on the North coast was watching Holland, and guarding against any invasion from England; Jourdan commanded the Army of the Danube, which had repassed the Rhine; Massena was at the head of the Army of Helvetia, and held Switzerland; and the fragment of the mighty host that Napoleon had himself led to victory, still called the Army of Italy.

Upwards of 350,000 men were now marched to various points of conflict with the European powers—England, Austria and Russia, together with Bavaria, Sweden, Denmark, and Turkey, which made a formidable array of enemies with whom Napoleon had to contend. The operations were conducted with the utmost secrecy. Napoleon had decided to strike the decisive blow against Austria in Italy, and to command there in person. An article in the new constitution forbade the First Consul taking the command of an army but he found a ready way to evade it. Berthier was superseded by Carnot as minister of war and given the nominal command of the Army of Italy. It was generally believed that the troops were to advance upon Italy.

Meantime, while Austria was laughing with derision at the French conscripts and "invalids" then at Dijon and amused itself with caricatures of some ancient men with wooden legs, and little boys twelve years old entitled "Bonaparte's Army of Reserve," the real Army of Italy was already formed in the heart of France and was marching by various roads towards Switzerland and was commanded by officers of recognized ability and courage. The artillery was sent piecemeal from different arsenals; the provisions, necessary to an army about to cross barren mountains, were forwarded to Geneva, embarked on the lake, and landed at Villeneuve, near the entrance of the valley of the Simplon.

The daring plan of Napoleon was to transport his army across the Alps; surmounting the highest chain of mountains in Europe, by paths which are dangerous and difficult to the unencumbered traveller; to plant himself in the rear of the Austrians, interrupt their communications, place them between his own army and that of Massena who was in command of the 12,000 men at Genoa, cut off their retreat and then give them battle under circumstances which must necessarily render one defeat decisive.

After dispatching his orders Napoleon joined Berthier at Geneva on May 8th, 1800. Here he met General Marescot, the engineer, who by his orders had explored the wild passes of the Alps. He described to the First Consul most minutely the all but insuperable obstacles that would oppose the passage of an army.

"Difficult, granted; but is it possible for an army to pass?" Napoleon at last impatiently inquired.

"It might be done," was the answer.

"Then it shall be; let us start," said the First Consul, and preparations for that most herculean task were at once made, the commander intending to penetrate into Italy, as Hannibal had done of old, through all the dangers and difficulties of the great Alps themselves.

For the treble purpose of more easily collecting a sufficient stock of provisions for the march, of making its accomplishment more rapid, and on perplexing the enemy on its termination, Napoleon determined that his army should pass in four divisions, by as many separate routes. The left wing, under Moncey consisting of 15,000 men, detached from the army of Moreau, was ordered to debouch by the way of St. Gothard. The corps of Thureau, 5,000 strong, took the direction of Mount Cenis; that of Chabran, of similar strength, moved by the Little St. Bernard. Of the main body, consisting of 35,000 men, although technically commanded by Berthier, the First Consul himself took charge, including the gigantic task of surmounting, with the artillery, the huge barriers of the Great St. Bernard. Once across he expected to rush down upon Melas, cut off all his communications with Austria, and then force him to a conflict.

BONAPARTE AT THE SIEGE OF ACRE

The main body of the army marched on the 15th of May from Lausanne to the village of St. Pierre, at the foot of the Great St. Bernard, at which point all traces of a practicable path entirely ceased. Field forges were established at St. Pierre to dismount the guns. The carriages and wheels were slung on poles and the ammunition boxes were to be carried by mules. To convey the pieces themselves a number of trees were felled, hollowed out, or grooved, and the guns being jammed within these rough cases, a hundred soldiers were attached to each whose duty it was to drag them up the steeps. All was now in readiness to commence the great march.

Botta in his description of this campaign says:

> The First Consul set forth on his stupendous enterprise, his forces being already at the foot of the Great St. Bernard. The soldiers gazed on the aerial summits of the lofty mountains with wonder and impatience. On the 17th of May the whole body set out from Martigny for the conquest of Italy. Extraordinary was their order, wonderful their gaiety, and astonishing also, the activity and energy of their operations. Laughter and song lightened their toils. They seemed to be hastening, not to a fearful war, but a festival. The multitude of various and mingled sounds were re-echoed from hill to hill, and the silence of these solitary and desolate regions, which revolving ages had left undisturbed, was for the moment broken by the rejoicing voices of the gay and warlike. Precipitous heights, strong torrents, sloping valleys, succeeded each other with disheartening frequency.
>
> Owing to his incredible boldness and order, Lannes was chosen by the First Consul to take the lead in every enterprise of danger. They had now reached an elevation where skill or courage seemed powerless against the domain of Nature. From St. Pierre to the summit of the Great St. Bernard there is no beaten road whatever, until the explorer reaches the monastery of the religious order devoted to the preservation of travellers bewildered in these regions of eternal winter. Every means that could be devised was adopted for transporting the artillery and baggage; the carriages which had been wheeled were now dragged—those which had been drawn were now carried. The largest cannon were placed in troughs and on sledges, and the smallest swung on sure-footed mules.

The ascent to be accomplished was immense. In the windings of the tortuous paths the troops were now lost and now revealed to sight. Those who first mounted the steeps, seeing their companions in the depths below, cheered them on with shouts of triumph. The valleys on every side re-echoed to their voices. Amidst the snow, in mists and clouds, the resplendent arms and coloured uniforms of the soldiers appeared in bright and dazzling contrast: the sublimity of dead Nature and the energy of living action thus united, formed a spectacle of surpassing wonder.

The consul, exulting in the success of his plans, was seen everywhere amongst the soldiers, talking with military familiarity to one and now another, and, skilled in the eloquence of camps, he so excited their courage that, braving every obstacle, they now deemed that easy which they had adjudged impossible. They soon approached the highest summit, and discerned in the distance the pass which leads from the opening between the towering mountains to the loftiest pinnacle. With shouts of transport they hailed this extreme point as the termination of their labours and with new ardour prepared to ascend. When their strength occasionally flagged under excess of fatigues, they beat their drums, and then, reanimated by the spirit-stirring sound, proceeded forward with fresh vigour.

At last they reached the summit and there felicitated each other as if after a complete and assured victory. Their hilarity was not a little increased by finding a simple repast prepared in front of the monastery, the provident Consul having furnished the monks with money to supply what their own resources could not have afforded for such numbers. Here they were regaled with wine and bread and cheese, enjoyed a brief repose amid dismounted cannon and scattered baggage, amidst ice and conglomerated snow; while the monks passed from troop to troop in turn, the calm of religious cheerfulness depicted on their countenances. Thus did goodness and power meet and hold communion on this extreme summit.

The troops made it a point of honour not to leave their guns in the rear; and one division, rather than abandon its artillery, chose to pass the night upon the summit of a mountain, in the midst of snow and excessive cold.

Thus did this brave army reach the Hospice of St. Bernard, singing amidst the precipices, dreaming of the conquest of that Italy where they had so often tasted the delights of victory, and having a noble presentiment of the immortal glory which they were about to acquire; as they climbed up and along airy ridges of rock and eternal snow, where the goatherd, the hunter of the chamois, and the outlaw smuggler, are alone accustomed to venture; amidst precipices where to slip a foot is death; beneath glaciers from which the percussion of a musket-shot is often sufficient to hurl an avalanche.

The labour was not so great for the infantry, of which there were 35,000 including artillery. As for the 5,000 cavalry, these walked, leading their horses by the bridle. There was no danger in ascending but in the descent, the path being very narrow, obliging them to walk before the horse, they were liable, if the animal made a false step, to be dragged by him into the abyss. Some accidents of this kind, not many, did actually happen, and some horses perished but scarcely any of the men.

After a brief rest at the hospice the army resumed its march and descended to St. Remy without any unpleasant accident. Napoleon rested and took a frugal repast at the convent, after which he visited the chapel, and the three little libraries, lingering a short time to read a few pages of some old book. He performed the descent on a sledge, down a glacier of nearly a hundred yards, almost perpendicular. The whole army effected the passage of the Great St. Bernard in the space of three days.

The transfer of the gun carriages, ammunition wagons and cannon was the most difficult of all, but the genius of Napoleon accomplished even this seemingly impossible feat. The peasants of the environs were offered as high as a thousand francs for every piece of cannon which they succeeded in dragging from St. Pierre to St. Remy. It took a hundred men to drag each; one day to get it up and another to get it down.

It has been said that Napoleon had his fortune to make at this period; but, at the moment of crossing Mount St. Bernard, he had fought twenty pitched battles, conquered Italy, dictated peace to Austria,—only sixty miles distant from Vienna,—negotiated at Rastadt, with Count Cobentzel for the surrender of the strong city of Mentz, raised nearly three hundred millions in contributions,—which had served to supply the army during two years,—created the Cisalpine Army, and paid some of the officers of the government at Paris. He had sent to the museum three hundred *chef d'oéuvres*, in statuary and painting; added to which he had conquered Egypt, suppressed the factions at home and totally eradicated the war in La Vendée.

Napoleon has been pictured crossing the Alpine heights mounted on a fiery steed. As a matter of fact he ascended the Great St. Bernard in that gray *surtout* which he usually wore, sometimes upon foot, and again upon a mule, led by a guide belonging to the country, evincing even in the difficult passes the abstraction of mind occupied elsewhere, conversing with the officers scattered on the road, and then, at intervals, questioning the guide who attended him, making him relate the particulars of his life, his pleasures, his pains, like an idle traveller who has nothing better to do. Thiers says:

> This guide, who was quite young, gave him a simple recital of the details of his obscure existence, and especially the vexation he felt because, for want of a little money, he could not marry one of the girls of his valley. The First Consul, sometimes listening, sometimes questioning the passengers with whom the mountain was covered, arrived at the hospice, where the worthy monks gave him a warm reception. No sooner had he alighted from his mule than he wrote a note which he handed to his guide, desiring him to be sure and deliver it to the quartermaster of the army, who had been left on the other side of the St. Bernard. In the evening the young man, on returning to St. Pierre, learned with surprise what powerful traveller it was whom he had guided in the morning, and that General Bonaparte had ordered that a house and a piece of ground should be given to him immediately, and that he should be supplied, in short, with the means requisite for marrying, and for realizing all the dreams of his modest ambition.

This mountaineer lived for a number of years, and when he died was still the owner of the land given him by the First Consul. The only thing remembered by this attendant in after years of the conversation of Napoleon during his trip was, when shaking the rain-water from his hat he exclaimed, "There! See what I have done in your mountains—spoiled my new hat!—Well, I will find another on the other side."

The passage of the Alps had been achieved long before the Austrians knew Napoleon's army was in motion. So utterly unexpected was this sudden apparition of the First Consul and his army, that no precaution whatever had been taken, and no enemy appeared capable of disputing his march towards the valley of Aosta. After a brief engagement at the fortress of St. Bard and other minor battles in which the French were victorious, they now advanced, unopposed down the valley to Ivrea which was without a garrison. Here Napoleon remained four days to recruit the strength of his troops.

Napoleon now took the road for Milan. The Sesia was crossed without opposition; the passage of the Tesino was effected after a sharp conflict with a body of Austrian cavalry, who were put to flight; and, on the 2nd of June, the First Consul entered Milan, amidst enthusiastic acclamations of the people, who had all believed that he had died in Egypt and that it was one of his brothers who commanded this army. He was conducted in triumph to the ducal palace, where he took up his residence. He remained six days in Milan during which time he gained the most important information, all the dispatches between the court of Vienna and General Melas falling into his hands. From these he learned the extent of the Austrian reinforcements now on their way to Italy; the position and state of all the Austrian depots, field-equipages, and parks of artillery; and the amount and distribution of the whole Austrian force. Finally, he clearly perceived that Melas still continued in complete ignorance of the strength and destination of the French army. His dispatches spoke with contempt of what he called "the pretended army of reserve," and treated the assertion of Napoleon's presence in Italy as a "mere fabrication." Possessed of all this valuable information Napoleon knew how to proceed with clearness and precision.

The eyes of the Austrian general were at length opened and he was preparing to meet the emergency with all the energy that the orders from Vienna and his great age of eighty years permitted; but his delay had been sufficient to render his situation critical. His army was divided into two portions, one under Ott near Genoa; the other, under his own command at Turin. The greatest risk existed that Napoleon would, according to his old plan, attack and destroy one division before the other could form a junction with it. To prevent such a disaster, Ott received orders to march forward on the Tesino, while Melas, moving towards Alessandria, prepared to resume his communications with the other division of his army.

Napoleon now advanced to Stradella where headquarters were fixed. On the 9th of June, Lannes, who continued to lead the vanguard of the French Army was attacked by an Austrian division superior in numbers and commanded by Ott. The battle, though severely contested, ended in the complete defeat of the Austrians, who lost three thousand killed and six thousand prisoners. The Battle of Montebello was won by sheer hard fighting, there being little opportunity for skill or manoeuvre, the fields being covered with full-grown crops of rye. The shower of balls from the Austrian musketry was at one time so intense, that Lannes, speaking of it afterwards, described its effect with a horrible graphic homeliness. "Bones were cracking in my division" he said, "like a shower of hail upon a skylight." Lannes was subsequently created Duke of Montebello.

Napoleon remained stationary for three days at Stradella, employing the time in concentrating his army, in hopes that Melas would be compelled to give him battle in this position; he was unwilling to descend into the great plain of Marengo, where the Austrian cavalry and artillery which was greatly superior in numbers, would have a fearful advantage. Meanwhile he dispatched an order to Suchet to march on the river Scrivia, and place himself in the rear of the enemy.

General Desaix now joined the army with his *aides-de-camp* Rapp and Savary, he having returned from Egypt and landed in France almost on the very day that Napoleon left Paris, and had immediately received a summons from him to repair to the headquarters of the Army of Italy, wherever they might be situated. Desaix and Napoleon were warmly attached to each other and their meeting was a great and mutual pleasure. Desaix was appointed to the command of a division, the death of General Boudet having left one vacant, and was extremely anxious to signalize himself. Under the impression that the Austrians were marching upon Genoa, Napoleon dispatched Desaix's division in form of the van-guard upon his extreme left, while Victor, arriving at Marengo from Montebello, where he had assisted Lannes, routed a rear guard of four or five thousand Austrians and made himself master of the village of Marengo.

The French and Austrian armies finally came together on June 14th on the plains of Marengo, to decide the fate of Italy.

Marengo was a day ever to be remembered by those who participated in the stubborn struggle. Napoleon fought against terrible odds in numbers and position. A furious cannonading opened the engagement at daybreak along the whole front, cannon and musketry spreading devastation everywhere—for the armies were but a short distance apart, their pieces in some cases almost touching. The advance under Gardanne, was obliged to fall back upon Victor,—who had been stationed with the main body of the first line,—for more than two hours and withstood singly the vigorous assaults of a far superior force; Marengo had been taken and retaken several times by Victor ere Lannes, who was in the rear of him, in command of the second line, received orders to reinforce him. The second line was at length ordered by Napoleon to advance, but they found the first in retreat, and the two corps took up a second line of defence, considerably to the rear of Marengo. Here they were again charged furiously, and again after obstinate resistance, gave way. The retreat now became general, although Lannes fell back in perfect order.

The Austrians had fought the battle admirably. Their infantry had opened an attack on every point of the French line, while the cavalry debouched across the bridge which the French had failed to destroy, and assailed the right of their army with such fury and rapidity that it was thrown into complete disorder. The attack of the Austrians was successful everywhere; the centre of the French was penetrated, the left routed, and another desperate charge of the cavalry would have terminated the battle. The order for this, however, was not given; but the retreating French were still in the utmost peril. Napoleon had been collecting reserves between Garafolo and Marengo and now sent orders for his army to retreat towards these reserves, and rally round his guard which he stationed in the rear of the village of Marengo and placed himself at their head.

To secure a position more favourable for resisting the overpowering numbers of the enemy, Bonaparte now seized a defile flanked by the village of Marengo, shut up on one side by a wood and on the other by lofty and bushy vineyards. Here from the astonishing exertions of their commander the French made a firm stand, and fought bayonet to bayonet with Austrian infantry, whilst exposed at the same time to a battery of thirty pieces of cannon, which was playing upon them with deadly effect. Every soldier seemed to consider this the defile of Thermopylae, where they were to fight until all were slain. With a heroism worthy of the Spartan band they withstood the tremendous shock of bayonets and artillery, the latter not only cutting the men in pieces, but likewise the trees, the large branches in falling killing many of the wounded soldiers who had sought a refuge under them.

At this awful moment Bonaparte, unmoved, seemed to court death, and be near it, the bullets being observed repeatedly to tear up the ground beneath his horse's feet. Alarmed for his safety the officers exhorted him to retire, exclaiming, "If you should be killed all would be lost." But the hero of Lodi and Arcola would not retire. Undismayed and unmoved amidst this dreadful tempest, he observed every movement and gave orders with the utmost coolness. The soldiers could all see the First Consul with his staff, surrounded by the two hundred grenadiers of the guard and the sight kept their hopes from flagging. The right wing, under Lannes, quickly rallied; the centre, reinforced by the scattered troops of the left, recovered its strength; the left wing no longer existed; its scattered remains fled in disorder, pursued by the Austrians. The contest continued to rage, and was obstinately disputed; but the main body of the French army, which still remained in order of battle, was continually, though very slowly, retreating.

The First Consul now dispatched his *aide-de-camp*, Bruyere, to Desaix, with an urgent message to hasten to the field of battle. Desaix on his part, had been arrested in his march upon Novi, by the repeated discharges of distant artillery; he had in consequence made a halt, and dispatched Savary, then his *aide-de-camp*, with a body of fifty horse, to gallop with all possible haste to Novi, ascertain the state of affairs there, according to the orders of Napoleon, while he kept his division fresh and ready for action.

Savary found all quiet at Novi; and returning to Desaix, after the lapse of about two hours, with this intelligence, was next sent to the First Consul. He spurred his horse across the country, in the direction of Marengo, and fortunately met General Bruyere, who was taking the same short cut to find Desaix. Giving him the necessary directions, Savary now hastened towards Napoleon. He found him in the midst of his guard, who stood their ground on the field of battle; forming a solid body in the face of the enemy's fire, the dismounted grenadiers were stationed in front and the place of each man who fell was instantly supplied from the ranks behind.

Maps were spread out before Napoleon; he was planning the movement which was to decide the action. Savary made his report and told him of Desaix's position.

"At what hour did he leave you?" said the First Consul pulling out his watch. Having been informed he continued, "Well he cannot be far off; go, and tell him to form in that direction (pointing with his hand to a particular spot); let him quit the main road, and make way for all those wounded men, who would only embarrass him, and perhaps draw his own soldiers after them."

It was now three o'clock in the afternoon; had Melas pursued the advantage with all his reserve the battle was won to the Austrians; but that aged general (he was eighty years old) doubted not that he had won it already. At this critical moment, being quite worn out with fatigue, he retired to the rear leaving General Zach to continue what he now considered a mere pursuit.

Napoleon's army was still slowly retiring from the field, one corps occupying three hours in retiring three quarters of a league, when Desaix, whose division was now forming on the left of the centre, rode up to the commander, and taking out his watch, said in reply to a question: "Yes, the battle is lost; but it is only three o'clock; there is time enough to gain another!"

Bonaparte was delighted with the opinion of Desaix, whose division had arrived at a full gallop after a force march of thirty miles, and prepared to avail himself of the timely succour brought to him by that far-seeing general, and of the advantage insured to him by the position he had lately taken. Napoleon quickly explained the manoeuvre he was about to effect and gave the orders instantly. He now drew up his army on a third line of battle, and riding along said to the different corps: "Soldiers! We have fallen back far enough. You know it is always my custom to sleep on the field of battle." The whole army now wheeled its front up the left wing of its centre, moving its right wing forward at the same time. By this movement Napoleon effected the double object of turning all the enemy's troops, who had continued the pursuit of the broken left wing and of removing his right at a distance from the bridge, which had been so fatal to him in the morning. The artillery of the guard was reinforced by that which belonged to Desaix's division, and formed an overwhelming battery in the centre.

The Austrians made no effort to prevent this decisive movement; they supposed the First Consul was only occupied in securing his retreat. Their infantry, in deep close columns, was advancing rapidly, when at the distance of a hundred paces they suddenly halted, on perceiving Desaix's division exactly in front of them. The unexpected appearance of six thousand fresh troops, and the new position assumed by the French, arrested the battle: very few shots were heard; the two armies were preparing for a last effort.

The First Consul rode up in person to give the order of attack while he dispatched Savary with commands to Kellerman, who was at the head of about six thousand heavy cavalry, to charge the Austrian column in flank, at the same time Desaix charged it in front. Both generals effected the movement rapidly and so successfully that in less than half an hour the French had put the enemy to rout on nearly all sides. A final charge was now made, when Desaix, whose timely arrival with reinforcements had saved the day, and who was then in the thickest of the engagement, was shot dead, just as he led a fresh column of 5,000 grenadiers to meet and check the advance of Zach. But a few moments before Desaix said to Savary, "Go and tell the First Consul that I am charging, and that I am in want of cavalry to support me." As the brave man fell he said: "Conceal my death, it might dishearten the troops." Napoleon embraced him for an instant, and said, as his eyes filled with tears: "Alas, I must not weep now—" and mounting his horse again plunged into the thickest of the battle.

The whole army fought with renewed vigour on learning of Desaix's death, every soldier being bent on avenging individually the loss of their leader. The combined forces now concentrated themselves and hurled their invincible columns upon the Austrian lines, marching victorious at last over thousands of slain. General Zach, and all his staff, were here made prisoners. The Austrian columns behind, being flushed with victory, were advancing too carelessly, and were unable to resist the general assault of the whole French line, which now pressed onward under the immediate command of Napoleon. Post after post was carried. The terrified cavalry and broken infantry fled in confusion to the banks of the Bormida, into which they were plunged by the French cavalry who swept the field. The Bormida was clogged and crimsoned with corpses, and whole corps, being unable to effect the passage, surrendered.

The victory, which had seemed quite secure to the Austrians at 3 o'clock was completely won by the French at six. Napoleon's conduct throughout the day and the bravery of his troops were beyond all praise; and it is no less a fact, that the appearance of victory in one or two parts of the extended field roused the courage of the Austrians to enthusiasm and in some cases fatal recklessness. They pressed forward to complete their triumph when the Consular guard, called the "wall of granite," met and successfully resisted the shock. The eye of Napoleon fixed the fortune of the day: he foresaw that the enemy, in the ardour of success, would extend his line too far; and what he had conjectured happened. Then it was that Desaix's division rushed amidst the all but triumphant foe, divided his ranks, and finally completed his ruin.

In this sanguine engagement the Austrians lost about 8,000 men in killed and wounded, and 4,000 more were taken prisoners—one-third of their army. The life of Desaix was the sacrifice. The French loss amounted to 6,000 killed or wounded and about 1,000 of them were taken prisoners, a loss of about one-fourth out of 28,000 soldiers present at the battle.

In the estimation of the First Consul this loss was great enough to diminish the joy that he felt for the victory. When Bourrienne, his secretary, congratulated him on his triumph saying, "What a glorious day!" he replied: "Yes it would have been glorious indeed, could I but have embraced Desaix this evening on the field of battle. I was going to make him minister of war; I would have made him a prince if I could." The triumph of this decisive victory was poisoned by Desaix's death. It seems that he never loved, nor regretted, any man so much and he never spoke of him without deep feeling. Desaix met his death at the early age of thirty-three, and France lost in him a great general and a man of rare promise. Savary, who was much attached to him, sought for his body amongst the dead, and found him completely stripped of his clothes, lying among many others in the same condition.

"France has lost one of her most able defenders and I my best friend," Napoleon said after the battle; "No one has ever known how much goodness there was in Desaix's heart; how much genius in his head." Then after a short silence, with tears starting into his eyes, he added, "My brave Desaix always wished to die thus; but death should not have been so ready to execute his wish."

Though the vast plain of Marengo was drenched with French blood, joy pervaded the army. Soldiers and generals alike were merited for their gallant conduct and were fully aware of the importance of the victory to France. Thus ended the Battle of Marengo, one of the most decisive which had been fought in Europe, and one which opened to Napoleon the gates of all the principal cities of northern Italy. By one battle he regained nearly all that the French had lost in the unhappy Italian campaign of 1799 while he was in Egypt. He had also shown that the French troops were once more what they had been when he was in the field to command them.

In talking with Gohier one day, Napoleon said: "It is always the greater number which defeats the lesser."

"And yet," said Gohier, "with small armies you have frequently defeated large ones."

"Even then," replied Napoleon, "it is always the inferior force which was defeated by the superior. When with a small body of men I was in the presence of a large one, collecting my little band, I fell like lightning on one of the wings of the hostile army, and defeated

Return of the French Army from Syria

it. Profiting by the disorder which such an event never failed to occasion in their whole line, I repeated the attack, with similar success, in another quarter, still with my whole force. I thus beat it in detail. The general victory which was the result was still an example of the truth of the principle, that the greater force defeats the lesser." One of his favourite maxims is said to have been, "*God always favours the heaviest battalions.*"

The Austrians were completely enveloped, and had no alternative but to submit to the law of the conqueror. Melas sent a flag of truce to Napoleon at daybreak on the following morning, and peace negotiations were at once began. In the meeting which followed Bonaparte required that all the fortresses of Liguria, Piedmont, Lombardy and the Legations should be immediately given up to France, and that the Austrians should evacuate all Italy as far as the Mincio.

The surrender of Genoa was strongly objected to by Melas, but the conqueror would not waive this point. The baron sent his principal negotiator to make some remonstrances against the proposed armistice. The First Consul with some warmth said,:

> Sir, my conditions are irrevocable. It was not yesterday that I began my military life; your position is as well known to me as to yourselves. You are in Alessandria, encumbered with dead, wounded, sick, destitute of provisions; you have lost the best troops of your army, and are surrounded on all sides. There is nothing that I might not require, but I respect the gray hair of your general, and the valour of your troops, and I require, nothing more than is imperatively demanded by the present situation of affairs. Return to Alessandria; do what you will, you shall have no other conditions.

The treaty of peace was signed at Alessandria, the same day, June 15th, 1800, as originally proposed by General Bonaparte. He then started for Paris by way of Milan, where preparations had been made for a solemn *Te Deum* in the ancient cathedral, and at which the First Consul was present. He found the city illuminated, and ringing with the most enthusiastic rejoicings. The streets were lined with people who greeted him with shouts of welcome. Draperies were hung from the windows, which were crowded by women of the first rank and who threw flowers into his carriage as he passed. He set off for Paris on the 24th of June and arrived at the French capital in the night between the 2nd and 3rd of July, having been absent less than two months. Massena remained as commander-in-chief of the Army of Italy.

To one of his travelling companions with whom he conversed on the journey to Paris about his remarkable victory at Marengo, he said: "Well, a few grand deeds like this campaign and I may be known to posterity."

"It seems to me," said his companion, "that you have already done enough to be talked about everywhere for a time."

"Done enough," said Bonaparte quickly, "You are very kind! To be sure in less than two years I have conquered Cairo, Paris and Milan; well, my dear fellow, if I were to die tomorrow, after ten centuries I shouldn't fill half a page in a universal history!"

At night the city of Paris was brilliantly illuminated and the inhabitants turned out en masse. Night after night every house was illuminated. The people were so anxious to show their pleasure at Napoleon's miraculous victory that they stood in crowds around the palace contented if they could but catch a glimpse of the preserver of France. These receptions so deeply touched him that twenty years afterwards, in loneliness and in exile, a prisoner at St. Helena, he mentioned it as one of the proudest and happiest moments of his life.

On the day following his return to the capital the president of the Senate—the entire body having waited upon him in state—complimented the conqueror of Marengo in language such as kings were formerly addressed in, and in closing his address said: "We take pleasure in acknowledging that to you the country owes its salvation; that to you the Republic will owe its consolidation, and the people a prosperity, which you have in one day made to succeed ten years of the most stormy of revolutions."

In November following Napoleon's return to the capital he received a letter addressed to him by Count de Lille (afterwards Louis XVIII.) which the exiled prince of the House of Bourbon evidently believed would place him on the throne of France. He said:

> You are very tardy about restoring my throne to me; it is to be feared that you may let the favourable moment slip. You cannot establish the happiness of France without me; and I, on the other hand, can do nothing for France without you. Make haste, then, and point out, yourself, the posts and dignities which will satisfy you and your friends.

The First Consul answered thus:

I have received your Royal Highness' letter. I have always taken a lively interest in your misfortunes and those of your family. You must not think of appearing in France—*you could not do so without marching over five hundred thousand corpses.* For the rest, I shall always be zealous to do whatever lies in my power towards softening your Royal Highness' destinies, and making you forget, if possible, your misfortunes. Bonaparte.

The Battle of Marengo was celebrated at Paris by a *fête* on the 14th of July, which presented a singularly interesting spectacle owing to the appearance of the "wall of granite," the members of which, just as the games were about to begin, marched into the field. The sight of those soldiers, covered with the dust of their march, sun-burned and powder-stained, and bearing marks of heroic deeds on the battlefield, formed a scene so truly affecting that the populace could not be restrained by the guards from violating the limits, in order to take a nearer view of those interesting heroes.

5

Ulm and Austerlitz

Napoleon had now reached such a point of power that the Bourbons resigned all hopes of restoration through his agency, and as the next best means of obtaining control of the throne of France assassination was decided upon. The First Consul had scarcely been in Paris a month, after the engagement at Marengo when Ceracchi, a sculptor of some fame, attempted Bonaparte's life as he was entering the theatre. But for his betrayal by a co-conspirator the plot would have succeeded. This attempt by means of the dagger was followed by the explosion of an infernal machine, which consisted of a barrel of gunpowder surrounded by an immense quantity of grape shot. On the night of October 10th the machine was placed at Nacaise, a narrow street through which Napoleon was to pass on his way to the opera house.

Some years later, in telling of the narrow escape he had on that night, he said:

> I had been hard at work all day, and was so overpowered by sleep after dinner that Josephine, who was quite anxious to go to the opera that night, found it quite difficult to arouse me and persuade me to go. I fell asleep again after we had entered the carriage, and I was dreaming of the danger I had undergone some years before in crossing the Tagliamento at midnight by the light of torches, during a flood, when I was waked by the explosion of the infernal machine. 'We are blown up,' I said to Bessieres and Lannes, who were in the carriage, and then quickly commanded the coachman to drive on.
>
> The coachman, who was intoxicated, heard the order, and having mistaken the explosion for a salute, lashed his horses furiously until

the theatre was reached. The machine had been fired by a slow match, and the explosion took place just twenty seconds too soon. Summary justice was executed upon the perpetrators of this infamous deed, and some time later the Duke d'Enghien atoned for the part, whatever it might have been, that the Bourbons had taken in these murderous schemes.

Austria delayed for several months final negotiations of the treaty agreed upon after the engagement at Marengo, evidently reassured by the attempts made on the First Consul's life. Preliminaries of peace had been signed at Paris, between the Austrian general, Saint Julian, and the French government. Duroc was dispatched to the Emperor of Austria, to obtain his ratification of the articles; but having reached the headquarters of the Army of the Rhine, he was refused a pass to proceed on his journey.

Napoleon immediately ordered Moreau to recommence hostilities, unless the emperor delivered up the fortresses of Ulm, Ingolstadt and Phillipsburg as pledges of his sincerity. Austria, accordingly, purchased a further protraction of the armistice at this heavy price; at the same time offering to treat for peace on new grounds. News of the occupation of the three fortresses by the French troops, was announced in Paris on the 23rd of September 1800, where the fresh hopes of peace caused universal satisfaction.

These hopes, however, proved delusive. Austria delayed and equivocated, until it became evident the emperor would make no peace separate from England, and that the latter power was prepared to support her ally.

Napoleon, perceiving that he was being trifled with, now gave orders (in November, 1800) to all his generals to put their divisions in march all along the frontiers of the French dominions. The shock was instantaneous, from the Rhine to the Mincio. Brune overwhelmed the Austrians on the Mincio; Macdonald held the Tyrol, and Moreau achieved the glorious victory of Hohenlinden after a desperate and most sanguinary battle. This latter contest decided the fate of the campaign. Thus with three victorious armies, either of which could have marched triumphantly into Vienna, Napoleon hesitated long enough before taking that final step, to allow Austria to sign an honest and definite peace. The treaty of Luneville was at last signed in good faith on February 9th, 1801. By the peace of Luneville, Napoleon for the second time effected the pacification of the Continent. Of all the powerful coalition which threatened France in 1800, England alone continued hostile in 1801 if we except Turkey, with which no arrangement could be made until the affairs of Egypt were settled.

On the 8th of March, 1801, a British army of 17,000 men landed in Egypt under the command of Sir Ralph Abercromby. The French were very ill-prepared for an attack. The English army overcame the resistance of the forces which opposed their landing through the heavy surf formed on the beach, and advanced upon their enemy. No general action occurred until the 21st when the English obtained a decisive victory and drove Menou,—who had succeeded to the command of the troops in Egypt at the death of Kléber,—with great loss within the walls of Alexandria. Here he was blockaded and General Belliard, cut off from all communication with him, capitulated after which Menou submitted. Each capitulated on condition of being taken back to France with all his troops and their arms and baggage. Thus ended the conquest of Egypt by Napoleon. The French admiral, Gantheaume, had long been making fruitless efforts to land reinforcements in Egypt, but had been unable to elude the British ships. He was now ordered to return to Toulon, where preparations were made to receive the French troops.

After the news of the reverses of the French army in Egypt, and the great sea victory of Copenhagen by Nelson, Napoleon was determined to bring England to negotiations of peace and a recognition of the French Republic, and with this in view he gathered an army of 100,000 men on the coasts of France, with a flotilla sufficiently large to effect a landing in England, whenever circumstances seemed to favour such a movement. At this very moment it was, that Fulton, the inventor of steamboats, communicated his discovery to the First Consul. Napoleon thus had the first chance placed in his hands of possessing exclusively for a time, the greatest and most diversified means of physical power ever known in the world. Scarcely deigning to bestow a thought upon the subject the First Consul treated the inventor as a "visionary."

Whether or not Napoleon ever intended to invade Great Britain, he succeeded at all events in convincing the world for a time that such was his design, and when the peace of Amiens was signed on March 25th, 1802, Paris and London rejoiced, as did all civilized nations. The peace of Amiens left the military resources of France unemployed on the hands of Bonaparte. This induced him to think of profiting by the European calm, and effect the conquest of St. Domingo. He gave the command of the expedition to his brother-in-law, Leclerc; but it was unsuccessful.

The inauguration of Christian worship once more in France in 1802 gave Napoleon an opportunity to show that he had the interest of the people at heart. France was an infidel nation, and it was the fashion to believe there was no God. The signing of the Concordat by Pope Pius VII. gave to France what she had long needed—a form of religious worship. It required no little strength of purpose to take this step. "Religion is a principle which cannot be eradicated from the heart of man;" said Napoleon. "Last Sunday I was walking here alone, and the church bells of the village of Ruel rang at sunset. I was strongly moved, so vividly did the memory of early days come back with that sound. If it be thus with me, what must it be with others? In re-establishing the Church, I consult the wishes of the great majority of my people."

A grand religious ceremony took place at Notre Dame Cathedral to celebrate the proclamation of the Concordat, at which the First Consul presided with great pomp, attended by all the ministers and general officers then in Paris. Another measure, adopted at this period, was the decree permitting the return of the emigrants, provided they appeared and took the oath to the government within a certain period. It is estimated that a hundred thousand exiles returned to their country in consequence of this decree.

It was about this period, too, that the First Consul turned his attention to the system of a national education. He also commenced the herculean task of preparing a code of law for the French nation with the result that the "Code Napoleon" is known to every civilized nation of the earth. Public improvements, formerly projected, were now carried out, and sciences and the arts progressed as never before.

The order of the Legion of Honour owes its inception to Napoleon Bonaparte, and it was he who placed it on such a footing in France that it has since thrived there as has no similar institution on the Continent. When established by him, after months of careful consideration, he believed it necessary to France. To his Counsellors of State he said:

> They talk about ribbons and crosses being the playthings of monarchs, and say that the old Romans had no system of honorary rewards. The Romans had patricians, knights, citizens and slaves,—for each class different dresses and different manners— mural crowns, civic crowns, orations, triumphs and titles. When

the noble band of patricians lost its influence, Rome fell to pieces—the people were a vile rabble. It was then that you saw the fury of Marius, the proscriptions of Scylla, and afterward of the emperors. In that manner Brutus is talked of as the enemy of tyrants; he was an aristocrat, who stabbed Caesar because Caesar wished to lower the authority of the senate. You call these ribbons and crosses child's rattles—be it so: It is with such rattles that men are led.

I would not say that to the multitude, but in a council of wise men and statesmen one may speak the truth.... Observe how the people bow before the decorations of foreigners. Voltaire calls the common soldiers 'Alexanders at five *sous* a day.' He was right. It is just so. Do you imagine you can make men fight by reasoning? Never! You must bribe them with glory, with distinctions and rewards.... In fine, it is agreed that we have need of some kind of institutions. If this Legion of Honour is not approved, let some other be suggested. I do not pretend that it alone will save the State, but it will do its part.

The Legion of Honour was instituted on the 15th of May 1802. When Napoleon had seen the fruits of it, he said:

This order was the reward of everyone who was an honour to his country, stood at the head of his profession, and contributed to the national prosperity and glory. Some were dissatisfied because the decoration was conferred alike on officers and soldiers; others, because it was given for civil and military merits indiscriminately; but if this order ever cease to be the recompense of the brave private, or be confined to military men alone, it will cease to be what I made it,—the Legion of Honour.

The First Consul was, in right of his office, captain general of the legion and president of the council of administration. The nomination of all the members was for life. The grand officers were endowed with a yearly pension of upwards of $1000. Pensions, decreasing in amount, were also affixed to the subordinate degrees of rank in the order. All the members were required to swear, upon their honour, to defend the government of France, and maintain the inviolability of her empire, to combat, by every lawful means against the re-establishment of feudal institutions, and to concur in maintaining the principle of liberty and equality. On the day the order was instituted, Napoleon, by act of the Senate was appointed Consul for life. The First Consul accepted the offered prolongation from the Senate, on the condition that the opinion of the people should be consulted on the subject. The question put to them, as framed by Cambacérès and Le Brun, was: "Napoleon Bonaparte—Shall he be Consul for life?" Registers were opened in all municipalities; and the answer of the people qualified to vote was decisive. Upwards of three million five hundred thousand voted for the proposal; 8,300 against it. In the month of August Napoleon was formally declared Consul for life and a decree of the Senate immediately consolidated his power, by permitting him to appoint his successor.

This personal elevation had its ample share in contributing to the number of Napoleon's enemies. In fact it appears in some measure astonishing how any individual could persuade a whole nation, day after day, to yield him up such a portion of its rights and privileges. However, among many instances that might be adduced of his powers of persuasion, one which occurred about this period is not the least remarkable. In the beginning of the summer of 1802 some officers of rank, enthusiastic republicans, took umbrage at Napoleon's conduct, and determined to go and remonstrate with him upon the points that had given them offense, and speak their minds freely. On the evening of the same day, one of the party gave the following account of the interview:

> I do not know whence it arises, but there is a charm about that man, indescribable and irresistible. I am no admirer of his; I dislike the power to which he has risen; yet I cannot help confessing that there is something in him which seems to speak him born to command. We went into his apartment, determined to declare our minds; to expostulate with him warmly; and not to depart till our subject of complaint should be removed. But in his manner of receiving us there was a certain tact which disarmed us in a moment; nor could we utter one word of what we had intended to say. He talked to us for a length of time, with an eloquence peculiarly his own, explaining with the utmost clearness and precision, the necessity of steadily pursuing the line of conduct he had adopted, and, without contradicting us in direct terms, controverted our opinions so ably, that we had not a word to offer in reply, we therefore retired, having done nothing but listen to, instead of expostulating with him,

fully convinced, at least for the moment, that he was right, and that we were altogether in the wrong!

Towards the close of the year 1802 it became evident that the peace of Amiens was based on a hollow foundation, and was destined at no distant period to be overthrown. At an interview held with Lord Whitworth, an ambassador from England, Napoleon said:

> No consideration on earth shall make me consent to your retention of Malta; I would as soon agree to put you in possession of the Faubourg St. Antoine. Every wind that blows from England brings nothing but hatred and hostility towards me. An invasion is the only means of offense that I can take against her, and I am determined to put myself at the head of the expedition. There are a hundred chances to one against my success; but I am not the less determined to attempt the descent, if war must be the consequence of the present discussion.

He now quickly brought matters to a crisis. He attacked the ambassador in vigorous language at a diplomatic meeting at the Tuileries which ended in an abrupt termination of the conference by Napoleon leaving the room.

The armistice lasted until March 18th, 1803, when England again declared war upon France. All commerce of the French nation was ordered seized, wherever found, and two hundred vessels, containing at least $15,000,000 worth of property fell into the hands of England. Napoleon retaliated by arresting upwards of ten thousand Englishmen then in France. The tocsin of war was sounded in every part of Europe, and 160,000 French soldiers were marshalled on the coasts of France, again threatening an invasion of England. France at this time was totally unprepared for war; a proof sufficient to show that the First Consul had not desired the termination of peace. The army was completely on a peace establishment; great numbers of the troops were disbanded and the parks of artillery were broken up. New plans for re-casting the artillery had been proposed, and they had already begun to break up the cannon to throw them into the furnaces. The navy was in a still less serviceable condition. In an address to the Senate Napoleon said:

> The negotiations are ended and we are attacked; let us at least fight to maintain the faith of treaties and the honour of the French name.

The nation responded with enthusiasm to the call; sums of money were voted by the large towns for building ships and the army was rapidly recruited.

The first hostile movement of Napoleon was upon the continental domains of George III. General Mortier invaded the Electorate of Hanover with 15,000 men and the Hanoverian army laid down its arms. The second movement of the First Consul was the occupation of Naples. No resistance was attempted. These measures, besides enabling Napoleon to maintain his army by levies on the foreign states he occupied, also crippled the commerce of England by shutting up all communication with many of the best markets on the Continent. The First Consul now visited the principal towns, accompanied by Josephine, where he made observations and gave orders respecting the fortifications. These measures were all preparatory on the part of Napoleon to his determined plan to attempt the invasion of England. Funds were secured in part by the sale of Louisiana to the United States.

Assassination was now again resorted to that Napoleon might be overthrown; but every attempt, as heretofore, proved futile. Conspiracy after conspiracy was detected—all traced to Napoleon's political enemies. The First Consul resolved on retaliation and ordered the arrest of the Duke d'Enghien at his castle in the Duchy of Baden. Three days afterwards the duke was conveyed to Paris, and after a few hours' imprisonment, was taken to the old State Prison of France, where he was tried by court martial, and in a most summary and hasty manner pronounced guilty of having fought against the Republic and condemned to death. He was led down a winding stairway by torchlight, and shot in a ditch in the castle at six o'clock in the morning. All Europe shuddered at the deed, but it produced exactly the result Napoleon intended by it; he was safe from attempts on his life forever afterwards.

Before the discovery of this plot the French Senate had sent an address to Napoleon congratulating him on his escape from a former conspiracy in which one hundred persons had schemed to take his life. In answer he said:

> I have long since renounced the hope of enjoying the pleasures of a private life; all my days are employed in fulfilling the duties which my fate and the will of the French people have imposed upon me. Heaven will watch over France, and defeat

the plots of the wicked. The citizens may be without alarm; my life will last as long as it will be useful to the nation; but I wish the French people to understand that existence, without their confidence and affection, would be to me without consolation, and would for them have no object.

The title of First Consul, by which Napoleon had been distinguished for more than four years, was exchanged on the 18th of May 1804 for that of emperor by the advice of the Senate, where it was first publicly broached, and by the universal assent of the French nation. Upwards of 3,500,000 voted for the measure and about 2,000 against it. The debates in the Senate were somewhat protracted and so great was the impatience of the military that the garrison of Paris had resolved to proclaim their chief as emperor, at the first review; and Murat, governor of the city, was obliged to assemble the officers at his house, and bind them by a promise to restrain the troops. The spirit of the army at Boulogne was soon manifested, by their voting the erection of a colossal statue of Napoleon, in bronze, to be placed in the midst of the camp. Every soldier subscribed a portion of his pay for the purpose; but there was a want of bronze. Soult, who presided over the completion of the undertaking, went, at the head of a deputation to Napoleon, and said: "Sire, lend me the bronze, and I will repay it in enemy's cannon at the first battle," and he kept his word.

On the 27th of May Napoleon received the oath of the Senate, the constituted bodies, the learned corporations and the troops of the garrison of Paris. Louis XVIII. immediately addressed a protest to all the sovereigns of Europe against the usurpation of Napoleon. Fouché, who was the first who heard of this document, immediately communicated the intelligence to the emperor, with a view to prepare the necessary orders to watch over those who might attempt its circulation; but great was his surprise, on receiving directions to have the whole inserted in the *Moniteur* the following morning, where it actually appeared. This was all the notice taken of the matter by Napoleon.

On December 1st of the same year, the lists of votes in favour of the establishment of the hereditary succession of the empire in his family were publicly presented by the Senate to Napoleon, and on the following day, in the midst of one of the most imposing and brilliant scenes ever enacted in France, Napoleon and Josephine were crowned Emperor and Empress of France by Pius VII., the Pontiff of Rome, in

ALLEGORIAL REPRESENTATION OF NAPOLEON CROSSING THE ALPS

the Cathedral of Notre Dame.

The emperor took his coronation oath as usual on such occasions, with his hand upon the Scripture, and in the form repeated to him by the Pope; but in the act of coronation itself there was a marked deviation from the universal custom. The crown having been blessed by the Pope, Napoleon took it from the altar with his own hands and placed it on his brow. He then put the diadem on the head of Josephine. The heralds proclaimed that "the thrice glorious and thrice august Napoleon, Emperor of the French, was crowned and installed;" and so ended the pageant. "Those who remember having beheld it," says Sir Walter Scott, "must now doubt whether they were waking, or whether fancy had formed a vision so dazzling in its appearance, so extraordinary in its origin and progress, and so ephemeral in its endurance."

The senators of the Italian Republic soon afterwards requested that Napoleon be crowned as their king, and on the following May 1805, in the ancient cathedral of Milan, he assumed the Iron Crown of the Lombard kings, saying as he did so, "God has given it to me; let him beware who would touch it!"

The new order of knighthood, that of the Iron Crown, with these words for its motto, arose out of this ceremony.

On the 8th of May, while on the road to Milan, Napoleon expressed a wish to visit the battlefield of Marengo, on which he had reconquered Italy five years before. All the French troops in that part of Italy were therefore mustered there, to the number of 30,000. Covered with the hat and uniform which he wore on the day of that memorable conflict—the emperor passed the army in review on horseback, and distributed crosses of the Legion of Honour, with the same ceremonies which had been observed on the Champ de Mars and the same return of enthusiastic devotion on the parts of the troops. Bourrienne says:

> It was remarked that the worms, who spare neither the costumes of living kings, nor the bodies of deceased heroes, had been busy with the trophies of Marengo, which, nevertheless, Bonaparte wore at the review.

Napoleon did not continue his journey until after he had laid the first stone of the monument consecrated to those who had been slain on the battlefield, and on the same day he made his entry into Milan. Meanwhile the activity in France continued unabated, and scarcely a day passed without some trifling engagement, brought on by the rigorous pursuit of the squadrons of the French fleet, as they advanced to Boulogne.

Scarcely had the emperor entered Paris after his return from the coronation in Italy, before he learned that a new coalition had been formed against him, and that England, Russia, Austria and Sweden, with half a million men, were preparing once more for war. The objects proposed were, briefly, the independence of Holland and Switzerland; the evacuation of Hanover, and the north of Germany by the French troops; the restoration of Piedmont to the King of Sardinia; and the complete evacuation of Italy by France. Great Britain, besides affording the assistance of her forces by sea and land, was to pay large subsidies for supporting the armies of the coalition. Napoleon had, in a great degree, penetrated the schemes of the allied powers, but was not prepared for the sudden assumption of arms by Austria without any declaration of war; a measure which Austria justified by referring to the increasing encroachments of France in Italy.

As the emperor desired leisure to prosecute and perfect the great public works he had begun, or projected, he most earnestly wished for peace, and he again addressed a letter to the King of England, and which was treated with contempt. An envoy was sent to Frankfort-on-the-Main to ascertain definitely whether Austria really intended to trample another treaty in the dirt, and so soon after the fatal day at Marengo. The messenger soon returned with the best maps of the German Empire, and opening them on the council table of the Tuileries, said: "The Austrian general is advancing on Munich: the Russian army is in motion, and Prussia will join them."

The Emperor of Russia had pushed on to Berlin to win over the Prussian monarch to the great Bourbon coalition, and to make the compact more impressive, he asked his royal brother to visit with him the tomb of Frederick the Great. They descended by torchlight to the vault, and there, over the honoured dust of Frederick, Francis, his heir, took a solemn oath, as he pointed to the sword of his ancestor as it lay on the coffin, to join the European coalition. Some weeks afterwards Napoleon visited the tomb as a conqueror, and said to his attendant, as he seized the precious relics: "These orders and sword shall witness no other such scene of perjury over the ashes of Frederick!"

The young Emperor of France now gathered his eagles to lead them toward the Danube. To the French Senate, whom Napoleon informed of the hostile conduct of Russia and Austria, the emperor said:

> I am about to quit my capital to place myself at the head of my army in order that I may render prompt assistance to my allies, and defend the dearest interests of my people. . . . I groan for the blood which it will cost Europe; but it will be the means of adding new lustre to the French name.

Another campaign against the kings of Europe was inevitable, and he proceeded to achieve the destruction of Mack's army, not as at Marengo by one general battle, but by a series of grand manoeuvres, and a train of partial actions necessary to execute them, which rendered assistance and retreat alike impossible.

The great army that had been assembled on the coast of France to invade England was now relieved from its inactivity and directed to march upon the German frontiers. The Count de Ségur, who had command of the detachment of the Guard at the Tuileries, and accompanied Napoleon on this campaign, relates in his *Memoirs* a remarkable scene in the emperor's private quarters at Boulogne before Napoleon started for the frontier. The emperor had just received news that Admiral Villeneuve had taken the French fleet to Ferrol and left the channel. On learning this the emperor at once decided that the contemplated invasion of England was then impossible. Ségur then says: "Sit there," Napoleon said to M. Daru, then acting as *intendant*-general of the army "and write."

And then, without a transition, without any apparent meditation, with his brief and imperious accent, he dictated to him, without hesitation, the plan of the campaign of Ulm as far as Vienna! The army of the coast, fronting the ocean for more than two hundred leagues, was at the first signal to turn round and march on the Danube, in several columns! The order of the marches, their duration, points of concentration, of reunion of the columns, surprises, attacks, various movements, the enemy's mistakes—all was foreseen. . . . The battlefields, the victories, even the dates on which we were to enter Munich and Vienna—all was then written just as it happened, and this two months in advance, at this very hour of the 13th of August, and from this quarter-general on the coast.

Daru, however accustomed to the inspirations of his chief, remained dumfounded, and he was even more surprised when afterwards he saw these oracles realized. The emperor returned to Paris without delay, and there laid before the Senate the state of the army and announced the commencement of hostilities.

It was five years since the soldiers had been in battle; and for two and a half years they had been waiting in vain for an opportunity to cross over into England. It would be difficult to form any conception then of their joy or of their ardour when they learned they were going to be employed in a great war. Old and young ardently longed for battles, dangers, distant expeditions. They had conquered the Austrians, the Prussians, the Russians; they despised all the soldiers of Europe and did not imagine there was an army in the world capable of resisting them. They set off singing, and shouting, "*Vive l'Empereur!*"

At the same time Massena received orders to assume the offensive in Italy, and force his way, if possible, into the hereditary States of Austria. The two French armies, one crossing the Rhine and the other pushing through the Tyrolese, looked forward to a junction before the walls of Vienna. After appointing Joseph Bonaparte to superintend the government in his absence Napoleon quitted Paris on the 24th of September 1805, accompanied as far as Strasbourg by Josephine: here they separated. The emperor put himself at the head of his army and crossed the Rhine on the 1st of October. He now begun a series of grand manoeuvres and partial actions, requiring consummate skill, with a view to the destruction of the great Austrian army under General Mack.

Mack, at the head of the Austrian forces, established his headquarters on the western frontier of Bavaria, at Ulm. Prudence would have suggested that he occupy the line of the River Inn, which, extending from the Tyrol to the Danube at Passau, affords a strong defence to the Austrian territory, and on which he might have awaited, in comparative safety, the arrival of the Russian forces, then on the march to aid Austria in the campaign.

Napoleon hastened to profit by Mack's error, and by a combination of manoeuvres with his different divisions, the great body of the French Army advanced into the heart of Germany by the left of the Danube, and then throwing himself across the river, took ground in the Austrian general's rear, when he expected to be assaulted in front of Ulm. As it was, Mack's communication with Vienna was interrupted, and he was completely isolated.

Never was astonishment equal to that which filled all Europe on the unexpected arrival of the French Army. It was supposed to be on the shores of the ocean, and in twenty days, scarcely time enough for the report of its march to spread to this point, it appeared on the Rhine.

Napoleon did not effect his purpose of taking up a position in the rear of Mack without resistance, but in the various engagements with the different divisions of the Austrian army at Wertingen, Gunzburgh, Memingen and Elchingen, the French were uniformly successful. At Memingen General Spangenburg was forced to capitulate, and 5,000 men laid down their arms. Not less than 20,000 prisoners fell into the hands of the French between the 26th of September and the 13th of October.

The emperor passed in review the dragoons of the village of Zumershausen when he ordered to be brought before him a dragoon named Marente, of the 4th regiment, one of the gallant soldiers who, at the passage of the Lech, had saved his captain, by whom he had, a few days before, been cashiered from his rank. Napoleon then bestowed upon him the eagle of the Legion of Honour.

"I have only done my duty," observed the soldier, "my captain degraded me on account of some violation of discipline but he knows I have always proved a good soldier."

The emperor expressed his satisfaction to the dragoons for the bravery they had displayed at the Battle of Wertingen and ordered each regiment to present a dragoon, on whom he also bestowed the decoration of the Legion of Honour.

Napoleon looked upon the Battle of Elchingen which followed the actions at Wertingen and Gunzburgh as one of the finest feats of arms that his army had ever accomplished. From this field of battle he sent the Senate forty standards taken by the French army in the various battles which had succeeded that of Wertingen, he wrote:

> Since my entry on this campaign I have disposed of an army of 100,000 men. I have taken nearly half of them prisoners; the rest have either deserted, are killed, wounded, or reduced to the greatest consternation...Assisted by Divine Providence I hope in a short time to triumph over all my enemies.

By the 13th of October General Mack found himself completely surrounded at Ulm with a garrison of fully 20,000 good troops. On this day Napoleon made an exciting address to his soldiers on the bridge of the Lech, amid the most intense cold, the ground being covered with snow, and the troops sunk to the knees in mud. He warned them to expect a great battle, and explained the desperate condition of the enemy. He was answered with acclamations and repeated shouts of, "*Vive l'Empereur!*" In listening to his exciting words, the soldiers forgot their fatigues and privations and were impatient to rush into the fight.

As Napoleon passed through a crowd of prisoners, an Austrian colonel expressed his astonishment on beholding the Emperor of the French drenched with rain, covered with dirt, and as much, or even more fatigued than the meanest drummer in his army. An *aide-de-camp* present having explained to him what the Austrian officer said, the emperor ordered this answer to be given:

"Your master wished me to recollect that I was a soldier; I hope that he will allow that the throne and the imperial purple have not made me forget my original profession."

From the height of the Abbey of Elchingen Napoleon now beheld the city of Ulm at his feet, commanded on every side by his cannon; his victorious troops ready for the assault, and the great Austrian army cooped up within the walls. Four days later a flag of truce came from General Mack.

Napoleon had called upon the commander to surrender, and unlike the brave Wurmser, who held Mantua to extremity during the campaign of Alvinzi, he capitulated without hazarding a blow. On the previous day Mack had published a proclamation urging his troops to prepare for the "utmost pertinacity of defence" and forbidding, on the pain of death, the very word "surrender" to be breathed within the walls of Ulm. He announced the arrival of two powerful armies, one of Austrians, the other of Russians, whose appearance "would presently raise the blockade." He even declared his intention of eating horseflesh rather than listen to any terms of capitulation!

On the morning of October 15th Napoleon finally resolved to bring the affair to a close, and gave orders to Marshal Ney to storm the heights of Michaelsberg. All at once a battery unmasked by the Austrians, poured its grape-shot upon the imperial group. Lannes, who was to flank Ney, abruptly seized Napoleon's horse to lead him out of the galling fire. The latter had taken up a position to watch Ney, who had set his columns in motion. Changing to a safe position, the emperor saw this intrepid leader climb the intrenchments raised on Michaelsberg, and carry them with the bayonet. Lannes secured another point of attack a moment later.

Napoleon then suspended the combat until the next day, when he ordered a few shells to be thrown into Ulm, and in the evening sent Ségur to General Mack summoning him to surrender. The envoy had great difficulty in getting into the place. He was led blindfold before

Mack, who, striving to conceal his anxiety, was nevertheless unable to dissemble his surprise and grief on learning the extent of his disaster and hopeless position.

On the 17th Mack signed articles by which hostilities were immediately ceased and he with all his men agreed to surrender(!) themselves as prisoners of war within ten days, unless some Austrian or Russian force should appear and attempt to raise the blockade. On the 19th, after a personal visit to Napoleon's camp, Mack submitted to a "revision" of the treaty, and on the 20th a formal evacuation of Ulm took place.

Thirty-six thousand soldiers filed off and laid down their arms before Napoleon and his staff. A large watch-fire had been made, near which the Emperor posted himself to witness the ceremony. General Mack came forward and delivered his sword, exclaiming, with grief: "Here is the unfortunate Mack!" Napoleon received him and his officers with the greatest courtesy. Eighteen generals were dismissed on parole, an immense quantity of ammunition of all sorts fell into the hands of the victor, and a wagonful of Austrian standards was sent to Paris.

Napoleon enforced the strictest silence on his troops while this ceremony, so painful to their enemies continued. In one instance he instantly ordered out of his presence one of his own generals from whom his quick ear caught some witticism passed on the occasion.

All the Austrian officers were allowed to return home, on giving their word of honour not to serve against France until a general exchange of prisoners should take place.

This campaign is perhaps unexampled in the history of warfare for the greatness of its results in comparison with the smallness of the expense at which they were obtained. Of the French Army, scarcely fifteen hundred men were killed and wounded; while the Austrian Army of almost ninety thousand men was nearly annihilated; all, with the exception of 15,000 who escaped, being killed, wounded, or prisoners; and having lost also, 200 pieces of cannon and ninety flags. It was a common remark among the troops, "The emperor has found a new method of carrying on war; he makes us use our legs instead of our bayonets." Five-sixths of the French Army never fired a shot, at which the troops were much mortified!

Massena was also successful in his advance from Lombardy, the Archduke Charles, who commanded an army of 80,000 men for Austria, being forced to abandon Italy, and Marshal Ney whom Napoleon had detached from his own main army with orders to advance in the Tyrol, was no less successful. The number of prisoners taken in this campaign was so great that Napoleon distributed them amongst the agriculturists that their work in the fields might make up for the absence of the conscripts, whom he had withdrawn from such labour.

Rumours of the approach of the Russians, headed by the Emperor Alexander in person, came fast and frequent. The divisions of Massena and Ney were now at the disposal of Napoleon, who was concentrating his forces for the purpose of attacking Vienna, and, with the main body, now moved on the capital of the Austrian emperor. The Emperor Francis, perceiving that Vienna was incapable of defence, quitted his palace on the 7th of November, and proceeded to the headquarters of Alexander at Brunn.

While Napoleon was riding on horseback on the Vienna road, he perceived an open carriage approaching, in which were seated a priest, and a lady bathed in tears. The emperor was dressed, as usual, in the uniform of a colonel of the *chasseurs* of the guard. The lady did not recognize him. He inquired the cause of her distress and where she was going.

"Sir," said she, "I have been robbed, about two leagues hence, by a party of soldiers, who have killed my gardener. I am going to request that your emperor will grant me a guard; he once knew my family well, and lay under obligations to them."

"Your name?" inquired Napoleon.

"De Brunny" answered the lady. "I am the daughter of M. de Marbeuf, formerly governor of Corsica."

"I am delighted to meet with you *madame*" exclaimed Napoleon with the most charming frankness, "and to have an opportunity of serving you,—I am the emperor."

The lady expressed much surprise and passed on agreeing to wait for the commander at headquarters. Here she was furnished a piquet of chasseurs.

On the 13th the French entered Vienna, and Napoleon took up his residence in the Imperial Palace of Schoenbrunn, the home of the Austrian Cæsars. While at this point Napoleon learned of the success of the English at Trafalgar on October 19th,—the day after Mack surrendered at Ulm. It was a battle sternly contested and resulted in the final annihilation of the French fleet. Great as the triumph was for England, it was dearly purchased—for Nelson fell, mortally wounded, early in the action. He lived just long enough to hear the cheers of victory, and as he passed away, said, "Thank God! I have done my duty!"

The tidings of Trafalgar served but as a new stimulus to Napoleon's energy. "Heaven has given the empire of the sea to England," he said, "but to us has fate decreed the dominion of the land." But though such signal success had crowned the commencement of the campaign, it was necessary to defeat the haughty Russians before the object of the war could be considered as attained. The broken and shattered remnant of the Austrian forces had rallied from different quarters around the yet untouched army of Alexander; Napoleon had therefore waited until the result of his skilful combinations had drawn around him the greatest force he could expect to collect, ere venturing upon a general battle. He then quitted Vienna and put himself at the head of his columns which soon found themselves within reach of the Russian and Austrian forces, at length combined and ready for action, and under the eye of their emperors.

Now it was to be a battle of three emperors,—France, Russia and Austria. Napoleon fixed his headquarters at Brunn, where he arrived on the 20th of November, and riding over the plain between this point and Austerlitz, a village about two miles from Brunn, said to his generals: "Study this field well,—we shall, ere long, have to contest it."

Napoleon, on learning that the Emperor Alexander was personally in the hostile camp, sent Savary to present his compliments to that sovereign, and of course "incidentally to observe as much as he could of the numbers and condition of the enemy's troops." The messenger reported that the Russians laboured under a belief that the reverses of the previous campaign were the result of unpardonable cowardice among the Austrians, and the first general battle would show the sort of warriors the Russians were. Savary said that from the conversations he had for three days with nearly thirty coxcombs about the person of Alexander, that presumption, inconsiderateness, and imprudence, reigned in the decisions of the military as much as in the political cabinet, and that an army so conducted must of necessity commit great faults.

The *Czar* sent a young *aide-de-camp* to return the compliment carried by Savary, and he found the French soldiery engaged in fortifying their position—a position which Napoleon had some time before determined to occupy; but the negotiations were of no avail: Napoleon wanted either an overwhelming battle or peace. The *aide-de-camp* sent by Alexander was impressed with what appeared to him to be evidence of fear and apprehension on the part of the French. The placing of strong guards and fortifications, thrown up with such haste, appeared to him like the precautions of an army half beaten. The Russian prince discussed every point with an air of impertinence difficult to be conceived. He spoke to Napoleon as if he had been conversing with a Russian officer; but the emperor repressed his indignation, and the young man returned under a full conviction that the French Army was on the brink of ruin.

Several old Austrian generals, who had made campaigns against Napoleon, are said to have warned the Russian council against too much confidence as they were to march against old soldiers and able officers. They said they had seen Napoleon, when reduced to a handful of men, repossess himself of victory, under the most difficult circumstances, by rapid and unforeseen operations, in which manner he had destroyed numerous armies. The presumptuous young man declared that the presence of the Russian emperor would inspire the troops to victory especially as they would be aided by the picked troops of the imperial guard of Russia.

On the 1st of December, on seeing the Russians begin to descend from a chain of heights on which they might have received an attack with great advantage to themselves, and have remained in safety until the Archduke Charles could come up with the 80,000 men in Bohemia and Hungary, Napoleon exclaimed rapturously, as he witnessed the rash manoeuvre: "In twenty-four hours that army will be mine!" In the meantime, withdrawing his outposts and concentrating his forces, he continued to imitate a conscious inferiority, which was far from existing. In the order of the day (December 1) before the Battle of Austerlitz, Napoleon inserted the following proclamation:

> Soldiers, the Russians are before you, to avenge the Austrian army at Ulm. They consist of the same battalions you beat at Hollenbrun and have constantly pursued. The positions we occupy are formidable; and, while they march to my right, they shall present me their flank.—Soldiers, I will direct myself all your battalions. I shall keep at a distance from the firing, if, with your accustomed bravery, you carry confusion and disorder into the enemy's ranks; but, should victory appear for a moment doubtful, you shall see your emperor expose himself to the first blows; for victory cannot hesitate on this day, in

which the honour of the French infantry, of so much importance to the whole army, is concerned. Suffer not the ranks to be thinned, under pretence of carrying off the wounded; but let each man be well persuaded that we must conquer the hirelings of England, who are animated with so deep a hatred of our nation. This victory must terminate our campaign; when we shall resume our winter quarters, and be joined by the new armies forming in France. The peace which I make will be worthy of my people, of you and myself.

(Signed)

Napoleon.

At one o'clock on the morning of the 2nd of December, Napoleon, having slept for an hour by a watch-fire, got on horseback and proceeded to reconnoitre the front of his position. He wished to do so without being recognized, but the soldiers penetrated the secret, and, lighting great fires of straw along the line, 80,000 men received him from post to post with great enthusiasm. They reminded him that it was the anniversary of his coronation, and declared that they would celebrate the day in a manner worthy of his glory.

"Only promise us," cried one old grenadier, "that you will keep yourself out of the fire: I promise you in the name of the grenadiers of the army that you will have to fight only with your eyes, and we will bring you the flags and artillery of the Russian army to celebrate the anniversary of your coronation."

"I will do so," answered the emperor, "but I shall be with the reserve *until you need us*." This promise Napoleon soon repeated in his proclamation. As he threw down his pen after signing this document, he exclaimed:

This is the noblest evening of my life; but I shall lose too many of these brave fellows tomorrow. The anguish which I experience at this idea makes me feel they are really my children; and truly I am vexed with myself for these sensations, as I fear they will unman me on the field of battle.

In his preparations for this decisive contest which he made immediately, ten battalions of the Imperial Guard, with ten of Oudinot's division, were to be kept in reserve in the rear of the line, under the eyes of Napoleon himself, who destined them, with forty field-pieces, to act wherever the fate of battle should render their services most necessary.

French Troops Crossing the Great St. Bernard

Ségur says:

> The battle was planned by Napoleon in every detail, just as he had planned the strategic movements of the army. In the early morning he sent for all his *aides-de-camp* to come to the small house where he had spent the night. We had a slight repast, which, like himself, we ate standing; after which, putting on his sword, he said, 'Now gentlemen, let us go and begin a great day.' We all ran to our horses. A moment afterwards we saw, on the top of the hill which the soldiers called 'the Emperor's hill,' arriving from the various points of our line, followed each by their *aides-de-camp*, all the chiefs of our army corps, Murat, Lannes, Bernadotte, Soult, Davoust,—all coming to receive final orders. If I were to live as long as the world shall last, I would never forget that scene.

After a hazy, misty daybreak, the sun at last arose with uncommon brilliancy, so bright in fact that "the sun of Austerlitz" afterwards fell into a proverb with the French soldiery, who hailed similar dawns with exultation and as a sure omen of victory. The emperor said, as he passed in front of several regiments: "Soldiers, we must finish this campaign by a thunderbolt which shall confound the pride of our enemies." Immediately they raised their hats on the bayonets' points and cries of, "Live the emperor!" formed the actual signal for battle. A moment afterwards the horizon cleared up and as the sun darted forth its glistening rays the cannonading was heard at the extremity of the right line. The great battle of Austerlitz had begun.

At the opening of the engagement, Kutusoff, the Russian general-in-chief, fell into a snare laid for him by Napoleon, and sent a large division of his army to turn the right of the French. His troops, detached for this, met with unexpected resistance from Davoust, and were held in check. Napoleon at once seized the opportunity given him by the enemy in leaving a deep gap in their line, and upon that space Soult forthwith poured a force which entirely cut off all communication between the Russian centre and left.

The *Czar* quickly perceived the fatal consequences of the movement, and ordered his guards to rush to the eminence called the hill of Pratzen, where the encounter was taking place, and beat back Soult. The Russians succeeded in driving the French before them, when Napoleon ordered Bessieres to their rescue with the Imperial Guards. The Russians had become somewhat disordered from the impatience of their temporary victory, and although they resisted Bessieres sternly, they were finally broken and fled. The regiment of the Grand Duke Constantine, who gallantly led the Russians, was now annihilated and the duke only escaped by the fleetness of his horse.

The French centre now advanced, and the charges of Murat's cavalry were most decisive, while the left wing, under the command of Lannes, marched forward, *en echelons*, by regiments, in the same manner as if they had been exercising by divisions. A tremendous cannonade then took place along the whole line; two hundred and three pieces of cannon, and nearly two hundred thousand men, being engaged, so that it was indeed a giant combat. Success could not be doubtful: in a moment the Russians were all but routed, their colonel, artillery, standards and everything being already captured. At 1 o'clock the victory was decided; it had never been doubtful for a moment; and not a man of the reserves was required.

From the heights of Austerlitz the Emperors of Russia and Austria beheld the total ruin of their centre as they had already of their left. The right wing only remained unbroken, it having contested well the impetuous charge of Lannes; but Napoleon could now gather round them on all sides, and, his artillery plunging incessant fire on them from the heights, they at length found it impossible to hold their ground and were driven from position to position. They were at last forced down into a hollow where some frozen lakes offered them the only means of escape from the closing cannonade. As they did so the French broke the ice about them by a storm of shot from 200 heavy cannon, and nearly 2,000 men died on the spot, some swept away by artillery, but the greater part being drowned beneath the broken ice.

The cries of the dying Russians, as they sank beneath the waters, were drowned, however, by the victorious shouts of the French, who were pursuing the scattering remnants of the enemy in every direction. In the bulletin of the engagement Napoleon compared the scene to that at Aboukir, "when the sea was covered with turbans."

The emperor had addressed his soldiers on the evening preceding the battle to heighten their courage, and presage to them the victory; he did not forget to address himself to them again after the fight, and felicitate them upon having so nobly contributed to verify his prediction. He said to them:

> Soldiers, you have on this day of Austerlitz justified all that which I expected from your intrepidity. You have decorated your ea-

gles with immortal glory. When all that is necessary to assure the happiness and prosperity of our country is accomplished, I will lead you back to France. There you will be the objects of my tenderest solicitude. My people will joyously greet you again, and it will suffice for you to say: 'I was at the battle of Austerlitz,' and for them to reply, 'Behold a brave man!'

In later years Napoleon said of this engagement:

I have fought thirty battles like that, but I have never seen so decisive a victory, or one where the chances were so unevenly balanced.

At another time while at St. Helena he said:

If I had not conquered at Austerlitz I should have had all Prussia on me.

It was with great difficulty that the Emperors of Russia and Austria rallied some fragments of their armies around them, and, terror-stricken, effected their retreat. With the conqueror there remained 20,000 prisoners, 40 pieces of artillery, and all the standards of the Imperial Guard of Russia. Such was the battle of Austerlitz, or as the French soldiers delighted to call it, "The Battle of the Emperors;" and thus did Napoleon's army fulfil its pledge to celebrate the anniversary of his coronation.

The fleeing emperors halted at midnight for council, and decided to send a messenger to Napoleon at daylight with proposals for peace. The envoy was courteously received, and arrangements were at once made for a meeting of the Austrian and French emperors at ten o'clock the next day. They met about three leagues from Austerlitz, near a mill. Napoleon was the first to arrive on the ground; he at once ordered that two fires be made, and with a squadron of his Guard drawn up at a distance of about two hundred paces, awaited the arrival of Francis and his personal suite. When Francis came in sight, accompanied by several princes and generals, and an escort of Hungarian cavalry, Napoleon advanced to his carriage, and embraced him. The two emperors, each with an attendant, then went to one of the fires near the entrance to a military hut, while the suites of the two sovereigns drew around the other fire, a few paces distant.

"Such are the palaces you have compelled me to occupy for these three months," said Napoleon, pointing to his modest quarters.

"You have made such good use of them," answered Francis, "that you ought not to complain of their accommodation."

The defeated emperor is represented as having thrown the blame of the war upon the English. "They are a set of merchants," he said, "who would set the continent on fire, in order to secure themselves the commerce of the world."

When the two great leaders separated, after an interview lasting an hour, they again embraced, Napoleon saying in the hearing of the gentlemen of the suites,—Prince John of Lichtenstein, near Francis, and Marshal Berthier, near Napoleon—: "I agree to it; but your Majesty must not make war upon me again."

"No, I promise you I will not," said Francis in reply; "I will keep my word"—a promise that was soon violated.

It was understood that the Emperor of Russia, although not present, was to abide by the agreement for an armistice. Alexander so assured Marshal Davoust, who had pursued him the night of the battle, and the Russians were allowed by Napoleon to retire unmolested to their own territory, on the royal word of Francis that Russia would adhere to his ally of Austria.

"The Russian Army is surrounded," said Napoleon to Francis; "Not a man can escape me but I wish to oblige their emperor, and will stop the march of my columns if your Majesty promises me that these Russians shall evacuate Germany, and the Austrian and Prussian parts of Poland."

"It is the purpose of the Emperor Alexander to do so," was the reply. No other engagement was required of the *Czar* than his word.

When the negotiations had been completed, and the Emperor Francis had departed, Napoleon walked hurriedly to and fro for a short time, and after a deep silence he was heard to say: "I have acted very unwisely. I could have followed up my victory, and taken up the whole of the Austrian and Russian Armies. They are both entirely in my power. But—let it be. It will at least cause some less tears to be shed."

Napoleon then went over the field of battle, ordering the wounded to be removed, when some of those unfortunates, forgetting their sufferings asked, "Is the victory quite certain?" The foot guards of the Emperor, not having been permitted to engage, actually wept and insisted upon doing something to identify them with the victory.

"Be satisfied," said Napoleon, "you are the reserve; it will be better if you have nothing to do today."

The commander of the artillery of the imperial Russian guard having lost his cannon, met the French emperor and said, "Sire, order me to be shot, I have lost my cannon."

"Young man," replied Napoleon, "I esteem your grief; but one may be beaten by my army, and still retain some pretension to glory."

The brief campaign was followed by a treaty with the Emperor of Austria, signed December 15th, 1805, and another with Prussia, signed December 26th at Vienna. The victor of Austerlitz made his own terms in the negotiations. Austria gave up the last of her Italian usurpations to be annexed to the Kingdom of Italy, and the Tyrol to Bavaria, and yielded other stipulations which the conqueror demanded, but which were so moderate that they excited the wonder and admiration of all Europe.

Previous to Napoleon's departure for Schoenbrunn on the 27th of December he issued the following proclamation to his army:

> Soldiers! Peace between myself and the Emperor of Austria is signed. You have, in this late season of the year, made two campaigns. You have performed everything I expected. I am setting out for my capital. I have promoted and distributed rewards to those who have most distinguished themselves. I will perform everything I have promised. You have seen that your emperor has shared all your dangers and fatigues; you shall likewise behold him surrounded by all that grandeur and splendour which become the sovereign of the first nation in the world. In the beginning of the month of May, I will give a grand festival in Paris; you shall all be there. We will celebrate the memory of those who, in these campaign have fallen on the field of honour. The world shall see that we are ready to follow their example, and, if necessary, do more than we have done, against those who suffer themselves to be misled by the gold of the eternal enemy of the continent.

The news of the success of the army was received with the greatest enthusiasm by the majority of the French people.

Madame de Rémusat in writing to her husband from Paris after the receipt of the news of the Battle of Austerlitz, said:

> You cannot imagine how excited everyone is. Praise of the Emperor is on everyone's lips; The most recalcitrant are obliged to lay down their arms, and to say with the Emperor of Russia, 'He is a man of destiny.'

The campaign had consolidated the Empire of Napoleon, and when he returned to France he was received with exultation by the citizens, who tendered him *fête* after *fête* such as had not been witnessed at the capital for years. This was followed by the elevation of many of his kinsmen and heroes to thrones of pomp and power, coronation following coronation in rapid succession, princedoms and dukedoms being accompanied with grants of extensive estates in the countries which the French armies had conquered. From that moment, the fanaticism of military glory quite effaced the few remaining impressions made by the love of liberty.

6

The Battle of Jena

The establishment of the Confederation of the Rhine, which was one of the great consequences of Austerlitz, rendered Napoleon in effect, sovereign of a large part of Germany. The kings of Bavaria and Wurtemberg, Prince Murat, the Grand Duke of Berg, and several other sovereigns of Germany, had leagued together in an alliance with the French Empire; and they constituted so formidable a power that the Emperor added a new title to his name—the "Protector" of this confederacy. Thus Napoleon became sovereign of a principal part of Germany, and his allies were obliged to furnish, at his call, 60,000 armed men. The only method of counteracting the consolidation of French power over all Germany seemed to be that of creating another confederacy in the Northern circles, capable of balancing the league of the Rhine, and to be known as the Northern Alliance. This alliance Napoleon determined to suppress. The relations between France and Prussia continued in an unsettled state, Prussia refusing on the one hand to embrace the Confederation proposed by the cabinet of Berlin, and yet declining on the other to form part of the Rhenish league to which Bonaparte had frequently and urgently invited it.

A year had elapsed since the Emperor of Russia had signed the famous treaty of Potsdam, wheedling the pliant King of Prussia and his wife with all sorts of promises, including an offer on the part of England to pay the costs of another campaign against Napoleon and his Empire. For some weeks strong hopes were entertained of a satisfactory conclusion to peace overtures, but in the end the negotiations broke up, on the refusal of Napoleon to concede Malta to England, unless England would permit him to conquer Sicily from the unfortunate sovereign whose Italian kingdom had already been transferred to his brother Joseph.

The death of Fox, according to Napoleon himself, was the immediate cause of the failure of these negotiations. The emperor maintained that had the great English statesman lived—he died on the 23rd of January, 1806—the negotiations would have been resumed and pushed to a successful close. When the Emperor of Russia went to Berlin he offered Prussia all the forces of his own great Empire. Warlike preparations of every kind filled the Kingdom of Prussia during August and September 1806. Notwithstanding the protestations made almost daily by the Prussian government, through its minister at Paris, towards the middle of August her preparations assumed such a decided character that her real object could no longer be concealed. A friendly letter was even dispatched from the King of Prussia to Napoleon and the French ambassador at Berlin was treated with due consideration but which was far from honest at heart.

On the 21st of September Napoleon wrote to the princes of the Confederation of the Rhine, requesting them to furnish their contingent troops for his army, and which was complied with, according to treaty. On the 25th the emperor quitted his imperial residence to place himself at the head of the army. While at the theatre at St. Cloud he received a dispatch from Murat containing an account of an attack made on French troops by some Prussian detachments. "I see they are determined to try us," he said to Count Rapp and orders were immediately given to prepare for departure to the frontier. He arrived at Mayence on the 28th and on the 1st of October passed the Rhine.

On this same day the Prussian minister at Paris presented a note to Talleyrand, Minister of Foreign Affairs, an ultimatum in which Prussia demanded, among other things, that the formation of a Confederacy in the North of Germany should no longer be thwarted by French interference, to renounce the kingdoms of Holland and Italy, and that the French troops within the territories of the Rhenish league should recross the Rhine into France by the 8th of the same month of October,—a virtual declaration of war.

The conduct of Prussia in thus rushing into hostilities, without waiting for the advance of her allies, the Russians, was as rash as her holding back from Austria during the campaign of Austerlitz was cowardly. Napoleon had not patience to finish reading this document, conveying those demands, but threw it down with contempt.

Napoleon made answer to the Prussian note from his headquarters at Bamberg on October 6th. He addressed a proclamation to his army to inform them of the enemy they were about to fight. He said:

Soldiers, the war-cry has been heard at Berlin; for two months our provocation has been increased each day ... Let us march—let the Prussian army meet with the same fate it evinced fourteen years ago on the plains of Champagne.

Thiers, the eminent historian, says in his *History of the Consulate and the Empire of France under Napoleon*:

> It was the height of imprudence on the part of Prussia to enter into a contest with Napoleon at a moment when the French army, returning from Austerlitz, was still in the heart of Germany, and more capable of acting than any army ever was.

It was evident that Napoleon did not feel the least concern about the approaching war. He wrote to his brothers in Naples and in Holland at this time assuring them that the present struggle would be terminated more speedily than the preceding. He called upon them to observe in what manner a German sovereign still dared to insult the soldiers of Austerlitz. Napoleon was then on the German side of the Rhine in person. The Prussian Council had directed their army to advance towards the French instead of lying on their own frontier, and the army accordingly invaded the Saxon provinces. The Elector of Saxony was compelled to accept the alliance which the cabinet of Berlin urged on him, and reluctantly joined his troops with those of Prussia.

At Bamberg, on the same day he issued his proclamation to his soldiers, Napoleon said to Berthier:

> Marshal, we have a rendezvous of honour appointed for the 8th; a Frenchman never fails to keep them; but as we are told that a beautiful queen wishes to be a witness of the fight, let us be courteous, and march, without sleeping, for Saxony.

Napoleon alluded to the Queen of Prussia who was with the Prussian Army, dressed as an Amazon, wearing the uniform of her regiment of dragoons, "writing twenty letters a day" said the first bulletin sent to Paris, "to fan the flame in all parts."

No sooner did Napoleon learn that the Prussians had advanced into the heart of Saxony than he formed his plan of campaign: and they, persisting in their advance, and taking up a position on the Saale, afforded him the means of repeating at their expense, the very manoeuvres which had ruined the Austrians in the preceding campaign. The French commander at once perceived that the Prussian Army was extended upon too wide a line, thus enabling him the better to destroy it in detail. He also discovered that the enemy had all its principal stores and magazines at Naumburg to the rearward, and he resolved to commence operations by an attempt to turn the flank and seize the magazines ere the main body of the Prussians, lying at Weimar, could be aware of his movement. The emperor quitted Bamberg on the 8th, at three in the morning, and arrived on the same day at Cronach. Every corps of the army was then in motion.

The French came forward in three great divisions; the corps of Ney and Soult in the direction of Hof; Davoust, Murat and Bernadotte towards Saalburg and Schleiz, and Lannes and Augereau upon Coburg and Saalfeld. These last generals were opposed at Saalfeld with much firmness by Prince Louis of Prussia, cousin-german to the king, who imprudently abandoned the bridge over the Saale,—which he might have defended with success,—and came out into the open plain where his troops were overpowered by the French. Fighting hand to hand with a subaltern who ran up to him and cried, "Surrender, General!" the brave young officer in brilliant uniform and adorned with all his decorations, replied with a sabre cut, and was immediately struck down by a mortal thrust in the face with a sabre, which occasioned it to be remarked in the second bulletin that "the first blow of the war had killed one of its authors."

Prince Frederick Christian Louis of Prussia had been very impatient to commence the war and urged and hastened hostilities. He was, besides, a man of great courage and talent. Rapp[1] in his *Memoirs* says:

> Napoleon, who did not like this petulant eagerness, was conversing with us one evening respecting the generals of the enemy's army. Someone present happened to mention Prince Louis. 'As for him' said he, 'I foretell that he will be killed in this campaign.' Who could have thought the prediction would so soon have been fulfilled?

The Prussians fled, leaving the bridge which gave the French access to the country behind the Saale. The flank of the Prussian position was turned; the French army passed entirely around them, and Napoleon seized and blew up the magazines at Naumburg. The explosion announced to the King of Prussia and his *generalissimo*, the Duke of Brunswick, that Napoleon was in their rear. From this mo-

---

1. *Rapp: the Last Victor* by Jean Rapp also published by Leonaur.

ment the Prussians were isolated and completely cut off from all their resources—as completely as the army of Mack was at Ulm the year before. The engagement at Schleiz contributed to hasten the retreat of the enemy which threw away upon the roads a great number of muskets and hats, and leaving in the hands of the French 400 prisoners and as many killed or wounded. But the moral effect of the action was greater than the material, the Prussians learning for the first time the sort of soldiers they had to deal with.

Napoleon was extremely pleased with this first action at Schleiz, as it proved how little the Prussian cavalry, though excellently mounted and very skilful in the management of its horses, was to be feared by his solid infantry and bold horse soldiers.

The Duke of Brunswick who flattered himself that the French could not debouch, hastily endeavoured to concentrate his forces for the purpose of cutting his way back again to the frontier which he had so rashly abandoned. Napoleon, meanwhile, had posted his divisions so as to watch the chief passages of the Saale, and awaited the coming of his outwitted opponent.

The manifesto of Frederick William had arrived at the capital a day or two after Napoleon had quitted Paris for the camp, and it was now that he found time to answer it by calling on his own marshals to witness how "The French Army has done as it was bidden; this is the 8th of October, and we have evacuated the territories of the Confederation of the Rhine!"

To the King of Prussia Napoleon wrote:

> Believe me, my strength is such that your forces cannot long balance the victory. But wherefore shed so much blood? To what purpose? I will hold to your Majesty the same language I held to the Emperor Alexander two days before the battle of Austerlitz: 'Why should we make our subjects slay each other? I do not prize a victory which is purchased by the lives of so many of my children.' If I were just commencing my military career, and if I had any reason to fear the chances of war, this language would be wholly misplaced. Sire, your Majesty will be vanquished; you will have compromised the repose of your life, the existence of your subjects, without the shadow of a pretext. At present you are uninjured, and may treat with me in a manner conformable with your rank; before a month has passed you will treat, but in a different position.

On learning of the fall of Naumburg, the Prussian king knew full well the imminent danger of his position. His army was at once set in motion in two great masses, one commanded by himself, advancing towards Naumburg, the other attempting in like manner to force its passage through the French line in the neighbourhood of Jena. The king's march was arrested at Auerstadt by Davoust, who, after a severely contested action, at length repelled the assailant. Napoleon himself, meanwhile, was engaged with the other great body of the Prussians.

Arriving on the evening of the 13th of October at Jena, he at once perceived that the enemy was ready to attempt the advance next morning, while his own heavy train was still thirty-six hours' march in his rear. As the emperor said in his bulletin of the battle fought next day:

> But there are moments in war when no consideration can balance the advantage of being before-hand with the enemy, and of attacking first.

On the heights from Jena to Landgrafenberg he placed Gazan's division on the left, in the right Souchet's division, and in the centre and rear the foot guard. He made the latter encamp in a square of 4000 men, and in the centre of this square overlooking the plains below, he established his bivouac. Ever since that time the people have called that height "Napoleonsberg," marking by a heap of rough stones the spot where the emperor had spent part of that memorable night.

The emperor laboured hard, torch in hand, directing and encouraging his soldiery to cut a road through a ledge of rocks and draw up by that means such light guns as he had at command to a position on a lofty plateau in front of Jena. It was a most formidable position, and one that was destined to prove more decisive than that of a much larger one might have been under other circumstances. Napoleon spent the entire night among the men, helped drag the guns to the cliffs, and offering rewards for every piece of cannon that should be placed on the heights. He reminded his followers that the Prussians were about to fight—not for honour, but for their lives. Napoleon says:

> The night offered a spectacle worthy of observation; that of the two armies, one of which embraced with its front an extent of six leagues, and peopled the atmosphere with its fires, the other, whose apparent fires were concentrated in a small point, and in both encampments activity and motion. The fires of the two armies were within half cannon-shot; the sentinels almost

Capitulation of General Mack at Ulm

touched each other, and not a movement could be made without being heard.

At about 5 o'clock Napoleon asked Marshal Soult, "Shall we beat them?"

"Yes, if they are there," answered the marshal; "I am only afraid they have left."

At that moment the first musketry was heard, "There they are," said the emperor joyfully; "there they are! The business is beginning."

Napoleon then rode through the ranks addressing his soldiers. He bade them remember that, a year ago, at the same period, they had conquered Ulm and recommended that they be on their guard against the Prussian cavalry, which had been represented as so formidable. "This cavalry," he said, "must be destroyed here, before our squares, as we crushed the Russian infantry at Austerlitz." He told them that if they should succeed in endeavouring to fight their way through any point, the corps that would suffer them to pass, must forfeit its honour and character.

The soldiers answered his animated discourse by demanding to be led against the enemy; and the cries of, "Forward! Let us march!" were heard in every direction.

Again, as at Austerlitz, a cloud of mist completely enveloped the contending hosts. Both armies were almost in the heat of battle before the different divisions were distinguishable. Augereau commanded the right wing, Soult the left, Cannes the centre and Murat the reserve of cavalry. Escorted by men carrying torches, Napoleon again went along in front of the troops, talking to the officers and soldiers. He exhorted them to keep on their guard against the Prussian cavalry and to receive it in square with their usual firmness. His words everywhere drew forth shouts of "Forward! *Vive l'Empereur!*" At that moment the corps of Lannes set itself in motion on a signal from Napoleon.

The battle began on the right and left and the conflict proved terrible. Davoust, in particular, was placed in a situation sufficient to try a man of the most determined courage and firmness but Bernadotte refused to support him. He paraded around Apolda, while 26,000 French troops were engaged with 60,000 picked men, commanded by the Duke of Brunswick and the King of Prussia. Thus, says General Gourgaud, he caused the death of five or six thousand Frenchmen and hazarded the success of the day, for which he experienced a very short disgrace. Napoleon on this occasion observed that Bernadotte did not behave well, and that he would have felt gratified had Davoust been defeated; "but," added the emperor, "the affair reflects the highest honour on the conqueror, and the more so, as Bernadotte rendered his situation a most difficult one." Bernadotte's conduct was such that a decree was signed by Napoleon that must have resulted in his being shot, but out of regard to his wife the emperor destroyed the order the moment he was about to put it into the hands of one of his officers.

A hand to hand struggle followed the first charge of the Prussians. It was received by Soult and was a doubtful engagement until Ney appeared with a fresh division and drove the Prussians back. Nothing but the smoke of battle now obstructed the view, the famous sun of Napoleon having mounted the heavens was throwing a flood of light on a terrific engagement. Charge after charge followed, both sides maintaining their positions with firmness and valour. The commanders were constantly executing manoeuvres as though on parade. At one time the Emperor observed Ney, whom he had supposed to be in the rear, engaged with the Prussians. He hastened up greatly displeased, but on discovering the brave marshal defending himself in the centre of two weak squares against the whole of the Prussian cavalry, his displeasure gave way to admiration, and an immediate relief was ordered and brought up by Bertrand and Lannes.

During the time that elapsed before relief arrived he fought as intrepidly as before, and was not in the least disconcerted by his hazardous position. Davoust's plans were so well laid, and his generals and troops displayed such courage and skill, that Blücher, with 12,000 cavalry, had not the satisfaction of penetrating through a single company. The king, the guards, and the whole army, attacked the French without obtaining better success. Amidst the deluge of fire that surrounded them on all sides, they preserved all their national gaiety. A French soldier, nick-named "the Emperor" impatient at the obstinacy of the Prussian guards, exclaimed, "On with me, grenadiers! Come, follow the emperor!" when, rushing into the thickest of the battle, the troops followed, and the enemy was penetrated. For this deed he was raised to the rank of a corporal.

Napoleon, field-glass in hand, at length ordered a general onslaught all along the lines, to be followed by a bold charge of Murat's cavalry at a point where the emperor had detected a weakness in the enemy's lines. As the signal blast for advancing was sounded, the eager squadrons that had been smelling the smoke of battle for hours with impatience, rushed onward to glory or to death. On, on they charged with all the vehemence and impetuosity of the French cavalryman, each of whom believed that on him, and him alone, rested the fate of the day, and as on so many similar occasions, they were victorious. The sturdy Prussian columns were broken,—infantry, cavalry, guards and grenadiers were mowed down by thousands. The French infantry gave fresh proof of their valor and sustained their reputation at this engagement. In one of the charges which the divisions under Morand had to sustain from the numerous Prussian cavalry under Prince Henry, the 17th regiment, before presenting arms, placed their caps at the ends of their bayonets, crying, "*Vive l'Empereur!*"

"Why not fire then?" exclaimed Colonel Lanusse who apprehended the enemy would be upon them before they were ready.

"Oh, time enough for that" they replied, "at fifteen paces you shall see."

In fact a murderous discharge at that distance made the Prussians turn their horses' heads and retire.

The ardor of the troops on this important day was such that some corps, which circumstances prevented from taking part in the engagement, loudly expressed their dissatisfaction. One of these traits is sufficiently characteristic of the soldier and the emperor under whose eyes they fought. At an early period of the conflict, while the French cavalry was anxiously expected, Napoleon seeing his infantry wings in a state of agitation, being threatened by the enemy's cavalry, set off at a full gallop to direct the manoeuvres and change the front into squares. The infantry of the imperial guard, seeing all the rest of the troops engaged, while the emperor left them in inaction, many voices were heard to cry "Forward!"

"Who is that?" asked the emperor quickly, as he presented himself in front of the battalions; "This is some beardless young man, who wishes to anticipate what I intend to do. Let him wait until he has commanded in thirty pitched battles, before he pretends to give me advice."

Out of the 70,000 Prussians who had appeared on the field of battle, not a single corps remained entire, not one retreated in order. Out of the 100,000 French, composed of the corps of Marshals Soult, Lannes, Augereau, Ney, Murat and the Guard, not more than 50,000 had fought, and they had been sufficient to overthrow the Prussian Army.

This rout ended in the complete breaking up of the Prussian Army, horse and foot all flying together, in the confusion of panic, upon the road to Weimar. At that point the fugitives met and mingled with their brethren, flying as confusedly as themselves, from Auerstadt.

In his account of the Battle of Jena Napoleon spoke with pleasure of the enthusiasm shown by his soldiers during the heat of battle. In conclusion he said:

> In so warm a fight, in which the enemy lost almost all their generals, we should thank that Providence which watched over our army, that no man of note has been killed or wounded. Marshal Lannes had his breast scratched without being wounded. Marshal Davoust had his hat carried away and a great number of balls in his clothes.

To Josephine, who was awaiting the results of the campaign at Mayence, he wrote on October 16th:

> Everything has turned out as I planned, and never was an army more thoroughly beaten and destroyed.

The emperor confessed, that, during the night before the battle of Jena, he had been exposed to the most imminent danger, and might have disappeared without anyone knowing clearly his fate. He had approached the bivouacs of the Prussians in the dark, to reconnoitre, having only a few officers about his person. The French Army was almost everywhere on the alert, under a persuasion that the Prussians were strongly addicted to nocturnal attacks. Returning from that survey, the emperor was fired at by the first sentinel of his own camp, which proved a signal for the whole line; and he had no resource left but to throw himself flat on his face until the mistake should be discovered. His principal apprehension, however, was not realized; he feared least the Prussian line, then very near him, might act in the same manner.

When the conflict ended 20,000 Prussians lay dead on the battle field, or were taken prisoners, including twenty generals. Among the trophies of war were 300 cannon and sixty royal standards.

The Queen of Prussia was a fearless horsewoman and had faced great dangers at Jena. When she rode before her troops in her helmet of polished steel, shaded by a plume, in her glittering golden cuirass, her tunic of silver stuff, her red boots with gold spurs, she resembled Tasso's heroines. The soldiers burst into cries of enthusiasm as they saw their warlike queen: before her were bowed the flags she had embroidered with her own hands and the old, torn, and battle-stained standards of Frederick the Great. After the battle she was obliged to take flight, at full gallop, to avoid being captured by the French hussars.

The Duke of Brunswick, who had contended with Napoleon in this memorable engagement, was wounded in the face with a grape-shot early in the battle and was carried off the field never to recover.

The various routed divisions roamed about the country seeking separately a means of escape, and fell an easy prey to the French. The Prince of Hohenlohe at length drew together not less than 50,000 of these wandering soldiers and threw himself at their head into Magdeburg, but that great fortress had been stripped of all its stores for the service of the Duke of Brunswick's army before Jena, and Hohenlohe was compelled to retreat. He was defeated in a number of skirmishes, and at length, finding himself devoid of ammunition or provisions, laid down his arms. The Duke of Wurtemburg, one of the Prussian generals, had taken a position at Halle and Bernadotte marched upon him. He attacked the enemy with the bayonet, killing and routing all who dared oppose him. The slaughter was dreadful and Napoleon, visiting the field of battle the ensuing day, was struck with the sight of the heaps of dead surrounding the bodies of the French soldiers. Observing on the uniforms some of the buttons of the 32nd, he said with a sigh, "So many of that regiment were killed in Italy, Egypt, and elsewhere, I thought none could be remaining."

General Blücher was shortly afterwards compelled to lay down his arms after a loss of 4,000 men out of 10,000 at Lubeck, where a severe action was fought in the streets of the town on the 6th of November. The fortresses of the Prussian monarch now capitulated as fast as their commanders were requested to do so, and Napoleon entered Berlin in triumph on the 25th of October. The honour of taking possession of that city Napoleon reserved for Davoust's corps, which had contributed so much to the victory at Jena.

The Prussians could not comprehend the rapid marches and the promptitude with which they were met in their flights. As the emperor said in his 14th bulletin:

> These gentry are doubtless accustomed to the manoeuvres of the 'Seven Years' War.' They would demand three days to bury their dead. 'Think of the living' replied the emperor, 'and leave the care of interring the dead to us; there is no need of a truce for that.'

Thus in a campaign of a week's duration had the proud Prussian monarchy been levelled to the ground. The people, believing that the fall of the military meant necessarily the fall of the monarchy itself, the pride and strength of the nation disappeared and every bond of union among the various provinces of the crown seemed to be at once dissolved.

On the 25th of October, 1806, after passing in review the Imperial foot guards, commanded by Lefebvre, Napoleon visited the tomb of Frederick the Great at Potsdam where were stored a number of mementos of the great warrior. The court of Prussia had fled with so much precipitancy from Potsdam, that nothing had been carried away. Even the sword of Frederick the Great, the belt and the cordon of his orders, were left there.

On finding that the court had not thought of placing these relics out of the reach of invasion, the emperor took possession of them. As he displayed the sword of Frederick, he said:

> I prefer these trophies to all the King of Prussia's treasures. I will send them to my veterans who served in the campaigns of Hanover. I will present them to the governor of the Hospital of the Invalides, who will preserve them as a testimony of the victories of the army, and the revenge it has taken for the disasters of Rosbach.

General Ségur says:

> The door of the monument was open, Napoleon paused at the entrance in a grave and respectful attitude. He gazed into the shadow enclosing the hero's ashes, and stood thus for nearly ten minutes motionless, silent, as if buried in deep thought. There were five or six of us with him: Duroc, Caulaincourt, an *aide-de-camp* and I. We gazed at this solemn and extraordinary scene, imagining the two great men face to face, identifying ourselves with the thoughts we ascribed to our emperor before that other genius whose glory survived the overthrow of his work, who was as great in extreme adversity as in success.

During his stay at Berlin Napoleon issued the famous "Berlin Decrees" by which he attempted to establish the "continental system," whose object was to shut out the commerce and intercourse of Great Britain from the Continent of Europe. The ruin of France's maritime power at Trafalgar, and the almost universal supremacy of the French Empire on land left Napoleon in his own judgment, no other means of retaliation. Through this continental system he endeavoured, for several years, to annihilate all commercial intercourse between the continent and England.

The Prince of Hatzfeld was detected, during Napoleon's stay at Berlin, in sending secret information of the state and movements of the French Army to the enemy. One of his letters fell into the hands of the French and he was arrested. His wife gained access to Napoleon's apartments, and, ignorant of her husband's conduct, spoke with the boldness of innocence in his favour. On being handed the letter written by her husband she was completely overcome and fell on her knees before the emperor, imploring his forgiveness. "Throw that paper into the fire, madam," said Napoleon, "and the military commission will then have no proof of his guilt."

With a cry of joy the princess did as she was directed and the order of arrest, which would have resulted in Hatzfeld's death in an hour, was recalled.

While at Berlin the emperor addressed his troops in a proclamation in which he said:

> Our entrance into Potsdam and Berlin had been preceded by the fame of our victories. We have made 60,000 prisoners, taken sixty-five standards, among which are the colours of the King of Prussia's guards, six hundred pieces of cannon, and three fortresses. Among the prisoners there are upwards of twenty generals; yet, notwithstanding all this, more than half our troops regret their not having fired a single shot . . . . Soldiers, the Russians boast of coming to meet us, but we will advance to encounter, and save them half their march; they shall meet another Austerlitz in the heart of Prussia. A nation that can so soon forget our generous treatment after that battle,—owed their safety only to the capitulation we granted them,—is a power that cannot successfully contend against us. We will not again be the dupes of a treacherous peace.

Before leaving Berlin Napoleon received a deputation of the Senate, sent from Paris to congratulate him on the success of his campaign. Accompanied by representatives from the army, he made them the bearer of the trophies of his recent victories. He then prepared to extinguish whatever resistance existed in a few garrisons of the Prussian monarchy and to meet, before they could reach the soil of Germany, those Russians who were now advancing, too late, to the assistance of Frederic William.

7

The Battle of Eylau

Before opening the great campaign with Russia Napoleon received the explanation of the Elector of Saxony, who truly stated that Prussia had forced him to take part in the war. The apology was accepted, and from this time the elector adhered to the league of the Rhine and was a faithful ally of Napoleon. On November 25th, 1806, the Emperor of France left Berlin and established himself on the 27th at Posen, a central town of Poland, which country began to manifest an agitation arising from the animating prospect of restored independence. The unfortunate but brave Poles entreated his aid; but Napoleon could not make them a positive promise of their restoration as a kingdom. His observation on the subject was, "that, if the match should once be lighted, there was no knowing how long it might continue to burn."

From the headquarters at Posen, Napoleon addressed his soldiers on December 2nd, saying:

> It is a year ago today, at this very hour, that you were on the battlefield of Austerlitz. The dismayed Russian battalions fled in disorder, or, surrounded, gave up their arms to their victors. The next day they sued for peace, but we were imposed on: scarcely escaped by our, perhaps, overweening generosity, from the disasters of a third coalition, they ventured upon a fourth. ... Soldiers, we will not lay down our arms until the general peace shall have fixed and assured the power of our allies and restored to our commerce its safety and its colonies.

The proclamation produced an exhilarating effect on the soldiers and throughout Germany.

In the meantime Warsaw was put in a state of defence, and the auxiliary forces of Saxony and the new confederates of the Rhine were brought up by forced marches, while strong reinforcements from France repaired the losses of the early part of the campaign.

The French Army at length advanced in full force and crossed successively the Rivers Vistula, the Narew and Bug, forcing a passage wherever it was disputed, the Russian detachments being repulsed as often as they presented themselves. But it was not the intention of Bennigsen, the Russian general, to give battle to forces superior to his own, and he therefore retreated behind the Wkra. On the 23rd of December Napoleon arrived in person upon the Wkra and ordered the advance of his army in three divisions. He was fully aware that he was approaching a conflict of a very different kind from that which he had maintained with Austria, and more lately against Prussia. These troops, however highly disciplined, wanted that powerful and individual feeling which was a strong characteristic of the Russians,—a feeling that induces the soldier to resist to the last moment, even when resistance can only assure him of revenge.

They were, in fact, those same Russians of whom Frederick the Great said, "that he could kill, but could not defeat them." They were also of strong constitution and inured to the iron climate in which Frenchmen were now fighting for the first time. The Cossacks are trained from early childhood to the use of the lance and sword, and familiarized to a horse peculiar to the country,—tractable, hardy, swift and sure-footed, beyond any breed perhaps in the world. On the actual field of battle the Cossack's mode of attack is singular; instead of acting in line, a body of them about to charge disperse at the word of command, and joining in a loud yell and hurrah, each acting individually upon the object of attack, whether infantry, cavalry or artillery, to all of which they have been in this wild way of fighting most formidable assailants.

In this campaign the Cossacks took the field in great numbers, under their celebrated hetman Platoff. The Russians also had in their service Tartar tribes who resemble the Cossacks in warfare; but they were little better than hordes of roving savages. On the plain between the town of Pultusk and the wood the right of the Russian position was formed, and on December 26th they were attacked by the French division of Lannes and Davout with but partial success. The French lost nearly 8,000 men, killed and wounded, while the Russian loss amounted to about 5,000. The French retreated after nightfall. On the same day another division engaged in action at Golymin, driving back the French after which the Russian commander retreated for the purpose of concentrating his forces with the Grand Army. Both engagements were without immediate results, and instead of pressing their operations, the French retreated into winter quarters, Napoleon withdrawing his guard as far as Warsaw, while the other divisions were cantoned in the towns to the eastward.

Bennigsen was now placed in supreme command of the Russian forces, amounting to 90,000 men, and he at once resolved not to wait for Napoleon's onset, but chose rather to anticipate him, wisely concluding that his enemy's desire of desisting from active operation, as evinced by cantoning his troops in winter quarters, ought to be a signal to the Russians to again take the field. Thus the French emperor found himself forced into a winter campaign, and he at once issued general orders for drawing out his forces for the purpose of concentrating them at Willenberg, in the rear of the Russians, who were then stationed at Mohringen. The duration of the winter quarters, in which the French troops had been placed, lasted no longer than the weather would permit.

The army reposed almost the whole of the month of December, and towards the beginning of January 1807, movements on both sides seemed to indicate more serious operations. It appeared the Russians had adopted a vast plan of defence. Their generals seemed to have regained confidence, on seeing Napoleon stop amidst the advantages he had acquired, and imputed that to fear which arose in him from motives of prudence. They could not imagine what other reason he could possibly have for going into cantonments upon the Vistula.

Napoleon now proposed to force his enemies eastward towards the Vistula, as at Jena he had compelled the Prussians to fight with their rear turned to the Rhine. Bernadotte had orders to engage the attention of Bennigsen upon the right, and detain him in his present situation; or rather, if possible, to induce him to advance eastward so as to facilitate the operations he meditated.

The Russian commander learned Bonaparte's intention from an intercepted dispatch, and changed his purpose of advancing on Ney and Bernadotte. Marches and counter-marches took place, through a country at all times difficult, and now covered with snow. Bennigsen was aware that it was to his advantage to protract the campaign in this manner, as he was near his reinforcements, and the French were distant from theirs:—every loss therefore telling more in proportion to the enemy than to his own army.

Notwithstanding this apparent advantage, the distress of the Russian army was so extreme from the lack of suitable provisions that it induced General Bennigsen, against his judgment, to give battle at all risks, and for this purpose to concentrate his forces at Preuss-Eylau, which was decided upon as the field which he proposed to contest with Napoleon.

It had been the intention to maintain the town itself which Bennigsen had entered on the 7th of February, and a body of troops had been left for that purpose; but in the confusion attending the movement of so large an army, the orders had been misunderstood, and the division designed for this service evacuated the place as soon as the rearguard had passed through it. A Russian division was hastily ordered to re-occupy the town; but they found the French already in possession, and although they dislodged them, they were themselves driven out in turn by another division of French to whom Napoleon had promised unusual rewards. A third division of Russians now advanced, Bennigsen being desirous of protracting the contest for the town until the arrival of his heavy artillery which joined him by a different route. When it came up he would have discontinued the struggle for Eylau but it was impossible to control the ardour of the Russian columns who persevered in advancing, with drums beating, rushed into the town and surprised the French in the act of sacking it,—putting many of them to death by the bayonet.

Another division of the French now advanced under cover of the hillocks and broken ground which skirt the village, threw their fire upon the streets and the Russians once more retreated with considerable loss. The town was now once more and finally occupied by the French. Night fell and the combat ceased only to be renewed with increased fury the next day.

The Russians occupied a space of uneven ground, about two miles in length and a mile in depth, with the village of Serpallen on their left. In the front of their army lay the town of Preuss-Eylau, situated in a hollow and in possession of the French. The latter occupied Eylau with their left, while their centre and right lay parallel to the Russians, upon a chain of heights which commanded, in a great measure, the ground possessed by the enemy. The French also expected to be reinforced by Ney's division which had not yet come up, and which was destined to form on the extreme left. The space between the hostile armies was open and flat, covered with snow and intersected with frozen lakes. The soldiers could trace each other's positions by the pale glimmer of watch lights upon the snow.

Battle of Austerlitz

Napoleon, who slept but three or four hours that night in a chair in the postmaster's house, placed the corps of Marshal Soult at Eylau itself, partly within the town, partly on the right and left of it, Augereau's corps and Imperial Guard a little in the rear, and all the cavalry upon the wings till daylight should enable him to make his final disposition of the fifty odd thousand men, exclusive of Ney's corps, and which were to meet the ninety thousand Russians and Prussians.

At daybreak on the 8th of February, 1807, two strong columns of the French advanced for the purpose of turning the right and storming the centre of the Russians, who had commenced the firing at one and the same time; but they were driven back in great disorder by the heavy and sustained fire of the Russian artillery. An attack on the enemy's left was equally unsuccessful. The Russian infantry stood like stone ramparts, each time repulsing the French assault—their cavalry then came to the support, pursued the retiring assailants and took standards and eagles.

About mid-day a heavy snowstorm set in, which the wind drove right in the faces of the Russians, adding to the obscurity caused by the smoke of the burning village of Serpallen that rolled along the line. The snow having now ceased, a melancholy spectacle presented itself. Thousands of dead and wounded lay on the ground, and several of the divisions were still *hors de combat*. Augereau's two divisions had been swept down by an unmasked battery of seventy-two pieces, and Augereau, wounded himself, but more affected by the disaster of his corps than by his personal danger, was carried to the cemetery of Eylau to the feet of Napoleon. To the emperor he complained, not without bitterness, of the failure to send him timely succour. Silent grief pervaded every face in the imperial staff. Napoleon, calm and firm, addressed a few soothing words to Augereau, then sent him to the rear, and took measures for repairing the mischief.

Dispatching in the first place the chasseurs of the Guard and some squadrons of dragoons which were at hand, he sent for Murat and ordered him to make a decisive effort on the line of the infantry which formed the centre of the Russian Army, and which, taking advantage of Augereau's disaster began to press forward. At the first summons Murat came up at a gallop: "Well," said Napoleon, "are you going to let those fellows eat us up?" He then ordered the heroic chief of his cavalry to collect the *chasseurs*, the dragoons, the *cuirassiers*, and to fall upon the Russians with eighty squadrons, to see what effect such a mass of horse, charging furiously, would have on an infantry reputed not to be shaken. The cavalry of the Guard was brought forward ready to add its shock to that of the cavalry of the army.

The moment was critical, for if the Russian infantry were not stopped it would soon attack the cemetery, the centre of the French position, and Napoleon had but six foot battalions of the Imperial Guard to defend it. Murat galloped off, collected his squadrons, made them pass between the cemetery and Rothenen where Augereau's corps had marched to almost certain destruction. Charge after charge was made and successfully resisted. At length one of them, rushing on with more violence, broke the enemy's infantry at one point and opened the breach through which *cuirassiers* and dragoons rushed, each eager to penetrate first. The Russians' first and second lines being broken, they turned the batteries of their artillery on the confused mass, killing as many of their own soldiers as those of the French, not caring whether they killed friends or foes so that they got rid of the formidable French force; but their efforts were useless.

Napoleon, graver than usual, in a gray riding-coat and Polish cap, sat motionless in the cemetery, in which were heaped bodies of a great number of his officers; his Guard was behind him and before him the *chasseurs*, the dragoons, the *cuirassiers*; they formed anew and were ready to devote themselves as he might direct. The emperor waited long before determining definitely on his last attack. Never had he nor his soldiers been engaged in such a hotly contested fight. The bullets whistled around and a shell burst within a few paces of him. Augereau's arm was broken and Lannes was wounded but not severely.

Under cover of darkness six columns of the French now advanced with artillery and cavalry and were close on the Russian position ere they were opposed. Bennigsen, at the head of his staff, brought up the reserve in position, and, on uniting with the first line bore the French back at the point of the bayonet. Their columns, partly broken, were driven again to their own position where they rallied with difficulty. A French regiment of *cuirassiers*, which during this part of the action had made an opening in the Russian line, were charged by the Cossacks, and found their defensive armour no protection against the lance. All but eighteen were slain.

At the moment when the Russians appeared to be the victors Davoust's division, which had been manoeuvring since the beginning of the action to turn the left and gain the rear of the Russian line, now made its appearance on the field. The effect was sudden and demoralizing to the Russians; Serpallen was lost, the Russian left wing, and a portion of its centre were thrown into disorder, and forced to retire and change front.

At this point in the contest the Prussian reinforcements, long expected, appeared in turn suddenly on the field, and passing the left of the French and right of the Russians, pushed down in three columns to redeem the battle on the Russian centre and rear. The Prussians, under their gallant leader L'Estocq, never fired until within a few paces of the enemy and then used the bayonet with fearful effect. They redeemed the ground which the Russians had lost and drove back in their turn the troops of Davoust and Bernadotte who had lately been victorious. Ney, in the meantime appeared on the field with his advanced guard and occupied Schnaditten, a village on the road to Konigsberg. As this endangered the communication of the Russians with that town, it was thought necessary to carry it by storm; a resolution which was successfully executed, the enemy's rearguard retreating in disorder.

This was the last act of that bloody day at Eylau. It was ten o' clock at night and darkness put an end to the combat. After fourteen hours of fighting both armies occupied the same positions taken in the morning. It was in fact the longest and by far the severest battle Napoleon had yet been engaged in. At the beginning of the contest, Augereau was scarcely in his senses, from the severity of rheumatic pain to which he was subject; but the sound of the cannon awakens the brave: he flew at full gallop at the head of his corps, after causing himself to be tied to his horse! He was constantly exposed to the hottest of the fire, and was only slightly wounded.

A few days after the battle Napoleon sent to Paris sixteen stands of colours taken on that occasion and ordered the cannon to be melted down and made into a statue of General d' Haulpoult, in the uniform of his regiment, he having gallantly commanded the second division of *cuirassiers*, when he was killed in the action.

In three letters which the emperor wrote to Josephine during the month of February he alluded with the deepest affection to the horrors of this engagement. He said:

> We had yesterday a great battle. The victory was mine, but I have been deprived of a great many men. The loss of the enemy, still more considerable, does not console me.

He adds in a second letter:

> The land is covered with dead and wounded. This is not the noble portion of war. One is pained, and the soul is oppressed

at the sight of so many victims.

In the biting frost, in face of thousands of dead and dying, when the gloomy day was sinking into a night of anguish, the emperor had said: "This sight is one to fill rulers with a love of peace and a horror of war," and in his bulletin of the engagement he said:

> Imagine, on a space of a league square, nine or ten thousand corpses, four or five thousand dead horses, lines of Russian knapsacks, fragments of guns and sabres; the earth covered with bullets, shells, supplies; twenty-four cannon, surrounded by their artillerymen, slain just as they were trying to take their guns away; and all that in plainest relief on the stretch of snow!

Twelve of Napoleon's eagles were in the hands of the Russians, and the field between them was covered with 50,000 corpses, of whom at least half were French. Each leader claimed the victory. The Russians retired from Eylau towards Konigsberg the very night after the battle, and the French made no effort to pursue but remained on the field nine days to allow the troops some repose.

It was in truth a drawn battle. The point of superiority on this dreadful day would have been hard to decide, but the victory, if rightly claimed by either party, must be pronounced to have remained with Napoleon; for Bennigsen retreated and left him master of the field of battle where he slept and remained for days; but it was a ghastly triumph. During the whole time the contest lasted Napoleon's countenance was never observed to change; nor did he show any emotion whatever; but all accounts agree that he was deeply impressed with the horrors of the succeeding night.

Finally, on the 19th of February, Napoleon left Eylau and retreated with his whole army to Osterode on the Vistula. Here he established his headquarters, living in a sort of barn, governing his empire and controlling Europe. The doubtful issue of the Battle of Eylau had given a shock to public opinion and it required all the emperor's prudence and address to overcome it. Great despondency was produced in Paris by the bulletin of the battle and a marked depression took place in the funds.

8

Friedland and Peace of Tilsit

Napoleon soon decided that it would be fatal rashness to engage in another campaign in Poland while several fortified towns, and above all, Dantzic, held out in his rear. He determined to capture all these places and to summon new forces from France before again meeting in the field such enemies as the Russians had proved themselves to be.

Dantzic was at length compelled to surrender on May 7th 1807, Marshal Lefebvre receiving the title of Duke of Dantzic in commemoration of his important success, after which event Napoleon's extraordinary exertions in hurrying supplies from France, Switzerland and the Rhine country, and the addition of the division of 25,000 men which had captured Dantzic, enabled him to take the field again by the first of June at the head of not less than 280,000 men. The Russian general had also done all in his power to recruit his army which was now reinforced by 90,000 men, during this interval.

The Russians were in the field by the 5th of June and were the first assailants; but nothing but skirmishes resulted until the Russian army was forced to retire towards Heilsberg where they halted, and there concentrating their forces, made a most desperate stand. They were, however, overpowered by superior numbers, after maintaining their position during a whole day. The battle had continued until midnight upon terms of equality, and when the morning dawned the space between the Russians and French was literally sheeted over with the bodies of the dead and wounded.

The Russians retired after the battle, crossing the River Aller, and on the 13th of June reached Friedland, a town of some importance on the west side of the stream, communicating with the eastern, or right bank of the river by a long wooden bridge. It was the intention of Napoleon to induce the Russian general to pass by this narrow bridge by the left bank, and then to decoy him into a general action, in a position where the general difficulty of defiling through the town, and over the bridge, must render retreat almost impossible. For this purpose he showed only such portion of his forces as induced General Bennigsen to believe that the French troops on the western side of the Aller consisted only of Oudinot's division, which had been severely handled in the battle of Heilsberg, and which he now hoped to altogether destroy. Under this deception Bennigsen ordered a Russian division to pass the bridge, defile through the town and march to the assault.

The French took great care to offer no such resistance as would show their real strength, and Bennigsen supposing he had only a single division of the French Army before him, and forgetting the usual promptitude of combination for which Napoleon was distinguished, had pushed on and brought an action which he believed he could terminate quickly and triumphantly. He was soon led to reinforce this first division with another. This was followed by other still divisions, and as the engagement was now becoming heated the Russian general at length transported all his army, one division excepted, to the left bank of the Aller, by means of the wooden bridge and three pontoons, and arrayed them in front of the town of Friedland, to overpower, as he supposed, the crippled division of the French to which alone he believed himself exposed. But no sooner had he taken this irretrievable step than the mask was dropped.

Napoleon was at first unable to believe that Bennigsen would venture to leave any part of his army for any period in so perilous a position as that in which he had placed it, maintaining a doubtful combat with no means of retreat but through the entanglement of the town of Friedland, and across the long narrow bridge of the Aller. His astonishment was great, therefore, when he learned from the officers he sent to reconnoitre that the whole Russian army was crossing the bridge, with the exception of one small division, and forming in front of the town. He had secured a victory by his numbers and position, but his remark to Savary, who carried him the information of the Russian movement, was characteristic, "Well," said he, "I am ready now, I have an hour's advantage of them, and will give them the battle, since they wish for it."

The French skirmishers advanced in force, heavy columns of infantry began to show themselves, batteries of cannon were placed in position, and Bennigsen found himself in the presence of the whole French Army. His position, a sort of plain surrounded by woods and broken ground, was difficult to defend; with the town and a large river in the rear it was dangerous to attempt a retreat, and an advance was prevented by the inequality of his force. Bennigsen found it expedient to detach 6,000 men to defend the bridge at Allerberg, some six miles from Friedland on the Aller, and with the rest of his forces he resolved to maintain his present position until night, hoping for Prussian reinforcements from General L'Estocq, *via* the town of Wehlau.

At about 10 o'clock on the morning of the 14th the French advanced to the attack. "This is the 14th of June; it will be a fortunate day for us," said Napoleon, recurring to the most glorious day of his life; "it is the anniversary of the Battle of Marengo." The broken and wooded country which the French occupied enabled them to maintain and renew their efforts at pleasure, while the Russians in their exposed position could not make the slightest movement without being observed. At about noon the French seemed to be sickening of the contest and about to retire.

This, however, was only a feint to give repose to such of the forces as had been engaged, and to bring up reinforcements. The cannonading continued until after 4 o'clock, the Russian line having sustained charge after charge and had neither recoiled or broken before infantry or cavalry. Napoleon, from his point of observation near the battlefield, had witnessed the failure of every stratagem and the charge of every division, and at last finding the day waning, drew up his full force in person for the purpose of making one of those desperate and generally irresistible efforts to which he often resorted to force a decision of a doubtful day.

There was not a marshal in his empire under whom the troops would not behave gallantly, but when the emperor put himself at the head of his army and led them to the charge, nothing could resist the shock. The brave Oudinot, hastening up with coat perforated by balls, and his horse covered with blood, exclaimed to the emperor: "Make haste, sire, give me a reinforcement, and I will drive all the Russians into the water!" The day was far advanced, and some of Napoleon's lieutenants were of the opinion that they ought to defer the final and decisive movement till the morrow.

"No! No!" replied Napoleon. "One does not catch an enemy twice in such a scrape." He then made his disposition of the several corps for the final attack.

Surrounded by his lieutenants, he explained to them, with energy and precision, the part which each of them had to act. Grasping the arm of Marshal Ney, and pointing to Friedland, the bridges, the Russians crowded together in front, he said: "Yonder is the goal, march to it without looking about you; break into that thick mass whatever it costs you; enter Friedland, take the bridges, and give yourself no concern about what may happen on your right, on your left or on your rear. The army and I shall be there to attend to that."

Ney at once set out at a gallop to accomplish the formidable task. Struck with his martial attitude Napoleon, addressing Marshal Mortier, said with much satisfaction: "That man is a lion!"

The order for attack all along the line with cavalry, infantry and artillery was now given, and simultaneously the Russians began to yield, the French advancing at the same time with shouts of assured victory. The Russians were now obliged to retreat in front of the enemy, and in half an hour the rout was complete. In vain did the enemy make all their reserves advance; Friedland was at last carried, but in the midst of a horrible carnage. The enemy left 20,000 men on the field, of whom 15,000 were killed and 5,000 wounded, and among the number thirty generals.

Dupont, who had been sent to assist Ney, met him in the heart of Friedland, then in flames, and they congratulated one another on the glorious success: Ney had continued to march straight forward, and Napoleon, placed in the centre of the divisions which he kept in reserve, had never ceased to watch his progress. It was now half past ten at night. Napoleon in his vast career had not gained a more splendid victory. He had for trophies eighty pieces of cannon, few prisoners, it is true, for the Russians chose rather to drown themselves than surrender. Twenty-five thousand Russians were killed as against 8,000 French. Out of 80,000 French 25,000 had not fired a shot. Meanwhile the bridge and pontoons were set on fire to prevent the French who had forced their way into the town, from taking possession of them. The smoke rolling over the scene increased the horror of the surroundings.

The Russian centre and right, which remained on the west side of the Aller, effected a retreat by a circuitous route, leaving on the right the town of Friedland with its burning bridges no longer practicable for friend or foe, and passed the Aller by a ford found in the very moment of extremity further down the river. Napoleon sent no cavalry in pursuit, though he had forty squadrons who might have cut them to pieces. Many animadversions have been cast upon him for not improving his victory in this manner; but the reason appeared clear: his object was to make peace with the Emperor Alexander, and the butchery of the broken battalions of the Russian guard would in no way have forwarded that object, and no power remained to oppose itself to the immense force under France's victorious warrior.

Thus ended the great Battle of Friedland. Napoleon wrote to Josephine:

> My children have worthily celebrated the Battle of Marengo. The Battle of Friedland will be equally celebrated and glorious for my people. . . . It is a worthy sister of Marengo, Austerlitz and Jena.

Napoleon visited the battlefield the next morning and beheld a frightful spectacle. The order of the Russian squares could be traced by a line of heaps of slain; and the position of their artillery might be guessed by the dead horses. As Savary well says:

> It might be truly said that sovereigns ought to have great interests of their subjects at stake to justify such dreadful sacrifices.

The Emperor Alexander, overawed by the genius of Napoleon which had triumphed over troops more resolute than had ever before opposed him, and alarmed for the consequences of some decisive measure towards the reorganization of the Poles as a nation, began to think seriously of peace. On the 21st of June General Bennigsen asked for an armistice and to this the victor of Friedland gave an immediate assent on his arrival at Tilsit. On the 22nd of June a proclamation was addressed by Napoleon to his army in which he said:

> From the banks of the Vistula, we have arrived upon those of the Niemen with the rapidity of the eagle's flight. You celebrated at Austerlitz, the anniversary of the coronation, and you have this year celebrated, in an appropriate manner, the Battle of Marengo, which put a period to the second coalition. Frenchmen, you have proved worthy of yourselves and me. You will return to France covered with laurels after having obtained a glorious peace, which carries with it the guarantee for its duration.

It was known that the Emperor Alexander was on the other side of the Niemen, at a village not far distant, and Napoleon addressed his reply to the sovereign in person. Its purport was to the effect that he was quite ready to make peace but would not consent to an armistice, if war were to continue. The result was a proposal on the part of Alexander that an interview should take place between the Emperor of France and himself, which was accepted. The armistice was ratified on the 23rd of June and on the 25th the emperors of France and Russia met personally, each accompanied by a few attendants, on a raft moored midstream in the river Niemen, near Tilsit, the town which gave its name to the secret treaty agreed upon at this time. The sovereigns embraced as they met, with their armies on the two banks of the river and retiring under a canopy, amid the cheers of the troops, had a long conversation, to which no one was a witness.

At its termination the appearance of mutual good will and confidence was marked, and the two emperors established their courts there and lived together, in the midst of the lately hostile armies, more like old friends than enemies and rivals, attempting by diplomatic means the arrangement of differences which had for years been deluging Europe with blood. By this treaty the King of Prussia was admitted as a party, Napoleon restoring to Frederick William ancient Prussia and the French conquests in Upper Saxony,—the king agreeing to adopt the "Continental System."

The beautiful and fascinating Queen of Prussia also arrived at Tilsit, but too late to obtain more favourable terms for her country than had already been granted her husband. "Forgive us," she said, as Napoleon received her, "forgive us this fatal war; the memory of the great Frederick deceived us; we thought ourselves his equal because we are his descendants; alas! we have not proved such!"

The queen used every stratagem which wit and genius could devise, and every fascination to which beauty could lend a charm, but without avail. Foiled in her ambition she died soon after, it is said, of chagrin.

No single episode in the career of Napoleon Bonaparte has been more adversely commented on than his alleged breach of faith with the Queen of Prussia, when the domain of her husband was absolutely at his feet. He always denied that he had broken his word, and according to his own story, as told after his final retirement, the queen had no cause of complaint. He said:

> The Queen of Prussia was still a beautiful woman, but she had lost many of the charms of youth. She evidently expected to

use her powers of persuasion on me for the benefit of Prussia. At dinner I took a beautiful rose from the table and presented it to her. She took it, smiled sweetly, and exclaimed: 'At least with Magdeburg, I hope.' I answered: 'Your majesty will observe that I am doing the giving and you are receiving what I give.'

I hastened the preparations for the completion of the treaty, and it was signed. When the Queen learned that Magdeburg had not been given to Prussia she was very angry. She went to the Czar Alexander, and said, with tears in her eyes: 'That man has broken his word with me.' 'Oh, no!' the *Czar* answered. 'I can hardly think that. I believe I have been present on every occasion when you have met Napoleon, and I have listened more carefully than you have thought. But, if you can prove to me that he made any promise that he has not kept, I pledge you my word as a man I will see that he keeps it.'

'Oh, but he gave me to understand—'

'That is precisely the point,' responded the *Czar*. 'He has promised nothing.' The queen turned quickly and left the apartment. She was too proud to acknowledge that in her effort to outwit me she had been outwitted.

At a subsequent meeting with Napoleon the queen said, "Is it possible, that, after having the honour of being so near the hero of the century and of history, he will not leave me the power and satisfaction of being enabled to assure him he has attached me to him for life?"

"Madam" replied the emperor, in a serious tone, "I am to be pitied; it is the result of my unhappy stars." He then took leave of the queen, who, on reaching her carriage, threw herself on the seat in tears.

Alexander was charmed by the presence of Napoleon. They spent some days at Tilsit together, and never did he leave the French emperor without expressing his unbounded admiration of him. "What a great man," he said incessantly to those who approached him; "What a genius! What extensive views! What a captain! What a statesman! Had I but known him sooner how many faults he might have spared me! What great things we might have accomplished together!"

In July Napoleon hastened back to Paris, arriving there on the 27th. He was received by the Senate and other public bodies as well as by the people with demonstrations similar to those which had been shown him on his return from the victory at Austerlitz. *Fêtes* and celebrations in honour of his achievements dazzled the world. He had

MEETING BETWEEN NAPOLEON AND FRANCIS II. OF AUSTRIA

now wrung from the last of his reluctant enemies, except England, the recognition of his imperial power, which already embraced a wider territory and a far greater number of subjects than Charlemagne ruled over, as Emperor of the West, a thousand years before. The power of Napoleon, the prosperity of France, and the splendour of Paris may be said to have been at their greatest height at this period. The regulation of the whole empire lay in the hand of Napoleon himself, and as the glory of France had always been, and continued to be his grand object, every faculty of his intellect was bent to its promotion.

Napoleon said one day to Gourgaud at St. Helena on being asked at what time he was happiest:

> I am inclined to think that I was happiest at Tilsit, I had experienced vicissitudes, cares, and reverses. Eylau had reminded me that fortune might abandon me, and I found myself victorious, dictating peace, with emperors and kings to form my court. After all that is not a real enjoyment. Perhaps I was really more happy after my Italian victories hearing the people raise their voices, only to bless their liberator, and all that at twenty-five years of age! From that time I saw what I might become, I already saw the world flying beneath me, as if I had been carried through the air.

Napier, the eminent historian, and himself an actor in many of the scenes he describes, says:

> Up to the peace of Tilsit, the wars of France were essentially defensive; for the bloody contest that wasted the Continent so many years was not a struggle for pre-eminence between ambitious powers—not a dispute for some acquisition of territory—nor for the political ascendancy of one or another nation—but a deadly conflict to determine whether aristocracy or democracy should predominate—whether aristocracy or privilege should henceforth be the principle of European governments.

On the 15th of August the emperor repaired in great pomp to Notre Dame, where the *Te Deum* was sung and thanksgiving offered up for the peace of Tilsit—a peace that gave much glory to France, but which as has generally been conceded, was "poor politics;" but, as Thiers has well said:

> In war Napoleon was guided by his genius, in politics by his passions.

9

War With Spain

At the signing of the treaty of Tilsit Napoleon had attained an eminence which, had his career ended at that time, would have left him a name revered by all the world—except, perhaps, it be by those enemies whom he had defeated on the field of battle. His star of destiny, however, was soon to be dimmed by acts which he ever afterwards regretted, and which, as he himself more than once declared, were the means to the end which finally caused his decline and fall.

Napoleon now turned his attention to Spain, where scenes shocking to morality were being enacted under the protection of Charles IV., the old and imbecile Bourbon king, in order, as he then believed, to insure the success of his "continental system." Ferdinand, the crown prince, had formed a party against his father and was attempting to dethrone him, while murderous courtiers filled the halls of the royal palace of Madrid, and dictated laws to the crumbling monarchy.

The vast extent to which the prohibited articles and colonial manufactures of England found their way into the Spanish peninsula, and especially into Portugal, and thence through the hands of whole legions of audacious smugglers into France itself, had fixed the attention of Napoleon, who was exasperated at the violation of his "Berlin decrees" against the continental traffic with England. In truth, a proclamation issued at Madrid shortly before the Battle of Jena, and suddenly recalled on the intelligence of that great victory, had prepared the emperor to regard with keen suspicion the conduct of the Spanish court, and to trace every violation of his system to its deliberate and hostile connivance. Napoleon knew that the Spanish cabinet, like that of Austria, was ready to declare itself the ally of Russia, Prussia and England, when the Battle of Jena came to deceive the hopes of the coalition. The last hour of the ancient regime was at hand beyond the Pyrenees; Napoleon felt himself called upon to give the signal to sound the fearful knell of its interment.

A treaty was ratified at Fontainebleau on the 29th of October 1807 between France and Spain, providing for the immediate invasion of Portugal by a force of 28,000 French soldiers, under the orders of Junot, and of 27,000 Spaniards; while a reserve of 40,000 French troops were to be assembled at Bayonne ready to take the field by the end of November, in case England should lend an army for the defence of Portugal, or the people of that country meet Junot by a national insurrection. Junot forthwith commenced his march through Spain, where the French soldiery were everywhere received with coldness and suspicion, but nowhere by any hostile movement of the people. He arrived in Portugal, on a peremptory order from Napoleon, late in November. The contingent of Spaniards arrived there also, and placed themselves under Junot's command.

On November 29th, and but a few hours before Junot made his appearance at the gates of Lisbon, the prince-regent fled precipitately and sailed for the Brazils. The disgust of the Portuguese at this cowardly act was eminently useful to the invaders, and with the exception of one trivial insurrection, when the conqueror took down the Portuguese arms and set up those of Napoleon in their place, several months passed in apparent tranquillity. "The House of the Braganza (Bourbon's), had ceased to reign," as announced in the *Moniteur* at Paris.

Napoleon thus saw Portugal in his grasp; but he had all along considered it as a place of minor importance, and availing himself of the treaty of Fontainebleau,—although there had been no insurrection of the Portuguese, he ordered his army of 40,000 men, named in the treaty, to proceed slowly but steadily into the heart of Spain and, without opposition. The royal family quietly acquiesced in this movement for some months, being apparently much more interested in its own petty conspiracies and domestic broils. A sudden panic at length seized the king and his minister, who prepared for flight. On the 18th of March, 1808, the house of Godoy, the court favourite, was sacked by the populace, Godoy himself assaulted, and his life saved with extreme difficulty by the royal guards, who placed him under arrest. At this Charles IV. abdicated his throne in terror, and on the 20th of March Ferdinand his son was proclaimed king at Madrid amid a tumult of popular applause.

Murat had, ere this, assumed command of all the French troops in Spain, and hearing of the extremities to which the court factions had gone, he now moved rapidly on Madrid, surrounded the capital with 30,000 troops and on the 23rd of March took possession of it in person at the head of 10,000 more. Charles IV., meanwhile, dispatched messengers both to Napoleon and to Murat asserting that his abdication had been involuntary, and invoking their assistance against his son.

Ferdinand entered Madrid on the 24th, found the French general in command of the capital, and in vain claimed his recognition as king. Napoleon heard with regret of the action of Murat, who had risked arousing the pride and anger of the Spaniards. He therefore sent Savary, in whose practiced skill he hoped to find a remedy for the military rashness of Murat, and who was to assume the chief direction of affairs at Madrid.

Ferdinand was at length persuaded by Savary that his best chance of securing the aid and protection of Napoleon lay in meeting him on his way to the Spanish capital and strive to gain his ear before the emissaries of Godoy should be able to make an impression concerning Charles' rights. Ferdinand, therefore, took his departure, and passing the frontier, arrived at Bayonne on the 20th of April where he was received by Napoleon with courtesy. In the evening he was informed by Savary, who had accompanied him, that his doom was sealed,—"that the Bourbon dynasty had ceased to reign in Spain," and that his personal safety must depend on the readiness with which he should resign all his pretensions into the hands of Napoleon.

Murat was now directed to employ means to have the old king and queen repair also to Bayonne, which they did, arriving there on May 4th. Following a bitter family quarrel, Charles IV. resigned the crown of Spain for himself and his heirs, accepting in return from the hands of Napoleon a safe retreat in Italy and a splendid mansion. At the first interview Charles IV. and his son were irrevocably judged. Napoleon said later:

> When I beheld them at my feet, and could judge of all their incapacity, I took pity on the fate of a great nation; I seized the only opportunity which fortune presented me with, for regenerating Spain, separating her from England and closely uniting her with our system.

A few days afterward Ferdinand VII. followed the example of his father and executed a similar act of resignation.

A suspicion that France meditated the destruction of the national independence in Spain now began to spread, and on the 2nd of May when Don Antonio, president of the Council of Regency at Madrid, and uncle of Ferdinand, began preparations for departing from the capital, the inhabitants became much enraged. A crowd collected around the carriage intended, as they concluded, to convey the last of the royal family out of Spain; the traces were cut and imprecations heaped upon the French. Colonel La Grange, Murat's *aide-de-camp*, happening to appear on the spot, was cruelly maltreated, and in a moment the whole capital was in an uproar. The French soldiery were assaulted everywhere, about seven hundred being slain. The French cavalry, hearing the tumult, entered the city and a bloody massacre ensued. Many hundreds were made prisoners. The troops then charged through the streets from end to end, released their comrades, and ere nightfall had apparently restored tranquillity. Murat ordered all the prisoners to be tried by a military commission, which doomed them to instant death.

The reports of the insurrection spread rapidly throughout the peninsula, and in almost every town in Spain depredations were committed against the French citizens, many of the acts being fomented by agents of England, whose navies hung along the coast inflaming the passions of the multitude.

Napoleon received this intelligence with alarm, but he had already gone too far to retreat. He proceeded, therefore, to act precisely as if no insurrection had occurred. Tranquillity being re-established in Madrid the Council of Castile was convoked and Napoleon's brother Joseph was chosen by an imperial decree as their ruler. Ninety-five notables met him in Bayonne and swore fealty to him and a new constitution. Joseph on entering Spain was met by many demonstrations of disapproval and hatred, but the main road being occupied with Napoleon's troops, he reached Madrid in safety.

England now became anxious to afford the Spaniards every assistance possible. On the 4th of July the king addressed the English parliament on the subject, declaring that Spain could no longer be considered the enemy of Great Britain, but was recognized by him as a natural friend and ally. Supplies of arms and money were liberally transmitted thither, and Portugal, catching the flame, and bursting into general insurrection, a treaty of alliance, offensive and defensive was soon concluded between England and the two kingdoms of the peninsula.

It was impossible for Napoleon to concentrate the whole of his gigantic strength of 500,000 men on the soil of Spain, as his relations with those powers on the Continent whom he had not entirely subdued, were of the most unstable character. His troops, moreover, being drawn from a multitude of different countries and tongues, could not be united in heart or discipline like the soldiers of a purely national army. On the other hand the military genius at his command had never been surpassed in any age or country. His officers were accustomed to victory, and his own reputation exerted a magical influence over both friends and foes.

At the moment when the insurrection occurred, 20,000 Spanish troops were in Portugal under the orders of Junot; 15,000 more under the Marquis de Roma were serving Napoleon in Holstein. There remained 40,000 Spanish regulars, 11,000 Swiss and 30,000 militia to combat 80,000 French soldiers then in possession of half of the chief fortresses of the country.

After various petty skirmishes, in which the French were uniformly successful, Bessieres came upon the united armies of Castile, Leon and Galicia, commanded by Generals Cuesta and Blak on the 14th of July at Riosecco, and defeated them in a desperate action in which not less than 20,000 Spaniards were killed. This calamitous battle opened the gates of Madrid to the new king, who arrived at the capital on the 20th of the month only to quit it again in less than a fortnight to take up his head quarters at Vittoria to preserve his safety. The English government, meanwhile, had begun its preparations for interfering effectually in the affairs of the peninsula. Thousands of English troops were landed, Dupont, Lefebvre and Junot meeting with reverses that resulted finally in the evacuation of the whole French army from Portugal.

The Battle of Baylen was one of the first and most fatal reverses of the French. Here, after a desperate engagement on the 23rd of July, upwards of 18,000 men, under General Dupont, surrendered to the Spaniards, defiled before the Spanish army with the honours of war, and deposited their arms in the manner agreed on by both parties. General Dupont and all the officers concerned in the capitulation, who were permitted to return to France, were arrested and held in prison. Napoleon deeply appreciated the importance of the reverse which his armies had sustained, but he still more bitterly felt the disgrace. It is said that to the latest period of his life he manifested uncontrollable emotion at the mention of this disaster. Subsequently an imperial decree appeared, which prohibited every general, or commander of a body of men, to treat for any capitulation while in the open field; and declared disgraceful and criminal, and as such, punishable with death, every capitulation of that kind, of which the result should be to make the troops lay down their arms.

The catastrophe at Baylen and the valiant defence of Saragossa had in some measure opened the eyes of Napoleon to the character of the nation with whom he was contending. He acknowledged, too late, that he had imprudently entered into war, and committed a great fault in having commenced it with forces too few in number and too wildly scattered. On hearing of the ill-luck of his three generals, he at once perceived that affairs in the peninsula demanded a keener eye and a firmer hand than his brother's, and he at once resolved to take the field himself, to cross the Pyrenees in person at the head of a force capable of sweeping the whole peninsula "at one fell swoop," and restore to his brother's reign the auspices of a favourable fortune.

When setting out from Paris in the early part of October, 1808, the emperor announced that the peasants of Spain had rebelled against their king, that treachery had caused the ruin of one corps of his army, and that another had been forced by the English to evacuate Portugal. Recruiting his armies on the German frontier and in Italy, he now ordered his veteran troops to the amount of 200,000, including a vast and brilliant cavalry and a large body of the Imperial Guards, to be drafted from those frontiers and marched through France towards Spain.

As these warlike columns passed through Paris Napoleon addressed to them one of those orations that never failed to fill them with enthusiasm. He said at a grand review which was held at the Tuileries on the 11th of September Comrades:

> After triumphing on the banks of the Danube and the Vistula, with rapid steps you have passed through Germany. This day, without a moment of repose, I command you to traverse France. Soldiers, I have need of you. The hideous presence of the English leopard contaminates the peninsula of Spain and Portugal. In terror he must fly before you. Let us bear our triumphant eagles to the pillars of Hercules; there also we have injuries to avenge. Soldiers! You have surpassed the renown of modern armies; but you have not yet equalled the glory of those Romans, who, in one and the same campaign were vic-

torious on the Rhine and the Euphrates, in Illyria and on the Tagus! A long peace, a lasting prosperity, shall be the reward of your labours. A real Frenchman could not, should not rest, until the seas are free and open to all. Soldiers, what you have done and what you are about to do, for the happiness of the French people, and for my glory, shall be eternal in my heart.

Having thus dismissed his faithful troops, Napoleon himself travelled rapidly to Erfurt, where he had invited the Emperor Alexander to confer with him. Here they addressed a joint letter to the King of England, proposing once more a general peace, but as they both refused to acknowledge any authority in Spain save that of King Joseph, the answer was in the negative. Austria also positively refused to recognize Joseph Bonaparte as King of Spain, and this answer was enough to satisfy Napoleon that she was determined on another campaign.

On the 14th of October the conference at Erfurt terminated, Napoleon sincerely believing himself the friend of Alexander, and little thinking he would one day say of him: "He is a faithless Greek!" Ten days later Napoleon was present at the opening of the legislative session at Paris, where he spoke with confidence of his designs and hopes in regard to Spain. He said:

> I depart in a few days to place myself at the head of my troops, and, with the aid of God, to crown the king of Spain in Madrid, and plant my eagles on the forts of Lisbon.

Two days later he left the capital and reached Bayonne on the 3rd of November, where he remained directing the movements of the last columns of his army until the morning of the 8th. He arrived at Vittoria, the headquarters of his brother Joseph, on the same evening. At the gates of the town he was met by the civil and military authorities, where sumptuous preparations had been provided, but instead of accepting their hospitality, entered the first inn he observed, and calling for maps and a detailed report of the position of all the armies, French and Spanish, proceeded instantly to draw up his plan for the prosecution of the war. Within two hours he had completed his task. Soult, who had accompanied him from Paris, set off on the instant, and within a few hours the whole machinery of the army, comprising 200,000 men, was in motion.

Ere long Napoleon saw the main way to Madrid open before him, except some forces said to be posted at the strong defile of the Somosierra, within ten miles of the capital. Saragossa on the east, the British

Army in Portugal on the west, and Madrid in front were the only far-separated points on which any show of opposition was still to be traced from the frontiers of France to those of Portugal, and from the sea coast to the Tagus.

Having regulated everything on his wings and rear, the emperor with his Imperial Guards and the first division of the army, now marched towards Madrid, his vanguard reaching the foot of the Somosierra chain on the 30th of November. Here he found that a corps of 12,000 or 13,000 men had been assembled for the defence of that pass under General San Juan, an able and valiant officer who had established an advance guard of 3,000 men at the very foot of the slope which the French would have to ascend, and then distributed over 9,000 men at the pass of Somosierra, at the bottom of the gorge; there the advancing army would be obliged to go through. One part of San Juan's force, posted on the right and left of the road, which formed numerous windings, was to stop the advance of the French by a double fire of musketry. The others barred the causeway itself, near the most difficult part of the pass, with the battery. The defile was narrow and excessively steep, and the road completely swept by sixteen pieces of cannon.

At daybreak on the 1st of December the French began their attempts to turn the flank of San Juan, who imagined himself invincible in his position. Three battalions scattered themselves over the opposite sides of the defile and a warm skirmishing fire had begun. At this moment Napoleon came up, at the head of the cavalry of his Guard rode into the mouth of the pass, surveyed the scene for an instant, and perceiving that his infantry was making no progress, at once conceived the daring idea of causing his brave Polish lancers to charge up the causeway in face of the battery.

The emperor had stopped near the foot of the mountain and attentively examined the enemy's position, the fire from which seemed to redouble, many balls falling near him, or passing over his head. Colonel Piré was first dispatched at the head of the Poles and having reconnoitred the position, countermanded the advance, and sent an officer to notify Napoleon "that the undertaking was impossible." Upon this information the emperor much irritated and striking the pommel of his saddle exclaimed, "Impossible! Why, there is nothing impossible to my Poles."

General Wattier, who was present endeavoured to calm him but he still continued to exclaim, "Impossible! I know of no such word.

What, my Guard checked by the Spaniards,—by armed peasants?" At this moment the balls began to whistle about him and several officers came forward and persuaded him to withdraw. Among these Napoleon observed Major Philip Ségur; to him he said, "Go, Ségur, take the Poles, and make them take the Spaniards, or let the Spaniards take them."

Colonel Piré, having informed Kozietulski, commander of the Polish troops, of what the emperor had said, that officer replied, "Come then alone with me, and see if the devil himself, made of fire as he is, would undertake this business."

Advancing, they saw 13,000 Spaniards placed as if in an amphitheatre in such a way that no one battalion was masked by another, and they could only join in columns. From that point the Poles had to sustain forty thousand discharges of musketry and as many of cannon, every minute. However, the order was positive.

"Commandant," said Ségur, "let us go, it is the emperor's wish; the honours will be ours; Poles advance. *Vive l'Empereur!*" Napoleon wished to teach his soldiers that with the Spaniards they must not consider danger, but drive them wherever found.

The smoke of the skirmishers on the side hills mingled with the thick fog and vapours of the morning, and under this veil the brave cavalry of the Guard led the way fearlessly and rushed up the ascent. A brilliant cavalry officer, General Montbrun, at this time somewhat out of favour with the emperor, advanced at the head of the Polish light horse, a young troop of elite which Napoleon had formed at Warsaw that he might have all nations and costumes in his Guard. General Montbrun with those gallant young soldiers dashed at a gallop upon the cannon of the Spaniards, and in defiance of a horrible fire of musketry. The first squadron received a discharge which threw it into disorder, sweeping down thirty or forty men in the ranks; but those that followed, passing beyond the wounded, reached the pieces, cut down the gunners and took all the cannon.

As the rushing steeds passed the Spanish infantry the latter fired and then threw down their guns, abandoned their intrenchments and fled. The brave San Juan, covered with blood, having received several wounds, strove in vain to stop his soldiers, who fled to the right and to the left in the mountains, leaving colours, artillery, 200 wagons with stores and almost all the officers in the hands of the victors. By the time the emperor reached the top not only was the French flag found floating over Buitrago, but Montbrun's cavalry was pursuing the routed Spanish a league beyond the town.

Napoleon was delighted to have proved to his generals what the Spanish insurgents were, what his soldiers were, and in what estimation both were to be held, and to have overcome an obstacle which some had seemed to think extremely formidable. The Poles had about fifty men killed or wounded. That evening Napoleon complimented and rewarded the survivors and included in the distribution of his favours M. Philippe de Ségur who had received several shot wounds in this charge; he also destined him to carry to the Legislative Body at Paris the colours taken at Somosierra and appointed Montbrun general of division.

On the morning of the 2nd three divisions of French cavalry made their appearance on the high ground to the north-west of the capital. The inhabitants of Madrid for eight days had been preparing to resist an invasion. Six thousand regular troops were within the town, and crowds of citizens and of the peasantry of the adjacent country were in arms with them. The pavement had been taken up, the streets barricaded, the houses on the outskirts loop-holed and occupied by a strong garrison. Many persons, suspected of adhering to the side of the French, were put to death, and amid the ringing of the bells of churches and convents, a general uprising for all means of defence was in operation when the French cavalry appeared.

The day was the anniversary of Napoleon's coronation and of the Battle of Austerlitz, and for the emperor as well as his soldiers a superstition was attached to that memorable date. The fine cavalry, on beholding its glorious chief, raised unanimous acclamations, which mingled with the shouts of rage sent up by the Spaniards on seeing the French at their portals.

At noon the town was summoned to open its gates. The young officer carrying the message barely escaped with his life, the mob being determined to massacre him. Only the interference of the Spanish regulars saved his life by snatching him out of the hands of the assassins. The Junta directed a Spanish general to convey a negative answer to the summons of the French. When sent back he was assured that firing would commence immediately, although told that in resisting they would only expose a population of women, and children and old men to the slaughter, and was informed that the city could not hold out long against the French Army.

Napoleon waited until his artillery and infantry came up in the evening and then the place was invested on one side. The emper-

Napoleon at the Battle of Jena

or made a reconnaissance himself on horseback around Madrid and formed the plan of attack which might be divided into several successive acts, so as to summon the place after each of them, and to reduce it rather by intimidation than by the employment of formidable military means.

At midnight the city was again summoned and the answer still being defiant, the batteries began to open. Terror now began to prevail within, and shortly afterward the city was summoned for the third time. Thomas de Morla, the governor, came to demand a suspension of arms. He said that all sensible men in Madrid were convinced of the necessity of surrendering; but that it was necessary to make the French troops retire and allow the Junta time to pacify the people and to induce them to lay down their arms.

Napoleon replied with some show of anger that Morla himself had excited and misled the people, he said:

> Assemble the clergy, the heads of the convents, the *alcaldes*, the principal proprietors, and if between this and six in the morning the city has not surrendered it shall have ceased to exist. I neither will nor ought to withdraw my troops. . . . Return to Madrid. I give you till six tomorrow morning. Go back, then; you have nothing to say to me about the people but to tell me that they have submitted. If not, you and your troops shall be put to the sword.

Morla returned to the town and urged the necessity of instantly capitulating, to which all the authorities but Costellas, the commander of the regular troops agreed. The peasantry and citizens continued firing on the French outposts during the night and then Costellas, seeing that further resistance was useless, withdrew his troops and sixteen cannon in safety.

At eight o'clock on the morning of the 4th Madrid surrendered. The Spaniards were at once disarmed and the French troops filled the town and established themselves in the great buildings. Napoleon took up his residence in a country house near the capital. He gave orders for a general and immediate disarming, and tranquillity was once more restored, the shops and theatres being opened as usual.

Napoleon now exercised all the rights of a conqueror and issued edicts abolishing, among other evils, the Inquisition of the Jesuits, as well as the feudal institutions of the Middle Ages. He received a deputation of the chief inhabitants who came to signify their desire to see his brother Joseph among them again. His answer was that Spain was his own by right of conquest; that he could easily rule it by viceroys; but if they chose to assemble in their churches, priests and people, and swear allegiance to Joseph, he was not indisposed to listen to their request. He distinctly affirmed that he would, in case they proved disloyal, put the crown upon his own head, treat the country as a conquered province and find another kingdom for his brother: "for" added he, "God has given me both the inclination and the power to surmount all obstacles."

Meanwhile Napoleon was making arrangements for the completion of his conquest. His plan was to invade Andalusia, Valencia and Galicia by his lieutenants, and march in person to Lisbon.

On learning on December 19th that the English army under Sir John Moore, amounting to 20,000, men, had put itself in motion, had advanced into Spain and left Salamanca to proceed to Valladolid; that a separate British corps of 13,000 men under Sir David Baird had recently landed at Corunna with orders to march through Galicia and effect a junction with Moore, either at Salamanca or Valladolid, Napoleon resolved to advance in person and overwhelm Moore. His resolution was instantly taken with that promptness of decision and unerring judgment which never forsook him. He instantly put himself at the head of 50,000 men and marched with incredible rapidity, with the view of intercepting Moore's communications with Portugal, and in short hemming the English commander in between himself and Soult.

Moore no sooner heard that Napoleon was approaching than he perceived the necessity of an immediate retreat; and he commenced, accordingly, a most calamitous one through the naked mountains of Galicia, in which his troops displayed a most lamentable want of discipline. They ill-treated the inhabitants, straggled from their ranks, and in short lost the appearance of an army except when the trumpet warned them that they might expect the French to charge.

Leaving Chamartin on the morning of the 22nd of December Napoleon arrived at the foot of the Guadarrama as the infantry of his Guard was beginning to ascend it. The weather, which till then had been superb, had suddenly become terrible, and at the very moment when forced marches were to be performed, as it was necessary that they lose no time in coming up with the English.

Napoleon, seeing the infantry of his Guard accumulating at the entrance of the gorge, in which the gun-carriages were also crowded together, spurred his horse into a gallop, and gained the head of the column which he found detained by the hurricane. The peasants declared that it was impossible to pass without being exposed to the greatest dangers. This, however, was not sufficient to stop the conqueror of the Alps. He made the *chasseurs* of his Guard dismount, and ordered them to advance first in close column, conducted by guides. These bold fellows, marching at the head of the army, and trampling down the snow with their own feet and those of their horses, formed a beaten track for the troops who followed.

The emperor himself climbed the mountain on foot, amidst the chasseurs of his Guard, merely leaning, when he felt fatigued, on the arm of General Savary. The cold, which was as severe as at Eylau, did not prevent him from crossing the Guadarrama. General Marbot, who accompanied Napoleon on the journey, says in his *Memoirs*:

> A furious snowstorm, with a fierce wind, made the passage of the mountains almost impracticable. Men and horses were hurled over precipices. The leading battalions had actually begun to retreat; but Napoleon was resolved to overtake the English at all cost. He spoke to the men, and ordered that the members of each section should hold one another by the arm. The cavalry, dismounting, did the same. The staff was formed in similar fashion, the emperor between Lannes and Duroc, we following with locked arms; and so, in spite of wind, snow and ice, we proceeded, though it took us four hours to reach the top. Half way up the marshals and generals, who wore jackboots, could go no farther. Napoleon, therefore, got hoisted on to a gun, and bestrode it; the marshals and generals did the same, and in this grotesque order they reached the convent at the summit. There the troops were rested and wine served out. The descent though awkward, was better.

Napoleon spent the night in a miserable post-house in the little village of Espinar. On the mules laden with his baggage had been brought the wherewithal to serve him with supper, and which he shared with his officers, cheerfully conversing with them on that series of extraordinary adventures which had commenced at the school of Brienne—to end, he knew not where!

Next day the emperor proceeded with his Guard; but the infantry advanced with difficulty and the artillery could not stir owing to the frightful quagmires. The stragglers and baggage came up slowly while Napoleon, anxious to meet the fleeing English troops, pushed on with his advance guard and with his chasseurs until Benevento was reached. Here he came up with his own troops in pursuit of Moore at Benevento, on the 29th of December, and enjoyed for a moment, from his headquarters established there, the spectacle of the English army in full retreat.

The French columns seemed to rival each other in their efforts to overtake the enemy. In their precipitation the English abandoned their sick, hamstrung their horses, when unable to keep up with them, and destroyed the greater part of their ammunition and baggage.

Marshal Soult, who had taken another road, was much nearer the enemy. His orders to follow the English intermission were difficult of accomplishing as the mud was deep and the soldiers sank up to their knees.

Napoleon now decided that Moore was no longer worthy of his own attention and intrusted the consummation of his ruin to Soult, who was ordered to pursue the English to the last extremity, and "with his sword at their loins." He therefore set out at once, his troops marching past the emperor.

Soult hung close on the rear of the English; he came up with them in the mountains of Leon and continued to pursue them until they reached the port of Corunna. Here Moore perceived that it would be impossible to embark without a convention or battle and he chose the latter. The attack was made by the French on the 16th of January in heavy columns and with their usual vivacity; but it was sustained and repelled by the English and they were permitted to embark without further molestation. Sir John Moore fell in the action mortally wounded by a cannon shot. His body was wrapped in a military cloak, instead of the usual vestments of the tomb, and deposited in a grave hastily dug on the ramparts of the citadel of Corunna, while the guns of the enemy paid him funeral honours. The next morning the grenadiers of France, who had been struck with admiration at the chivalry of the English commander, gathered reverently around the new-made grave, and while the English fleet was yet visible on the bosom of the Mediterranean, they erected a monument over his body and placed thereon an appropriate inscription.

Napoleon, having been informed of the embarkation of the English Army, instead of returning to Madrid to complete his Spanish conquest, proceeded at once towards Astorga where his fears with reference to Austria were heightened by news from Paris by courier. The storm that was gathering once more along the shores of the Danube was of more vital consequence to France than the kingdom of Joseph Bonaparte. On his arrival at Astorga he changed all his plans. General Marbot says:

> It was late at night when the emperor and Lannes, escorted only by their staffs, and some hundred cavalry, entered Astorga. So tired and anxious for shelter and warmth was everyone that the place was scarcely searched. If the enemy had had warning of this, and returned on their tracks, they might perhaps have carried off the emperor; fortunately they were in too great a hurry, and we did not find one of them in the town. Every minute fresh bodies of French troops were coming up and the safety of the Imperial headquarters was soon secured.

Proceeding to Valladolid with his Guard, which he wished to keep as near to events in Germany as himself, after placing Joseph on the throne at Madrid again, he soon afterwards hastened to Paris with all speed, riding on post horses on one occasion not less than eighty-five miles in five and one-half hours. He had traversed Spain with the rapidity of lightning, followed by his Guard, to the spot where new dangers and triumphs awaited him. He left behind a feeble king, equally as incapable of keeping as obtaining a conquest; and marshals who, no longer restrained by the presence of an inflexible chief, for the most part delivered themselves over to their own self-love or private jealousies.

In his *Memorial* written in exile at St. Helena, Napoleon said "that the war of Spain destroyed him, and that all the circumstances of his disasters connect themselves with this fatal knot."

He said at another time:

> In the crisis France was placed in, in the struggle of new ideas in the great cause of the age against the rest of Europe, we could not leave Spain behind.

10

War With Austria, 1809

Before Napoleon returned to Paris from Spain he learned that, yielding to England's instigations, Austria was about to take advantage of his being so far away, to cross its borders, invade Bavaria, carry the war to the banks of the Rhine, and then effect the liberation of Germany. The opportunity was an excellent one for attempting such an undertaking. The emperor had been compelled to send the pick of his battalions to the other side of the Pyrenees, thus greatly reducing the number of French foes in Germany. The French Minister of Foreign Affairs, Talleyrand, had during Napoleon's absence made every effort to conciliate the Emperor Francis, but the warlike preparations throughout the Austrian dominions proceeded with increasing vigour.

After the declaration of war by Austria on the 6th of April, couriers were at once dispatched with orders to the armies on the Rhine, and beyond the Alps, to concentrate themselves on the field. To the ambassadors at Paris the emperor spoke most freely of the coming conquest, he said:

> They have forgotten the lessons of experience there. They want fresh ones; they shall have them, and this time they shall be terrible I promise you. I do not desire war; I have no interest in it, and all Europe is witness that my whole attention and all my efforts were directed towards the field of battle which England had selected, that is to say, Spain. Austria, which saved the English in 1805 when I was about to cross the straits of Calais, has saved them once more by stopping me when I was about to pursue them to Corunna. She shall pay dearly for this new diversion in their favour. Either she shall disarm instantly, or she

shall have to sustain a war of destruction. If she disarms in such a manner as to leave no doubt on my mind as to her further intentions, I will myself sheathe my sword, for I have no wish to draw it except in Spain against the English; otherwise the conflict shall be immediate and decisive, and such that England shall for the future have no allies on the Continent.

The instant Napoleon ascertained that Bavaria was invaded by the Archduke Charles, he at once proceeded, without guards, without equipage, accompanied solely by the faithful Josephine, to Frankfort and thence to Strasbourg. Here he assumed command of the army on the 13th of April, and immediately formed the plan of his campaign. He found the two wings of his army, the one under Massena, the other under Davoust, at such a distance from the centre that, had the Austrians seized the opportunity, the consequences might have been fatal to the French.

On the 17th of April, while at Donawerth, Napoleon commanded Davoust and Massena to march simultaneously towards a position in front, and then pushed forward the centre in person, to the same point. The Archduke Louis, who commanded the Austrian divisions in advance, was thus hemmed in unexpectedly by three armies, moving at once from three different points.

At Donawerth Napoleon addressed his troops in a proclamation in which he said:

Soldiers, the territory of the Confederation has been violated. The Austrian general expects us to fly at the sight of his arms, and to abandon our allies to him. I arrive with the rapidity of lightning. Soldiers, I was surrounded by you when the sovereign of Austria came to my camp in Moravia; you have heard him implore my clemency, and swear an eternal friendship towards me. Victors, in three wars Austria has owed everything to your generosity; three times has she perjured herself. Our past successes are a safe guarantee of the victory which awaits us. Let us march, and at our aspect may the enemy acknowledge his conqueror.

It should be remembered that at this time, while Napoleon was astonishing Europe by the rapidity of his movements, and the display of the resources of his military and political genius, he had left an army in the Peninsula, distributed over an immense space of territory, weakened by diseases, reduced by partial combats, and without receiving reinforcements from the interior of the empire. During the whole of the German campaign of 1809, the French in Spain were merely able to maintain themselves in the positions they had occupied soon after Napoleon's departure.

Austria had reckoned on the absence of Napoleon and his Guard, and on the veteran troops of Marengo and Austerlitz being far distant. She knew that there did not remain more than 80,000 French scattered throughout Germany, while her army divided into nine bodies, under the orders of the Archduke Charles, had not less than 500,000 men.

The Archduke Louis was defeated and driven back at Abensberg on the 20th, and utterly routed at Landshut on the 21st, losing 9,000 men, thirty guns and all his stores. Those unfortunate Austrians who had been led from Vienna singing songs, under a persuasion that there was no longer a French army in Germany, and that they should only have to deal with Wurtemburgers and Bavarians, experienced the greatest terror when they came to conflict and found themselves defeated. The Prince of Lichtenstein and General Lusignan, were wounded, while the loss of the Austrians in colonels, and officers, of lower rank was considerable.

In the Battle of Abensberg which occurred on the 20th, Napoleon was resolved to destroy the corps of the Archduke Louis, and of General Keller, amounting to sixty thousand men. The enemy only stood his ground for an hour and left eighteen thousand prisoners. The cannonade of the French was successful at all points and the Austrians, disconcerted by Napoleon's brilliant movements, beat a hasty retreat leaving eight standards and twelve pieces of cannon. The French loss was very small.

Before this engagement Napoleon saw defile before him on the plateau in front of Abensberg the Wurtemberg and Bavarian troops, allies of the French, who were going to put themselves in line and whom the pride of fighting under a general of his renown filled with enthusiasm. The emperor caused them to be drawn up and proceeded to harangue them, one after the other, the officers translating his words to the troops. He said that he was making them fight, not for himself, but for themselves; against the ambition of the house of Austria, which was enraged at not having them, as of yore, under its yoke; that this time he would soon restore them peace, and forever, and with such an increase of power that for the future they should be able to defend themselves against the pretensions of their old dominators.

His presence and words electrified his German allies, who were flattered to see him amongst them, he trusting entirely to their honour, for at that moment he had no other escort than some detachments of Bavarian cavalry.

When Napoleon arrived that evening at Rotterburg he was intoxicated with joy. The engagement, which was of short duration, had cost the Austrians 7,000 or 8,000 men, and he saw his adversary driven back on the Iser at the very beginning of the campaign, and the Austrian soldiers disheartened, like the Prussians after Jena.

The Battle of Landshut completed the defeat of the preceding evening. On this day General Mouton, at the head of a column of grenadiers rushed through the flames that were consuming one of the bridges of the Iser; "Forward, but reserve your fire!" he shouted to the soldiers in a voice of thunder; and in a few moments he had penetrated into the town, which then became the seat of a sanguinary struggle, and which the Austrians were not long in abandoning.

Next day Napoleon executed a variety of manoeuvres, considered as amongst the most admirable of his science, by means of which he brought his whole force, by different routes, at one and the same moment upon the position of the Archduke Charles, who was strongly posted at Eckmuhl with 100,000 men. On both sides all was ready for a decisive action. Until 8 o'clock a thick fog enveloped that rural scene which was soon to be drenched with the blood of thousands of men. As soon as it cleared away both sides prepared for action. Not a musket or a cannon shot was fired before noon, however.

There was no need of a signal for battle as the terrible contest began on both sides simultaneously about 2 o'clock in the afternoon, Napoleon commanding and leading the charge, and accompanied by Lannes and Massena. One of the most beautiful sights war could produce now presented itself; one hundred and ten thousand men were attacked on all points, turned to their left, and successively driven from all their positions, although not a half of the French troops were engaged. The battle was stern and lasted until twilight, ending with the utter defeat of the Archduke's army, and leaving Napoleon with 20,000 prisoners, fifteen imperial standards and a vast number of cannon in his hands, while the defeated and routed enemy fled back in confusion on the city of Ratisbon. The Austrian cavalry, strong and numerous, attempted to cover the retreat of the infantry, but was attacked by the French both on the right and left. The Archduke Charles was only indebted for his safety to the fleetness of his horse, when darkness at length compelled the victors to halt.

While the French were galloping along the road in pursuit of the Austrians, finding the plain to which they had retreated swampy, they endeavoured to regain the road, and thus became mingled with the mass of victorious cavalry. A multitude of single combats then took place by the uncertain light of the moon, and nothing was heard but the clashing of sabres on their *cuirasses*, the shouts of the commandants, and the heavy tramp of horses. The French *cuirassiers*, wearing double *cuirasses*, which covered them all round, could more easily defend themselves than the Austrians, who, having only breastplates, fell in great numbers, mortally wounded by the thrusts dealt them from behind. Night put an end to a contest where there were scenes of carnage that had not been equalled in years.

At the Battle of Abensberg the emperor beat separately the two corps of the Archduke Louis and General Keller; at the Battle of Landshut he took the centre of their communications and the general depot of their magazines and artillery; and, finally, at the Battle of Eckmuhl, the corps of Hohenzollern, Rosenberg, and Lichtenstein, were defeated.

The Austrians, astonished by rapid movements beyond their calculation, were soon deprived of their sanguine hopes, and precipitated from a delirium of presumption to a despondency bordering on despair. Two days later the Archduke made an attempt to rally his troops, and not only to hold Ratisbon, but to meet Napoleon. He was obliged to give up the place at the storming of the walls by the French, who drove the Austrians through the streets. All who resisted were slain. The enemy's commander fled precipitately into Bohemia, abandoning once more the capital of the Austrian Empire to the mercy of the conqueror.

Napoleon was wounded in the foot during the storming of Ratisbon. He had approached the town amidst a fire of sharpshooters kept up by the Austrians from the walls, and by the French from the edge of a ditch. Whilst he was looking through a telescope he received a ball in the instep, and said, with the coolness of an old soldier: "I am hit!" When the emperor received his wound he was talking with Duroc. "This," said he to his marshal, "can only come from a Tyrolean; no other marksman could take an aim at such a distance; those fellows are very clever."

The wound might have been dangerous for had it been higher up the foot would have been shattered and amputation inevitable. The first surgeon of the Guard, Dr. Larrey, being near took off his boot and prepared to dress the wound, which was not serious.

At the news that the emperor was wounded the troops crowded around him in great alarm. Officers and soldiers ran up from all sides; in a moment he was surrounded by thousands of men, in spite of the fire which the enemy's guns concentrated on the vast group. The emperor, wishing to withdraw his troops from this useless danger, and to calm the anxiety of the more distant corps who were getting unsteady in their desire to come and see what was the matter, mounted his horse the instant his wound was dressed and rode down the front of the whole line amid loud cheers. Those around remonstrated with him for continually exposing his person, to which he replied: "What can I do? I must see how things are going on."

General Marbot says:

> It was at this extempore review, held in presence of the enemy, that Napoleon first granted gratuities to private soldiers, appointing them Knights of the Empire and members, at the same time, of the Legion of Honour. The regimental commanders recommended, but the emperor also allowed soldiers who thought they had claims, to come and represent them before him; he then decided upon them himself.

An old grenadier, who had made the campaigns of Italy and Egypt, not hearing his name called, came up, and in a calm tone of voice asked for the cross.

"But," said Napoleon, "what have you done to deserve it?"

"It was I, sir, who, in the desert of Joppa, when it was so terribly hot, gave you a watermelon!"

"I thank you for it again," said the emperor, "but the gift of the fruit is hardly worth the cross of the Legion of Honour." Then the grenadier, who up till then had been as cool as ice, working himself up into a frenzy, shouted at the top of his voice, "Well, and don't you reckon seven wounds received at the bridge of Arcola, at Lodi, at Castiglione, at the Pyramids, at Acre, Austerlitz, Friedland; eleven campaigns in Italy, Egypt, Austria, Prussia, Poland—."

But the emperor cut him short laughing, and mimicking his excited manner, cried;—"There, there, how you work yourself up when you come to the essential point! That is where you ought to have begun; it is worth much more than your melon. I make you a Knight of the Empire, with a pension of 1200 *francs*. Does that satisfy you?"

Entry of Napoleon into Berlin

"But your Majesty, I prefer the cross."

"You have both one and the other since I make you a Knight."

"Well, I would rather have the cross," and the worthy grenadier could not be moved from that point. It took much explaining to make him understand that the title of Knight of the Empire carried with it the Legion of Honour. He was not appeased on this point until the emperor had fastened the decoration on his breast, and he seemed to think a great deal more of this than of his annuity of 1200 *francs*.

It was by familiarities of this kind that the emperor made the soldiers adore him, but as Marbot again well says, it was a means that was only available to a commander whom frequent victories had made illustrious; any other general would have impaired his reputation by it.

Napoleon now sent an *aide-de-camp* to Lannes urging him to expedite the taking of Ratisbon. This intrepid marshal had directed all his artillery against a projecting house which rose above the wall surrounding the town. The house was knocked down and the ruins fell into the ditch. Still there were two fortified positions to take. Ladders were procured and placed at the critical points by the grenadiers, but every time one of them appeared he was instantly brought down by the well-aimed balls of the Austrian sharpshooters. After some men had been thus struck, the rest appeared to hang back. Thereupon Lannes advanced, covered with decorations, seized one of the ladders and cried out: "You shall see that your marshal, for all he is a marshal, has not ceased to be a grenadier!" Two *aides-de-camp* sprang forward and snatched the ladder out of his hands, and the grenadiers followed them, took the ladders, and, notwithstanding the continued fire of the sharpshooters, made the crossing in safety, followed by hundreds of others in an instant.

The walls being scaled, the town was soon in the hands of the French, who rushed along the blazing streets taking prisoners in all directions. Suddenly they were stopped with a cry of terror uttered by the Austrians; "Take care, we shall all be blown up!" shouted an officer. There were some barrels of powder left in the street which were in danger of being fired by the shots exchanged on either side. The belligerents stopped with one accord and joined hands in removing the barrels to a place of safety. The Austrians then withdrew and left the town to the French troops.

After the taking of Ratisbon Napoleon issued an address to his soldiers complimenting them highly on their valour. He said:

You have justified my expectations. You have made up for numbers by your courage; you have gloriously marked the difference which exists between the soldiers of Cæsar and the armies of Xerxes. In a few days we have triumphed in the three battles of Tann, Abensberg and Eckmuhl, and the affairs of Peising, Landshut and Ratisbon. One hundred pieces of cannon, fifty thousand prisoners, three equipages, three thousand baggage wagons, all the funds of the regiments, are the results of the rapidity of your marches, and of your courage.... Before a month we shall be in Vienna!

Thus in five days, in spite of inferiority of numbers and of the unfavourable manner in which his lieutenants had distributed an inferior force; by the sole energy of his genius, did Napoleon triumph over the main force of his opponent. The emperor reviewed his army on the 24th, distributing rewards of all sorts with a lavish hand. Upon Davoust he bestowed the title of Duke of Eckmuhl.

On May 3rd a body of 30,000 Austrians remaining from the army of Landshut, fell back upon Ebersberg, where Massena engaged in a stubborn battle, General Claparéde being obliged to defend himself for three hours with but 7,000 men against 30,000 Austrians. Reinforcements at last arrived and the enemy retired in disorder upon the Ens, where they burned the bridge so as to protect their flight in the direction of Vienna. The battle cost the Austrians 12,000 men, of whom 7,500 were prisoners. The field of carnage was hideous, and the town of Ebersberg was so wrapped in flames that the wounded could not be withdrawn. To prevent the fire from reaching the bridge it had been necessary to cut off the approach at either end, so that communication was interrupted for several hours between the troops who had crossed the river and those coming to their aid. Napoleon had galloped up on hearing the cannonade, and though inured to all the horrors of war, is said to have been greatly shocked at the sight he beheld.

Passing before the ruins of the castle of Dirnstein, on an eminence beyond the Molck, and in the direction of Vienna, whither he was going, Napoleon said to Marshal Lannes, who was at his side:

Look! Behold the prison of Richard Coeur de Lion. Like us, he went to Syria and Palestine. Coeur de Lion, my brave Lannes, was not braver than thou. He was more fortunate than I at St. Jean d'Acre. The Duke of Austria sold him to an emperor of Germany who had him imprisoned there. That was in the barbarous ages. How different to our own civilization! You have seen how I treat the Emperor of Austria, whom I could have taken prisoner. Ah! well! I shall treat him again in the same manner. It is not my wish, but that of the age!

From Molck the headquarters of the emperor were transferred to St. Polten and two days later, at 9 o'clock in the morning, Napoleon was at Vienna, which he desired to take forthwith, but to take without destroying if possible.

Meeting with resistance in entering the city, the inhabitants having prepared for a vigorous defence, Napoleon began to play with his heavy batteries upon the city. The bombardment soon convinced them that it was hopeless to resist, and Vienna surrendered May 12th after suffering severely. In a few hours eighteen hundred shells had fallen in the city. The streets were narrow, the houses high, and the population crowded within the narrow fortifications, were terrified and infuriated at the sight of the damage caused by the shells which started fires in every direction. Who would have said to the Viennese, who were then hurling all manner of imprecations at Napoleon, the author of all their woes, that ten months later they would be singing the praise of this detested emperor, and would be voluntarily setting French flags in their windows as symbols of friendship?

All the royal family had fled except the young Archduchess Marie Louise, who was detained in the palace, suffering from small-pox. When Napoleon heard she was sequestered there he ordered that no battery should be directed to that part of the town in which lay she who was destined to be his bride within less than a year! At this time Napoleon himself would no doubt have laughed heartily had he been told that in that palace was a woman who was to succeed Josephine in his struggle for a dynasty, to be Empress of the French, and later, to bear him the long wished for son and heir.

That Marie had no such thoughts or inclinations can readily be guessed from the fact of the present campaign in which her father, the emperor, was battling for his empire. The Emperor Francis had left his capital on April 8th, 1809, leaving there his wife and children, but all of whom departed, except Marie, on May 5th. From Vienna Marie wrote frequently to her father. A rumour had reached the capital that the Battle of Eckmuhl had been a brilliant victory for the Austrians, and the young archduchess wrote to her father on April 25th:

We have heard with delight that Napoleon was present at the great battle which the French lost. May he lose his head as well! There are a great many prophecies about his speedy end, and people say that the Apocalypse applies to him. They maintain that he is going to die this year at Cologne, in an inn called the 'Red Crawfish.' I do not attach much importance to these prophecies, but how glad should I be to see them come true!

On May 13th the capitulation of the Austrian capital was signed, and Napoleon's army again entered Vienna, the emperor taking up his old quarters at the imperial palace of Schoenbrunn. He said to his soldiers:

> The people of Vienna, according to the expression of the deputation, wearied, deserted, widowed, shall be the object of your regards. I take the inhabitants under my special protection. As for the turbulent and ill-disposed, I will make a severe example of them. Let us be kind towards the poor peasants, towards these good people, who have so many claims upon our esteem. Let us not be vain of all our successes; but look upon them as a proof of that divine justice which punishes ingratitude and perjury.

11

The Battle of Wagram

The Austrian Army, in abandoning the capital of the empire, had not renounced the war, although in thirty-three days Napoleon had, with one stroke of his sword, cut in two the mass of their armies, and with a second burst open the gates of Vienna. He was now firmly established in that capital, and master of the main resources of the monarchy; but his work was far from being done, either in Austria or in Germany. A great difficulty remained to be overcome,—that of crossing a vast river in the face of the enemy, and to give battle with the river behind him. This difficulty Napoleon had been unable to prevent, and it resulted inevitably from the nature of things. On leaving Ratisbon he had been obliged to take the route which was shortest, thus keeping the two main divisions of the Austrian army separated from each other. He was consequently obliged to march along the right bank of the Danube, abandoning the left to the Austrians, but securing to himself exclusively the means of crossing from the one to the other.

The Archduke Charles was soon tempted to quit the fastness of Bohemia, and try once more the fortune of a battle. Having re-established the order, and recruited the numbers of his army to 100,000 men, he was soon posted on the banks of the Danube. Opposite were the French, and the river being greatly swollen, and all the bridges destroyed, the two armies seemed separated by an impassable barrier. Napoleon determined to pass it and after an unsuccessful attempt at Nussdorff, met with better fortune at Ebersdorff, where the river is broad and intersected by a number of low and woody islands, the largest of which bears the name of Lobau. Here Massena had thrown several bridges over the arms of the Danube.

On these islands Napoleon established the greater part of his army on May 19th, and on the following day made good his passage by means of a bridge of boats to the left bank of the Danube, where he took possession of the villages of Asperne and Essling, with so little show of opposition that it became evident that the archduke wished the inevitable battle to take place with the river between his enemy and Vienna.

On the 21st, at daybreak, the archduke appeared on a rising ground, separated from the French position by an extensive plain. His whole force was divided into five heavy columns and protected by not less than two hundred pieces of artillery. The battle began at 4 o'clock in the afternoon with a furious assault on the village of Asperne, which was taken and retaken several times, and remained at nightfall in the occupation partly of the French and partly of the assailants, who had established themselves in the church and churchyard. Essling sustained three attacks also, but there the French remained in complete possession. At one time Lannes, who defended this point, was so hard pressed, that he must have given way had not Napoleon relieved him, and obtained him a breathing spell by a well-timed and terrific charge of cavalry under Bessieres, which fell upon their centre.

Night finally interrupted the action, the Austrians exulting in their partial success; and Napoleon surprised that he should not have been wholly victorious. On either side the carnage had been terrible, and the pathways of the villages were literally choked with the dead.

Just as Napoleon was about to retire for a few hours' rest he was interrupted by a violent altercation between two of his chief lieutenants, Bessieres and Lannes, the former of whom complained of the language used by the latter, his inferior in rank, in giving a necessary order for a charge of *cuirassiers* and *chasseurs*, then under the orders of Marshal Bessieres himself. Massena, who was on the spot, was obliged to interfere between these gallant men, who after having braved for a whole day the cross-fire of 300 pieces of cannon, were ready to draw their swords for the sake of their offended pride. Napoleon allayed their quarrel, which was to be terminated next day by the enemy in the saddest way for themselves and for the army.

Next morning the battle recommenced at 4 o'clock with equal fury, the French recovering Asperne; but the Austrian right wing renewed its assaults on that point, and in such numbers that Napoleon guessed that their centre and left had been weakened for the purpose of strengthening their right. Believing this he instantly moved such masses upon the Austrian centre that the Archduke's line was shaken, and for a moment it seemed as if the victory of the French was secure. In fact it was extremely doubtful if the Austrian centre could withstand the mass of 20,000 infantry and 6,000 horse which Lannes had thrown upon it.

The Archduke Charles now hastened to the spot to prevent the catastrophe that threatened his centre, and in this critical moment discharged at once the duties of a general and a common soldier. He brought up reserves, replaced the gaps which had been made in his line by the furious onslaught of the French, and while awaiting the execution of these orders, seized a standard and himself led the grenadiers to the charge, while his bravest officers were struck down by his side. Lannes, who also headed his soldiers in person, seeing the Austrian infantry disordered, let loose upon them Bessieres and his own *cuirassiers*, who, charging Hohenzollern's corps, broke several squares and took prisoners, cannon and flags.

Success now seemed certain, and Lannes sent a staff officer to acquaint Napoleon of his progress and asked him to cover his rear whilst he was advancing in the plain and leaving so large a space between him and Essling. The officer found Napoleon watching the grand spectacle of which he was the director. He did not express anything like the satisfaction he might have been expected to feel at such a communication. The fact was, an unfortunate accident had occurred. At this critical moment the bridge connecting the island of Lobau was being wholly swept away by means of fire-ships sent down the river by the Austrians.

Napoleon at once perceived that if he wished to preserve his communication with the right of the Danube, where his reserve still lay, he must instantly fall back on Lobau. The want of troops, however, was not the first consequence of the rupture of the bridge, for the 60,000 already passed over were enough to beat the Austrians. What was most to be regretted was the want of ammunition, a prodigious quantity of which had already been consumed, and of which there would soon be a scarcity.

Napoleon therefore resolved upon a painful sacrifice in order not to expose himself to risks which prudence forbade him to brave. Having formed this resolution, in an instant he ordered the staff officer to return to Lannes as fast as possible and tell him to suspend the movement and fall back gradually on the Essling and Asperne line. He was also to recommend the marshal to be sparing of ammunition.

On receiving this order Lannes and Bessieres were compelled, to their deep regret, to halt in the midst of the vast plain of Marchfield. No sooner did the French troops commence their backward movement than the Austrians recovered their order and zeal, charged in turn, and finally made themselves masters of Asperne.

Essling, where Massena commanded, held firm, and under the protection of that village and numerous batteries erected near it, Napoleon succeeded in withdrawing his whole force during the night. The commander had sent earlier in the day to inquire of Massena if he could rely on the possession of Asperne; for as long as it and Essling remained, the safe retreat of the army was insured. The staff officer who took the message found Massena on a heap of rubbish, harassed with fatigue, with blood-shot eyes, but with unabated energy of spirit.

On receiving the message he stood up and replied with extraordinary emphasis: "Go tell the emperor I will hold out two hours,—twenty-four—so long as it is necessary for the safety of the army!"

It was during this exciting retreat that a dreadful calamity befell the army. Whilst Lannes was galloping in front of the line from one corps to another, encouraging the soldiers by his voice and example, an officer who was alarmed at seeing him exposed to so much danger, entreated him to dismount for greater safety. He followed the advice, though it was far from his habit to be careful of his life. At that instant he was struck by a cannon ball that shattered both his knees. Bessieres and an aide raised him up, and found him bathed in blood and almost senseless. Bessieres, with whom he had quarrelled on the preceding day, pressed his weak hand. He was laid on a *cuirassier's* cloak and carried to a little bridge where an ambulance was stationed. The news soon spread through the army and filled it with sorrow. The surgeon declared his wounds to be mortal.

In his frenzy the brave marshal called for Napoleon, his friend. The latter observed a group advancing, supporting Lannes on a bier formed of crossed fire-locks and some branches of oak. Twelve old grenadiers, covered with blood and dust, bore this illustrious warrior along. As soon as the emperor saw it was the Duke of Montebello he hastened to meet him. The grenadiers stopped, and Napoleon, throwing himself upon his old companion-in-arms, who had fainted from the loss of blood, in a voice scarcely articulate, said, several times, "Lannes, my friend, do you know me? It is the emperor, it is Bonaparte, your friend."

At these words Lannes opened his eyes, till then closed, collected his spirits, and made some attempts to speak; but, being unable, he could only lift his dying arms to pass them round the neck of Napoleon. The fear of exhausting the little life still remaining in the marshal determined the emperor to leave him.

Sometime later Napoleon visited his wounded friend and conversed with him briefly. "My noble marshal," said the emperor, "It is all over."

"What!" cried the dying man, "can't *you* save me?" He died in delirium some days later in the arms of his chief, who wept over him as he had done at the death of Desaix at Marengo.

The French soldiery delighted to call him the "Roland of the Camp," and Napoleon said, "It was impossible to be more brave than Lannes." No man could inspire his troops with more confidence than could this brave soldier who had been the companion of the fortunes and glory of Napoleon from the very beginning of his public career.

Napoleon had charged Lannes to maintain Essling at all hazards and he valiantly fulfilled his task. At length, at nine at night, the sanguinary conflict ceased; the French preserving the position they had occupied in the morning, and the Austrians bivouacking where they were. Both sides sustained an equal loss, from fifteen to twenty thousand men having been killed, or wounded, on both sides. Among the Austrians were four field-marshals, eight generals and six hundred and sixty-three officers killed or wounded.

On the morning of the 23rd of May the French were cooped up in Lobau and the adjacent islands,—Asperne and Essling—the whole left bank of the river, remaining in the possession of the Austrians. On either side a victory was claimed. In the eyes of Europe it was a check for Napoleon, accustomed to crush his enemy, to have been unable at this time to drive the Austrians from their position.

The situation of the French emperor was imminently hazardous; he was separated from Davoust and his reserves, and, had the enemy either attacked him in the islands, or passed the river higher up and so overwhelmed Davoust and relieved Vienna, the results might have been fatal. But the archduke's loss in these two days had been very great; and, in place of risking an offensive movement, he contented himself with strengthening the position of Asperne and Essling, and awaiting quietly the moment when his enemy should choose to attempt once more the passage to the left bank, and the reoccupation of these stubbornly contested villages.

Napoleon availed himself of this pause with his usual skill. That he had been checked was true, and that the news would be heard with enthusiasm, he well knew. It was necessary, therefore, to regain the fame which had surrounded the beginning of the campaign, and he made every preparation for another decisive battle. Some weeks elapsed ere he ventured to assume the offensive.

On the 4th of July, 1809, Napoleon at last re-established his communication with the right bank, and arranged the means of passing to the left at a point where the archduke had made hardly any preparation for receiving him. On the 5th of July, at 10 o'clock at night, the French began to cross from the islands in the Danube to the left bank. Gunboats prepared for the purpose silenced some of the Austrian batteries; others were avoided by passing the river out of reach of their fire on bridges that had been secretly erected by the French. When Napoleon had a river to be crossed he began the operation by suddenly conveying some determined men to the opposite side in boats. These proceeded to disarm or kill the enemy's advanced posts, and to fix the moorings to which the boats were to be attached that were to carry the bridge. The army then passed over as quickly as possible.

The first of these operations was the most difficult in presence of an enemy so numerous and so well prepared as were the Austrians. To facilitate it, Napoleon had large flat boats constructed, capable of carrying 300 men each, and having a moving gunwale to protect the men from musketry, which on being let down, would serve instead of planks for landing. Every corps was provided with five of these flat-boats, which made an advance guard of 1500 men carried over at once, and the enemy, not knowing exactly where the crossing would be made, could not confront the French with advanced posts in sufficient numbers to prevent their landing.

The Austrians having rashly calculated that Asperne and Essling must needs be the object of the next contest, as of the preceding, they were taken almost unawares by Napoleon's appearance in another quarter. They changed their line on the instant and occupied a position, the centre and key of which was the little town of Wagram. Here, on the 6th of July, the final and decisive battle was to be fought. Adding together the troops of Massena, Oudinot, Davoust, Bernadotte, Prince Eugene, Macdonald, Marmont, de Wrede and the Guard, there appeared to be 150,000 men; of whom 26,000 were cavalry and 12,000 artillerymen serving 550 guns; an enormous force, such as Napoleon had never yet mustered on a field of battle, and according to some authorities, such a host as had never been brought into action by any leader.

Besides this vast force Napoleon had with him the invincible Massena, who was then suffering from a fall from his horse, but who was capable of mastering all physical sufferings on a day of battle; the stubborn Davoust, the impetuous Oudinot, the intrepid Macdonald, and a multitude of others who were ready to purchase the triumph of the French arms with their blood. The heroic Lannes was the only one missing. Fate had forbidden him to witness a victory to which he had powerfully contributed by his conduct in this campaign.

When the day dawned on the banks of the river, about 4 o'clock in the morning, a most imposing spectacle presented itself to both armies. The sun glistened on thousands of bayonets and helmets, and seventy thousand men were already in line of battle on the enemy's side of the river capable of making a good fight with the Archduke's forces. Seeing Napoleon ride along the front of the lines his soldiers raised their shakos on their bayonets and cried: "*Vive l'Empereur!*" The ground covered by the two armies was about two leagues in extent. The troops nearest were about 1200 fathoms from the city of Vienna, so that the towers, steeples, and tops of the highest houses, were covered by the numerous population, thus become spectators of the terrible contest then preparing.

The archduke had extended his line over too wide a space, and his former error enabled Napoleon to at once see an opportunity to ruin him by his old device of pouring the full shock of his strength on the centre. In fact, so apparently weak was the position of the Austrians at this time that the emperor, in his bulletin of the engagement sent to Paris, had this to say:

> This disposition of the army appeared so absurd that some snare was dreaded, and the emperor hesitated some time before ordering the easy dispositions which he had to make in order to annul those of the enemy, and render them fatal to him.

At sunrise the cannonade commenced upon the two lines. Napoleon, perceiving that the Prince of Rosemberg was moving upon Marshal Davoust, repaired in person to the right wing, which he reinforced with the *cuirassiers* under General Arrighe, and caused twelve pieces of light artillery to advance upon the flank of the enemy's columns. After an obstinate engagement of two hours' duration, Davoust succeeded in repulsing his adversary as far as Neusiedel.

While the French Army thus signalized itself by success in the beginning of the day, the battle was carried along the rest of the line with great determination. The fire of musketry and cannon was now general on that vast front of nearly three leagues, along which 300,000 men and 1100 pieces of cannon were arrayed against each other. It was a principle of Napoleon's that by concentrating on one point the action of certain special arms that grand effects were to be produced, and therefore it was that he bestowed an immense amount of artillery on the Guard and had kept under his hand a reserve of fourteen regiments of *cuirassiers*.

The emperor now ordered that the whole of the artillery of the Guard, together with all that could be spared by the several corps, advance at a gallop. Just then General de Wrede arrived on the ground with twenty-five pieces of excellent artillery, and solicited the honour of taking part in the decisive movement, to which Napoleon consented. He then sent for General Macdonald, his design being to shake the Austrian centre with 100 guns, and then pierce it with Macdonald's bayonets and Nansouty's sabres. These orders were obeyed on the instant.

While awaiting the carrying out of these movements, impatient for the arrival of Macdonald and Lauriston, Napoleon rode about the field on his Persian horse of dazzling whiteness, giving orders to his *aides* constantly. The cannonading had by this time acquired the frequency of musket-firing, and everybody shuddered at the thought of seeing the man, on whose life so many destinies depended, struck by one of those blind messengers of death. The hundred guns were now ranged in line and instantly began the most tremendous slaughter ever known to those who witnessed it. Napoleon observed with his glass the effect of that formidable battery, saw the enemy's artillery dismounted, and was satisfied with the correctness of his own conceptions. But artillery was not sufficient to break the Austrian centre; bayonets, too, were requisite.

The intrepid Macdonald now advanced at the head of his corps under a deluge of fire, leaving the ground covered at every step with his dead and wounded, still closing the ranks without wavering, and communicating his own gallant bearing to his soldiers. "What a brave man!" Napoleon exclaimed several times, as he saw him thus march under the shower of grape and bullets. The archduke's centre, shaken by the fire of a hundred pieces of ordinance, retreats, as does also his right. Davoust now shakes the Austrian left wing, and as he does so Napoleon exclaims: "The battle is won!,"—and so it was. Lauris-

Napoleon at the Battle of Eylau

ton, with a hundred pieces of cannon, and Macdonald at the head of a chosen division, charged the Austrians in the centre and broke through it. The victory was for the French once more.

At length the Austrian Army fell into disorder, their centre was driven back two or three miles out of the line; cries of alarm were heard, the right wing gave way and the left soon followed. The rout was now complete. At the close of the battle there remained 20,000 prisoners, besides all the artillery and baggage in the hands of the French. Napoleon showed all his courage and talents on this day, and was ever in the hottest of the action, though the appearance of his retinue drew on him showers of grape by which he was repeatedly endangered. From early morning, he was occupied in galloping through the different lines, encouraging the troops by his presence and persuasive eloquence; many being killed by the balls that flew about him. It was observed that the enemy's fire was particularly directed against the emperor; in consequence of which Napoleon was obliged to change his *surtout* three times. The *aides-de-camp* and officers of the staff were also given to understand that they should keep more at a distance, and the regiments were instructed not to salute the emperor with acclamations at the moment he was passing.

On the following morning, after surveying the field of battle, Napoleon went to place himself in the midst of his troops who were about to pursue the retreating enemy. He walked round the bivouacs without either hat or sword, his hands being crossed behind him, and as he talked with the soldiers of his Guard his manner and countenance expressed the utmost satisfaction and confidence. On passing Macdonald, with whom he had lost favour, and who had not followed the fortunes of the emperor for some years, Napoleon stopped and held out his hand, saying:

> Shake hands, Macdonald; no more animosity between us, we must henceforth be friends; and, as a pledge of my sincerity, I will send you your marshal's staff, which you so gloriously earned in yesterday's battle.

The general, pressing the emperor's hand affectionately, exclaimed: "Ah, sire; with us it is henceforth for life and for death." The act was heightened by the grace and good will with which it was performed. The same rank was granted a few days after to General Oudinot and the Duke of Ragusa (Marmont), for their eminent services.

After the battle Napoleon recognized among the dead a colonel who had displeased him. He stopped and looked at the mangled body for a moment and then said, "I regret not having told him before the battle that I had forgotten everything."

The archduke fled in great confusion as far as Znaim in Moravia, abandoning, as trophies of his defeat, ten standards, forty pieces of cannon, nearly 18,000 prisoners, nine thousand wounded, and a great quantity of equipage.

The loss of the French, while much less than that of the enemy, was 6,000 wounded and 2,600 killed. Marshal Bessieres was among the former. The French Army had to lament the loss of the valiant LaSalle, one of the first generals of light cavalry. His death was greatly regretted both by the emperor and the army. He was considered the best light cavalry officer for outpost duty and had the surest eye. He could take in a whole district in a moment, and seldom made a mistake, so that his reports on the enemy's position were clear and precise. He was a handsome man of bright wit, an excellent horseman and brave to the point of rashness. He first attracted the notice of General Bonaparte at the Battle of Rivoli when he galloped down a descent to which the fleeing Austrians had resorted to escape, and took some thousand prisoners under the eyes of General Bonaparte and the army. From that time LaSalle was in high favour with Napoleon who promoted him rapidly and took him to Egypt where he made him colonel. He distinguished himself at Austerlitz and in Prussia.

The Imperial Council perceived that further resistance was useless and an armistice was agreed to at Znaim. Napoleon, on returning to Vienna, continued occupied until October. For the third time he found himself master of the destinies of the House of Lorraine, which he had accused of ingratitude and perjury before Europe and in the face of history; for the third time this conqueror, so violent in his menaces, so overwhelming in his reproaches, eagerly received the proposals of those who had provoked the war, whose hopes had been overthrown, and whose resources were destroyed on the day of Wagram. The results of the battle, without being as extraordinary as those of Austerlitz, Jena or Friedland, were great nevertheless.

The announcement of the armistice with Austria put an end, in effect, to all hostile demonstrations on the Continent, except in the Peninsula, and Germany in apparent tranquillity awaited the result of the negotiations of Vienna.

A few days after Napoleon had returned to Schoenbrunn from Moravia he narrowly escaped the dagger of a young man who rushed upon him at a grand review of the Imperial Guard, and while in the midst of all his staff. Berthier and Rapp threw themselves upon the would-be assassin and disarmed him at the moment when his knife was about to enter the emperor's body.

Napoleon demanded to know what motive had actuated the assassin. "What injury," said he, "have I done to you?"

"To me personally, none," answered the youth, "but you are the oppressor of my country; the tyrant of the world; and to have put you to death would have been the highest glory of a man of honour."

The youth, a son of a clergyman of Erfurt named Staaps, was condemned to death. It is said Napoleon wished to pardon Staaps, whose frankness and courage had struck him, and in whom, besides, he saw but a blind instrument of the passions incited by the monarchy; but his orders arrived too late. The young German met his death with the greatest coolness, exclaiming: "Hail, Liberty! Germany forever! Death to the tyrant!"

The length to which the negotiations with Austria were protracted excited much wonder, but Napoleon, who was occupied incessantly with his ministers and generals, and seldom showed himself in public, had other business on hand besides his treaty with the Emperor Francis. His long-standing quarrel with the Pope now reached its crisis, growing out of the Concordat, involving affairs in Spain and Portugal, and finally by a refusal of the *pontiff* to acquiesce in the Berlin and Milan decrees against England's commerce. On the 17th of May Napoleon had issued from Vienna his final decree declaring the temporal sovereignty of the Pope to be wholly at an end, incorporating Rome with the French Empire, and declaring it to be his second city, settling a handsome pension on the holy father in his spiritual capacity, and appointing a committee of administration for the civil government of Rome. The Pope replied with a bull of excommunication against Napoleon which finally resulted in the removal of His Holiness to Fontainebleau where he continued a prisoner, though treated personally with respect and magnificence, during more than three years.

The treaty with Austria was at last signed at Schoenbrunn on the 14th of October, Austria giving up territory to the amount of 45,000 square miles, with a population of four millions, and depriving her of her last seaport. Yet, when compared with the signal triumphs of the campaign at Wagram, the terms on which the conqueror signed the peace were universally looked upon as remarkable for moderation. Napoleon afterwards expressed himself as highly culpable in having left Austria too powerful after the affair at Wagram, using the following words on that occasion:

"The day after the battle I ought to have published in the order of the day that I would ratify no treaty with Austria, until after a previous separation of the crown of Austria, Hungary, and Bohemia; to be placed on three different heads."

Napoleon quitted Vienna on the 16th of October, and was congratulated by the public bodies of Paris at Fontainebleau on the 14th of November as "the greatest of heroes, who never achieved victories but for the happiness of the world." When he reappeared at the palace at Fontainebleau on Oct. 26th 1809, crowned with the victory of Wagram, there was one to whom dark forebodings came—Josephine felt that her fate was sealed. In fact, as a modern writer has said, the immediate result of Wagram was the divorce from the empress.

The first public intimation of a measure which had for a considerable period occupied Napoleon's thoughts came from the emperor himself when he said, in an imperial speech in which he described the events of the past year, and the state of France:

> I and my house will ever be found ready to sacrifice everything, even our own dearest ties and feelings, to the welfare of the French people.

12

Campaign of Russia

Long before Napoleon assumed the imperial title his hopes of offspring from the union with Josephine were at an end, but the empress lived for a time in hope that the emperor would be content to adopt her son Eugene. Louis Bonaparte married Hortense Beauharnais, daughter of Josephine, and an infant son became so much the favourite of Napoleon that the empress, as well as others, come to regard this boy as the heir of France. But the child died early and the emperor then began to direct his thoughts towards the best means of dissolving his marriage with Josephine, in order that he might form an alliance with some daughter of Russia, or other imperial family. The Emperor Alexander was approached on this subject, and informed that one of his sisters, the Grand Duchess Anne, would be acceptable, but the empress-mother hesitated, and this being taken by Napoleon as a refusal, he sought the hand of the Archduchess Marie Louise, daughter of the Emperor Francis of Austria.

On the 15th of December, 1809, the emperor summoned his council and announced to them, that at the expense of all his personal feelings, he, devoted wholly to the welfare of the State, had resolved to separate himself from his most dear consort. He said:

> Arrived at the age of forty years I may conceive the hope of living sufficiently long to elevate, in my mind and after my ideas, the children with which it shall please Providence to bless me. God knows how much this resolution has cost my heart; .... I should also add, that, far from ever having to complain, I have on the contrary, only had cause to laud the attachment and tenderness of my beloved wife. She has adorned fifteen years of my life. The recollection thereof will always remain graven

on my heart.

Josephine then appeared among them, and not without tears, expressed her acquiescence in the decree. She said:

> I believe I acknowledge all these sentiments by consenting to the dissolution of a marriage which, at present, is an obstacle to the welfare of France, which deprives it of being one day governed by the descendants of a great man, so evidently raised by Providence to efface the ills of a terrible revolution, and reestablish the altar, the throne, and social order.

The council, after addressing the emperor and empress on the nobleness of their mutual sacrifice, accepted and ratified the dissolution of marriage. The title of empress was preserved to Josephine for life and a pension of two million *francs*, to which Napoleon afterwards added a third million from his privy purse. She then retired from the Tuileries, residing thenceforth mostly at Malmaison, and in the course of a few weeks Austria was called upon for her daughter.

Having given her hand at Vienna on the 11th of March, 1810, to Berthier, who had the honour to represent the person of the emperor, the young archduchess set out for France on the 13th.

On the 28th, as her carriage was proceeding towards Soissons, Napoleon rode up to it, in a plain dress, altogether unattended, and introduced himself to his proxy bride. She had never seen his person till then, and it is said her first exclamation was, "Your Majesty's pictures have not done you justice."

They spent the evening at the *château* of Compiegne and a religious marriage was celebrated on the 1st of April at St. Cloud amidst every circumstance of splendour; the next day they made their entry into the capital. Napoleon in his exile said that "the Spanish ulcer" and the Austrian match were the two main causes of his ruin;—and they both contributed to it largely, although by no means equally. The exile's own opinion was that the error lay, not in seeking a bride of imperial birth, but in choosing her at Vienna. Had he persisted in his demands, the *Czar*, he doubted not, would have granted him his sister; the proud dreams of Tilsit would have been realized, and Paris and St. Petersburg become the only two capitals of Europe. Possibly, then, he would not have had occasion to say that he "set his foot upon an abyss of roses" when he married Marie.

Had he married a daughter of France, or even an imperial princess of Russia, he could have done so without the sacrifice of the prestige of the nobility, and even the divinity of the people he had so gloriously contended for; but when it was announced that he had contracted an alliance with the House of Hapsburg,—that hated race against whom and whose principles he had fought a hundred battles, they were convinced that no good would come of it—and they were right.

The war, meanwhile, continued without interruption in the Peninsula; whither, but for his marriage Napoleon would certainly have repaired in person, after the peace of Schoenbrunn left him at ease. So illy was that Spanish campaign conducted during Napoleon's absence that not an inch of soil could be counted by the French beyond their outposts. Their troops were continually harassed and thinned by the indomitable guerrillas who acted singly or in bands as occasion offered.

The emperor's marriage was speedily followed on the 20th of April, 1811, by the birth of a son and heir whom Napoleon announced to the waiting courtiers in these words: "It is a King of Rome!" The happy event, announced to the populace by the firing of one hundred and one guns, was received with many demonstrations of loyal enthusiasm. Even Josephine joined in expressing her satisfaction at the event which seemed to portend so much for the founding of a Napoleonic dynasty which the emperor now saw possible by direct lineage.

When the Emperor of Russia was informed of Napoleon's approaching nuptials with the Austrian princess his first exclamation was, "Then the next thing will be to drive us back into our forests." In truth the conferences at Erfurt had but skinned over a wound which nothing could have cured but a total alteration of Napoleon's policy. The Russian nation suffered so much from the continental system that the *Czar* soon found himself compelled to relax the decrees drawn up at Tilsit in the spirit of those previously declared at Berlin and Milan. Certain harbours were opened partially for the admission of colonial produce and the export of native productions; and there ensued a series of indignant reclamations on the part of Napoleon, and haughty evasions on that of the *Czar*, which, ere long, satisfied all near observers that Russia would not be slow to avail herself of any favourable opportunity of once more appealing to arms.

During the summer of 1811 the relations of Russia and France were becoming every day more dubious and when towards the close of it the Emperor of Austria published a rescript granting a free passage through his territories to the troops of his son-in-law, England, ever watchful of her great enemy, perceived clearly that France was about to have an ally. Alexander had long since ceased to regard the friendship of the great man as a blessing of heaven. Of the solemn cordiality of Tilsit, and the more recent meeting at Erfurt, there remained in the soul of the *Czar* naught but the displeasure and resentment arising from extinct affection and deceived hopes.

From the moment in which the Russian government began to reclaim seriously against certain parts of his conduct, Napoleon increased by degrees his military force in the north of Germany, and the Grand Duchy of Warsaw, and advanced considerable bodies of troops nearer and nearer to the *Czar's* Polish frontier. These preparations were met by similar movements on the other side; yet, during many months, the hope of terminating the differences by negotiations was not abandoned. The regulations of the Continental System were especially objected to by Russia, and the *Czar* having lent his ear to the representations of the English cabinet, asked that they be dispensed with as he declared he could no longer submit to see the commerce of an independent empire trammelled for the purpose of serving the policy of a foreign power.

Napoleon admitted that it might be necessary to modify the system complained of, and expressed his belief that it would be found possible to devise some middle course by which the commercial interests of France and Russia might be reconciled. A very considerable relaxation in the enforcement of the Berlin code was at last effected, and a license system arranged which admitted Alexander to a share in the pecuniary advantages. Had there been no cause of quarrel between these powers except what appeared on the face of their negotiations, it is hardly to be doubted but a new treaty might have been effected. The *Czar*, however, from the hour of Marie Louise's marriage, felt a conviction that the diminution of the Russian power in the north of Europe would form the next great object of Napoleon's ambition. The *Czar* therefore assured himself that if war must come, there could be no question as to the policy of bringing it on before Austria had entirely recovered from the effects of the campaign of Wagram, and, above all, while the Peninsula continued to occupy 200,000 of Napoleon's troops.

As concerned the Spanish armies, it might still be said that King Joseph was in military possession of all but some fragments of his kingdom. The English had been victorious in Portugal and the French troops in Spain lost more lives in this incessant struggle, wherein no glory could be achieved, than in any similar period spent in any regular campaign; and Joseph, while the question of peace or war with Russia was yet undecided, became so weary of his situation, that he earnestly entreated Napoleon to place the crown of Spain on some other head. Such were the circumstances under which the eventful year of 1812 began.

Most persuasive appeals were made to Napoleon by his ministers to refrain from entering into a campaign of aggression against Russia. To Fouché, minister of police, Napoleon is reported to have said, in reply:

> Is it my fault that the height of power which I have attained compels me to ascend to the dictatorship of the world? My destiny is not yet accomplished,—the picture exists as yet only in outline. There must be one code, one court of appeal, and one coinage for all Europe. The states of Europe must be melted into one nation, and Paris be its capital.

In the arguments used by Napoleon's advisers at this time they attempted to show him, among other things, the great extent of Alexander's resources,—his 400,000 regulars, and 50,000 Cossacks, already known to be in arms—and the enormous population on which he had the means of drawing for recruits; the enthusiastic national feeling of the Muscovites; the distance of their country; the severity of their climate; the opportunity which a war would afford to England of urging her successes in Spain; and the chance of Germany rising in insurrection in case of any reverses.

With the greater part of the population of France, and especially with the army, the threatened war was exceedingly popular. Russia, the most extensive empire in Europe, it was fondly imagined, was on the point of falling before the power of the Great Nation; and England would then be left to struggle, unaided, for mastery with France. It was deemed a certain pledge of victory, since the emperor himself was to lead his veteran legions to the new scene of triumph.

Cardinal Fesch, uncle of the emperor, appealed to him on other grounds. The cardinal had been greatly affected by the treatment of the Pope, and he contemplated this new war with dread,—as likely to bring down the vengeance of heaven upon the head of one who had dared to trample on its vice-regent. Napoleon led the cardinal to the window, opened it, and pointing upwards, said, "Do you see yonder star?"

"No Sire," replied the cardinal.

"But I see it," answered Napoleon; and the churchman was dismissed.

Trusting to this star,—his "Star of Destiny" in which he yet firmly believed,—he was far from being awed when in April, 1812, Russia declared war against France. It was an indefensible violation of the treaty of Tilsit, but it showed Napoleon that Europe was determined to crush him, and he rallied the forces of his empire for a more terrible conflict than he had yet been summoned to.

Not satisfied with disposing everything for war in the bosom of the empire, Napoleon, who wished to march into Russia at the head of his vast army of Europe, busied himself in forming and cementing, externally, powerful allies. Two treaties were concluded to this effect; the one with Prussia and the other with Austria on the 24th of February and 14th of March, 1812.

Alexander's minister was ordered in the beginning of April to demand the withdrawal of the northern troops, together with the evacuation of the fortress in Pomerania, in case the French Government still entertained a wish to negotiate. Napoleon replied that he was not accustomed to regulate the distribution of his forces by the suggestions of a foreign power. The ambassador then demanded his passports and quitted Paris.

The Emperor of France was confident, and seems to have entertained no doubt of his success in the coming campaign. He said:

> The war is a wise measure, called for by the true interests of France and the general welfare. The great power I have already attained compels me to assume an universal dictatorship. My views are not ambitions. I desire to obtain no further acquisition; and reserve to myself only the glory of doing good, and the blessings of posterity.

Leaving Paris with the empress on the 9th of May, 1812, on his way to join the Grand Army then forming on the Polish frontier, the imperial pair were accompanied by a continual triumph. Not merely in France but throughout Germany the ringing of bells, music and the most enthusiastic greetings awaited them wherever they appeared. On May 16th, the emperor arrived at Dresden where the Emperor of Austria, the Kings of Prussia, Naples, Wirtemberg, and Westphalia and almost every German sovereign of inferior rank had been invited to meet him. He had sent to request the *Czar* also to appear in this brilliant assemblage, as a last chance of an amicable arrangement, but the messenger could not obtain admission to Alexander's presence.

Marie Louise was now sent back to France and the Russian campaign began. Marshal Ney, with one great division of the army, had already passed the Vistula; Junot, with another, occupied both sides of the Oder. The *Czar* was known to be at Wilna, collecting the forces of his immense empire and entrusting the general arrangements of the approaching campaign to Marshal Barclay de Tolly, an officer who had been born and educated in Germany. The season was advancing and it was time that the question of peace or war should be forced to a decision.

Napoleon, before leaving the gay court of Dresden, where he was hailed as "the king of kings," dispatched Count de Narbonne to the Emperor Alexander to make a fresh attempt at negotiation in order to spare the shedding of more blood. On his return Narbonne stated that "he had found the Russians neither depressed nor boasting; that the result of all the replies of the *Czar* was, that they preferred war to a disgraceful peace; that they would take special care not to risk a battle with an adversary so formidable; and, finally, that they were determined to make every sacrifice to protract the war, and drive back the invader."

Napoleon arrived at Dantzic on the 7th of June, and during the fortnight which ensued, it was known that the final communications between him and Alexander were taking place. On the 22nd the French emperor broke silence in a bulletin in which he said:

> Soldiers, Russia is dragged on by her fate; her destiny must be accomplished. Let us march; let us cross the Niemen, let us carry war into her territories. Our second campaign of Poland will be as glorious as the first; but our second peace shall carry with it its own guarantee. It shall put an end forever to that haughty influence which Russia has exercised for fifty years over the affairs of Europe.

The *Czar* announced the termination of the negotiations by stating the innumerable efforts to obtain peace and concluded in these words:

> Soldiers, you fight for your religion, your liberty and your native land. Your emperor is amongst you; and God is the enemy of the aggressor.

Napoleon reviewed the greater part of his troops on the battlefield of Friedland, and having assured them of still more splendid victories over the same enemy, issued his final orders to the chief officers of his army. The disposition of his forces when the campaign commenced was as follows:—

The left wing, commanded by Macdonald, and amounting to 30,000 men, had orders to march through Courland, with the view, if possible, of outflanking the Russian right, and gaining the possession of sea coast in the direction of Riga. The right wing, composed almost wholly of Austrians, 30,000 in number, and commanded by Schwartzenberg, was stationed on the Volhynian frontier. Between these moved the various corps forming the grand central army under the general superintendence of Napoleon himself, *viz.*, those of Davoust, Ney, Jerome Bonaparte, Eugene Beauharnais, Prince Poniatowski, Junot and Victor; and in numbers amounting to 250,000 men. The communication of the centre and the left was maintained by the corps of Oudinot, and those of the centre and the extreme right by the corps of Regnier, who had with him the Saxon auxiliaries and the Polish legion of Dombrowski. The chief command of the whole cavalry of the host was assigned to Murat who was in person at the headquarters of the emperor, having immediately under his order three divisions of horse—those of Grouchy, Montbrun and Nantousy. Augereau, with his division was to remain in the north of Germany to watch over Berlin and protect the communications with France. Napoleon's base of operations extended over full one hundred leagues, and the heads of his various columns were so distributed that the Russians could not guess whether St. Petersburg or Moscow formed the main object of his march.

The Russian Army, under de Tolly, had its headquarters at Wilna, and consisted, at the opening of the campaign, of 120,000 men. Considerably to the left lay "the second army," as it was called, of 80,000 men under Bagration with whom were Platoff and 12,000 of his Cossacks; while at the extreme of that wing, "the army of Volhynia," 20,000 strong, commanded by Tormazoff, watched Schwartzenberg. On the right of de Tolly was Witgenstein with 30,000 men and between these again and the sea, the corps of Essen 10,000 strong. Behind the whole line two armies of reserve were rapidly forming at Novogorod and Smolensk, each, probably, of about 20,000 men. The Russians actually in the field at the opening of the campaign were, then, as nearly as can be computed, 260,000; while Napoleon was prepared to cross the Niemen at the head of 470,000 men.

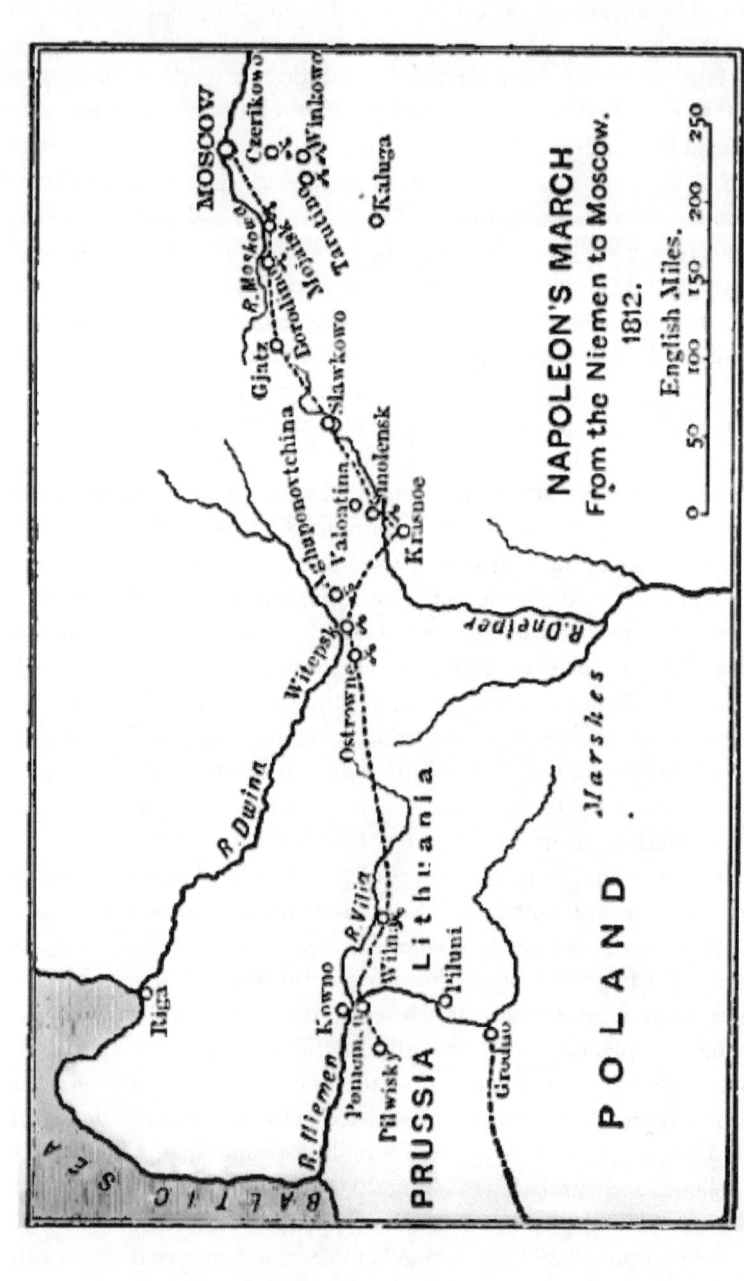

The *Czar* was resolved from the beginning to act entirely on the defensive and to draw Napoleon, if possible, into the heart of his own country ere he gave him battle. The various divisions of the Russian force had orders to fall back leisurely as the enemy advanced, destroying whatever they could not take with them, and halting only at certain points where intrenched camps had already been formed for their reception.

The difficulty of feeding half a million men in a country deliberately wasted beforehand, and separated by so great a space from Germany, to say nothing of France, was sure to increase at every hour and every step. Alexander's great object was, therefore, to husband his own strength until the Polar winter should set in around the strangers, and bring the miseries which he thus foresaw to a crisis.

Napoleon, on the other hand, had calculated on being met by the Russians at, or even in advance of their own frontier, (as he had been by the Austrians in the campaign of Austerlitz and by the Prussians in that of Jena); of gaining a great battle, marching immediately either to St. Petersburg or Moscow, and dictating a peace within the walls of one of the *Czar's* own palaces.

On June 24th the Grand Imperial Army, consolidated into three masses, began their passage of the Niemen,—Jerome Bonaparte at Grodno, Eugene at Pilony, and Napoleon himself near Kowno. The emperor rode on in front of his army at two o'clock in the morning to reconnoitre the banks, escaping observation by wearing a Polish cloak and hat; his horse stumbled and he fell to the ground. "A bad omen—a Roman would return," someone remarked. After a minute investigation he discovered a spot near the village of Poinemen, above Kowno, suitable for the passage of his troops, and gave orders for three bridges to be thrown across at nightfall. The first who crossed the river were a few sappers in a boat. All was deserted and silent on the foreign soil, and no one appeared to oppose their proceedings with the exception of a single armed Cossack, who asked, with an appearance of surprise, who they were and what they wanted. "Frenchmen," was the reply; "we come to make war upon your emperor; to take Wilna, and deliver Poland."

The Cossack struck spurs into his horse and three French soldiers discharged their pieces into the gloomy depths of the woods, where they had lost sight of him, in token of hostility. There came on at the same moment a tremendous thunderstorm. Thus began the fatal invasion.

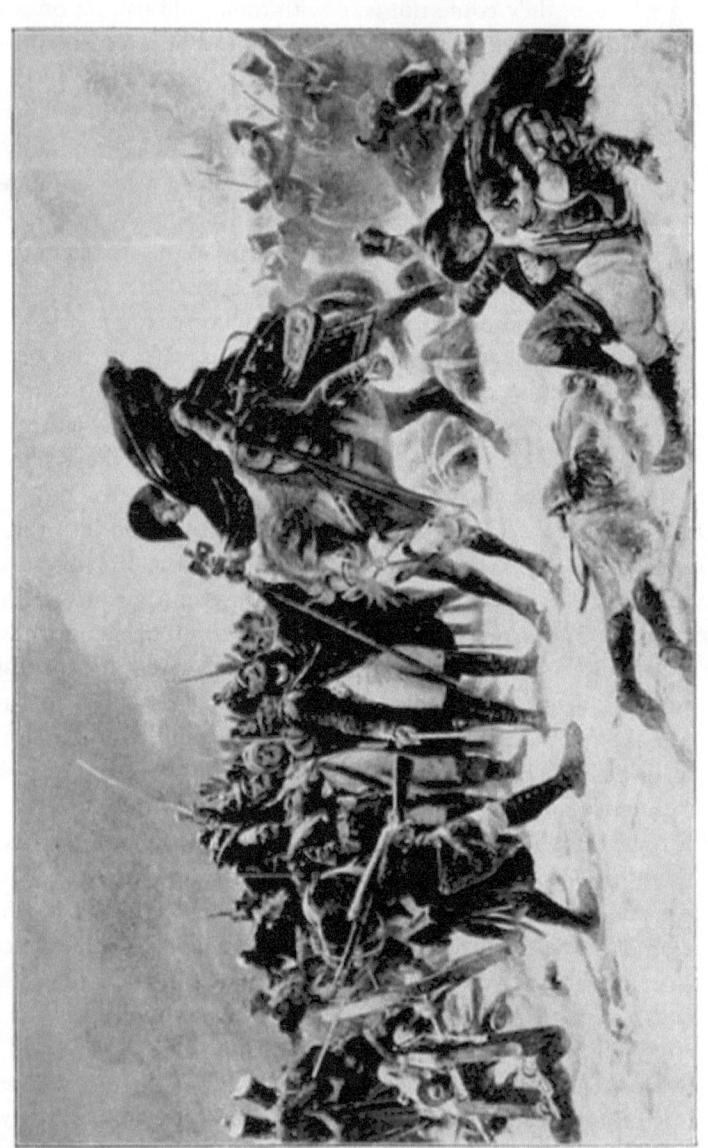

The 14th Line at Eylau

The passage of the troops was impeded for a time; as the bridge over the Vilia, a stream running into the Niemen, had been broken by the Russians. The emperor, however, despising this obstacle, ordered a Polish squadron of horse to swim the river. They instantly obeyed; but on reaching the middle the current proved too strong for them, broke their ranks, and swept away and engulfed many of them. Even during their last struggles the brave fellows turned their faces towards the shore, where Napoleon was watching their unavailing efforts with the deepest emotion, and shouted with their dying breath, "*Vive l'Empereur!*"

Three of these noble-spirited patriots uttered this cry when only a part of their faces was above the waters. The army was struck with a mixture of horror and admiration. Napoleon watched the scene apparently unmoved, but gave every order he could devise for the purpose of saving as many of them as possible, though with little effect. It is probable that his strongest feeling, even at the time, was a presentiment that this disastrous event was but the beginning of others, at once tremendous and extensive.

As these enormous hosts advanced into the Russian territory Alexander withdrew his armies as deliberately as the invader pushed on. Wilna, the capital itself, was evacuated two days before the French came in sight of it, and Napoleon took up his quarters there on the 28th of June. Here it was found that all the magazines, which he counted on seizing, had been burnt before the Russians withdrew. Already the imperial bulletins began to denounce the "barbarous method" in which the enemy resolved to conduct his defence.

Napoleon remained twenty days at Wilna during which time he redoubled his efforts to secure quantities of provisions which were to be conveyed along with his army; these were to render him independent of the countries through which he might pass. The destruction of the magazines at Wilna reassured him that he had judged well in departing from the old system of marauding, which had been adopted in previous campaigns with success. At the end of this period Napoleon became aware that while the contracts entered into by his war minister were adequate for the army's needs, the handling of such enormous quantities of provisions, under the most favourable circumstances, must be slow and in some degree uncertain. Thus the emperor found himself under the necessity, either of laying aside his invasion for another year, or of urging it in the face of every difficulty, all of which he had foreseen except the slowness of a commissariat department.

When Napoleon arrived at Wilna, he was regarded by the people as their liberator. A deputation was sent to him by the Diet of Warsaw entreating his assistance towards the restoration of their ancient kingdom, the re-establishment of Poland having been proclaimed. They came, they said, to solicit Napoleon the Great to pronounce these few words: "Let the kingdom of Poland exist!" and then it would exist; that all the Poles would devote themselves to the orders of the fourth French dynasty, to whom ages were but a moment, and space no more than a point.

Napoleon's reply was not satisfactory, "In my position, I have many interests to reconcile," he said "and many duties to fulfil." His answer was so extremely guarded, that the Poles became dissatisfied and offered little or no support to the French. Bourrienne says:[1]

> Had Poland been regenerated Napoleon would have found the means of succeeding in his expedition. In his march upon Moscow, his rear and supplies would have been protected, and he would have secured that retreat which subsequent reverses rendered but too needful.

During this delay Alexander was enabled to withdraw the troops which he had been maintaining on the flanks of his European domains and bring them all to the assistance of his main army. The enthusiasm of the Russian nation appeared in the extraordinary rapidity with which supplies of every kind were poured at the feet of the *Czar*. From every quarter he received voluntary offers of men, money, and whatever might assist in the prosecution of the war. The Grand Duchess Anne, whose hand Napoleon had solicited, set the example by raising a regiment on her estate. Platoff, the veteran *hetman* of the Cossacks, promised his only daughter and 200,000 *rubles* to the man by whose hand Napoleon should fall. Noblemen everywhere raised troops, and displayed their patriotism by serving in the ranks themselves and entrusting the command to experienced officers chosen by the government.

Napoleon at length re-entered the field without having done much to remedy the disorders of his commissariat. He at first determined to make St. Petersburg his mark, counting much on the effects which a triumphal entry into the capital would produce throughout the coun-

---

1. *Memoirs of Napoleon Bonaparte:* in Volumes 1, 2 and 3 by Louis Antoine Fauvelet de Bourrienne also published by Leonaur.

try, but his troops meeting with some reverses at Riga and Dunaburg, he changed his plans and resolved to march on Moscow instead.

The centre of the army was now thrown forward under Davoust with the view of turning Barclay's position and cutting off his communication with Bagration. This brought about an engagement with the latter on the 23rd of July near Mohilow, the French remaining in possession of the town. The Russian commander in retreating informed Barclay that he was now marching, not on Vitepsk, but on Smolensk.

During the three days of the 25th, 26th and 27th of July the French were again victorious. Napoleon halted at Vitepsk for several days in order to allow his troops to recuperate. On the 8th of August the emperor quitted Vitepsk and after a partial engagement at Krasnoi on the 14th, came in sight of Smolensk on the 16th. On the 10th of August Napoleon was observed to write eight letters to Davoust, and nearly as many to each of his commanders. He said in one of his letters to Davoust:

> If the enemy defends Smolensk as I am tempted to believe he will, we shall have a decisive engagement there, and we cannot have too large a force. Orcha will become the central point of the army. Everything induces me to believe that there will be a great battle at Smolensk.

The day on which the combat at Krasnoi was fought happened to be the emperor's birthday. There was no intention of keeping it in these immense solitudes, and under the present circumstances of peril and anxiety. There could be no heartfelt festival without a complete victory. Murat and Ney, however, on giving in the report of their recent success, could not refrain from complimenting the emperor on the anniversary of his nativity. A salute from a hundred pieces of artillery was now heard,—fired according to their orders.

Napoleon, with a look of displeasure, observed, that in Russia it was important to be economical of French powder; but he was informed in reply, that it was Russian powder, and had been taken the night before. The idea of having his birthday celebrated at the expense of the Russians made Napoleon smile.

Prince Eugene also paid his compliments to the emperor on this occasion, but was cut short by Napoleon saying, "Everything is preparing for a battle. I will gain that, and then we will see Moscow." Ségur says that Eugene was heard to observe, on leaving the imperial tent, "Moscow will destroy us!"

The first and second armies of the *Czar*, under Bagration and Barclay, having at length effected a junction, retired with 120,000 men behind the river which flows at the back of this town.

As soon as Napoleon saw these masses of men approaching from the distance he clapped his hands with joy, exclaiming, "At last I have them!" The moment that was to decide the fate of Russia or the French Army, had apparently arrived.

Napoleon passed along the line, and assigned to each commander his station, leaving an extensive plain unoccupied in front between himself and the Dneiper. This he offered to the enemy as a field of battle, but instead of accepting the challenge Barclay and Bagration were seen next morning in full retreat.

During the night the Russian garrison had withdrawn and joined the army across the river. Before they departed they committed the city to flames, and, the buildings being chiefly of wood, the conflagration, according to the French bulletin, "resembling in its fury an eruption of Vesuvius."

"Never," said Napoleon, "was war conducted with such inhumanity; the Russians treat their own country as if it were that of an enemy." It now, however, began to be difficult in the extreme to extinguish the flames created by the retreating Russians. The emperor in person used every effort to stop the progress of the devouring element and render succour to the wounded. Gourgaud says:

> Napoleon is of all generals, whether ancient or modern, the one who has paid the greatest attention to the wounded. The intoxication of victory never could make him forget them, and his first thought, after every battle, was always of them.

It was very evident that the Russian commander had no desire that Napoleon should establish himself in winter quarters at this point. From Smolensk the Russians retreated to Dorogoburg, and thence to Viasma; halting at each of these towns and deliberately burning them in face of the enemy. Having returned to Smolensk, Napoleon became a prey to the most harassing reflections on the opportunity which had so lately escaped him of destroying the whole of the Russian army, and attaining a speedy conclusion of peace. Uncertainty began to gain ground with him; vague presentiments made him desire to terminate as soon as possible this distant campaign. The emperor said on arriving at Ougea:

We are too far engaged to fall back, and if I only proposed to myself the glory of warlike exploits, I should have but to return to Smolensk, there plant my eagles, and content myself with extending my right and left arms which would crush Witgenstein and Tormasoff. These operations would be brilliant; they would finish the campaign very satisfactorily, but they would not terminate the war. Our troops may advance, but are incapable of remaining stationary, motion may keep them together: a halt or retreat would at once dissolve them. Ours is an army of attack, not of defence; of operation, not of position. We must advance upon Moscow, gain possession of that capital, and there dictate terms of peace to the *Czar!* Peace is before us; we are but eight days march from it; when the object is so nearly attained, it would be unwise to deliberate. Let us, therefore, march upon Moscow!

At this period Barclay was appointed to the war ministry at St. Petersburg, and Kutusoff, who assumed the command in his stead, was beginning to doubt whether the system of retreat had not been far enough persisted in. Napoleon ordered a vigorous pursuit of the enemy, hoping to come up with and crush him, before he could reach his ancient capital. The honour of marching with the advance guard devolved upon Marshal Ney, who gloriously justified the confidence of Napoleon by the intelligence and bravery which he displayed at the battle of Valoutina. This was a most sanguinary fight. Four times were the Russians driven from their positions, and on each occasion, brought up reinforcements, and retook them; at length they were finally overthrown by the valorous Gudin who charged at the head of his division, the vigour and impetuosity of which led the enemy to believe that they were exposed to the shock of the Imperial Guard.

Thirty thousand men were brought into action on either side, and the slaughter was terrible. Much individual bravery was also displayed on this occasion. But for the failure of Junot,—who had begun to show signs of approaching insanity,—to faithfully execute his orders, the victory might have been decisive. The emperor was much gratified, however, at the conduct of his troops at Valoutina. He repaired in person to the field of battle and passed in review the divers regiments which had distinguished themselves there. Gourgaud says:

Arrived at the 7th Light Infantry, he ordered the captains to advance, and said to them, 'Show me the best officer of the regiment.' 'Sire, they are all good—' 'that is no answer; come at least to the conclusion of Themistocles; "I am the first; the second is my neighbour."'

At length Captain Moncey, who was absent on account of his wounds, was named.

"What," said the emperor, "Moncey who was my page! the son of the marshal! Seek another!"

"Sire, he is the best."

"Ah, well!" said Napoleon, "I shall give him the decoration."

Up till this time the 127th regiment had marched without an eagle, having had no opportunity of distinguishing itself. The Imperial ensign was now delivered to it by Napoleon's own hands.

The new Russian general at length resolved to comply with the clamorous entreaties of his troops and fixed on a strong position between Borodino and Moskowa on the highroad to Moscow, where he determined to await the attack of Napoleon who was pushing the war vigorously, sword in hand, in the hopes of closing hostilities by one pitched battle.

On the 5th of September Napoleon came in sight of the position of Kutusoff and succeeded in carrying a redoubt which had been erected to guard the high-road to Moscow. This was effected at the bayonet point, though not without great slaughter on either side.

The next day the two armies lay in presence of each other preparing for a great contest. On the eve of, and before daybreak on the 6th, the emperor was on horseback, wrapped in his gray coat, and exhibited all the alacrity of his younger days. On his return to headquarters he found a courier had arrived with dispatches announcing Marmont's defeat and the deliverance of Salamanca into the hands of Wellington. M. de Beausset also arrived bringing from Paris a portrait of Napoleon's son which deeply moved the emperor. He caused the picture to be placed outside his tent where it was viewed by his officers. He then said to his secretary, "Take it away, and guard it carefully; he sees a field of battle too early."

The Russians were posted on an elevated plain; having a wood on their right flank, their left on one of the villages, and a deep ravine, the bed of a small stream, in front. Extensive field-works covered every prominent point of this naturally very strong ground; and in the centre of the whole line, a gentle eminence was crowned by an enormous battery, serving as a species of citadel. The Russian Army numbered about 120,000 men against which were opposed almost an equal number of French troops. In artillery, also, the armies were equal. The emperor fixed his headquarters in the redoubt whence he had issued the order for battle in the morning; the elevation of the ground permitted him to observe the greatest part of the Russian line, and the various movements of the enemy. The young guard and the cavalry were before him, and the old guard in his rear.

Before the engagement Napoleon addressed his troops: "Here is the battle you have looked for,"—he said, "for it brings us plenty; good winter-quarters, and a safe retreat to France. Behave yourselves so that posterity may say of each of you,—'He was in that great battle beneath the walls of Moscow.'"

At 4 o'clock on the morning of the 7th the French advanced under cover of a thick fog, and assaulted at once the centre, the right, and the left of Kutusoff's position. Such was the impetuosity of the charge that they drove the Russians from their redoubts but this was for a short time only as they rallied under every line of the fire from the French, and instantly advanced. Russian peasants who, till that hour, had never seen war, and who still wore their usual rustic dress, distinguished only by a cross sewed on it in front, threw themselves into the thickest of the combat. As they fell, others rushed on and filled their places.

Some idea may be formed of the obstinacy of the contest from the fact that one division of the Russians which mustered 30,000 in the morning only 8,000 survived. These men had fought in close order, and unshaken, under the fire of eighty pieces of artillery. The Russians had the advantage of ground, of speaking but one language, of one uniform, of being a single nation, and fighting for the same cause. By 2 o'clock, however, according to the imperial bulletin, all hope had abandoned the enemy; the battle was at an end, although the cannonade was not yet discontinued. The Russians fought for their retreat and safety, but no longer for the victory.

The result of this terrible day, in which the French fired sixty-six thousand cannon balls, was that while the Russians were defeated they were far from routed. Ségur says:

> However great may have been the success of this day, it might have been still more so if Napoleon, instead of finishing the battle at 4 o'clock in the afternoon had profited by the remainder of the day to bring his Guard into the field, and thus changed the defeat of the enemy into a complete rout.

That the emperor suffered intensely during the day is well-known. He had passed a restless night and a violent and incessant cough cut short his breathing.

As to his desire of preserving a reserve uninjured, and forming it from a chosen and devoted body, such as his Guard, Napoleon explained it to his marshals by saying: "And if there should be a second battle tomorrow, what could I oppose to it?"

General Gourgaud has added:

> If the Guard had been destroyed at the Battle of Moskowa, the French army, of which their guard constantly formed the core, and whose courage it supported during the retreat, could scarcely have ever repassed the Niemen.

This refusal of Napoleon to engage his Guard is generally held to have been one of his greatest military lapses. At the time they were demanded by Ney and others the enemy was all but beaten and the appearance of the emperor at their head would in all probability have closed the day with a great victory to his credit, and, according to the opinions of many military men of this day, have ended the Russian campaign by this one battle.

Night found either army on the ground they had occupied at daybreak. The number of guns and prisoners taken by the French and the Russians was about equal; and of either host there had fallen not less than 40,000 men. Some accounts give the total number of the slain as 100,000.

The Russian commander fought desperately but was at last compelled to retire. His army was the mainstay of the country and had it been destroyed, the *Czar* would have found it difficult to form another. Having ascertained then the extent of his loss and buried his dead, among whom was the gallant Bagration, the Russian withdrew from his intrenchment and marched on Mojaisk. Marshal Ney was rewarded for the noble share he had in the success of this battle, by the title of Prince of the Moskowa.

The small number of prisoners taken at Moskowa,—or Borodino as the battle is frequently called,—the circumstance of the Russians being able to carry away their wounded, and many other considerations amply prove that such another contest would have ruined Napoleon. The Russians ordered *Te Deums* to be chanted at Moscow in honour of what they termed a victory for themselves and Napoleon sent similar instructions to his bishops in France.

Napoleon was so fortunate as to be joined exactly at this time by two fresh divisions from Smolensk which nearly restored his muster to what it had been when the battle began, and thus reinforced commanded that the pursuit be pushed. On the 9th the French vanguard came in sight of the Russian rear again and Napoleon prepared for battle but once more Kutusoff fled precipitately in the direction of the capital.

The emperor reached the "Hill of Salvation,"—so called because from that eminence the Russian traveller obtains his first view of the ancient metropolis affectionately called "Mother Moscow," and hardly less sacred in his eyes than Jerusalem. The soldiery beheld with joy and exultation the magnificent extent of the place; its mixture of Gothic steeples and oriental domes; and high over all the rest the huge towers of the Kremlin, at once the palace and citadel of the old *Czars*. The cry of "Moscow! Moscow!" ran through the lines. Napoleon himself reined in his horse, and exclaimed, "Behold, at last, that celebrated city!"

It was soon observed that no smoke came from the chimneys, and again, that no military appeared on the battlements of the old walls and towers. Murat, who commanded the van, now came riding up and informed the emperor that he had held a parley with Milarodowitch, general of the Russian rearguard, and that he had declared that unless two hours were granted for the safe withdrawing of his troops, he would at once set fire to Moscow. Napoleon immediately granted the armistice. When the emperor halted at the barrier he had the exterior of the city reconnoitred; Eugene was ordered to surround it on the north, and Poniatowski to embrace the south, whilst Davoust remained near the centre; the Guard was then ordered to march, and, under the command of Lefebvre, Napoleon entered Moscow, and prepared to establish himself in the city.

He found the capital deserted by all but the very lowest and most wretched of its vast population. The French soldiers soon spread themselves over its innumerable streets filling the magnificent palaces, the bazaars of the merchants, the churches, convents and public buildings of every description. The meanest soldier clothed himself in silk and furs and drank at his pleasure the costliest wines. Napoleon, perplexed at the abandonment of so great a city, had great difficulty in keeping together 30,000 men under Murat, who followed Milarodowitch, and watched the walls on that side.

At midnight the emperor, who had retired to rest in a suburban

Napoleon at the Battle of Freidland

palace, was awakened by the cry of "Fire!" The chief market-place was in flames and it was some hours before it could be extinguished. While the fire still burned Napoleon established his quarters in the Kremlin, and wrote by that fatal light, a letter to the *Czar*, containing proposals for peace. In his letter he assured the *Czar*, "that whatever might be the vicissitudes of war, nothing could diminish the esteem entertained for him by his friend of Tilsit and Erfurt."

The letter was committed to a prisoner of rank but no answer was ever received to it. On the next day the flames broke out again and in a short time various detached parts of the city were in flames, combustibles and matches were found in many places, and the water-pipes cut so that attempts to control the spreading flames were almost useless. The wind changed three times in the course of the night and the flames always broke out again with new vigour in the quarter from which the prevailing breeze blew right on the Kremlin. It was now found that the governor, in abandoning the city, had set all the malefactors in the numerous jails at liberty.

For four days the fire continued with more or less fury and four-fifths of the city was wholly consumed. Karamsin the Russian author says:

> Palaces and temples, monuments of arts and miracles of luxury, the remains of ages long since past, and the creation of yesterday, the tombs of ancestors, and the cradles of children were indiscriminately destroyed. Nothing was left of Moscow save the memory of her people, and their deep resolution to avenge her fall.

On the third night the equinoctial gale arose, the Kremlin itself, from which point Napoleon had witnessed the spread of this fearful devastation, took fire and it became doubtful whether it would be possible for the emperor to withdraw in safety.

About 4 o'clock in the morning, one of Napoleon's officers awoke him, to inform him of the conflagration. He had thrown himself on the bed only a few minutes before, after having dictated orders to the various corps of his army, and laboured with his secretaries. He watched from the windows the course of the fire which devoured his fair conquest, and the exclamation burst from him: "This is then how they make war! The civilization of St. Petersburg has deceived us; they are indeed Scythians!"

During several hours he remained immovable at the Kremlin. The palace was now surrounded by the flames and he consented to be conducted out of the city. He rode out through streets in many parts arched over with flames, and buried, where this was not the case, in one dense mantle of smoke. Ségur says:

> It was then that we met the Prince of Eckmuhl (Davoust). This marshal, who had been wounded at the Moskowa, had desired to be carried back among the flames to rescue Napoleon, or to perish with him. He threw himself into his arms with transport; the emperor received him kindly, but with that composure which in danger he never lost for a moment.

"Not even the fictions of the burning of Troy" said the emperor, "though heightened by all the powers of poetry, could have equalled the destruction of Moscow."

It was in the afternoon of the 16th that Napoleon left Moscow and before nightfall had reached Petrowsky, a country palace of the *Czar*, about a league distant, and where he fixed his headquarters.

On the 20th, the flames being at length subdued, or exhausted, Napoleon returned to the Kremlin still hoping that the *Czar* would relent on learning of the destruction of his ancient and sacred metropolis. Day after day passed and still there came no answer from Alexander. The emperor's position was becoming hourly more critical. On every side there was danger; the whole forces of Russia appeared to be gathering around him. Then, too, the season was far advanced; the stern winter of the North was at hand and the determined hostility of the peasants prevented the smallest supplies of provisions from being introduced into the capital.

Daru advised the emperor to draw in all his detachments, convert Moscow into an intrenched camp, kill and salt every horse, and trust to foraging parties for the rest—in a word to lay aside all thoughts of keeping up communication with France, or Germany, or even Poland; and issue forth from Moscow, with his army entire and refreshed, in the commencement of the Spring. But Napoleon feared, and not without reason, that were he and his army cut off from all communication, during six months, the Prussians and the Austrians might throw off the yoke; while, on the other hand, the Russians could hardly fail, in the course of so many months, to accumulate, in their own country, a force before which his isolated army, on re-issuing from their winter quarters would appear but a mere speck.

Another letter was now sent by Napoleon to the headquarters of

Kutusoff for Alexander. Count Lauriston was received by the commander in the midst of his generals and answered with such civility that the envoy doubted not of success. In the end, however, he was informed that no negotiations could be entertained and he declared his inability to even sanction the journey of any French messenger to St. Petersburg, without the authorization of his master. Kutusoff offered, finally, to send Napoleon's letter by one of his own *aides-de-camp*, and to this Lauriston was obliged to agree. The interview occurred on the 6th of October; no answer could be expected before the 20th. There had already been one fall of snow, and the dangers attendant on a longer sojourn in the ruined capital were increasing every hour.

It was under such circumstances that Napoleon lingered on in the Kremlin until the 19th of October when he decided to depart from Moscow. That evening several divisions were put in motion and the metropolis was wholly evacuated on the morning of the 22nd. This sudden departure was due in part to Murat's engagement with Bennigsen at Vincovo on the 18th, the day on which the suspension of arms expired, causing him to lose 3,000 prisoners and forty pieces of artillery. General Milarodowitch, during a conversation with Murat a few days before, talked very frankly of the situation. Murat looked upon peace as indispensable to Russia, and was enlarging upon "the continued success of the French" and having opened for them the gates of Moscow. "Yes General," replied Milarodowitch, briskly, "the campaign is over with the French, and it is now time it should commence with the Russians."

On the 19th of October the emperor with 6,000 chosen horse began his journey towards Smolensk, the care of bringing up the main body being given to Eugene Beauharnais, while Ney commanded the rear.

As Napoleon left Moscow he said to Mortier:

> Pay every attention to the sick and wounded. Sacrifice your baggage,—everything to them. Let the wagons be devoted to their use, and, if necessary your own saddles. This was the course I pursued at St. Jean d'Acre. The officers will first relinquish their horses, then the sub-officers, and finally the men. Assemble the generals and officers under your command, and make them sensible how necessary, in their circumstances, is humanity. The Romans bestowed civic crowns on those who preserved their citizens; I shall not be less grateful.

From the commencement of this march hardly a day elapsed in which some new calamity did not befall those hitherto invincible legions. The Cossacks of Platoff came upon one division at Kolotsk, near Borodino, on the 1st of November, and gave them a total defeat. A second division was attacked the day after and with nearly equal success, by the irregular troops of Count Orloff Denizoff. The French now became separated by attacks made by Milarodowitch and the soldiers began to suffer from extreme hunger. On the 6th of November their miseries were heightened by the setting in of the Russian winter. Thenceforth, between the heavy columns of regular troops which on every side watched and threatened them, the continued assaults of the Cossacks who hung around them in clouds by day and by night, rushing on every detached party like the Mamelukes of Egypt, disturbing every bivouac, breaking up bridges before, and destroying every straggler behind them, to the terrible severity of the climate, the frost, the snow, the wind—the sufferings of this once magnificent army were such as have hardly been equalled in the world's history.

The enormous train of artillery which Napoleon brought from Moscow was soon diminished and the roads were blocked up with the spoils of the city, abandoned of necessity, as the means of transport failed. The horses, having been ill-fed for months, were altogether unable to resist the united effects of cold and fatigue. They sank and stiffened by hundreds and by thousands. The starving soldiery slew others of these animals that they might drink their warm blood and wrap themselves in their yet reeking skins! All discipline had vanished.

They were able to keep together some battalions of the rearguard, and present a bold aspect to the pursuers, the heroic Marshal Ney not disdaining to bear a firelock, and share the meanest fatigues of his brave followers.

The main Russian Army, having advanced side by side with the French, was now stationed to the southwest of Smolensk, in readiness to break the enemy's march whenever Kutusoff should choose. Milarodowitch and Platoff were hanging close behind, and thinning every hour the miserable bands which had no longer heart, nor, for the most part, arms of any kind wherewith to resist them. All the reports brought to headquarters by the officers, represented Kutusoff as disposed to oppose the French Army and risk a battle, rather than abandon his positions which were on the road he wished to close against the continued retreat of the emperor. Napoleon was not convinced by these reports. At daybreak, mounted on horseback, he started out to reconnoitre the camp and disposition of the enemy who was preparing to dispute Kalouga. As the emperor arrived near Malojaroslawetz a body of Cossacks was seen approaching. Napoleon and his escort prepared to defend themselves. Rapp had scarcely time to seize his chief's bridle and say, "It is the Cossacks, turn back!" ere a fierce band galloped towards them. The emperor, scorning flight, drew his sword, and reigned his horse to the side of the road. The troop dashed past wounding Rapp and his horse. Rapp says in his *Memoirs:*

> When Napoleon saw my horse covered with blood, he demanded if I had been wounded. I replied that I had come off with a few bruises, upon which he began to laugh at our adventure, although I, for my part, found it anything but amusing.

The appearance of Marshal Bessieres, who arrived at the head of some squadrons of grenadiers of the Guard, sufficed to stay the disorder and put the Cossacks to flight.

The Grand Army had mustered 120,000 men when it left Moscow. Including the fragments of various divisions which met the emperor at Smolensk it was with great difficulty that 40,000 men could now be brought together in anything like fighting condition. These Napoleon divided into four columns, nearly equal in numbers; of the first which included 6,000 of the Imperial Guard, he himself took the command, and marched with it towards Krasnoi. The second corps was that of Eugene Beauharnais; the third Davoust's; and the fourth destined for the perilous service of the rear, and accordingly strengthened with 3,000 of the Guard, was intrusted to the guidance of Marshal Ney.

Eugene and Ney at length entered Smolensk. The name of that town had hitherto been the only spell that preserved any hope within the soldiers of the retreat. There, they had been told, they should find food, clothing, and supplies of all kinds, and there being once more assembled under the eye of Napoleon, speedily reassume an aspect such as none of the northern barbarians would dare to brave.

These expectations were far from realized. Smolensk had been almost entirely destroyed by the Russians in the early part of the campaign. Its ruined walls afforded only a scant shelter to the famished and shivering fugitives, and the provisions assembled there were so inadequate to the demands of the troops, that after the lapse of a few days Napoleon found himself under the necessity of once more renewing his disastrous march. While at Smolensk Napoleon received dispatches from France, informing him that a false report of his death had occasioned an outbreak and which threatened for a brief period the colossal empire he controlled. On receiving the news he exclaimed, with deep feeling, and in the presence of his generals:

> Does my power then, hang on so slender a thread? Is my tenure of sovereignty so frail that a single person can place it in jeopardy? Truly my crown is but ill-fitted to my head if, in my very capital, the audacious attempt of two or three adventurers can make it totter. After twelve years of government,—after my marriage—after the birth of my son—after my oaths—my death would have again plunged the country into the midst of revolutionary horrors. And Napoleon II., was he no longer thought of?

Napoleon left Smolensk on the 13th of November, 1812, having ordered that the other corps should follow him on the 14th, 15th and 16th respectively thus interposing a day's march between every two divisions.

It seems to be generally accepted that the name of Napoleon saved whatever part of his host finally escaped from the territory of Russia. Kutusoff appears to have exhausted the better part of his daring at Borodino and thenceforth adhered to the plan of avoiding battle. He seems to have been unable to again shake off that awe which had been the growth of a hundred of Napoleon's victories;—had he been able to do so the emperor would probably have died on some battlefield between Smolensk and the Beresina, or been taken a prisoner in the country which three months before he had invaded at the head of half a million of men. The army of Napoleon had been already reduced to a very small fragment of its original strength, and even that fragment was now split into four divisions against any one of which it would have been easy to concentrate a force overwhelmingly superior.

The emperor reached Krasnoi unmolested although the whole of the Russian Army, moving on a parallel road, were in full observation of his march; Eugene, who followed him, was, however, intercepted on his way by Milarodowitch, and after sustaining the contest gallantly against very disproportionate numbers, and a terrible cannonade, was at length saved only by the fall of night. During the darkness Eugene executed a long and hazardous *detour*, and joined the emperor at Krasnoi on the 17th; the two leading divisions now united, mustered scarcely 15,000 men. It was then thought advisable to await the arrival of Davoust's and Ney's divisions before proceeding. Kutusoff was again urged to seize this opportunity of pouring an irresistible force on the French position, and although he thinned the ranks of the enemy with 100 pieces of artillery well placed, he ventured on no closer collision than one or two isolated cavalry charges. Napoleon, therefore, held his ground in face of all that host, until nightfall, when Davoust's division, surrounded and pursued by innumerable Cossacks, at length was enabled to rally once more around his headquarters. Ney, however was still at Smolensk.

The emperor now pushed on to relieve Eugene who was in command of the van with orders to march on Liady and secure the passage of the Dneiper at that point.

Davoust and Mortier were left at Krasnoi with orders to hold out as long as possible in the hope of being there joined by Ney. Long, however, before that gallant leader could reach this point, the Russians, as if the absence of Napoleon had at once restored all their energy, rushed down and forced on Davoust and Mortier the battle which Napoleon had in vain solicited. On that fatal field the French left forty-five cannon and 6,000 prisoners, besides the slain and wounded. The remainder with difficulty effected their escape to Liady, where Napoleon once more received them, and crossed the Dneiper.

Ney, meanwhile, having as directed by the emperor, blown up whatever remained of the walls and towers of Smolensk, at length set his rearguard in motion and advanced to Krasnoi, without being harassed by any except Platoff whose Cossacks entered Smolensk ere he could wholly abandon it. Ney continued to advance on the footsteps of those who had thus shattered Davoust and Mortier and met with no considerable interruption until he reached the ravine in which the rivulet Losmina has its channel. A thick mist lay on the ground and Ney was almost on the brink of the ravine before he perceived that it was manned throughout by Russians, while the opposite banks displayed a long line of batteries deliberately arranged, and all the hills behind covered with troops.

A Russian officer appeared and summoned Ney to surrender. "A Marshal of France never surrenders!" was his intrepid answer, and immediately the batteries, distant only two hundred and fifty yards, opened a tremendous storm of grape-shot. Ney, nevertheless, had the hardihood to plunge into the ravine, clear a passage over the stream, and charge the Russians at their arms. His small band was repelled with fearful slaughter; but he renewed his efforts from time to time during the day, and at night, though with numbers much diminished, still occupied his original position in the face of a whole army interposed between him and Napoleon. The emperor had by this time given up all hopes of ever again seeing anything of his rear column.

During the ensuing night Ney effected his escape—an escape so miraculous that the history of war can scarcely furnish a parallel. The marshal broke up his bivouac at midnight, and marched back from the Losmina, until he came on another stream, which he concluded must also flow into the River Dneiper. He followed this guide, and at length reached the great river at a place where it was frozen over, though so thinly, that the ice bent and cracked beneath the feet of the men who crossed it in single files. The wagons laden with the wounded, and what great guns were still with Ney, were too heavy for this frail bridge. They attempted the passage at different points, and one after another went down, amid the shrieks of the dying and the groans of the onlookers.

The Cossacks had by this time gathered hard behind, and swept up many stragglers, besides the sick. But Ney had achieved his great object; and on the 20th of November he, with his small and devoted band of 1500 men, joined the emperor once more at Orcha. Napoleon, on seeing him received him in his arms, and exclaimed, "What a man! What a soldier!" He could not find words to express the admiration which the intrepid marshal had inspired him with; he hailed him as "the bravest of the brave" and declared with transport: "I have two hundred millions (of *francs*) in the cellars of the Tuileries, and I would have given them all to save Marshal Ney!"

The emperor was once more at the head of his united "grand army"—a sad remnant of its former glory and power. Between Smolensk and the Dneiper the Russians had taken 228 guns, and 26,000 prisoners. At leaving Smolensk Napoleon had mustered 40,000 effective men—he now could count only 12,000, after Ney joined him at Orcha. Of these there were but one hundred and fifty cavalry; and, to remedy this defect, officers still in possession of horses, to the number of 500, were now formed into a "sacred band," as it was called, commanded by General Grouchy, under Murat, for immediate attendance upon the emperor's person.

The Russians were now uniting all their forces for the defence of the next great river on Napoleon's route,—the Beresina. The emperor had hardly resolved to cross this river at Borizoff, ere, to renew all perplexities, he received intelligence that by a combat with Dombrowski there the enemy had retained possession of the town and bridge. Victor and Oudinot advanced immediately to succour Dombrowski and retook Borizoff; but the Russians burned the bridge before re-crossing the Beresina.

Napoleon now decided to pass the Beresina higher up, at Studzianska, and forthwith threw himself into the huge forests which border the river, adopting every stratagem by which his enemies could be puzzled as to the immediate object of his march. His 12,000 brave and determined men were winding their way amidst these dark woods, when suddenly the air around them was filled with sounds which could only proceed from the march of some far greater host. They were preparing for the worst when they found themselves in the presence of the advanced guard of the united army of Victor and Oudinot, who, although they had been defeated by Witgenstein, still mustered 50,000 men, completely equipped and hardly shaken in discipline.

Napoleon now continued his march on Studzianska, employing, however, all his wit to confirm the belief among the Russians that he meant to pass the Beresina at a different place, and this with so much success that the Russian rearguard abandoned a strong position commanding the river, during the very night which preceded the emperor's appearance there.

Two bridges were erected, and Oudinot had passed over before Tchaplitz, in command of the Russian rearguard, perceived his mistake, and returned again toward Studzianska. Discovering that the passage had already begun, and that in consequence of the narrowness of the only two bridges, it must needs proceed slowly, Tchichagoff and Witgenstein now arranged a joint plan of attack. Platoff and his indefatigable Cossacks joined Witgenstein arriving long before the rearguard of Napoleon could pass the river. The French that had made the passage were attacked by Tchaplitz, and being repelled by Oudinot left them in unmolested possession, not only of the bridges on the Beresina, but of a long train of wooden causeways extending for miles beyond the river over deep and dangerous morasses which but a few sparks were needed to ignite and destroy.

Victor with the rear division, consisting of 8,000 men, was still on the eastern side when Witgenstein and Platoff appeared on the heights. The still numerous retainers of the camp, crowds of sick, wounded, and women, and the greater part of the artillery were in the same situation.

When the Russian cannon began to open upon this multitude, crammed together near the bank, and each anxiously expecting the turn to pass, a shriek of utter terror ran through them, and men, women, horses and wagons rushed pell-mell upon the bridges. The larger of these, intended solely for wagons and cannon, ere long broke down precipitating all that were upon it into the dark and half-frozen stream. "The scream that arose at this moment," says one that heard it, "did not leave my ears for weeks; it was heard clear and loud over the hurrahs of the Cossacks, and all the roar of artillery."

The remaining bridge was now the only resource, and all indiscriminately endeavoured to gain a footing on it; exposed to the incessant shower of Russian cannonade they fell and died in thousands. Victor stood his ground bravely until late in the evening, and then conducted his division over the bridge. Behind was left a great number of the irregular attendants besides those soldiers who had been wounded during the battle, and guns and baggage-carts in great quantities. The French now fired the bridge and all those were abandoned to their fate. The Russian account states that when the Beresina broke up in the Spring 36,000 bodies were found in the bed of the river.

On the 3rd of December Napoleon reached Morghoni, and announced to his marshals that the news he had received from Paris at Smolensk concerning Mallet's attempt to overthrow his government by announcing the death of the Emperor, and the uncertain relations with some of his allies, rendered it indispensable for him to quit his army without further delay and return to Paris with all possible speed. They were now, he said, almost within sight of Poland; they would find plenty of everything at Wilna. It was his business to prepare at home the means of opening the next campaign in a manner worthy of the great nation.

At Morghoni, on the 5th, the garrison at Wilna met the emperor and then, having intrusted to these fresh troops, the protection of the rear, and given the chief command to Murat, he finally bade *adieu* to the rulers of his host. He set off in a sledge at midnight, accompanied by Caulaincourt, whose name he assumed. Having narrowly escaped being taken by a party of irregular Russians at Youpranoni, the emperor reached Warsaw at nightfall on the 10th of December. Here he met his ambassador, the Abbé de Pradt, to whom he said, "I quit my army with regret; but I must watch Austria and Prussia, and I have more weight on my throne than at headquarters. The Russians will be rendered foolhardy by their successes. I shall beat them in a battle or two on the Oder, and be on the Niemen again within a month— *Monsieur L'Ambassadeur*, from the sublime to the ridiculous there is but a step."

Resuming his journey, Napoleon reached Dresden on the evening of the 14th of December, where the King of Saxony visited him, and reassured him of his fidelity. He then resumed the road to his capital and arrived at the Tuileries on the 18th, late at night, after the Empress had retired.

The remnant of the Grand Army meanwhile moved on towards France in straggling columns. They passed the Niemen at Kowno, and the Russians did not pursue them into Prussian territory. Here about 1000 men in arms, and perhaps 20,000 more utterly demoralized, were received with compassion. They took up their quarters and remained for a time unmolested, in and near Konigsberg. The French Army crossed the Niemen on the ice, on the 13th of December, defended still by Ney, who had to fight with the Russians in Kowno. He now fought at the head of only thirty men and was the last individual of the French Army who left Russian territory, as he did so he threw his musket into the river defying the enemy with his last breath. When he came up with General Dumas in Prussian Poland he was scarcely recognizable, and on being asked who he was replied, with eyes red and glaring, "I am the rearguard of the Grand Army; I have fired the last musket shot on the bridge of Kowno!"

The few who survived all these horrors, men who had fought in all Napoleon's campaigns, and wore the cross of the Legion of Honour on their breasts, were now so wasted with famine that they wept when they saw a loaf of bread!

The total loss in this terrible campaign was somewhere near 450,000 men; fatigue, hunger and cold had caused the death of 132,000; and the Russians had taken prisoners of 193,000—including forty-eight generals and three thousand regimental officers. The eagles and standards left in the enemy's hands were seventy-five in number and the pieces of cannon nearly one thousand.

Review of Troops in the Place du Carrousel, Paris

13

The Campaign of 1813

To the premature cold, and burning of Moscow, Napoleon attributed the failure of his campaign in Russia. His arrival at the Tuileries had been preceded by the 29th bulletin in which the fatal events of the campaign were fully and graphically recited. While he had not been able to conquer the elements he found the Senate and all the public bodies full of adulation and willingness to obey his commands. However, what had been foreseen by almost every person of discernment, except Napoleon, soon followed, *viz.*, an alliance against France by Prussia, Russia and Austria.

New conscriptions were now called for and yielded; regiments arrived from Spain and Italy; every arsenal resounded with the preparation of new artillery. Scott says:

> The wonderful energies of Napoleon's mind, and the influence which he could exert over the minds of others, were never so striking as at this period of his reign. He had returned to the seat of his empire at a dreadful crisis, and in a most calamitous condition. His subjects had been ignorant for three weeks whether he was dead or alive. When he arrived it was to declare a dreadful catastrophe. . . . . Yet Napoleon came, and seemed but to stamp on the earth, and armed legions arose at his call: the doubts and discontents of the public disappeared as mists at sunrising, and the same confidence which had attended his prosperous fortunes, revived in its full extent, despite of his late reverses.

Ere many weeks had elapsed Napoleon found himself once more in a condition to take the field with not less than 350,000 soldiers. Such was the effect of his new appeal to the national feelings of the

French people. Meanwhile the French garrisons dispersed over the Prussian territory were wholly incompetent to overawe a nation which thirsted for vengeance. The king endeavoured to protect Napoleon's soldiers but it soon became manifest that their safety must depend on their concentrating themselves in a small number of fortified towns. Murat now resigned command of the troops, being succeeded by Eugene Beauharnais who had the full confidence of the emperor. The new commander found that Frederick William could no longer, even if he would, repress the universal enthusiasm of the Prussians who were clamorous for war.

On the 31st of January, 1813, the king made his escape to Breslau, in which neighbourhood no French were garrisoned, erected his standard and called on the nation to rise in arms. Eugene, thereupon, retired to Magdeburg and shut himself up in that great fortress, with as many of the troops as he could assemble to the west of the Elbe. When Napoleon heard that Prussia had declared war against France he said with perfect calmness, "It is better to have a declared enemy, than a doubtful ally."

It was now six years since the fatal day of Jena, and in spite of all of Napoleon's watchfulness the Prussian nation had recovered, in a great measure, its energies. The people answered the call as with the heart and voice of one man. Youths of all ranks, the highest and the lowest, flocked indiscriminately to the standard. The women poured their trinkets into the king's treasure, the gentlemen melted their plate,—England poured in her gold with a lavish hand. The thunder of the cannon of the Beresina had raised the hopes of the House of Bourbon until Louis XVIII. finally caused to be published in England, and distributed throughout the Continent, a proclamation in which he addressed himself to the people adroitly supporting the common opinion which attributed to Napoleon the prolongation of the war, and promising, among other things, "to abolish the conscription."

The Emperor of Russia was no sooner aware of this great movement, than he resolved to advance into Silesia. Having masked several French garrisons in Prussian Poland, and taken others, he pushed on with his main army to support Frederick William. Evidently he did not intend to permit the Prussians to stand alone the first onset of Napoleon, of whose extensive arrangements all Europe was aware.

The two sovereigns met at Breslau on the 15th of March. Tears rushed down the cheeks of Frederick William, as he fell into the arms of Alexander; "Wipe them," said the *Czar;* "they are the last that Napoleon shall ever cause you to shed."

The aged Kutusoff having died, the command of the Russian army was now given to Witgenstein; while that of the Prussians was intrusted to Blücher, an officer who had originally trained under the great Frederick and who, since the Battle of Jena, had lived in retirement. The soldiers had long before bestowed on him the title "Marshal Forwards" and they heard of his appointment with delight. Blücher hated the very names of France and Bonaparte, and once more permitted to draw his sword, he swore never to sheathe it until the revenge of Prussia was complete. Bernadotte, now the Crown Prince of Sweden, and an ingrate,—owing not only his position but his very existence to Napoleon,—now landed at Stralsund, and advanced through Mecklenburg while the sovereigns of Russia and Prussia were concentrating their armies in Silesia. It was announced and expected that German troops would join Bernadotte, so as to enable him to open the campaign on the lower Elbe with a separate army of 100,000 men. Wellington, too, was about to advance once more into Spain with his victorious armies. Three great armies, two of which might easily communicate with each other, were thus taking the field against Napoleon at once.

Ere the emperor once more left Paris, he named Marie Louise Empress-Regent of France in his absence. As the time approached when he was expected to assume the command of his army in the field his devoted subjects again and again expressed their loyalty to him and to France. He quitted Paris in the middle of April.

On starting to join his youthful and inexperienced army at Erfurt, Napoleon said:

> I envy the lot of the meanest peasant in my dominion. At my age he has fulfilled his duties to his country, and he may remain at home, enjoying the society of his wife and children; while I—I must fly to the camp and engage in the strife of war. Such is my fate.
>
> My good Louise is gentle and submissive, I can trust her. Her love and fidelity for me will never fail(!). In the current of events there may arise circumstances which decide the fate of an Empire. In that case I hope the daughter of the Cæsars will be inspired by the spirit of her grandmother, Maria Theresa.

In three months an army of 350,000 men was raised, equipped and brought together, and General Ségur says:

At any hour of the day or night the emperor, whatever he was doing, could have told the numbers, the composition, the strength of every one of the thousands of detachments of every branch of the service which he set in movement from every part of the empire, the way they were uniformed or equipped, the number of marches each one had to make, the day, the place, even the hour at which each was to arrive.

On the 18th he reached the banks of the Saale where the troops he had been mustering and organizing in France had now been joined by Eugene and the garrison of Magdeburg.

The *Czar* and his Prussian ally were known to be at Dresden, and it soon appeared that, while they meditated a march westwards on Leipsic, the French intended to move eastward with a view of securing the possession of that great city. He had a host nearly 200,000 strong concentrating for action while reserves of almost equal numbers were gradually forming behind him on the Rhine. Napoleon arrived at Erfurt on the 23rd of April, whilst Marshal Ney was taking possession of Weissenfels, after a contest which caused him to say "he had never at any one time, seen so much enthusiasm and *sang froid* in the infantry." And yet the veterans of Austerlitz, Jena, Friedland and Wagram had nearly all disappeared from the ranks, and the honour of those eagles, so long victorious, had been committed to young conscripts, hardly conversant with their exercise, and by no means habituated to the fatigues of war.

The armies met on the first of May,—sooner than Napoleon had ventured to hope,—near the town of Lutzen, then celebrated as the scene of the battle in which King Gustavus Adolphus died. The evening before the battle Marshal Bessieres was forcing a defile near Poserna, and having, according to custom, advanced into the very midst of the skirmishers, a musket-ball struck him in the breast, and extended him lifeless on the ground. His death was concealed from the brave men he had so long commanded and by whom he was greatly beloved, until after the victory of the following day.

The allies crossed the Elster suddenly, under the cover of a thick morning fog, and attacked the left flank of the French, who had been advancing in column, and who thus commenced the action under heavy disadvantages. But the emperor so skilfully altered the arrangement of his army, that, ere the day closed, the allies were more afraid of being enclosed to their ruin within his two wings, than hopeful of being able to cut through and destroy that part of his force which they had originally charged and weakened, and which had now become his centre.

Night interrupted the conflict and the next morning the enemy retreated, leaving Napoleon in possession of the field. His victory was less complete than was desirable although he lost but ten or twelve thousand men while the allies lost above twenty thousand.

A great moral effect was, however, produced by the battle. Napoleon, who had been regarded as already conquered, was again victorious. The emperor immediately sent dispatches to every court in alliance with France, to announce the event, he said:

> In my young soldiers I have found all the valour of my old companions-in-arms. During the twenty years that I have commanded the French troops I have never witnessed more bravery and devotion. If all the Allied Sovereigns, and the ministers who direct their cabinets, had been present on the field of battle, they would have renounced the vain hope of causing the Star of France to decline.

Beaten at Lutzen, Alexander and the King of Prussia fell back on Leipsic, thence on Dresden, and finally across the Elbe to Bautzen. A want of cavalry prevented their pursuit.

Napoleon entered Dresden on the 11th of May, and on the 12th was joined by the King of Saxony who still adhered to him. The Saxon troops once more decided to act in concert with the French. As Napoleon approached Dresden, he was waited upon by the magistrates who had been treacherous to him and to their king, and had welcomed the allies.

"Who are you?" Napoleon asked severely.

"Members of the municipality," replied the trembling burgomasters.

"Have you bread for my troops?" inquired Napoleon.

"Our resources," they answered, "have been entirely exhausted by the requisitions of the Russians and Prussians."

"Ah!" replied Napoleon, "it is impossible, is it? I know no such word. Get ready bread, meat and wine. You richly deserve to be treated as a conquered people. But I forgive all from regard for your king. He is the saviour of your country. You have been already punished by the presence of the Russians and Prussians, and having been governed by Baron Stein."

On becoming master of Dresden, the emperor, as usual, sent proposals of a pacific nature to the allies, suggesting that a general congress should assemble at Prague to treat for peace. Neither Russia nor Prussia, however, would listen favourably to what they considered would be an admission of their incapacity to realize their boast of speedily dethroning "the scourge and tyrant of Europe and mankind."

Austria had been sounded, and expressed her willingness to join the coalition on the first favourable opportunity. She was at this time increasing her military establishment largely, and a great body of troops was already concentrated behind the mountainous frontier of Bohemia. Austria, therefore, was enabled to turn the scale on whichever side she might choose.

Napoleon now determined to crush the army which had retreated from Lutzen, ere the ceremonious cabinet of Vienna should have time to come to a distinct understanding with the headquarters of Alexander and Frederick William. That victory was the best method of securing Austria's help, Napoleon clearly saw.

The allies, on their retreat, had blown up the magnificent bridge over the Elbe at Dresden, and this being replaced in part by some arches of wood, Napoleon now moved towards Bautzen and came in sight of the enemy on the morning of the 21st of May. The position of the allies was almost perfect: in their front was the river Spree; wooded hills supported their right, and eminences well fortified their left.

The action began with an attempt to turn their right, but Barclay de Tolly anticipated this movement and repelled it with such vigour that a whole column of 7,000 dispersed and fled into the hills of Bohemia for safety.

Napoleon now determined to pass the Spree in front of the enemy, and they permitted him to do so, rather than come down from their position. He took up his quarters in the town of Bautzen, and his whole army bivouacked in presence of the allies.

The battle was resumed at daybreak on the 22nd; when Ney on the right, and Oudinot on the left, attempted simultaneously to turn the flanks of the position; while Soult and Napoleon himself directed charge after charge on the centre. During four hours the struggle was maintained with unflinching obstinacy. The wooded heights, where Blücher commanded, had been taken and retaken several times, ere the allies perceived the necessity of retiring or losing the engagement. They finally withdrew, panic-stricken, continuing their retreat with such celerity as to gain time to rally on the roads leading to Bohemia, all others being closed against them. The want of cavalry, however, again prevented Napoleon from turning his success to account.

During the whole of the ensuing day Napoleon, at the head of the cavalry of the Guard, urged pursuit and exposed at all times his own person in the very hottest of the fire. By his side was Duroc, grand master of the palace—his dearest friend. "Duroc," said the emperor, on the morning of the battle, "fortune has a spite at us today."

About 7 o'clock in the evening, Duroc was conversing on a slight eminence, and at a considerable distance from the firing, with Marshal Mortier and General Kirgener,—all three on foot,—when a cannon-ball, aimed at the group, ploughed up the ground near Mortier, ripped open Duroc's abdomen and struck General Kirgener dead on the spot.

Napoleon hastened to Duroc as soon as he heard of the event and was deeply moved on beholding him. The latter, who was still conscious, said to the emperor: "All my life has been devoted to your service, and I only regret its loss for the use which it might still have been to you."

"Duroc," replied the emperor, "there is another life! it is there that you will await me and there we shall one day meet."

"Yes, Sire, but that will be in thirty years, when you shall have triumphed over your enemies, and realized the hopes of your country; I have lived an honest man and have nothing to reproach myself with. I leave a daughter, your Majesty will be a father to her."

At Duroc's own solicitation the emperor retired to spare him further grief. Napoleon had ordered his troops to halt, and he remained all the afternoon in front of his tent, surrounded by the Guard, who did not witness his affliction without tears. He stood by Duroc while he died and drew up with his own hand an epitaph, to be placed over his remains by the pastor of the place, and who received two hundred *napoleons* to defray the expense of a fitting monument. Thus closed the 22nd.

That night Napoleon, after dictating the bulletin of the battle, wrote the following decree, which Alison says:

> All lovers of the arts, as well as admirers of patriotic virtue, must regret was prevented by his fall from being carried into execution—A monument shall be erected on Mount Cenis; on the most conspicuous space the following inscription shall be written: 'The Emperor Napoleon, from the field of Wurschen,

has ordered the erection of this monument in testimony of his gratitude to the people of France and of Italy. This monument will transmit, from age to age, the remembrance of that great epoch, when, in the space of three months, twelve hundred thousand men flew to arms, to protect the integrity of the French Empire.'

The allies, although strongly posted during the most of the day, had lost 10,000 men. They continued to retreat into Upper Silesia, and Napoleon advanced to Breslau and released the garrison of Glogau. General Regnier obtained fresh advantage over the Russians in the affair of Gorlitz on the following day, and on the 24th Marshal Ney forced the passage of the Neiss and in the morning of the 25th was beyond the Quiess where he met the emperor.

Meanwhile, the Austrians, having watched these indecisive though bloody fields, and daily defeats of the allies, sought to bring about an armistice, but only with a view of gaining them time to recuperate. The sovereigns of Russia and Prussia expressed a willingness to accept it, and Napoleon also was desirous of bringing his disputes to a peaceful termination until the 10th of August. He agreed to an armistice, and in arranging its conditions, agreed to fall back out of Silesia, thus enabling the allies to reopen communications with Berlin. On the first of June the lines of truce to be occupied by the armies was signed, the French emperor returned to Dresden, and a general congress of diplomatists prepared to meet at Prague, England alone refusing to send a representative alleging that Napoleon had as yet signified no intention to recede from his position with regard to Spain.

The armistice was arranged purely to gain time. Napoleon's successes, while unproductive, were dazzling in their execution, and the allies found it of the utmost importance to stop hostilities until the advance of Bernadotte, and secure further time for the arrival of new reinforcements from Russia; for the completion of the Prussian organization and, above all, for determining the policy of Vienna.

While inferior diplomatists wasted much time in endless discussions at Prague one interview between Prince Metternich and Napoleon, at Dresden, brought the whole question to a definite issue. The emperor, during the course of their conversation, is said to have asked "What is your price? Will Illyria satisfy you? I only wish you to be neutral—I can deal with these Russians and Prussians singlehanded."

Metternich answered that the time in which Austria could be neutral was past; that the situation of Europe at large must be considered. He declared that the Rhenish Confederacy must be broken up, that France must be contented with the boundary of the Rhine and pretend no longer to maintain her unnatural influence in Germany. Napoleon replied, "Come Metternich, tell me honestly how much the English have given you to take their part against me?"

At length the Austrian Court sent a formal document containing its ultimatum, the tenor of which Metternich had indicated in his conversation. Napoleon was urged by his ministers, Talleyrand and Fouché, two arch-intriguers, to accede to the proffered terms. Their arguments were backed by intelligence of the most disastrous character from Spain. Wellington, on perceiving that Napoleon had greatly weakened his armies in that country, while preparing for his campaign against Prussia and Russia, had once more advanced and was now in possession of the supreme authority over the Spanish armies as well as the Portuguese and English, and had appeared in greater force than ever. The French had suffered defeat at several points and on the 21st of June, Joseph Bonaparte and Marshal Jourdan had sustained a total defeat, and the former was now retreating towards the Pyrenees.

Berthier concurred in pressing upon the emperor the desirability of making peace on the terms proposed, or to draw in his garrisons on the Oder and Elbe, whereby he would strengthen his army with 50,000 veterans and retire to the Rhine. There, it was urged, with such a force assembled on such a river, and with all the resources of France behind him, he might bid defiance to the united armies of Europe, and, at worst, obtain a peace that would leave him in secure tenure of a nobler dominion than any of the kings, his predecessors, had even hoped to possess. "Ten lost battles," he replied, "would not sink me lower than you would have me place myself by my own voluntary act; but one battle gained enables me to seize Berlin and Breslau and make peace on terms compatible with my glory."

Finally, Metternich suddenly broke off all negotiations, and on the 12th of August, Austria declared war against France. It was an act of bold and shameless perfidy; but Metternich was richly rewarded for his treachery by the crowned heads of Europe. It was then that Napoleon discovered the depth of the abyss on which he had set his foot. He had lived in the hopes that his alliance with the House of Austria, by marriage with Marie Louise, would prevent the Archduchess' father from taking the field against him, but in this he was sadly disappointed. Austria now signed an alliance, offensive and defensive, with Russia and Prussia. Thus was consolidated at last the great coalition. The sovereigns of the nations of Europe had leagued together and sworn to crush the Emperor of France.

On the night between the 10th and 11th rockets answering rockets, from height to height along the frontiers of Bohemia and Silesia, had announced to all the armies of the allies this accession of strength and the immediate recommencement of hostilities. Napoleon had now been several weeks with his army at Dresden and it had been fondly hoped by the populace that on the birthday of the French emperor, a peace with Europe would be signed. They had prepared a magnificent festival in his honour and to celebrate the restoration of peace. Their hopes were considerably lessened, however, by an order for the *fête* to take place on the 10th in conjunction with a grand review of the army. On the great plain of Ostra-Gehege, near Dresden, the imperial troops were drawn up, and in the presence of the King of Saxony, the emperor's brothers, marshals, and the chief dignitaries of the empire, Napoleon held his last review. Twenty thousand of the Old Guard, five thousand of whom were mounted on fine horses richly caparisoned, with the whole of his vast army, defiled before their Imperial Commander. At night a banquet was spread for his gallant veterans.

Military preparations had been progressing on both sides during the cessation of hostilities. Napoleon now had a force of 250,000 men distributed as follows: Macdonald lay with 100,000 at Buntzlaw, on the border of Silesia; another corps of 50,000 had their headquarters at Zittau, in Lusatia; St. Cyr, with 20,000 was at Pirna on the great pass from Bohemia; Oudinot at Leipsic, with 60,000; while with the Emperor himself at Dresden remained 25,000 of the Imperial Guard, the flower of France.

Behind the Erzgebirge, or Metallic Mountains, and having their headquarters at Prague, lay the grand army of the allies, consisting of 120,000 Austrians and 80,000 Russians and Prussians; commanded in chief by the Austrian general Schwartzenberg. The French corps at Zittau and Pirna were prepared to encounter these, should the attempt to force their way into Saxony, either on the right or the left of the Elbe. The second army of the allies, consisting of 80,000 Russians and Prussians,—called the army of Silesia,—and commanded by Blücher, lay in advance of Breslau. Lastly, the Crown Prince of Sweden, Bernadotte, who had been influenced by a belief that he was to succeed to the throne of France, was at Berlin, with 30,000 of his own troops, and 60,000 Russians and Prussians. Oudinot and Macdonald were so stationed that he could not approach the upper valley of the Elbe without encountering one of them, and they also had the means of mutual communication and support.

Napoleon had evidently arranged his troops with the view of making isolated assaults, and beating them in detail. He was opposed, however, by generals who were well acquainted with his tactics but none of whom, except Blücher, was above mediocre in generalship. The three allied commanders had prepared counter schemes to frustrate his arrangements, having agreed that whosoever of them should be first assailed or pressed by the French, they should on no account accept battle, but retreat; thus tempting Napoleon in person to follow, leaving Dresden open to the assault of some other great branch of their confederacy, and to enable them at once to seize all his magazines, to break the communications between the remaining divisions of his army, and interpose a hostile force in the rear of them all—between the Elbe and the Rhine.

This plan of campaign is believed to have been drawn up by two of Napoleon's old marshals—Bernadotte and Moreau—both traitors. The latter had just returned from America on the invitation of the Emperor Alexander, whither he had gone after being exiled, and had joined the Allies in their warfare on the French emperor.

The first movement was made by Blücher, and no sooner did Napoleon become aware that he was threatening the position of Macdonald than he quitted Dresden. He left with his Guard and a powerful force of cavalry on the 15th of August, and proceeded to the support of his marshal. The Prussian commander adhered faithfully to the general plan and retired across the Katsbach, in the face of his enemies. While in pursuit of him Napoleon was informed that Schwartzenberg had rushed down from the Bohemian hills and abandoning Blücher to the care of Macdonald, sent his Guard back to Dresden leaving for the same point himself on the 23rd.

Schwartzenberg made his appearance on the heights to the south of the Saxon capital on the 25th, having driven St. Cyr and his 20,000 men before him.

The army of St. Cyr had thrown itself into the city of Dresden and on the 26th were assailed in six columns, each more numerous than its garrison. The French marshal had about begun to despair when the Imperial Guard made its appearance, crossing the bridge from the eastern side of the Elbe, and in their midst was the emperor himself.

Insurrection in Madrid

His arrival was most timely and the two sallies executed by those troops, hot and tired from their long and tiresome march, caused the allies to be driven back some distance. Night then set in and the two armies remained very near together until the next morning when the battle was renewed amidst a storm of wind and rain.

The emperor, by movements most phenomenal, now had 200,000 men gathered round him, and he poured them out with such skill on either flank of the enemy's line, that ere the close of the day they were forced to withdraw. At 3 o'clock the Battle of Dresden was definitely gained for Napoleon. The allied monarchs, in danger of losing their communication with Bohemia, were obliged to provide for their safety and beat a retreat leaving in the power of the conqueror from twenty-five to thirty thousand prisoners, forty flags, and sixty pieces of cannon.

Napoleon remained on the field until his victory was decided, and then returned to Dresden on horseback; his gray-coat, and weather-worn hat streaming with water, and his whole appearance forming a singular contrast to that of Murat, who rode by his side with all the splendour of his usual battle-dress. The latter had, however, especially distinguished himself during the action.

On either side 8,000 men had been slain or wounded and one of the ablest of all the enemy's generals—Moreau, had fallen. Early in the day Napoleon had observed a group of reconnoitring officers and ordered that ten cannon be prepared at once. He believed that he recognized in the group "the traitor Moreau." He at once ordered that the heavy guns, charged with all their power, be pointed in that direction. He superintended the operation and decided himself the angle of elevation, the aim and the moment to fire. Ten pieces went off at once, carrying a storm of cannon-shot over the heads of the contending armies. This was followed by a movement which was thought to indicate that some person of importance had been wounded.

A peasant came in the evening and brought with him a bloody boot and a greyhound, both the property, he said, of a great man who was no more; the words on the dog's collar were: "I belong to General Moreau." Moreau was dead. Both his legs had been shot off. It is said he continued to smoke a cigar while the surgeon dressed his wounds, in the presence of Alexander, and died shortly after.

The fatigues Napoleon had undergone between the 15th and 28th of August now overcame him and he was unable to remain with the columns in the rear of Schwartzenberg, but returned to Dresden.

Here he learned of Vandamme's failure in an engagement in the valley of Culm with a Prussian corps commanded by Count D'Osterman, wherein the French lieutenant laid down his arms with 8,000 prisoners. This news reached Napoleon, still sick, at Dresden. "Such," he said to Murat, "is the fortune of war—high in the morning, low ere night; between triumph and ruin there intervenes but one step."

No sooner did Blücher perceive that Napoleon had retired from Silesia than he resumed the offensive, still carrying out Moreau's advice, "attack Napoleon where he is not!" and descended from the position he had taken at Jauer. He encountered Macdonald,—who was by no means prepared for him,—on the plains between Wahlstadt and the River Katsbach, on the 26th of August, and after a hard fought day, gained a complete victory. The French lost 15,000 men and 100 guns and fell back on Dresden. Oudinot was defeated on the 23rd of August by Bernadotte at Gross-Beeren and Ney suffered like reverses on the 7th of September at Dennewitz, leaving 10,000 prisoners and forty-six guns in the hands of Bernadotte.

Napoleon now recovered his health and activity, and the exertions he made at this time were never surpassed, even by himself. On the 3rd of September he was in quest of Blücher who had now advanced near to the Elbe, but the Prussians retired and baffled him as before. Returning to Dresden he received the news of Dennewitz and immediately afterwards heard that Witgenstein had a second time descended towards Pirna. He flew thither on the instant, the Russian gave way, according to the plan of campaign, and Napoleon returned once more to Dresden. Again he was told that Blücher on the one side, and Witgenstein on the other, were availing themselves of his absence, and advancing. He once more returned to Pirna; a third time the Russian retired. Napoleon followed him as far as Peterswald and once more returned to his centre point.

Bernadotte and Blücher finally effected a junction to the west of the Elbe, despite the heroic exertions of Ney who, on witnessing the combination of these armies retreated to Leipsic. Napoleon now ordered Regnier and Bertrand to march suddenly from Dresden to Berlin in the hope of recalling Blücher, but without success. Meantime Schwartzenberg was found to be skirting round the hills to the westward, as if for the purpose of joining Blücher and Bernadotte, in the neighbourhood of Leipsic.

It became manifest that Leipsic was now becoming the common centre towards which the forces of France and all her enemies were converging. Napoleon reached that venerable city on the 15th of October and almost immediately the heads of Schwartzenberg's columns began to appear towards the south. Napoleon, having made all his preparations, reconnoitred every outpost in person, and distributed eagles to some new regiments which had just joined him. The young soldiers, with a splendid ceremony, swore to die rather than witness the dishonor of France. Five hundred thousand men were now in presence of each other under the walls or in the environs of Leipsic and a grand battle had become inevitable.

At midnight three rockets, emitting a brilliant white light, sprang into the heavens to the south of the city. These marked the position on which Schwartzenberg—having with him the Emperor of Austria, as well as Alexander and Frederick William, had fixed his headquarters. They were answered by four rockets of a deep red colour ascending from the northern horizon.

Napoleon now became convinced that he was to sustain, on the morrow, the assault of Blücher and Bernadotte as well as the grand army of the allies. Blücher was indeed ready to co-operate with Schwartzenberg, and though the crown prince had not yet reached his ground, the numerical strength of the enemy was very great. Napoleon had with him to defend the line of villages to the north and south of Leipsic, 134,000 infantry and 22,000 cavalry; while, even in the absence of Bernadotte, who might be hourly looked for, the allies mustered not less than 340,000 combatants, including 54,000 cavalry.

At daybreak on the 16th of October, the battle began on the southern side, the allies charging the French line there six times in succession, and were as often repelled. But it was not sufficient for the emperor to resist with success and to hold his positions; he had, more than ever, need of a signal triumph, of a decisive victory; and when his enemies failed in their first attack, it was for him to attack them briskly in turn without giving them time to stay the disorder and discouragement of their columns, and to replace by fresh troops the fatigued and beaten soldiers; and this Napoleon did. He at once charged and with such effect, that Murat's cavalry were at one time in possession of a great gap between the two wings of the enemy.

The Cossacks of the Russian Imperial Guard, however, encountered the French horse, and pushed them back again, preserving the army of the allies from a total defeat. The combat raged without intermission until nightfall, when both armies bivouacked exactly where the morning light had found them. "The allies were so numerous" said Napoleon at St. Helena, "that when their troops were fatigued they were regularly relieved as on dress parade!" With such a numerical superiority, they could scarcely be definitely beaten; therefore, notwithstanding the prodigies of valour performed by the French Army, the victory remained almost undecided. In the centre and to the right the French had maintained their position but on the left treachery made them lose ground.

Marmont commanded on this side. Blücher attacked him with a vastly superior force in numbers and while nothing could be more obstinate than his defence, he lost many prisoners and guns, was driven from his original ground, and occupied when the day closed, a new position, much nearer the walls of the city.

Napoleon became convinced that he must at last retreat from Leipsic and he now made an effort to obtain peace. General Merfeld, the same Austrian officer who had come to his headquarters after the battle of Austerlitz, to pray for an armistice on the part of the Emperor Francis, had been made prisoner in the course of the day, and Napoleon resolved to employ him as his messenger. Merfeld informed him that the King of Bavaria had at length acceded to the alliance, thus adding greatly to his perplexities in finding a new enemy stationed on the line of his march to France.

The emperor asked the Austrian to request for him the personal intervention of Francis, he said:

"I will renounce Poland and Illyria, Holland, the Hanse Towns, and Spain. I will consent to lose the sovereignty of the kingdom of Italy, provided that state remain as an independent one, and I will evacuate all Germany. *Adieu!* Count Merfeld. When on my part you name the word armistice to the two emperors, I doubt not the sound will awaken many recollections."

Napoleon received no answer to his message. The allied princes had sworn to each other to entertain no treaty while one French soldier remained on the eastern side of the Rhine. He therefore prepared for the difficult task of retreating with 100,000 men, through a crowded town, in presence of an enemy already twice as numerous, and in hourly expectation of being joined by a third great and victorious army. During the 17th the battle was not renewed except by a distant and partial cannonade. The allies were determined to have the support of Bernadotte in the decisive contest.

On the morning of the 18th the battle began again about 8 o'clock and continued until nightfall without intermission. Never was Napoleon's generalship or the gallantry of his troops more thoroughly tested than on this terrible day. He again commanded on the south and again, in spite of the vast superiority of the enemy's numbers, the French maintained their ground to the end. On the north the arrival of Bernadotte enabled Blücher to push his advantages with irresistible effect; and the situation of Marmont and Ney was further perplexed by the shameful defection of 12,000 Saxons who went over with all their artillery to the enemy in the very midst of the battle. These Saxons, forming nearly a third of the left, ran over to the Russians, entered their ranks, and at Bernadotte's request discharged their artillery on the French, their fellow-soldiers, whom they had just abandoned!

The loss on either side had been very great. Napoleon's army consisted chiefly of very young men, many were merely boys, yet they fought as bravely as the Guard. The failure of the emperor was partly occasioned by a want of ammunition; as in the course of five days, having fired more than two hundred and fifty thousand shots, his troops had not sufficient to continue the firing two hours longer. As the nearest reserves were at Magdeburg and Erfurt, Napoleon determined to march for the latter place. He gave orders at midnight for the commencement of the inevitable retreat, and while the darkness lasted, the troops continued to file through the town, and across the two bridges, over the Pleisse, beyond its walls. One of these bridges was a temporary fabric and broke down ere daylight came to show the enemy the movement of the retreating French.

The confusion necessarily accompanying the march of a whole army, through narrow streets, and upon a single bridge, was fearful. The allies stormed at the gates on either side, and, but for the heroism of Macdonald and Poniatowski, to whom Napoleon intrusted the defence of the suburbs, it is doubted whether he himself could have escaped in safety. At 9 in the morning of the 19th Napoleon bade farewell to the King of Saxony who had remained all the while in the heart of his ancient city. The king was left to make whatever terms he could with the Allied Sovereigns.

The battle was now raging all round the walls and at 11 o'clock the allies had gathered close to the bridge. The officer to whom Napoleon had committed the task of blowing up the structure, when the advance of the enemy should render this necessary, set fire to the train much too soon. The crowd of men, urging each other on to a point of safety could not at once be stopped and soldiers, horses and cannon, rolled headlong into the deep, but narrow river. Marshal Macdonald swam the stream in safety, but the gallant Poniatowski, who defended the suburbs inch by inch, and had been twice wounded ere he plunged his horse into the current, sank to rise no more. This order was given to Poniatowski by the emperor himself:

"Prince" said Napoleon to him, "you will defend the southern *faubourg.*"

"Sire" he replied, "I have but few people."

"Ah! well! you will defend yourself with what you have."

"Ah! Sire, we will maintain it! We are always ready to perish for your Majesty."

The illustrious, unfortunate Pole kept his word; he was never again to behold the emperor. Later Napoleon said of him: "Poniatowski was a noble man, honourable and brave. Had I succeeded in Russia, I intended to make him king of Poland."

The body of the prince was found on the fifth day by a fisherman. He had on his gala uniform, the epaulets of which were studded with diamonds, and upon his fingers were several rings covered with brilliants, while his pockets contained snuff-boxes of considerable value, and other trinkets. Many of these were eagerly purchased by Polish officers who had been made prisoners. Twenty-five thousand Frenchmen, the means of escape being entirely cut off, now laid down their arms within the city with more than two hundred pieces of cannon. In killed, wounded and prisoners, Napoleon lost at Leipsic at least 50,000 men.

St. Amand says:

> This defeat at Leipsic was for Napoleon a combination of grief and surprise. Of all the battles he had fought, this was the first that he had lost. Up to that time he could boast that if he had been conquered by the elements he had never been conquered by man; and now he was to know for himself the sufferings he had inflicted on others. He was to learn by personal experience the bitterness of defeat, the anguish of retreat, the desperation of useless bloodshed. War, which up to this time had been a source of gratification to his unparalleled pride, now showed to him its horrors, with its humiliations and inexpressible anguish. The hour had struck when he could make tardy reflections on the emptiness of genius and glory on the intoxication of pride that had turned his head.
>
> The retreat of the French through Saxony was a sad ending to the

auspicious beginning which the emperor had opened the campaign with. Napoleon conducted himself as became a great mind amidst great misfortunes; he appeared at all times calm and self-possessed, receiving every day that he advanced new tidings of evil, for the peasantry was hostile, supplies scarce, and added to this was the persevering pursuit of the Cossacks who attacked at every opportunity.

The emperor halted for two days at Erfurt, where extensive magazines had been established, employing all his energies in the restoring of discipline. He resumed his march on the 25th of October, 1813, towards the Rhine. The Austro-Bavarians hastened to meet him and had taken up a position amidst the woods near Hanau before the emperor reached the Mayne. He came up with them on the morning of the 30th, and his troops charged on the instant with the fury of desperation. Napoleon cut his way through ere nightfall, and Marmont, with the rear, had equal success on the 31st. In these actions the French lost 6,000 men but the enemy had 10,000 killed or wounded, and lost 4,000 prisoners.

The mill on the River Kinzig which runs without the town, was the scene of many desperate struggles. Here the French drove the Bavarians to the banks, precipitating hundreds into the deep stream. The miller, however, at the risk of his life, at length coolly went out, amidst a shower of balls and stopped the flood-gates, so as to leave a safe retreat to the Bavarians over the mill-dam. The side of the town next to the scene of battle was constantly taken and retaken by the contending armies, and during the night of the 30th the watch-word was changed not less than seven times. Six of the Austro-Bavarian's generals were killed or wounded and both cannon and flags were left in the power of the conqueror.

The pursuit of Napoleon, which had been intrusted to the Austrians, was far from vigorous and no considerable annoyance succeeded the battle of Hanau. The relics of the French host, now reduced to 60,000 men, at length passed the Rhine; and the emperor, having quitted them at Mayence, arrived in Paris on the 9th of November.

14

The Invasion of France

By the defeat of the emperor in the campaign of 1813 the Confederation of the Rhine was dissolved forever. The princes who adhered to that league were now permitted to sue for forgiveness by bringing a year's revenue and a double conscription to the banner of the Allies. Bernadotte turned from Leipsic to reduce the garrisons which Napoleon had not seen fit to call in, and one by one they fell, though in most cases, particularly at Dantzic, Wirtemberg and Hamburg, the resistance was obstinate and long.

The Crown Prince of Sweden having witnessed the reduction of some of these fortresses, and intrusted the siege of others to his lieutenants, invaded Denmark and the government of that country severed its long adhesion to Napoleon by a treaty concluded at Kiel on the 14th of January, 1814. Sweden yielded Pomerania to Denmark; Denmark gave up Norway to Sweden; and 10,000 Danish troops having joined his standard, Bernadotte turned his face towards the Netherlands. Holland also revolted after Leipsic, the Prince of Orange returning in triumph from England and assumed administration of affairs in the November following. On the side of Italy, Eugene Beauharnais was driven beyond the Adige by an Austrian army headed by General Hiller, and it was not at all likely that he could hope to maintain Lombardy much longer.

To complete Napoleon's perplexity his brother-in-law, Murat, was negotiating with Austria and willing, provided Naples was guaranteed to him, to array the force of that state on the side of the Confederacy. Beyond the Pyrenees, Soult, who had been sent from Dresden to retrieve, if possible, the fortunes of the army defeated in June at Vittoria, had been twice defeated; the fortresses had fallen, and except a detached, and now useless force under Suchet in Catalonia, there remained no longer a single French soldier in Spain.

Such were the tidings which reached Napoleon from his Italian and Spanish frontiers at the very moment when it was necessary for him to make head against the Russians, the Austrians, and the Germans, chiefly armed and supplied at the expense of England, and now rapidly concentrating in three great masses on different points of the valley of the Rhine. The royalists, too, were exerting themselves indefatigably in the capital and the provinces, having recovered a large share of their ancient influence in the society of Paris even before the Russian expedition. The Bourbon princes watched the course of events with eager hope. The republicans, meanwhile, were not inactive. They had long since been alienated from Napoleon by his assumption of the imperial dignity, his creation of orders and nobles, and his alliance with the House of Austria; these men had observed, with hardly less delight than the royalists, that succession of reverses which had followed Napoleon in his last two campaigns. Finally, not a few of Napoleon's own ministers and generals were well prepared to take a part in his overthrow. Talleyrand, and others only second to him in influence, were in communication with the Bourbons, before the allies crossed the Rhine. "Ere then," said Napoleon, "I felt the reins slipping from my hands."

The Allied princes issued at Frankfort, a manifesto on the 1st of December in which the sovereigns announced their belief that it was for the interests of Europe that France should continue to be a powerful state, and their willingness to concede to her, even now, greater extent of territory than the Bourbon kings had ever claimed—the boundaries, namely, of the Rhine, the Alps, and the Pyrenees. Their object in invading France was to put an end to the authority which Napoleon had usurped over other nations. The hostility of Europe, they said, was against,—not France, but Napoleon—and even as to Napoleon, against not his person but his system. These terms were tendered to the emperor himself, and although he authorized Caulaincourt to commence negotiations in his behalf, it was merely for the purpose of gaining time.

Napoleon's military operations were now urged with unremitting energy. New conscriptions were called for, and granted; every arsenal sounded with the fabrication of arms. The press was thoroughly aroused and with its mighty voice warned the allies against an invasion of the sacred soil of France. The French Senate was somewhat reluctant, however; they ventured to hint to the emperor that ancient

France would remain to him, even if he accepted the proposals of the allies. The emperor cried:

> Shame on you, Wellington has entered the south, the Russians menace the northern frontier, the Prussians, Austrians, and Bavarians the eastern. Shame! Wellington is in France and we have not risen *en masse* to drive him back! All my allies have deserted—the Bavarian has betrayed me. No peace until we have burned Munich! I demand a levy of 300,000 men—with this and what I already have, I shall see a million in arms. I will form a camp of 100,000 at Bordeaux; another at Mentz; a third at Lyons. But I must have grown men: these boys only serve to incumber the hospitals and the roadsides. Abandon Holland! Sooner yield it back to the sea! Senators, an impulse must be given—all must march—you are fathers of families—the head of the nation—you must set the example. Peace! I hear of nothing but peace when all around should echo to the cry of war!

The Senate drew up and presented a report which renewed the emperor's wrath. He reproached them openly with designing to purchase inglorious ease for themselves, at the expense of his honour, he said:

> In your address you seek to separate the sovereign from the nation. I alone am the representative of the people. And which of you could charge himself with a like burden? The throne is but of wood, decked with velvet. If I believed you, I should yield the enemy more than he demands; in three months you shall have peace, or I will perish. It is against me that our enemies are more embittered than against France, but on that ground alone am I to be suffered to dismember the State? Do not sacrifice my pride and my dignity to obtain peace. Yes, I am proud because I am courageous; I am proud because I have done great things for France...... You wished to bespatter me with mud, but I am one of those men who may be killed yet not dishonoured. Return to your homes ..... even supposing me to have been in the wrong, there was no occasion to reproach me publicly; dirty linen should be washed at home. For the rest; *France has more need of me, than I have of France.*

Having uttered these words the emperor repaired to his council of state and there denounced the Legislative Senate as one composed of one part of traitors and eleven of dupes he said:

> In place of assisting they impede me. Our attitude alone could have repelled the enemy—they invite him. We should have presented a front of brass—they lay open wounds to his view. I will not suffer their report to be printed. They have not done their duty, but I will do mine—I dissolve the Legislative Senate!

The Pope was now released from his confinement and returned to Rome which he found in the hands of Murat, who had ere then concluded his treaty with Francis and was advancing into the north of Italy, with the view of co-operating in the campaign against Beauharnais, with the Austrians on one side and on the other with an English force recently landed at Leghorn, under Lord William Bentinck. Ferdinand also returned to Spain, after five years of captivity, amid universal acclamations. Bourrienne says:

> When first informed of Murat's treason, by the viceroy (Eugene), the emperor refused to believe it. 'No!' he exclaimed to those about him, 'It cannot be! Murat—to whom I have given my sister! Eugene must be misinformed. It is impossible that Murat has declared himself against me.' It was, however, not only possible but true." As St. Amand well says, in speaking of Murat's desertion: "He might have united his forces with those of Prince Eugene and have attacked the invasion in the rear; he would have saved the Empire of France; he would have died on the throne, covered with glory, instead of being shot!

For a time the inhabitants of the French provinces on the frontier believed it impossible that any foreign army would dare to invade their soil, and it was not until Schwartzenberg had crossed the Rhine between Basle and Schaffhausen on the 20th of December, that they were willing to believe in the sincerity of the Allies and their determination to carry the war into France itself. Disregarding the claim of the Swiss to preserve neutrality, Schwartzenberg advanced through that territory with his grand army, unopposed—an indefensible act in itself, and began to show himself in Franche-Compté, in Burgundy, even to the gates of Dijon.

On the 1st of January, 1814, the Silesian Army, under Blücher, crossed the river at various points between Rastadt, and Coblentz; and shortly after, the army of the north, commanded by Witzingerode and Bülow, began to penetrate the frontier of the Netherlands.

The Pyrenees had been crossed by Wellington and the Rhine by three mighty hosts, amounting altogether to 300,000 men and including every tongue and tribe from the Germans of Westphalia to the wildest barbarians of Tartary. Dumas says:

> Seven hundred thousand men trained by their very defeats in the great school of Napoleonic war, were advancing into the heart of France, passing by all fortified places and responding, the one to the other, by the single cry, 'Paris! Paris!'

The allies proclaimed everywhere as they advanced, that they came as the friends, not the enemies of the French nation, and that any of the peasantry who took up arms to oppose them must be content to abide the treatment of brigands; a flagrant outrage against the most sacred and inalienable rights of mankind.

Meanwhile, nearer and nearer each day the torrent of invasion rolled on, sweeping before it, with but slight resistance, the various corps which had been left to watch the Rhine. Ney, Marmont, Victor and Mortier, commanding in all about 50,000 men, retired of necessity before the enemy.

It now became apparent that the allies had resolved to carry the war into the interior without waiting for the reduction of the great fortresses on the Rhenish frontier. They passed on with hosts overwhelmingly superior to all those of Napoleon's lieutenants, who withdrew, followed by crowds of the rustic population, rushing onwards towards Paris by any means of transport. Carts and wagons, filled with terrified women and children thronged every avenue to the capital.

The emperor now resolved to break silence to the Parisians and prepared to reappear in the field. On the 22nd of January, 1814, the official news of the invasion appeared. The next morning—Sunday—the officers of the National Guard to the number of nine hundred were summoned to the Tuileries. Napoleon took his station in the centre of the hall and immediately the empress, with her son, the King of Rome, carried in the arms of Countess Montesquiou, appeared at his side.

The emperor said:

> Gentlemen, France is invaded; I go to put myself at the head of my troops, and with God's help and their valour, I hope soon to drive the enemy beyond the frontier.

Here he took Marie Louise in one hand and her son in the other,

Napoleon at the Battle of Wagram

and continued:

> But if they should approach the capital, I confide to the National Guard the empress and the King of Rome—my wife and my child!

Several officers stepped from their places and approached with tears in their eyes.

The emperor spent part of the 24th of January in reviewing troops in the courtyard of the Tuileries, while the snow was falling, and at 3 o'clock in the morning of the 25th once more left his capital, after having burnt his most secret papers, and embraced his wife and son for the last time, to begin his fifteenth campaign. Thiers says of this farewell:

> Napoleon, when he left, unconscious that he was embracing them for the last time, hugged tenderly his wife and son. His wife was in tears, and she feared she would never see him again. She was in fact fated never to see him, although the enemy's bullets were not to kill him. She would certainly have been much surprised if she had been told that this husband, then the object of all her care, was to die on a distant island, the prisoner of Europe, and forgotten by her. As for him, no prediction would have astonished him,—whether the cruellest desertion, the most ardent devotion,—for he expected anything from men; he knew them to the core, though he treated them as if he did not know what they really were.

The emperor again appointed Marie Louise[1] Empress-Regent, placed his brother Joseph at the head of her council, gave orders for raising military defences around Paris, and for converting many public buildings into hospitals. He arrived at Chalons ere midnight and found that Schwartzenberg with 97,000 men, and Blücher with 40,000 men, were now occupying an almost complete line between the Marne and the Seine. Blücher was in his own neighbourhood and he immediately resolved to attack the right of the Silesian army,—which was pushing down the valley of the Marne, while its centre kept the parallel course of the Aube,—ere the Prussian marshal could concentrate all his own strength or be supported by Schwartzenberg who was advancing down the Seine towards Bar.

---

1. *Marie-Louise and the Invasion of 1814* by Imbert de Saint-Amand also published by Leonaur.

On the 27th of January a sharp skirmish took place at St. Dizier; and Blücher, who had committed all sorts of excesses during the last two days, warned of Napoleon's arrival, at once called in his detachments and took a post of defence at Brienne—the same town where Bonaparte had received his military education.

The emperor marched through a thick forest upon the scene of his youthful studies and appeared there on the 29th, having moved so rapidly that Blücher was at dinner in the *château* when the French thundered at his gates, and with difficulty escaped to the rear through a passage, on foot and at the head of his staff.

The invaders maintained their place in the town courageously, and some Cossacks, throwing themselves upon the rear of the French, the emperor was involved in the *mêlée*; he quickly drew his sword and fought like a private dragoon and General Gourgaud shot a Cossack while in the act of thrusting a spear at Napoleon's back. The town of Brienne was burned to the ground by the Prussians in order to cover their retreat.

Alsusieff, the Russian commander, and Hardenberg, a nephew of the Chancellor of Prussia, were made prisoners and there was considerable slaughter on both sides. Blücher retired further up the Aube with a loss of 4,000 men and posted himself at La Rothiere, where Schwartzenberg, warned by the cannonade, hastened to co-operate with him.

While at St. Helena Napoleon said that during the charge of the Cossacks at Brienne defending himself, sword in hand, he recognized a particular tree under which, when a boy, he used to sit and read the *Jerusalem Delivered* of Tasso. The field had been in those days, part of the exercise-ground of the students, and the *château*, whence Blücher escaped so narrowly, their lodging.

Blücher now assumed the offensive, having joined Schwartzenberg, and on the 1st of February assaulted the rearguard of the French army. Proud of their numerical superiority they reckoned upon an easy triumph. The battle lasted all day. At nightfall the French were left in possession of their original positions. A battery of guns had been taken, however, and Napoleon lost on this occasion seventy-three guns, and some hundred prisoners, besides a number of killed and wounded. The result of this action was equivalent to a defeat of the French army. The cannoniers saved themselves, with their baggage, by forming a squadron and fighting vigorously as soon as they perceived that there was no time to use their pieces.

The Battle of Brienne and the defence of La Rothiere, Dienville and La Giberie, had gloriously opened the campaign, but Blücher and Schwartzenberg had such considerable forces at their disposal that Napoleon might fear being surrounded, or cut off from his capital, if he persisted in retaining his position in the environs of Brienne. The allies had now definitely resolved to march on Paris.

While the division of Marmont retired down the Aube before Blücher, Napoleon himself struck across the country to Troyes which he had reasons to fear must be immediately occupied by Schwartzenberg. Here he was joined by a considerable body of his Guard, in high order and spirits, whose appearance restored, in a great measure, the confidence of the troops who had been engaged in the defence of La Rothiere. On the 3rd of February the emperor received a dispatch from Caulaincourt, informing him that Lord Castlereagh, the English Secretary of State for Foreign Affairs, had arrived at the headquarters of the allies, that negotiations were to be resumed the morning after at Chatillon, and requesting him to intimate distinctly at what price he would be willing to purchase peace.

Napoleon replied by granting Caulaincourt full powers to do everything necessary "to keep the negotiations alive and save the capital." The duke was unwilling to act upon so broad a basis and sent back once more for a specific detail of the Emperor's purposes.

Napoleon had his headquarters at Nogent, on the Seine, some leagues below Troyes, when the dispatch reached him on the evening of the 8th of February, and his counsellors urged him to make use of this, probably last, opportunity. He was prevailed upon to agree to abandon Belgium, the left of the Rhine, Italy and Piedmont, but in the night after the consultation, and before the ultimatum had his signature, he received information which caused him to change all his views. When Maret visited him with his dispatches ready for signing Napoleon was poring over his maps, tracing the route of Blücher on Paris. "Oh here you are!" he exclaimed as Maret entered, "but I am now thinking of something very different—I am beating Blücher on the map. He is advancing by the road to Montmirail; I will set out and beat him tomorrow. Should this movement prove as successful as I expect it will, the state of affairs will be entirely changed, and we shall then see what can be done."

The emperor had learned that Blücher, instead of continuing his march down the Aube, and in communication with Schwartzenberg on the Seine, had transferred his whole army to the Marne, and was now advancing towards Paris by the Montmirail road.

The separation of their forces by the allies was a great blunder and the emperor, who at once detected it, could not resist the temptation which it presented to make one warlike effort more. Napoleon, therefore, refused to sign the dispatch on the morning of the 9th and having left small forces to defend the bridge over the Seine at Nogent and at Bray, commenced his march, with the main body of his army, upon Sezanne, prepared for one of the most extraordinary and successful manoeuvres which has ever been recorded in the annals of war.

Forty miles were traversed over a most difficult country, usually considered impassable in winter,—ere the troops halted with the dark. Next morning the army moved again with equal alacrity, and at length debouched on the road by which Blücher's army was advancing, at Champaubert.

The central division was passing when Napoleon suddenly appeared at this point, and was altogether unable to resist his assault. They dispersed in confusion with great loss and fled towards the Marne. The general-in-chief, Ousouwieff, at the head of twelve regiments was completely routed. He was taken with 6,000 of his men, and the remainder were drowned in a swamp, or killed on the field of battle. Forty pieces of cannon, and all the ammunition and baggage were left in the power of the victor. Napoleon had now interposed his army between the advanced guard of the Silesian Army, commanded by Sacken, and the rear commanded by Blücher himself.

The van of the same army turned, on hearing the cannonade of Champaubert, and countermarched with the view of supporting Alsusieff only to share the fate of the centre, and were put to flight after the loss of one-fourth of the division.

Now it was Blücher's turn to be beaten. Napoleon mounted his horse at midnight on the 13th and came up with him at Montmirail. At 8 o'clock in the morning the shouting of the soldiers announced the presence of the emperor. Blücher would gladly have declined battle, but it was out of his power. He was conquered but retreated with great skill and courage. After many hours of hard fighting his retreat became a flight. Blücher was frequently obliged to defend himself with his sabre during the day, surrounded by his staff, and chiefly owed his escape to the darkness of the night.

He retired in alternate squares, sustaining all day the charges of the French with much loss of life and at length cut his way, at Etoges, through a column of heavy horse, sent round to intercept him, and drawn up on the causeway.

On the following day there was a fresh success. A hostile column, endeavouring to protect Blücher's retreat, was taken at Château Thierry, where the French troops entered pell-mell upon the Russians and Prussians. Five generals of these two nations were among the prisoners.

Blücher finally crossed the Marne at Chalons. In five days Napoleon's armies had been successful three times; he had shattered and dispersed the Silesian army, and above all, recovered the spirits of his own soldiery.

A column of 7,000 Prussian prisoners, with a considerable number of guns and standards, reminded the Parisians that the commander of the French troops had not forgotten the art of warfare and their hopes were considerably heightened on hearing of these successes against the allies. But these allied armies, annihilated each day, reappeared incessantly, and always ready for battle. All Europe was now contending against the emperor and her beaten and dispersed soldiers were immediately replaced by fresh troops. Scott says:

"So alarmed were the Allies at the near approach of their terrible enemy, that a message was sent to Napoleon, from the Allied Sovereigns, by Prince Schwartzenberg's *aide-de-camp*, Count Par, stating their surprise at his offensive movements, since they had given orders to their plenipotentiaries at Chatillon to sign the preliminaries of peace, on the terms which had been assented to by the French envoy."

Napoleon had, however, learned the meaning of such messages in the course of his career, and paid no attention to this one.

Scarcely had the Parisians seen the prisoners from Montmirail marched along their *boulevards*, before they heard that the Cossacks were in possession of Fontainebleau. Napoleon had left small divisions of his army to guard the Seine at Nogent and Bray, and the enemy soon discovered that the emperor and his chief force were no longer in that quarter. While he was beating Alsusieff, Sacken and Blücher had made good the passage of the Seine at three different points, driving the discomfited guardians of these important places before them. Schwartzenberg now had his quarters at Nangis, and was, obviously, resolved to reach Paris, if possible, while Napoleon was on the Marne. The light troops of the grand allied army were scattering confusion on both sides of the Seine, and one party of them was so near the capital as Fontainebleau.

Napoleon now committed to Marmont and Mortier the care of

watching the Chalons road and the remains of Blücher's army, and marched with his main body on Meaux where on the 15th of February he received reinforcements of 20,000 veterans from Spain, commanded by Grouchy.

The latter's troops had aided Marmont on the 14th in a victory over Blücher at the village of Vauchamp which cost the allies ten thousand prisoners, ten flags, ten pieces of cannon and many prisoners, including General Ouroussoff, in command of the Russian rearguard.

On the 16th Victor and Oudinot were engaged with the van of Schwartzenberg, on the plains of Guignes, when the emperor came rapidly to their assistance. The enemy immediately drew back, and concentrated his strength at Nangis. Napoleon attacked that position on the morning of the 17th, and with such effect that the allies were completely routed and retreated after considerable loss. They halted, however, at Montereau and Victor, who commanded the pursuers on that route, failed to dislodge them because of greatly inferior numbers. Napoleon came up on the morning of the 18th and rebuked Victor; then dismissed him from the service. The marshal, with tears streaming down his face, said: "I will procure a musket, I have not forgotten my old trade; Victor will place himself in the ranks of the Guard."

The emperor was vanquished by this noble language. "Well! Well! Victor," said he, tendering his hand, "remain; I cannot restore you your corps, since I have given it to Gerard, but I award you two divisions of the Guard; go and take the command of them, and let there be no longer a question of anything between us."

The attack then commenced with fury and the bridge and town of Montereau were carried. The defence was long and stern, however, and Napoleon was occasionally seen pointing cannon with his own hand, under the heaviest of the fire. The artillerymen protested at the exposure of his person and entreated him to withdraw. He persisted in his work, answering gaily, "My children! the bullet that shall kill me is not yet cast." The inhabitants of Montereau associated themselves with this triumph by firing from their windows on the Austrians as they passed through the town.

After distributing praises and rewards to the generals who had contributed to gaining this battle, Napoleon thought of those who had delayed their march, or exhibited negligence in their command, and among those reprimanded were Generals Guyot, Digeon and Montbrun, the latter for having abandoned the forest of Fontainebleau to the Cossacks, without resistance.

Pursuing his advantage Napoleon saw the grand army of the invaders continue their retreat in the direction of Troyes, and on the morning of the 22nd arrived before Mery. This town he found occupied, much to his astonishment, not by a feeble rearguard of Schwartzenberg but by a powerful division of Russians, commanded by Sacken and therefore belonging to the apparently indestructible army of Blücher. These unexpected enemies were charged in the streets, and at length retired out of the town,—which was burnt to the ground in the struggle,—and thence beyond the Aube. The emperor then halted, and spent the night of the 22nd of February in a charcoal burner's cottage at Chatres.

Meanwhile negotiations were still pending at Chatillon. Caulaincourt, receiving no answer to his second dispatch sent to Napoleon at Nogent on the 8th of February, proceeded to act on the instructions dated at Troyes on the 3rd; and in effect accepted the basis of the Allies. When Schwartzenberg was attacked at Nangis, on the 17th, he had just received the intelligence of Caulaincourt's having signed the preliminary articles, and he, therefore, sent a messenger to ask why the emperor, if aware of his ambassador's act, persisted in hostilities; but received no answer.

Napoleon sent instead a private letter to the Emperor of Austria, once more trying to gain his friendship. The reply of Francis, written to him from Nangis, reached Napoleon at Chatres on the 23rd. It announced Francis' resolution on no account to abandon the general cause, but declared that he lent no support to the Bourbonists, and urged Napoleon to avert by concession, ere it was too late, total ruin from himself and his House. Napoleon returned the envoy with a note signifying that now he would not consent to a day's armistice, unless the Allies would fall back so as to leave Antwerp in their front. The same evening news came from Paris that the Council of State had discussed the proposals of the Allied Powers, and with only one dissenting voice, now entreated the emperor to accept them. He was urged, anew, to send to Chatillon and accept the basis to which Caulaincourt had agreed.

He answered that he had sworn at his coronation to preserve the territory of the Republic entire, and that he could not sign this treaty without violating his oath. "If I am to be scourged" said he, "let the whip come on me of necessity, and not through any voluntary stooping of my own." The truth of these attempts at negotiation is that the Allies merely desired a simple suspension of arms, in order to gain time to reinforce themselves, and also in order to interrupt the too rapid course of Napoleon's successes in the last eight days. This the emperor easily discerned through the maze of the contrary declarations of the foreign negotiators, and in fact is avowed by the historians of the campaigns of the Allies.

Napoleon now resolved to push on as far as Troyes, at the same time permitting proposals for an armistice to be considered at Lusigny, and negotiations for peace to proceed at Chatillon. The emperor had meanwhile requested Oudinot and Macdonald, with their divisions, to manoeuvre in the direction of Schwartzenberg, in order to keep the Austrians in check.

Napoleon learned at Troyes, in the night of the 26th of February, that the Prussian Army was in motion. His resolution was soon taken. He again hastened to the succour of his capital, and came, with the prodigious celerity which rendered his marches and manoeuvres so distinguishing, to fall upon the rear of Blücher, who still had Marmont and Mortier in front. Marching rapidly across the country to Sezanne he received intelligence that these two generals, finding themselves inferior in numbers to Blücher, had retired before him in the direction of Ferté-sous-Jouarre, and were in full retreat to Meaux. This point he considered as almost a suburb to Paris and he quickened his speed accordingly. Hurrying on, at Ferté-Goucher he was at once met and overtaken by evil tidings. Schwartzenberg, having discovered the emperor's absence, had immediately assumed the offensive, defeated Oudinot and Macdonald at Bar-sur-Aube on the 27th, and driven them before him as far as Troyes; and Augereau, who commanded in the neighbourhood of Lyons, announced the arrival of a new and great army of the Allies in that quarter.

On the 1st of March an important treaty was ratified at Chaumont between the sovereigns of Austria, England, Russia and Prussia, by which the four contracting powers bound themselves each to maintain in the field an army of one hundred and fifty thousand men until the objects of the war were attained; England, as usual, engaging, over and above, to furnish a subsidy of four millions sterling. In a second clause, each of the four powers was bound never to make a separate peace with the common enemy. About the same time the commissioners at Lusigny broke up the negotiations for an armistice, on the plea of inability to settle the line of demarcation.

Napoleon's operations were not checked, however. Having been detained for some time at Ferté, in consequence of the destruction of the bridge, he took the direction of Château Thierry and Soissons, where he hoped to receive Blücher, while Mortier and Marmont received orders to assume the offensive in front of Meaux. The emperor hoped in this manner to throw himself on the flank of Blücher's march, as he had done before at Champaubert; but the Prussian received intelligence of his approach and drawing his troops together, retired to Soissons. Napoleon proceeded thither with alacrity, believing that the French garrison intrusted with the care of that town, and its bridge over the Marne, was still in possession of it, and would enable him, therefore, to force Blücher into action with this formidable obstacle in his rear. He did not know that Soissons had been taken by a Russian corps, retaken by a French one and fallen once more into the hands of the enemy, ere the emperor came in sight of it. He assaulted the place with much vigour but the Russians repelled the attack. Learning that Blücher had filed his main body through the town and posted himself behind the Marne, Napoleon marched up the left bank of the river and crossed it also at Bery.

A few leagues in front of this place, on the height of Craonne, two Russian corps,—those of Sacken and Witzingerode,—were already in position, and the emperor lost no time in charging them there, in the hope of destroying them ere they could unite with Blücher. The battle of Craonne began at 11 a. m. on the 7th of March and lasted until 4 o'clock in the afternoon. The resistance of the enemy was most stubborn and the emperor was preparing for a final effort, when suddenly the Russians began to retreat and he remained master of the field. He followed them; but they continued to withdraw having been ordered to fall back on the plateau of Laon, in order to form thereon the same line with Blücher, who was once more eager for a decisive conflict,—having been reinforced by the vanguard of Bernadotte's army.

On the 9th of March Napoleon found his enemy strongly posted along an elevated ridge, covered with wood, and further protected in front by a succession of terrace walls,—the enclosures of vineyards. There was a heavy mist on the lower ground and the French were advancing up the hill ere their movement was discovered. They were met by a storm of cannonade which broke their centre, and on either flank the French were all but routed. On all points they were repelled, except at the village of Athies, where Marmont had some advantage. Night interrupted the contest, and the armies bivouacked in full view of each other. Napoleon, although he had suffered severely, resolved to renew the attack and mounted his horse accordingly at 4 o'clock in the morning of the 10th. At that moment news came that Marmont's corps had just been assaulted at Athies and were compelled to fly towards Corbeny.

The Battle of Laon continued, all day, however; Napoleon was unable to turn his adversaries and on the 11th he commenced his retreat, leaving thirty cannon and 10,000 men. Soissons had been evacuated by the allies when concentrating themselves for the battle of Laon, and Napoleon threw himself into that town, and was making rapid efforts to strengthen it in expectation of the Prussian advance, when he learned that a detached Russian corps had seized Rheims.

The possession of this city could hardly fail to establish Blücher's communications with Schwartzenberg, and Napoleon instantly marched thither in person leaving Marmont to hold out as well as he could in case that should be the direction of Blücher's march. The emperor came upon Rheims with his usual rapidity and on the 13th took the place by assault.

In this crisis, in which Napoleon was battling against numbers overwhelmingly his superior, it is remarkable to note the energy with which he turned from enemy to enemy, and behold his fearless assaults on vastly superior numbers, his unwearied resolution and exhaustless invention. In his every movement he seemed a perfect master of warfare; but he was battling against odds which even his indomitable will, courage and foresight, could not overcome. It should not be forgotten, also, that in addition to this extraordinary series of campaigns, he continued to conduct, from his perpetually changing quarters, the civil business of his Empire.

The Allies, by a series of victories in various quarters, were now, to all appearance, in full march upon Paris, both by the valley of the Marne, and by that of the Seine, at a moment when Napoleon had thought to defeat their movements by taking up a position between them at Rheims. When Schwartzenberg learned that the emperor was at this point his old terror returned, and the Austrian instantly proposed to fall back from Troyes. This did not please Lord Castlereagh who announced that the Grand Army might retire if the sovereigns pleased, but that if such a movement took place the subsidies of England must be considered at an end. The *Czar* also opposed the overcaution of Schwartzenberg, who then took courage, and his columns instantly resumed their march down the Seine, to offer battle to Napoleon at Arcis.

The emperor was now struggling to decide which of two courses to pursue; should he hasten after Blücher on the Marne, what was to prevent Schwartzenberg from reaching Paris ere the Silesians, already victorious at Laon, could once more be brought to action by an inferior force: should he throw himself on the march of Schwartzenberg, would not the fiery Prussian be at the Tuileries long before the Austrian could be checked on the Seine? There remained a third course—namely, to push at once into the country in the rear of the Grand Army and thus strike the advancing Allies, both the Austrians and Prussians, with terror, and paralyze their movements. Would they persist in their cry, "On to Paris!" when they knew Napoleon to be posting himself between them and their resources, and at the same time relieving and rallying around him all the garrisons of the great fortresses of the Rhine?

While Napoleon was thus tossed with anxiety for means to avert, if it were yet possible, the visitation of these mighty armies upon Paris, and unaware of Castlereagh's very effective threat, the capital showed small symptoms of sympathizing with him. The machinery of government was clogged in every wheel, and the necessity of purchasing peace by abandoning him was the common burden of conversation.

In this extreme situation, the gravity and peril of which he measured with a glance, the emperor felt that he could only escape by a striking and decisive action, and he did not hesitate to direct the intended blow towards Schwartzenberg, whose approach already spread alarm throughout the capital. The Emperor Alexander, on learning the successes of Napoleon at Craonne and Rheims, had feared that Schwartzenberg, by approaching the capital alone, would be again beaten separately, and that all these daily and isolated defeats would end by discouraging the troops of the Coalition, already filled with apprehension and alarm. The Czar, therefore, insisted in that council of war held at Troyes, that the two grand allied armies should forthwith manoeuvre so as to effect their junction in the environs of Chalons, in order to march thence on Paris, and crush everything which might be opposed to their passage.

This advice had prevailed and Napoleon met, on the 20th, before Arcis, the entire army of Schwartzenberg, which was bearing in a mass for this town, in order to cross the Aube, and rapidly gain the plains of Champagne where the junction was to be effected.

This sudden change of system in the military operations of the Allies completely disarranged all the plans of Napoleon, who quickly perceived the difficult and perilous position in which he was placed,

Arrival of the Grand Army at Moscow

by encountering an army three times as strong as his own, where he had only thought to find a rearguard. However, he quickly decided to take the chance by casting into the struggle the weight of his own example, and reckoning his personal dangers for nothing. His cavalry had orders to attack the Austrian light troops while the infantry debouched from Arcis; but they were repulsed by the overpowering numbers opposed to them and driven back upon the town.

In this extremity, Napoleon evinced the same heroic and almost reckless courage which he had shown at Lodi and Arcola, and on other occasions. He threw himself, sword in hand, among the broken cavalry, called on them to remember their former victories, and checked the enemy by an impetuous charge in which he and his staff-officers fought hand to hand with the invaders. Baron Fain, in a volume called *The Manuscript of 1814*, giving an account of the engagement at Arcis, says:

> Surrounded in the crowd by the charges of cavalry, he freed himself only by making use of his sword. On divers occasions, he fought at the head of his escort, and, far from avoiding the dangers, he seemed, on the contrary, to brave them. A shell fell at his feet; he awaited its bursting, and disappeared in a cloud of dust and smoke; he was believed to be lost; presently he arose, flung himself upon another horse, and again went to place himself beneath the fire of the batteries! .... Death would have nothing to do with him!

In spite of the prodigious efforts of the French Army, and the unchangeable heroism of its chief, the Battle of Arcis could not hinder the passage of the Aube, by the Austrians. The emperor retired in good order, on the 21st, after having done the enemy much harm, and held him in check for a whole day; but Schwartzenberg ended by gaining the road which was to conduct him to Blücher.

Napoleon now decided on throwing himself upon the rear of the Allies. They were for some time quite uncertain of his movements after he quitted Rheims, until an intercepted letter to Marie Louise informed them that he was at St. Dizier, where Napoleon had slept on the 23rd. He continued to manoeuvre on the country beyond this point for several days. Having seized the roads by which the Allies had advanced, he took many prisoners of distinction on their way to headquarters and at one time the Emperor of Austria himself escaped narrowly a party of French hussars. At St. Dizier, Caulaincourt rejoined the emperor and announced to him the definite rupture of the negotiations with the Allies. This, however, was no surprise; but was expected. The only real discomfiture it caused was among the malcontents in the army, whose chief regret was at being from Paris, and who asked each other, barely out of hearing of the emperor, "Where are we going? What is to become of us? If he falls, shall we fall with him?"

On the 26th of March the distant roaring of artillery was heard at intervals on the *boulevards* of Paris and the alarm began to be violent. On Sunday the 27th, Joseph Bonaparte held a review in the Place Carrousel. That same evening the allies passed the Marne at various points and at 3 o'clock in the morning they took Meaux. The regular troops now marched out of the capital, leaving all the barriers in charge of the National Guard. On the 29th the empress, her son, and most of the members of the Council of State, set off attended by 700 soldiers, for Rambouillet from which they continued their journey to Blois. Queen Hortense, afflicted at seeing the empress-regent and her son abandon the capital to intriguers and conspirators, strongly pressed her to remain, and said with a prophetic conviction: "If you leave the Tuileries, you will never see them again!"

Pons de L' Herault, a historian of the period, says:

> One of the most astonishing circumstances of the moment is undeniably, the obstinacy with which the King of Rome refused to depart. This obstinacy was so great, that it became necessary to use violence in order to remove the young prince. The cries of the infant-king were heart-rending. He repeated several times: 'My father told me not to go away!' All the spectators shed tears.

The young prince had declared again and again that "his papa was betrayed" and his declaration has never been satisfactorily accounted for and can only be explained by the supposition that he had heard the subject discussed among those who considered that all was lost in abandoning the capital.

Joseph now published the following proclamation

> Citizens of Paris! A hostile column has descended on Meaux. It advances; but the emperor follows close behind, at the head of a victorious army. The Council of Regency has provided for the safety of the empress and the King of Rome. I remain with you. Let us arm ourselves to defend this city, its monuments, its

riches, our wives, our children—all that is dear to us. Let this vast capital become a camp for some moments; and let the enemy find his shame under the walls which he hopes to overleap in triumph. The emperor marches to our succour. Second him by a short and vigorous resistance, and preserve the honour of France.

The appeal did not produce the results hoped for. Some officers urged Savary to have the streets unpaved and persuade the people to arm themselves with stones and prepare for a defence such as Saragossa. He answered, shaking his head, "the thing cannot be done."

On the 30th the Allies fought and won the final battle. The French occupied the whole of the range of heights from the Marne at Charenton, to the Seine beyond St. Denis; the Austrians beginning the attack about 11 o'clock towards the former of these points, while nearly in the midst between them, a charge was made by the Russians on Pantin and Belleville. The French troops of the line were commanded by Marmont and Mortier; those battalions of the National Guard, whose spirit could be trusted, and who were adequately armed, took their orders from Marshal Moncey and formed a second line of defence. The scholars of the Polytechnic School volunteered to serve at the great guns, and the artillery though weak in numbers, was well arranged.

At the barrier of Clichy, in particular, the Allies met with a spirited resistance. The pattern of the French soldiers, the brave Moncey, was there, with his son, and with him Allent, the leader of his staff; celebrated artists and distinguished writers surrounded him and shared his perils. Among the former was Horace Vernet whose Napoleonic pictures have since become famous in two continents. The defence of the city, while brave and determined was ineffectual, and courage was at length compelled to yield to numbers.

By 2 o'clock the Allies were victorious at all points except Montmartre. Marmont then sent several *aides-de-camp* to request an armistice and offer a capitulation in order to save the capital. The *Czar* and the King of Prussia professed their willingness to spare the city, provided the regular troops would evacuate it.

Blücher meanwhile continued pressing on at Montmartre and shortly after 4 o'clock, the victory being completed in that direction, the French cannon were turned on the city and shot and shells began to spread destruction within its walls. The capitulation was drawn up at 5 o'clock, close to the barrier St. Denis.

It was not until the 27th that Napoleon distinctly ascertained the fact of both the allied armies having marched directly on Paris. He instantly resolved to hasten after them, in hopes of arriving on their rear ere they had mastered the heights of Montmartre. Arriving at Doulevent on the 29th he received a message from Lavalette, his postmaster general, who wrote:

> The partisans of the stranger are making head, aided by secret intrigues. The presence of the emperor is indispensable—if he desires to prevent his capital from being delivered to the enemy. There is not a moment to be lost!

Urging his advance accordingly, Napoleon reached Troyes on the night of the 29th, his men having marched fifteen leagues since daybreak. General Dejean, his *aide-de-camp*, rode on before him bound for Paris to announce to the Parisians that the emperor flew to succour them.

On the 30th Macdonald attempted to convince him that the fate of Paris must have been decided ere he could reach it, and advised him to march, without further delay, so as to form a conjunction with Augereau. The marshal said:

> In that case we may unite and repose our troops, and yet give the enemy battle on a chosen field. If Providence has decreed our last hour, we shall at least die with honour, instead of being dispersed, pillaged and slaughtered by Cossacks.

The emperor was unwilling to abide by the counsel of his marshal, but continued to advance; finding the road beyond Troyes clear he threw himself into a post-chaise and travelled on before his army at full speed. At Villeneuve L'Archereque he mounted on horseback and galloping without a pause, reached Fontainebleau late at night. Here he ordered a carriage, and taking Caulaincourt and Berthier, drove on towards Paris. He was still of the belief that he was yet in time—until, while he was changing horses at an inn called "La Cour de France," but a few miles from Paris, General Belliard came up, at the head of a weary column of cavalry marching towards Fontainebleau, in consequence of the provisions of Marmont's treaty with the Allies. He was too late! Paris had capitulated!

Leaping from his carriage as the words reached his ears, the emperor exclaimed, "What means this? Why here with your cavalry, Belliard? And where are the enemy? Where are my wife and boy? Where Marmont? Where Mortier?"

Belliard, walking by his side, told him of the events of the day. Still the emperor insisted on continuing his journey although again informed there was no longer an army in Paris; that the regulars were all coming behind, and that neither they nor he himself, having left the city in consequence of a convention, could possibly return to it. It seemed impossible for him to comprehend the astounding intelligence of Belliard who said; "Paris is surrounded by one hundred and thirty thousand enemies."

Napoleon bade Belliard turn with his cavalry and follow him. "Come" said he "we must return to Paris,—nothing goes aright when I am away—they do nothing but blunder!" As he progressed he continued, "You should have held out longer—you should have raised Paris—they cannot like the Cossacks—they would surely have defended their walls. Go! Go! I see everyone has lost his senses. This comes of employing fools and cowards."

The emperor and Belliard continued Paris-ward, until they were met, a mile beyond the post-house, by the first column of the retreating infantry. Their commander, General Curial, reiterated what Belliard had said. "In proceeding to Paris," he said, "you rush on to death or captivity." The emperor then became at once perfectly composed and abandoned his design, gave orders that the troops, as they arrived, should draw up behind the little River Essonne, and dispatched Caulaincourt to Paris to ascertain if it were yet possible for him to interpose in the treaty. Having taken this measure he turned back towards Fontainebleau.

Caulaincourt reached the *Czar's* quarters at Pantin early in the morning of the 31st of March where he found a deputation from the municipality of Paris waiting to present the keys of the city and invoke the protection of the conqueror. The *Czar* received them immediately on arriving and promised that the capital, and all within it, should be treated with perfect consideration.

Caulaincourt then found his way to Alexander; but he was dismissed immediately. The Allies had practically agreed in favouring the restoration of the Bourbons, ere any part of their forces entered the capital, and a proclamation signed, "Schwartzenberg, Commander of the Chief of the Allied Armies" was distributed throughout Paris in which there were many phrases not to be reconciled with any other position. The royalists welcomed with exultation the dawn of the 31st and issued proclamations of their own appealing for restoration, besides parading the streets without interruption from either the civil authorities or of the National Guard, although decorated with the symbols of their cause.

At noon the first of the Allied troops began to pass the barrier and enter the city, and the triumphal procession lasted for several hours. Fifty thousand troops, horse, foot and artillery, marched along the boulevards and in their midst appeared the youthful *Czar* and the King of Prussia, followed by a dazzling suite of princes, ambassadors and generals.

The *Czar* repaired to the hotel of Talleyrand where a council was convened. Alexander and Frederick were urged to re-establish the House of Bourbon. They hesitated: "It is but a few days ago" said the *Czar*, "since a column of five or six thousand troops suffered themselves to be cut in pieces before my eyes, when a single cry of '*Vive le Roi!*' would have saved them." One of those present answered "Such things will go on as long as you continue to treat with Bonaparte even although at this moment he has a halter round his neck." The *Czar* did not understand this allusion until it was explained to him that the Parisians were busy pulling down Napoleon's statue from the top of the great pillar in the Place Vendome.

Alexander now signed a proclamation asserting the resolution of the Allies "to treat no more with Napoleon Bonaparte, or any of his family." That same evening the *Czar*, by his minister, declared that "Louis XVIII will immediately ascend the throne." A few days later myriads of hands were busy in every corner of the city pulling down the statues and pictures and effacing the arms of Napoleon.

Caulaincourt returned to Fontainebleau in the night between the 2nd and 3rd of April and informed Napoleon that the monarchs he had so often spared, and whose royal destinies he could have closed after Austerlitz, Jena, and Wagram, refused to treat with him,—and demanded his abdication. He added that the Allies had not yet, in his opinion, made up their minds to resist the scheme of a regency, but that he was commissioned to say that nothing could be arranged as to ulterior questions, until he, the emperor, had formally abdicated.

Napoleon was not yet prepared to give up his throne; the news both irritated him and made him indignant. He again wished to try the lot of arms; but his old companions-in-arms declared they would take no further part in the war. The next day, the 4th of April, he reviewed some of his troops, addressed them on "the treasonable proceedings in the capital," and announced his intention of instantly marching thither, being answered by shouts of "Paris! Paris!" Nearly 50,000 men were now stationed around Fontainebleau. On parade, Napoleon looked pale and thoughtful, while his convulsive motions manifested his internal struggles, and he did not stop many minutes. On retiring to the chateau, after the review, the emperor was followed by his marshals, who informed him that if he refused to negotiate on the basis of his personal abdication, and persisted in risking an attack on Paris, they would not accompany him. He paused for a moment in silence—then a long debate ensued, ending in his drawing up and signing the following:

> The Allied Powers having proclaimed that the Emperor Napoleon was the sole obstacle to the re-establishment of peace in Europe, he, faithful to his oath, declares that he is ready to descend from the throne, to quit France, and even to relinquish life, for the good of his country; which is inseparable from the rights of his son, from those of the regency in the person of the empress, and from the maintenance of the laws of the empire. Done at our Palace of Fontainebleau, April the 4th, 1814.
>
> Napoleon.

Caulaincourt was appointed to bear this document to Paris and the marshals proposed that Ney should accompany him. It was suggested that Marmont should also form a part of the deputation but he being in command at Essonne, Macdonald was named in his stead. The officers now desired to know on what stipulations, as concerned the emperor personally, they were to insist. "On none," he answered; "obtain the best terms you can for France—for myself I ask nothing." They then departed.

Shortly afterwards Napoleon asked Oudinot if the troops would follow him. "No, Sire" answered the marshal, "you have abdicated."

"Yes, upon certain conditions."

"The soldiers" resumed Oudinot, "do not comprehend the difference; they think you have no more any right to command them."

"Well then," said Napoleon, "it is no more to be thought of; let us wait for accounts from Paris."

Marmont, whom he had loaded with favours, had in the meantime joined the Allies, and by a nocturnal march of his army passed over into the midst of the enemy, enabling them to appear more exacting than ever, and which caused Napoleon to denounce his treason to the army by an order of the day in which he scanned the conduct of the Senate who had also, on April 2nd, declared Napoleon Bonaparte and his family expelled from the throne of France. Meneval says:

> Marshal Marmont's desertion was a mortal blow to the Imperial cause. It decided the Emperor Alexander, who till then had appeared to hesitate on the question of a regency, to exact in the name of the Allied Powers, the unconditional abdication of the emperor.

Talleyrand said dryly, when someone called Marmont a traitor, "his watch only went a little faster than the others," and in this he spoke truthfully, for officers of all ranks now rapidly abandoned the camp at Fontainebleau, and presented themselves to swear allegiance to the new government, impatient to enjoy in peace the honours and riches with which Napoleon had loaded them.

Caulaincourt, Ney and Macdonald, on being admitted to the presence of the *Czar*, the act of abdication was produced. Alexander was surprised that it should have contained no stipulations for Napoleon personally; "but I have been his friend" said he "and I will willingly be his advocate. I propose that he shall retain his imperial title, with the sovereignty of Elba, or some other island."

When Napoleon's envoys retired from the presence of the *Czar* it still remained doubtful whether the abdication would be accepted in its present form, or the Allies would insist on an unconditional surrender. At length they signified their intention to accept of nothing but an unconditional abdication. These terms were finally borne by the marshals to their waiting chief. The marshals returned in the night about twelve. Ney entered first: "Well, have you succeeded?", said Napoleon.

"Revolutions do not retrograde," answered the veteran marshal, "this has begun its course; it was too late: tomorrow the Senate will recognize the Bourbons."

"Where shall I be able to live with my family?"

"Where your Majesty pleases; for example, in the isle of Elba, with a revenue of six millions."

"Six millions! that is a great deal for a soldier as I am. I see very well I must submit."

The form of abdication submitted by the marshals was to the following purport:

1st. The imperial title to be preserved by Napoleon, with the free sovereignty of Elba, guards, and a navy suitable to the extent of that island; a pension, from France, of six millions of *francs* annually.

2nd. The Duchies of Parma, Placentia and Guastalla to be granted in sovereignty to Marie Louise and her heirs, and

3rd. Two millions and a half of *francs* annually to be paid, by the French government, in pensions to Josephine and other members of the Bonaparte family.

Napoleon hesitated when he received the formal ultimatum of the invading powers. He thought seriously of continuing the war, but the group of his personal followers had been rapidly thinned by desertion.

On the 11th of April he at length abandoned all hope and the next day executed an instrument called the treaty of Fontainebleau formally "renouncing for himself and his heirs, the thrones of France and Italy." Concerning the act Napoleon said:

> I blush for it; what avails a treaty, since they will not settle the interests of France with me. If only my personal interests are concerned, there is no need of a treaty. I am conquered; I yield to the fate of arms. All I ask is, not to be accounted a prisoner of war.

To all suggestions referring to his providing for his future wants he replied, "What matters it? A horse and a crown a day are all I want!"

Baron Fain, his secretary, says:

> Napoleon, when he affixed his name to the abdication, made two or three scratches, and a dent, with the stump of his pen, or back of a knife, on the little, round, claw-footed, yellow table, on which it was signed. After the resignation of the empire, he spent his time either in conversation in his apartment, or in a small English garden at the back of the palace.... Napoleon, during those days of distress, was seated alone for hours and amused himself by kicking a hole, a foot deep, with his heel, in the gravel beneath.... At the moment of Bonaparte's abdication, he remarked that instruments of destruction had been left in his way; he seemed to think that they were placed there purposely, in order that he might attempt his own life; and with a sardonic smile, said, 'Self-murder is sometimes committed for love—what folly! Sometimes for the loss of fortune—there it

is *cowardice*! Another cannot live after he has been disgraced—*what weakness*! But to survive the loss of empire, to be exposed to the results of one's contemporaries,—*that is true courage!*'

15

Exile To Elba

The armies of the Allies had gradually pushed forward from Paris and now nearly surrounded Fontainebleau. When the last of the marshals had quitted Napoleon's presence for the night, after imperiously demanding his resignation, he revolted at the humiliations he had to undergo and disgusted at their cowardice, exclaimed:

> These men have neither hearts nor entrails. I am conquered less by fortune than by the selfishness and ingratitude of my brothers-in-arms!

The same night, in a fit of despair he swallowed a weak poison contained in a bag that he had worn around his neck since 1808. The palace was aroused by his cries and Dr. Yvan hastily summoned by his valet. An antidote was given him and his life saved. To Caulaincourt he said an hour later:

> God would not allow it. I could not die. Why did they not let me die? It is not the loss of my throne that makes existence insupportable to me. My military career is enough glory for one man. Do you know what is more difficult to bear than reverses of fortune? It is the baseness, the horrible ingratitude of men. I turned my head away with horror from the sight of their meanness and their contemptible selfishness, and I am disgusted with life. What I have suffered during the last three weeks, no one can tell.

Some months later, while at Elba, Napoleon ascribed his ruin entirely to Marmont, to whom he had confided some of his best troops, and a post of the greatest importance, as a person on whose devotion to him he could most depend. "For how could I expect to be betrayed," he said, "by a man whom I had loaded with kindness from the time he was fifteen years of age? Had he stood firm, I could have driven the Allies out of Paris, and the people there,—as well as throughout France,—would have risen, in spite of the Senate, if they had had a few troops to support them."

The emperor remained long enough at Fontainebleau to hear of the restoration of the Bourbon Monarchy, and on the 20th of April, the commissioners of the Allied Sovereigns having arrived, he once more called his loyal officers about him and signified that they were summoned to receive his last *adieu*. A few of the marshals and others who had sworn fealty to the new monarch were also present. Napoleon said:

> Louis (the king), has talents and means: he is old and infirm; and will not, I think, choose to give a bad name to his reign. If he is wise, he will occupy my bed, and only change the sheets. He must treat the army well, and take care not to look back on the past, or his time will be brief. For you, gentlemen, I am no longer to be with you;—you have another government; and it will become you to attach yourselves to it frankly, and serve it faithfully as you have served me.

As he passed along he beheld all that now remained of the most brilliant and numerous courts in Europe, reduced to about sixteen individuals, who thus waited to manifest their regard and respect for the fallen emperor. Junot, had died the year before, and Caulaincourt and General Flahault were absent on missions. Napoleon shook hands with them all; then hastily passing the range of carriages, he advanced towards the relics of the Imperial Guard which he had desired to be drawn up in the courtyard of the castle. He advanced to them on horseback and tears dropped from his eyes as he dismounted in their midst he said:

> Soldiers of the Old Guard, I bid you farewell! During twenty years you have been my constant companions in the path of honour and glory. In our last disasters, as well as in the days of our prosperity, you invariably proved yourselves models of courage and fidelity. With such men as you, our cause could not have been lost; but a protracted civil war would have ensued, and the miseries of France would thereby have been augmented. I have, therefore, sacrificed all our interests to those of the country. I depart: you, my friends, will continue to serve France,

whose happiness has ever been the only object of my thoughts, and still will be the sole object of my wishes. Do not deplore my fate. If I consent to live, it is that I may still contribute to your glory. I will record the great achievements we have performed together. Farewell, my comrades! I should wish to press you all to my bosom. Let me at least embrace your standard.

At these words, General Petit took the eagle and came forward. Napoleon received the general in his arms, and kissed the flag. The silence of this affecting scene was only interrupted by the occasional sobs of the soldiers. Having kissed the flag, Napoleon said with great emotion, "Farewell once more my old comrades! Let this kiss be impressed on all your hearts!"

On this occasion the English commissioner who stood near him, and had previously been his inveterate enemy, was so deeply moved that he was affected in the same degree as Napoleon's attendants. When leaving Napoleon called for Rustan, his Mameluke servant, but the latter had concealed himself, though on the preceding day he had received from his master, at Fontainebleau, a present of 30,000 *francs* to provide for his wife and family during his absence. The emperor, in speaking afterwards of this man who nightly slept across his doorway, said:

> I am by no means astonished at his conduct, as he was imbued with the sentiments of a slave; and, finding me no longer master, he imagined his services might be dispensed with.

Napoleon now hurried through the group that surrounded him—stepped into his carriage, and instantly drove off. The carriages took the road to Lyons.

Four commissioners, one each from the great Allied Powers, Austria, Russia, Prussia and England, accompanied him on his journey. He was attended by the ever faithful Bertrand, Grand Master of the Palace, and some other attached friends and servants. While fourteen carriages were conveying him and his immediate suite towards Elba, 700 infantry and about 150 cavalry of the Imperial Guard,—all picked men and volunteers,—marched in the same direction to take on them the military duties of the exiled court.

Not far from Lyons Napoleon met Augereau, general-in-chief of the Army of the East, whose conduct during the late campaign had been that of a traitor. When Augereau had taken his leave from his ex-chief one of the commissioners ventured to express surprise that

Retreat from Moscow—1814

Napoleon should have treated him with such a show of affection. "Why should I not?" he asked.

"Your Majesty is perhaps unacquainted with his conduct. Sire, he entered into an understanding with us several weeks ago!"

The emperor afterwards confirmed this anecdote, adding:

"The conqueror of Castiglione might have left behind him a name dear to his country; but France will execrate the memory of the traitor of Lyons."

During the early part of his progress the exile was received respectfully by the civil functionaries of the different towns and departments, and many tokens of sympathy on the part of the people were expressed. As he increased the distance between himself and his capital, and was carried into provinces wherein his name had never been extremely popular, he was once or twice subjected to personal insult, and danger of violence, when the horses were changing. At Lyons, an old woman in mourning, and with a countenance full of enthusiasm, rushed forward to the door of the carriage. "Sire" said she, with an air of solemnity, "may the blessing of heaven attend your endeavour to make yourself happy. They tear you from us; but our hearts are with you, wheresoever you go."

The Austrian commissioner, quite disconcerted, said to his companion, "Let us go; I have no patience with this mad woman!"

At length Napoleon disguised himself and sometimes appearing in an Austrian uniform, at others riding on before the carriages in the garb of a courier, reached in safety the place of embarkation. A French vessel had been sent round from Toulon to Cannes, for the purpose of conveying him to Elba; but there happened to be an English frigate also in the roads and he preferred sailing under any flag rather than the Bourbon. The voyage to Elba was uneventful. Napoleon succeeded in making a favourable impression on the English crew and when, on finally leaving the *Undaunted*, he caused some two hundred *napoleons* ($800) to be distributed among the sailors, the boatswain undertook to return thanks in the name of the crew by "wishing him a long life—*and better luck next time!*" As he left the vessel a royal salute was fired.

The emperor of the little island of Elba came in view of his new dominions on the afternoon of May 4th, 1814, and went ashore in disguise the same evening, in order to ascertain for himself whether the feelings of the Elbans were favourable or otherwise. He found the people considered his residence as likely to increase in every way the importance and prosperity of their island, and returned on board the ship; at noon the day following he made his public entry into the town of Porto-Ferrajo amidst many popular demonstrations of welcome and respect. The English and Austrian commissioners landed with him, those from Russia and Prussia having departed at the coast of Provence. When the exile climbed to the hill above Ferrajo, and looked down upon the whole of his territory, as upon a map, he remarked to Sir Neil Campbell, the English commissioner, "It must be confessed that my island is very small."

The island, however, mountainous and rocky, for the most part barren, and of a circumference not exceeding sixty miles, was his. He forthwith devoted to it the same anxious care and industry that had sufficed for the whole affairs of France, and a large portion of Europe besides. In less than three weeks he had thoroughly acquainted himself with its history, resources and the character of its people, had explored every corner of the island "and projected more improvements of all sorts" according to one historian, "than would have occupied a lifetime to complete." He even extended his "Empire" by sending some soldiers to take possession of a small adjacent islet, hitherto unoccupied for fear of *corsairs*. He established residences in four different corners of Elba and was continually in motion from one to the other.

All the etiquette of the Tuileries was adhered to as far as possible, and Napoleon's eight or nine hundred veterans were reviewed as frequently and formally as if they had been the army of Austerlitz or Friedland, and over which hung the flag of Elba which the emperor had adopted, and which was that of the island,—white, striped with purple and studded with stars. Sometime later he adopted a new flag as King of Elba; silver with a red band, the latter having bees of gold on it. The emperor wore the uniform of the Colonel of the Horse Chasseurs of the Guard. He had substituted on his *chapeau* the red and white cockade of the island for the tri-coloured cockade. His presence gave a new stimulus to the trade and industry of the island and the port of Ferrajo was crowded with vessels from the opposite coast of Italy.

Napoleon received no money whatever from the Bourbon court, his pension having been entirely forgotten by his successors at the capital. His complaints on this head were not even considered, and the exchequer of the exile being rapidly depleted by his generous expenditures, he soon became in need of many necessities. These new troubles embittered the spirit of the fallen chief and but for the course of events at Paris, of which he was kept fully advised, would have become overpowered by a listlessness which at one time affected him seriously.

While on the island the emperor observed that his new flag had become the first in the Mediterranean. It was held sacred, he said, by the Algerians, who usually made presents to the Elban captains, telling them they were paying the debt of Moscow. Some Algerian ships once anchoring off the island, great alarm was caused among the inhabitants, who questioned the pirates, and asked them plainly whether they came with any hostile views. "Against the Great Napoleon;" they replied, "Oh! never; we do not wage war on God!"

Louis XVIII. had made his public entry into Paris on the 21st of April. He was advanced in years, gross and infirm in person, yet he was, perhaps, less unpopular than the rest of his family; but it was his fatal misfortune to continue to increase day by day the bitterness of those who had never been sincerely his friends. The king had been called to the throne by the French Senate in a decree which provided that he should preserve the political system "which Napoleon had violated," and which declared the legislative constitution as composed of a hereditary sovereign and two houses of assembly; to be fixed and unchangeable. Louis, however, though he proceeded to France on this invitation, did not hesitate to date his first act in the twentieth year of his reign.

The Senate saw in such assumptions the traces of those old doctrines of "the divine right of kings," of which Louis was a shining example, and which they, who though not originally of his party, had consented to his recall—although they had through life abhorred and combated such principles; and they asked themselves, why, if all their privileges were but the gifts of the king, they might not, on any tempting opportunity, be withdrawn by the same authority. They, whose titles had all been won since the death of Louis XVI., were startled when they found, that, according to the royal doctrine, *there had been no legitimate government all that time in France!*

The first tumult of the Restoration being over, and the troops of the Allies withdrawn, things began to so shape themselves that there were many elements of discontent amongst all classes, one of the most powerful of which was in the army itself. The Allies had restored, without stipulation, the whole of the prisoners who had fallen into their hands during the war. At least 150,000 veteran soldiers, all of whom had fought under Napoleon on many battlefields, were thus poured into France ere Louis was well seated on the throne; men, too, who had witnessed nothing of the last disastrous campaigns; who had sustained themselves in their exile by recounting their earlier victories; and who now, returning fresh and vigorous to their native soil, had but one answer to every tale of misfortune which met them: "These things could never have happened had we been here!"

The Empress Marie was at Blois at the time Napoleon signed his abdication, and Savary has described her grief as very great, but her own reverses were sufficiently severe to account for this, without any strong feeling for Napoleon. By direction of Napoleon she applied for protection to the Emperor of Austria and went to Rambouillet to meet him, where he explained to her that she was to be separated from her husband "for a time." The Emperor Alexander visited her also, very much against her will, and a few days afterwards she departed for Vienna.

Alexander also visited Josephine, and found her distress at Napoleon's abdication very great. She appears never to have recovered from the shock for she survived it only about six weeks. She died on the 29th of May, 1814, at Malmaison, and was buried in the church of Ruel. Her funeral was attended by several generals of the allied armies, and marshals and generals of France. The body was afterwards placed in a magnificent tomb of white marble, erected by her two children, and bearing the simple inscription:

Eugene and Hortense to Josephine.

Napoleon's mother, and sister Pauline, as well as a number of ancient and attached servants of his civil government and his army, visited him during the summer of 1814. Not the least of these was Pauline, who made repeated voyages to Italy, and returned again as mysteriously. In the circles of Ferrajo new and busy faces now appeared and disappeared—no one knew whence they had come or whither they went and an air of bustle and mystery pervaded the atmosphere of the place. The emperor continued to review his handful of veteran soldiers with as much pride as if they had been the innumerable hosts he had led to victory on the Continent, and seemed to be fairly well contented with his situation notwithstanding he had fallen from an eminence that had been reached by no other man in modern times. The only notable change observed in his habits was that he became grave, and reserved, and seemed no longer to take any interest in the improvements he had effected on the island.

It was evident, however, that something was preparing; but the commissioners who watched over Napoleon were unable to fathom it. They repeatedly remarked on the absurdity of the Allied Powers in withholding his pension, which they had solemnly pledged should be paid every quarter, thereby tempting him to release himself; but their reports were left unnoticed by those in whose hands they fell. This obliged the emperor to sell every luxury and comfort around him to raise the means of paying his current expenses. Then it was that he began to forecast the future and to contemplate a bold stroke, not only for liberty, but to regain his lost throne before he could be transported to St. Helena which he had been informed privately was being discussed at Vienna.

In this he was aided by a nation which was far from satisfied with the man whose possession of the royal sceptre had only been made possible by the force of foreign armies, and it was apparent to nearly everyone that Louis XVIII. could not long rule France tranquilly, even though Napoleon did not return.

Ere autumn closed Napoleon granted furloughs on various pretexts to about two hundred of his Guard, and these at once scattered themselves over France singing his praises. It now began to be whispered that the exile would return to the soil of France in the spring of the coming year. Among the soldiery and elsewhere he was toasted under the *sobriquet* of "Corporal Violet," a flower or a ribbon of its colour being the symbol of rebellion, and worn openly in the sight of the unsuspecting Bourbons. It was by this secret symbol that Napoleon's friends knew each other. Rings of a violet colour with the device, "It will reappear in the spring," became fashionable; women wore violet-coloured silks and the men displayed watch-strings of the same colour; while the mutual question when these friends met was generally, "Are you fond of the violet?" to which the answer of a confederate was, "Ah! well."

The representatives of all the European princes had met in Vienna to settle finally a number of questions left undecided at the termination of the war, including a division of the "spoils." Talleyrand was there for France, Wellington for England, Metternich for Austria. On the 11th of March these representatives, who were then discussing among other things "how to get rid of the Man of Elba," were thrown into a panic by the news that Napoleon Bonaparte had reared his standard once more in France and was marching on Paris!

Of the state of affairs in France Napoleon had been fully advised as well as of the sessions of the ministers at the Congress of Vienna, who had suggested that, as the French Government would not honestly pay his pension, he should be taken to some place of greater safety, and St. Helena was even mentioned at this time. This determined Napoleon to act, especially as he was fully convinced that he had a good chance of being well received by the twenty or thirty millions of people who were being treated with contempt by Louis XVIII. and his followers. The arrival also of M. Fleury de Chaboulon, with secret messages from Maret, (Duke of Bassano) then at Paris, had much to do with the hasty determination of Napoleon to quit Elba at the earliest moment possible. Reserved as the exile was with others he told his mother of his plans. He said to her:

> I cannot die on this island, and terminate my career in a repose unworthy of me. Besides, want of money would soon leave me here alone, exposed to the attack of my enemies.

His mother reflected for some time in silence and then replied:

> Go, my son—go and fulfil your destiny! You will fail perhaps, and your failure will soon be followed by your death. But I see with sorrow that you cannot remain here; let us hope that God, who has protected you amid so many battles, will save you once more!

Bertrand, who was sharing Napoleon's exile, was now informed of the emperor's decision as was also Druot who at once commenced secret preparations for the approaching expedition. Eleven hundred soldiers were collected of whom 800 belonged to the Guard and 300 to the 35th light infantry that Napoleon had found in the island. None of these men had any idea of the projected enterprise. Colonel Campbell, who was watching proceedings in Elba for the English, had left Ferrajo and gone to Leghorn. There remained then only the cruisers that were easily deceived or avoided. In order to keep his preparations a profound secret, Napoleon, two days before embarking, laid an embargo on the vessels in the harbours of Elba, and cut off all communication with the sea. He then ordered his ordnance officer, Vantini, to seize one of the large vessels lying in the port, which, with the *Inconstant* of twenty-six cannon, and six other smaller craft, making in all seven vessels, he secured the means of embarking his eleven hundred men and four pieces of field artillery. He had decided to commence his romantic enterprise on the 26th of February, 1815.

On this day he allowed his soldiers to remain at their usual employment until the middle of the day. They were suddenly summoned in the afternoon and after being lightly fed, were assembled with arms and baggage on the pier where they were informed that they were to go on board the vessels. The inhabitants of the island regretted the exile's departure as they feared its prosperity would go with him. Napoleon's staff and about three hundred men embarked on board the *Inconstant*, the others being distributed in the other vessels of the flotilla.

The discharge of a single cannon at about 7 o'clock in the evening was the signal agreed upon for weighing anchor, and when the sails were unfurled, and the little fleet steered its course, reiterated cries of "Paris or death!" were heard from the exultant troops. The emperor had said to them, "Grenadiers! we are going to France; we must march to Paris!"

The English commissioner immediately attempted to get Napoleon's mother and sister to betray his destination and being unsuccessful, at once pursued; but was unable to overtake his charge. On the voyage a French ship-of-war crossed his path; but the emperor made all his soldiers and those persons who could be suspected descend under the deck, and the steersman of the *Inconstant*, who happened to be well acquainted with the commanding officer, had received and answered the usual challenge without exciting any suspicion. In reply to the question of how they left the emperor at Elba, Napoleon himself made answer by signal that, "He was very well."

During the voyage he dictated two proclamations which were copied by almost all his soldiers and attendants who could write. These were to be duplicated on landing and distributed throughout France.

The emperor, having left Elba on the 26th of February, arrived off Cannes, near Fréjus, on March 1st,—the very spot he had touched when he arrived from Egypt, and from which he had embarked ten months before. He landed without opposition, and his handful of men,—500 grenadiers of the Guard, 200 dragoons and 100 Polish lancers, these last without horses and carrying their saddles on their backs, were reviewed and immediately began their march on Paris. He bivouacked that night in a plantation of olives, with all his men about him. As soon as the moon rose, the *reveillé* sounded. A labourer who was going thus early to work in the fields recognized the emperor's person, and uttering a cry of joy, said he had served in the Army of Italy and would join the ranks. "Here is a reinforcement already!" said

Napoleon to Bertrand, and after spending the balance of the evening in chatting familiarly with his Guard, the march towards Paris recommenced.

Early in the morning they passed through the town of Grasse, and halted on the height beyond it. There the whole population of the place surrounded them, some cheering and many others maintaining perfect silence; but none offered any show of opposition. The peasants blessed his return; but, on viewing his little band looked upon him with pity, and entertained no hope of his ultimate success. The roads were so bad that the pieces of cannon which they had with them were abandoned in the course of the day, but they marched full twenty leagues ere they halted for the night at Seranon. Thiers says:

> Before arriving at this stopping place the emperor stopped a few minutes in a hut, occupied by an old woman and some cows. Whilst he warmed himself before a brushwood fire he entered into conversation with the old country-woman, who little imagined what guests she entertained beneath her humble thatch, and was asked, 'What news from Paris?' She seemed surprised at a question to which she was little accustomed, and replied very naturally that she knew of none. 'You don't know what the king is doing then?' said Napoleon.
> 'The king?' answered the old woman, still more astonished, 'the king! You mean the emperor—he is always *yonder*.'

This dweller in the Alpine country was wholly ignorant that Napoleon had been hurled from his throne and replaced by Louis XVIII. All present were struck with astonishment at witnessing this extraordinary ignorance. Napoleon, who was not less surprised than the others, looked at Druot and said, "Well, Druot, of what use is it to disturb the world to fill it with one's name?"

On the 5th of March the emperor reached Gap, where he published his first proclamations,—one to the army and another to the French people. The former said:

> Soldiers! We have not been conquered. Two men, raised from our ranks, (Marmont and Augereau) have betrayed our laurels, their country, their prince, their benefactor. In my exile I have heard your voice. I have arrived once more among you, despite all obstacles, and in all perils. We ought to forget that we have been the masters of the world; but we ought never to suffer foreign interference in our affairs. Who dares pretend to be master

over us? Take again the eagles which you followed at Ulm, at Austerlitz, at Jena, at Eylau, at Friedland, at Tudela, at Eckmuhl, at Essling, at Smolensk, at Moskowa, at Lutzen, at Wurtchen, at Montmirail. Soldiers! come and range yourselves under the banners of your old chief. Victory shall march at the charging step. The eagle, with the national colours, shall fly from steeple to steeple, till it reaches the towers of Notre Dame! In your old age, surrounded and honoured by your fellow-citizens, you shall be heard with respect when you recount your high deeds. You shall then say with pride, 'I also was one of that great army which entered twice within the walls of Vienna, which took Rome, and Berlin, and Madrid and Moscow, and which delivered Paris from the stain printed on it by domestic treason, and the occupation of strangers.'

Between Mure and Vizele, Cambronne, who commanded Napoleon's advanced guard of forty grenadiers, met suddenly a battalion sent forward from Grenoble to arrest the march. The colonel refused to parley with Cambronne and either party halted until the emperor came up. Napoleon did not hesitate for a moment but dismounted and advanced alone; some paces behind him came about a hundred of his Guard, with their arms reversed. There was perfect silence on all sides until the returned exile was within a few yards of the men. He then halted, threw open his *surtout*, so as to show the star of the Legion of Honour, and exclaimed, "If there be among you a soldier who desires to kill his general—his emperor—let him do it now. Here I am!"

The old cry of "*Vive l'Empereur!*" burst instantly from every lip. Napoleon threw himself among them, and taking a veteran private, covered with scars and medals, by his beard, said, "Speak honestly, old Moustache, couldst thou have had the heart to kill thy Emperor?"

The old soldier dropped his ramrod into his piece to show that it was not loaded, and answered, "Judge if I could have done thee much harm—*all the rest are the same!*" The soldiers had now broken their ranks and were surrounding the emperor, kissing his hands and calling him their general, their emperor, their father. The commander of the 5th battalion, thus abandoned by his soldiers, knew not what to do, when Napoleon, freeing himself from the throng stepped forward, asked his name, his grade, his services and then added: "My friend, who made you chief of battalion?"

"You, Sire,"

"Who made you captain?"

"You, Sire,"

"And would you fire on me?"

"Yes" replied the brave man, "in the performance of my duty."

He then gave his sword to Napoleon, who took it, pressed his hand and in a voice that clearly indicated that the weapon would be restored at that point, said, "Meet me at Grenoble." Turning to Bertrand and Druot the emperor then said: "All is decided: within ten days we shall be in the Tuileries!"

Napoleon now gave the word, and the old adherents and the new began the march together towards Grenoble. Ere they reached that town Colonel Labedoyere, an officer of noble family, and who had been promoted by Louis XVIII., appeared on the road before them at the head of his regiment, the seventh of the line. These men and the emperor's little column, on coming within view of each other, rushed simultaneously from their ranks and embraced with mutual shouts of, "Live Napoleon! Live the Guard! Live the Seventh!"

Labedoyere now produced an eagle, which he had kept concealed about his person, and broke open a drum which was found to be filled with tri-coloured cockades. As these ancient ensigns were exhibited by the first officer of superior rank who voluntarily espoused the side of the returned exile, renewed enthusiasm was apparent on all sides. Napoleon then questioned young Labedoyere concerning the state of Paris, and France in general. That gallant officer answered with much frankness:

> Sire, the French will do everything for your Majesty; but your Majesty must do everything in return for them; no more ambition, no more despotism; we are determined to be free and happy. It is necessary, Sire, to renounce that system of conquest and power which occasioned the misfortune of France and yourself.

Napoleon replied, "I know that. I return to revive the glory of France, to establish the principles of the Revolution and to secure to the nation a degree of liberty which, though difficult at the commencement of my reign, is now become not only possible but necessary."

This act of Labedoyere was most decisive, for in spite of all the efforts of General Marchand, commandant at Grenoble, the whole of

Departure of Napoleon for Paris

that garrison, when he approached the walls, shouted "*Vive l'Empereur!*" Though welcoming Napoleon with their voices and shaking hands with his followers through the wicket below, they would not so far disobey the governor as to throw open the gates. Neither could any argument prevail upon them to open fire on the advancing party and in the very teeth of all their batteries Napoleon calmly planted a howitzer or two and blew the gates open. Then, as if the spell of discipline was at once dissolved, the garrison broke from their lines and dragging the emperor from his horse, bore him aloft on their shoulders towards the principal inn of the place, amidst the clamours of enthusiastic and delirious joy. The inhabitants of Grenoble, being unable to bring him the keys of the city, brought him with acclamations, the shattered gates instead, exclaiming: "For want of the keys of the good city of Grenoble, here are the gates for you!" Next morning he reviewed his troops, now amounting to about 7,000, and on the 9th recommenced his march.

On the 10th of March Napoleon came within sight of Lyons and was informed that Marshal Macdonald had arrived to take the command, had barricaded the bridge of Guillotierre, and posted himself at the head of a large force to dispute the entrance of the town. Nothing daunted with this intelligence, the column moved on, and at the bridge of Lyons, as at the gates of Grenoble, all opposition vanished when the person of the emperor was recognized by the soldiery. Macdonald was forced to retire and Napoleon entered the second city of France in triumph. Macdonald would have been taken prisoner by his own troops, had not some of them, more honourable than the rest, insisted on his escape being unobstructed. He thereupon returned to Paris where he once more hoped to make a stand.

A guard of mounted citizens who had been formed to attend on the person of Count d'Artois, the heir of the empire, and who had accompanied Macdonald, were the foremost to offer their services to the emperor after he reached the hotel; but he rejected their assistance and dismissed them with contempt. Finding that one of their number had followed the Prince until his person was out of all danger, Napoleon immediately sent to that individual the cross of the Legion of Honour.

Meanwhile, during the week that the emperor had continued his march Parisward without opposition, the newspapers of the capital were silent, and none ventured to make any allusion whatever to his successes. There then appeared a royal decree, proclaiming Napoleon

Bonaparte "an outlaw," and convoking, on the instant, the two Chambers. Next day the *Moniteur* announced that, surrounded on all hands by faithful garrisons and a loyal population, this "outlaw and invader" was already stripped of most of his followers, was wandering in despair among the hills, and certain to be a prisoner within two or three days at the utmost! Louis received many addresses full of loyalty and devotion from the public bodies of Paris, from towns and departments, and, above all, from the marshals, generals and regiments who happened to be near the capital. The partisans of Napoleon at Paris, however, were far more active than the royalists.

They gave out everywhere that, as the proclamation addressed "To the French people" from Gap had stated, Napoleon came back thoroughly cured of that ambition which had armed Europe against his throne; that he considered his act of abdication void, because the Bourbons had not accepted the crown on the terms which it was offered, and had used their authority in a spirit, and for purposes at variance with the feelings and the interests of the French people; that he was come to be no longer the dictator of a military despotism, but the first citizen of a nation which he had resolved to make the freest of the free; that the royal government wished to extinguish by degrees all memory of the Revolution; that he was returning to consecrate once more the principles of liberty and equality, ever hateful to the eyes of the old nobility of France, and to secure the proprietors of forfeited estates against all machinations of that dominant faction;—in a word, that he was fully sensible of the extent of his past errors, both of domestic administration and of military ambition, and desirous of nothing but the opportunity of devoting, to the true welfare of peaceful France, those unrivalled talents and energies which he had been rash enough to abuse in former days.

Napoleon's friends declared, too, and with much show of authority, that the army was, high and low, on the side of the emperor; that every detachment sent to intercept him would but swell his force so that nothing could prevent him from taking possession of the Tuileries ere a fortnight more had passed over the head of the Bourbon King.

Napoleon remained at Lyons from the 10th to the 13th of March. Here he formally resumed the functions of civil government, published various decrees, one of which commanded that justice be administered everywhere in his name after the 15th, another abolishing the Chambers of the Peers and the Deputies and summoning all the electoral colleges to meet in Paris to witness the coronation of

Marie Louise and her son, and settle definitively the constitution of the State; a third, ordering into banishment all those whose names had not been erased from the list of emigrants prior to the abdication of Fontainebleau; a fourth, depriving all strangers and emigrants of their commissions in the army; a fifth, abolishing the order of St. Louis, and bestowing all its revenues on the Legion of Honour; and a sixth restoring to their authority all magistrates who had been displaced by the Bourbon government.

These publications soon reached Paris and caused much alarm among the adherents of the king.

Marshal Ney now received orders from the Minister of War to take command of a large body of troops whose fidelity was considered sure, and who were about to be sent to Lons-le-Saunier, to intercept and arrest the returning exile before he could make further progress. Ney immediately rode to Paris from his retired country-seat and there, for the first time, learned of the disembarkation of Napoleon from Elba. He is even said to have declared that he would bring his former chief to Paris in a cage, like a wild beast, in the course of a week. On reaching Lons-le-Saunier he received a letter from Napoleon reminding him of their former campaigns and summoning him to join his standard as the "bravest of the brave."[1] Ney had a secret interview with a courier who brought this letter, with one from Bertrand. Generals Lecourbe and Bourmont, by whom the marshal was attended, advised him not to oppose a torrent which was too powerful for any resistance he could bring against it.

While in this state of doubt and indecision, sorely perplexed as to his exact duty, he received intelligence that his vanguard, posted at Bourg, had gone over to Napoleon, and that the inhabitants of Chalons-sur-Saone had seized the park of artillery. All this confirming what Ney had just been told by the courier, he exclaimed, "It is impossible for me to stop the incoming water of the ocean with the palm of my hand!" Accordingly, on the following morning, he published an order of the day, declaring that "the cause of the Bourbons was lost forever, and that the legitimate dynasty which the French nation had adopted was about to reascend the throne."

This order was read to the troops and was received by them with rapture; some of the officers, however, remonstrated and left their command. One, before he went away, broke his sword in two, and threw the pieces at Ney's feet, saying, "It is easier for a man of honour

---

1. *The Bravest of the Brave* by A. Hilliard Atteridge also published by Leonaur.

to break iron than to infringe his word."

Ney put his soldiery in motion forthwith, and joined the march of the emperor on the 17th of March at Auxerre, being received by Napoleon with open arms. Ney avowed later that he had chosen the part of Napoleon long ere he pledged his oath to Louis, adding that the greater number of the marshals were, like himself, original members of the Elban conspiracy to again place him on the throne.

In and about the capital there still remained troops sufficient in numbers to overwhelm the advancing column, and Louis intrusted the command of these battalions to Marshal Macdonald, who proceeded to establish himself at Melun with the king's army, in the hopes of being supported by his soldiers in the discharge of his commission.

On the 19th Napoleon slept once more in the *château* of Fontainebleau, and on the morning of the 20th he advanced through the forest, alone, and with the full knowledge of Macdonald's arrangements. About noon the marshal's troops, who had been for some time under arms on an eminence beyond the wood, perceived suddenly a single open carriage coming at full speed towards them from among the trees. A handful of Polish horsemen, with their lances reversed, followed the equipage. The little flat cocked hat; the gray *surtout*; then the person of Napoleon was recognized. In an instant the men burst from their ranks, surrounded him with the cries of "*Vive l'Empereur!*" and trampled their white cockades in the dust. Macdonald escaped to Paris but Louis had not awaited his last stand. He had set off from the Tuileries in the middle of the preceding night, amidst the tears and lamentations of several courtiers, taking the road to Lisle. McDonald soon overtook and accompanied him to the frontier of the Netherlands, which he reached in safety.

Napoleon once more entered Paris on the evening of the 20th of March. He came preceded and followed by the soldiery on horseback, and on whom alone he had relied. At the Tuileries he was received with every possible demonstration of joy and was almost stifled by the pressure of those enthusiastic adherents who, the moment he stopped in the court-yard of the palace, mounted him on their shoulders and carried him in triumph up the great staircase of the palace. The emperor, during this dramatic proceeding, continued to exclaim, "Be steady my good children; be steady I entreat you." A piece of his coat being either purposely or by accident torn off, was instantly divided into hundreds of scraps, for the procurement of each remnant of which, by way of relic, there was as much struggling as if the effort had been made to become possessed of so many ingots of gold. He found in the apartments, which the king had but lately vacated, a brilliant assemblage of those who had in former times filled the most prominent places in his own councils and court.

"Gentlemen," said Napoleon, as he walked round the circle, "it is disinterested people who have brought me back to my capital. It is the subalterns and the soldiers that have done it all. I owe everything to the people and the army."

All night long the cannon of Marengo and Austerlitz pealed forth their joyous sounds, the city was brilliantly illuminated, and all except the Bourbons, who, as Thiers happily says, "during twenty-five years had neither learned or forgotten anything," were rejoicing at the return of the exile. Napoleon had now proved that he was not only emperor of the army but of the citizens, the people, the peasantry, and the masses. With a handful of men he had marched from one end of the kingdom to the other, entered the capital and taken possession of the throne, and that without shedding even one drop of blood!

He assigned, among other reasons for leaving Elba, that in addition to the violation of the treaty of Fontainebleau in failing to pay his pension, that his wife and child had been seized, detained, and never permitted to join him; that the pensions to his mother and brothers were alike refused, and that assassins had been sent over to Elba, for the express purpose of murdering him. This last charge has also been made by Savary with much positiveness. "Last year," said Napoleon, "it was said that I recalled the Bourbons; this year they recall me; so we are equal!"

Previous to the morning of the 20th of March the nights had been rainy and the days sombre and cloudy; but on this morning, the anniversary of the birth of the young King of Rome, the day was ushered in by a brilliant sun and which produced a strong effect on the populace who again referred in their acclamations to the "sun of Napoleon" as they had that of Austerlitz, ten years before. On the following day the whole population of the capital directed their steps towards the Tuileries and repeated *anon* and *anon* their pleasure at the return of the emperor who had, between the 1st and the 20th of March, fulfilled that strange prophecy in which he said, victory would march at the charging step, and that the imperial eagle would fly, without pause, from steeple to steeple, to the towers of Notre Dame, even to the dome of the Palace of the Tuileries!

16

The Hundred Days. Waterloo

The instant that news of Napoleon's daring movement reached Vienna, the Congress, although on the point of dissolution, published a proclamation in which it was said:

> By breaking the convention which had established him in Elba, Bonaparte destroyed the only legal title on which his existence depended; and by appearing again in France, with projects of confusion and disorder, he has deprived himself of the protection of the laws, and has manifested to the universe that there can be neither peace or truce with him. The powers consequently declare, that Napoleon Bonaparte has placed himself without the pale of civil and social relations, and that as an enemy and disturber of the tranquillity of the world, he has rendered himself liable to public vengeance.

All Europe was now prepared once more for war. A formal treaty was entered into by which the four great powers, England, Austria, Russia and Prussia, bound themselves to maintain, each of them, at least 150,000 troops in arms until Napoleon should either be dethroned, or reduced so low as no longer to endanger the peace of Europe. The other states of the Continent were to be invited to join the alliance, furnishing contingents adequate to their respective resources.

It was stipulated that in case England should not furnish all the men agreed upon she would compensate by paying at the rate of $150 *per annum* for every cavalry soldier, and $100 for every foot soldier under the full number.

On the day following his return from Elba, Napoleon reviewed all the troops in Paris, and addressed them in one of those stirring and eloquent speeches which had never failed to excite their enthusiasm. In beginning his address, he said:

> Soldiers, I am returned to France with twelve hundred men, because I relied upon the love of the people, and the remembrance of me with the veteran troops. I have not been deceived in my expectations; I thank you, soldiers. The glory of all that is achieved is due to the people and yourselves. My only merit consists in having justly appreciated you.

Cries of "*Vive l'Empereur!*" filled the air and were redoubled when General Cambronne entered at the head of the officers of the battalion of the Guard, which had accompanied him to and from Elba, and carrying the imperial eagles. On observing the ancient emblems, Napoleon exclaimed:

> Behold the officers of the battalion who accompanied me in the hour of misfortune! They are all my friends; they are dear to my heart; whenever I beheld them, they presented to my view the different regiments composing the army; for, in the number of these six hundred brave men, there are individuals of every corps. In loving them, it is all of you, soldiers of the whole army, that I loved. They come to restore you those eagles; let them prove to you the rallying point! Swear that they shall be found everywhere, when the interests of the country shall require them; that the traitors, and those who would subjugate our territory, may never be able to support their view.

"We swear!" came the vociferous replies of the soldiers to the strains of the band playing: "Let us watch over the safety of the empire."

Among the peals that rent the air, those of the working class were particularly audible, their incessant cries being ouched in these terms: "The Great Contractor is returned; we shall now eat bread!"

Napoleon was hardly reseated on his throne ere he learned that he must in all likelihood defend himself against 225,000 Russians, 300,000 Austrians, 236,000 Prussians, an army of 150,000 men furnished by the minor States of Germany, 50,000 contributed by the government of the Netherlands, and 50,000 English, commanded by the Duke of Wellington; in all 1,100,000 soldiers! From the moment he re-established himself in the Tuileries, he began that period of his government, which has been designated the "Hundred Days," in order to meet this gigantic confederation. Carnot became once more

Minister of War, and showed the same energy he had manifested during the Consulate. Napoleon had the nation with him at that moment, notwithstanding the proclamations of Louis XVIII.,—which had found their way into the capital,—announced the speedy arrival of a million foreign soldiers under the walls of Paris to replace him on his throne and drive away the "usurper."

The Duchess d'Angoulême was the last of the royal family who remained in France. She had thrown herself into Bordeaux, trusting to the friendly feeling of the mayor and citizens. She made strong efforts to maintain the Bourbon cause, and behaved with so much spirit as to make Napoleon pass an eulogium on her as "the only man of her family." But her efforts failed.

The effective force of the army in France, when Napoleon landed at Cannes, consisted of but about 93,000 men. The cavalry had been greatly reduced, and the disasters of 1812, 1813 and 1814 were still visible in the deficiency of military stores, and arms,—especially of artillery. By almost incredible exertions, although now unable to adopt the old method of conscription, by the middle of May the emperor had over 375,000 men in arms,—including an Imperial Guard of 40,000 chosen veterans,—all in a splendid state of equipment and discipline; a large and brilliant force of cavalry, and a train of artillery of proportional extent and excellence. He had laboured unremittingly to raise the military strength of France to a height sufficient once more to repel the attack of all Europe, and was employed fifteen or sixteen hours a day during the whole of this period. Men, clothing, arms, horses, and discipline were wanting.

All the veterans were now recalled to the ranks. They came in crowds, leaving the employments to which they had applied themselves to the number of one hundred thousand men. All the officers on half pay were also summoned to action.

Napoleon made several attempts to open a negotiation with the Allies, and urged three arguments in defence of his "breach of the Convention" by which he had become sovereign of Elba: 1st, the detention of his wife and son by the Court of Austria: 2nd, the non-payment of his pension, and 3rd, the voice of the French nation which he had heard and obeyed, as evidenced by the fact that by the end of March the tri-coloured flag was displayed on every tower in France.

During the last days of the Congress of Vienna, Murat's possession of the throne of Naples was under discussion, and Talleyrand was endeavouring to dethrone him and place thereon the King of the Sicilies. When Napoleon landed on the shores of France, Murat resolved to rival his brother-in-law's daring and without further pause marched to Rome, at the head of 50,000 men, the Pope and cardinals fleeing at his approach. Murat then advanced into the north of Italy, inviting "all true Italians" to rally round him, and assist in the erection of their country into one free and independent state, with himself at their head.

The Austrian commander in Lombardy put his troops in motion at once to meet Murat, and the latter's followers fleeing in confusion, their leader sought personal safety in flight. On quitting his wretched remnant of an army he returned *incognito* to his capital on the evening of the 18th of May. As he embraced his queen,—Napoleon's sister,—he exclaimed, with emotion, "All is lost, Caroline, except my own life, and that I have been unable to throw away!"

He departed in a fishing vessel which landed him near Toulon about the end of May. Here he lingered for some time, entreating Napoleon to receive him at Paris, and being unsuccessful, after a series of extraordinary hardships, relanded on the coast of Naples after the King of the Two Sicilies had been re-established on that throne.

Murat hoped to invite an insurrection and recover what he had lost; but was seized, tried, and executed, meeting his fate with heroic fortitude. To those who took his life he said at the last moment, "Save my face; aim at my heart!" At St. Helena, Napoleon often said that the fortune of the world might have been changed had there been a Murat to head the French cavalry at Waterloo.

Austria was now concentrating all her Italian forces for the meditated re-invasion of France; the Spanish army began to muster towards the passes of the Pyrenees, the Russians, Swedes and Danes were already advancing from the north, while the main armies of Austria, Bavaria and the Rhenish princes were rapidly consolidating themselves along the Upper Rhine. Blücher was once more in command of the Prussians in the Netherlands; and Wellington, commanding in chief the British, Hanoverians and Belgians, had also established his headquarters at Brussels by the end of May. It was very evident to Napoleon that the clouds were thickening fast and he at once began preparations to defend himself ere his frontier had been crossed on all sides.

Among other preparations, the emperor had now strongly fortified Paris and all the positions in advance of it on the Seine, the Marne, and the Aube, and among the passes of the Vosgesian hills. Lyons, also, had been guarded by very formidable outworks. Massena, at Metz, and Suchet, on the Swiss frontier, commanded divisions which the emperor judged sufficient to restrain Schwartzenberg for some time on the Upper Rhine. Should he drive them, in the fortresses behind could hardly fail to detain him much longer.

Meanwhile Napoleon had resolved to himself attack the most alert of his enemies, the Prussians and the English, beyond the Sambre,—while the Austrians were thus held in check on the Upper Rhine; and ere the armies of the North could debouch upon Manheim, to co-operate by their right with Wellington and Blücher, and by their left with Schwartzenberg.

On the 14th of May, previously appointed as the day of procession and solemn festival of the "Federates,"—operatives and artisans of Paris—the emperor rode along their ranks, received their acclamations, and harangued them in his usual strain of eloquence. In the meantime, however, Fouché, Minister of Police, had already begun to hold traitorous communications with the Austrian government. In one instance Napoleon had discovered this fact, and had nearly caused him to be arrested; but he abstained, apparently from apprehension of the Republican party, amongst whom Fouché was a busy pretender.

The ceremony of the "*Champ-de-Mai*" took place on the 1st of June, in the open space facing the Military School. The Imperial and National Guards and troops of the line, amounting in all to 15,000 soldiers, were drawn up in squares in the Champ-de-Mars and an immense concourse of spectators thronged every vacant space from which a view of the scene could be gained. After a religious solemnity, a patriotic address was delivered to the emperor by the electors of the departments, to which he replied: "Emperor, Consul, Soldier—I hold all from the people. In prosperity, in adversity, in the field of battle, in council, on the throne, in exile, France has been the sole object of all my thoughts and actions."

The emperor then proceeded to the altar and took an oath to observe the new constitution, which had been adopted by upwards of a million and a half votes, and in which he was followed by his ministers and the electoral deputations. The ceremony concluded with the distribution of the eagles to the troops, and with loud and repeated acclamations, and cries of "*Vive l'Empereur!*" from the soldiers and multitude assembled. On the following day the emperor gave a grand *fête*, in the gallery of the Louvre, to the deputies of the army and the electors, on which occasion he was again greeted with every manifestation of devotion and fidelity. On the 4th of June, Napoleon attended in person the opening of the Chambers and delivered addresses which were both firm, open and sensible.

By this time the emperor had made most extraordinary progress in his preparations for war. The effective strength of the army had been raised to 365,000 men, of whom 117,000 were under arms, clothed, disciplined and ready to take the field. They were formed into seven grand corps, besides several corps of observation stationed along the whole line of the frontiers, which were then threatened on every side. What Napoleon now required was time to prepare the means of defence; but this his enemies were far from intending to allow.

Their immense armaments were already passing on towards the frontiers of France, in different lines, and at considerable intervals, for the convenience of subsistence. The emperors of Russia and Austria, and the King of Prussia, had once more placed themselves at the head of their respective armies. The Austrians, amounting to 300,000 men, commanded in chief by Schwartzenberg, were divided into two bodies, one of which was to enter France by Switzerland, the other by the Upper Rhine. Two hundred thousand Russians were marching towards Alsace, under the Archduke Constantine. The Prussian Army amounted to two hundred and thirty-six thousand men; of whom one half were already in the field. The minor states of Germany had furnished one hundred and fifty thousand; the Netherlands, fifty thousand; England, eighty thousand, including the King's German Legion, and other troops in British pay, under the command of the Duke of Wellington;—in all 1,016,000 soldiers!

Among these hosts it was the army commanded by the Duke of Wellington, and the Prussians under Blücher, which were first in the field. They occupied Belgium and amounted to upwards of two hundred thousand men, of whom rather less than one half were ranged under the English commander-in-chief.

Two plans of campaign presented themselves to the mind of Napoleon. One was to remain entirely on the defensive, leaving to the Allies the odium of striking the first blow against the liberties of nations. He believed that as they would not begin the invasion until the middle of July, it would be the middle of August before they could make their way through the fortresses, and appear in force before Lyons and Paris. Large armies, could, before that time, be concentrated by him under the walls of these two cities, and there the battles must be fought and decided.

Return of Napoleon from Elba

The second plan was to assume the offensive before the Allies had completed their operations, by marching into Belgium and attacking the armies of Wellington and Blücher. His numbers would be inferior, but his tactics would aim at preventing the junction of the two armies opposed to him and beating them separately, in which event Belgium would to a certainty rise and join his cause. He finally resolved on the latter plan of campaign. His calculations, were, in part, disturbed by a serious insurrection in La Vendée, which obliged him to send 20,000 men into that province, in order to quell it, and reduced his disposable forces to one hundred and twenty thousand men; but did not alter his determination. The army was put in motion, and every preparation made for the approaching struggle.

The emperor left Paris on the night between the 11th and 12th of June, as some writers declare "to measure himself against Wellington." The Imperial Guard had commenced its march on the 8th, and all the different corps of the army were in motion towards Maubeuge and Phillipville. When he had made known his intention of commencing the war, Caulaincourt solicited the favour of attending him. "If I do not leave you at Paris" answered Napoleon, "on whom can I depend?" Even then he felt that it was not the Allies alone that he had to contend against; and when he had left Paris he seemed less apprehensive of the enemies before, than those he had left behind him. To Bertrand's wife he said, as he took her hand at departing, "Let us hope, Madame Bertrand, that we may not soon have to regret the Island of Elba."

Napoleon arrived at Vervins on the 12th of June and assembled and reviewed at Beaumont on the 14th, the whole of the army which had been prepared to act immediately under his own orders. They had been most carefully selected, and formed, and it was, perhaps, the most perfect force, though far from the most numerous, with which he had ever taken the field. The returns showed that his army amounted to one hundred and twenty-two thousand four hundred men, with three hundred and fifty pieces of cannon. These included 25,000 of his Imperial Guard, 25,000 cavalry in the highest condition, and artillery admirably served. Count Labedoyere says:

> The whole army was superb and full of ardour; but the emperor, more a slave than could have been credited to recollections and old habits, committed the great fault of replacing his army under the command of its former chiefs, most of whom, not-

withstanding their previous addresses to the king, did not cease to pray for the triumph of the Imperial cause; yet were not disposed to serve it with that ardour and devotion demanded by imperious circumstances. They were no longer men full of youth and ambition, generously prodigal of their lives to acquire rank and fame; but veterans, weary of warfare, who, having attained the summit of promotion, and being enriched by the spoils of the enemy, or the bounty of Napoleon, indulged no other wish, than the peaceable enjoyment of their good fortune under the shade of those laurels, they had so dearly acquired.

The emperor reminded his soldiers, in a fiery proclamation issued on the 14th of June, that the day was the anniversary of the Battle of Marengo and of Friedland.

Then, as after Austerlitz and Wagram, we were too generous. We gave credit to the protestations and oaths of the princes whom we suffered to remain on their thrones. Now, however, having coalesced among themselves, they aim at the independence and the most sacred rights of France. They have commenced the most unjust of aggressions. Are we no longer the same men? Fools that they are! A moment of prosperity blinds them. The oppression and the humiliation of the French people are out of their power. If they enter France, there will they find their tomb. Soldiers! We have forced marches to make; battles to wage; perils to encounter; but with constancy the victory will be ours. The rights—the honour of the country—will be honoured. For every Frenchman who has a heart, the moment has now arrived either to conquer or perish!

The army of Blücher numbered at this time about 120,000 men. They communicated on their right with the left of the Anglo-Belgian Army, under Wellington, whose headquarters were at Brussels. Blücher's forces extended along the line of the Sambre and the Meuse, occupied Charleroi, Namur, Givet, and Liege. The Duke of Wellington's host amounted in all to 75,000 men; his first division occupied Enghien, Brain-le-Compte and Nivelles, communicating with the Prussian right at Charleroi. The second division,—Lord Hills',—was cantoned in Halle, Oudenard and Gramont, together with the greater part of the cavalry. The reserve, under Sir Thomas Picton, was quartered at Brussels and Ghent. The English and Prussian commanders had thus arranged their troops with the view of being able to support each other, wherever the French might hazard their assault.

In the night between the 14th and 15th, scouts returned to the headquarters of the French, reporting that there was no movement among the invaders at Charleroi, Namur or Brussels, thus verifying the emperor's belief that the plans for concealing the movements of his army during the last few days were successful. The Duke of Wellington, in a letter to Lord Bathurst, on the 13th, declared his disbelief in the report that Napoleon had joined the army, and it was not until the afternoon of the 15th that he possessed any knowledge of the position and intentions of Napoleon. On that day, an officer of high rank arrived at Wellington's headquarters in Brussels with the intelligence of Napoleon's decisive operations.

General Bourmont, a *protegé* of Ney, with Colonels Clouet and Villoutreys, and two other officers, had gone over to the enemy with all the emperor's plans. Napoleon knew from Marshal Ney that Bourmont had shown some hesitation, and he had been backward in employing him. Bourmont, however, having given General Gerard his word of honour to serve the emperor faithfully; and the general in question, whom Napoleon valued highly, having for his integrity, the emperor consented to admit him into the service. He had covered himself with glory in 1814, and it was not to be expected that he would in 1815 go over to the enemy on the eve of a battle. A drum-major, who deserted from the French ranks some hours before General Bourmont and his two companions, was conducted under an escort to the headquarters of Blücher, at Namur, where he gave the first intelligence of Napoleon's intended attack. This was confirmed by Bourmont, Clouet and Villoutreys who added details with which the drum-major could not possibly have been acquainted.

Later on, in speaking of these traitors, Napoleon said, "Their names will be held in execration so long as the French people form a nation. This desertion increased the anxiety of the soldiers."

The emperor immediately made those alterations in his plan of attack, as such unexpected treason rendered necessary, and then proceeded to carry out the details of his campaign. He had determined on first attacking the Prussians, as he believed Blücher would give him battle at once, in order to allow the English time to collect their forces. He believed also, that if the English Army were attacked first, Blücher would more rapidly arrive to the support of the English than the latter were likely to do if the Prussians were first attacked.

Ney had been placed in command of 43,000 men, with orders to advance on the road to Brussels and make himself master of the position of Quatre-Bras, at all points, so as to prevent Wellington from supporting the Prussians. He was to march at daybreak, on the 16th, occupy the position and intrench himself.

On Thursday, the 15th of June, the French drove in all the outposts on the west bank of the Sambre at daybreak and at length assaulted Charleroi, it being the intention of the emperor to crush Blücher ere he could concentrate all his own forces,—far less be supported by the advance of Wellington,—and then rush on Brussels. Zietten held out with severe loss at Charleroi; but long enough for the alarm to spread along the whole Prussian line and then fell back on a position between Ligny and Amand, where Blücher now awaited Napoleon's attack at the head of his whole army, except the division of Bülow, which had not yet come up from Liege.

The design of beating the Prussians in detail was not a success but the second part of the plan—that of separating them wholly from Wellington, might still succeed. With this view, while Blücher was concentrating his force about Ligny, the French held the main road to Brussels from Charleroi, beating some Nassau troops at Frasnes, and following them as far as Quatre-Bras, a farmhouse, so-called because it is there that the roads from Charleroi to Brussels, and from Nivelles to Namur cross each other.

On Thursday a Prussian officer arrived at Wellington's headquarters in Brussels, with the intelligence of Napoleon's decisive operations. It is still an open question just what hour this news was received by the Duke, the time being variously stated at from 1 to 6 o'clock p.m. This news was to the effect that the attack had commenced and the outposts of the Allies had been driven back—much to Wellington's surprise, as he was not wholly prepared for the news. There was to be a ball in Brussels on Thursday evening, at the Duchess of Richmond's hotel, attended by the Duke of Wellington and most of his general officers. Notwithstanding the intelligence, they all went; but a second dispatch arrived at 11 o'clock, announcing that "the French had entered Charleroi that morning, and continued to march in order of battle on Brussels; that there were one hundred and fifty thousand strong; and that the emperor was at their head!" It was now but too clear that no more time should be lost and the duke and all of his officers hurried out of the ballroom.

Wellington, now fully aware of his situation, at once issued orders for the breaking up of his cantonments, and the concentration of the forces, which were spread over a very great extent. He rode off at an early hour on the 16th, to Quatre-Bras, to visit the position, and thence to Bry, where he had an interview with Blücher.

Napoleon, whose manoeuvres had thus far succeeded to his wish, on coming up from Charleroi about noon on the 16th, was undecided whether Blücher at Ligny, or Wellington at Quatre-Bras, ought to form the main object of his attack. He at length determined to give his own personal attention to Blücher.

The advanced guards met at the village of Fleurus, and those belonging to the Prussians having retreated, their army now appeared drawn up in battle array;—their left on Sombref; their centre on Ligny; their right on St. Amand. The reserves were on the heights of Bry. Upon the summit of this high ground the mill of Bry was conspicuous, and behind the mill, in a depression, stood the village of Bry, whose steeple only was visible.

The Prussian forces occupied a line nearly four miles in extent. The French Army, not including Ney's division, amounting to 60,000 men, halted and formed. The emperor now rode to some windmills on the chain of outposts on the heights, and reconnoitred the enemy.

The Prussians displayed to him a force of about 80,000 men. Their front was protected by a deep ravine; but their right was exposed, and had Ney's division at Quatre-Bras, as the emperor supposed, in the rear. A staff officer now arrived from Ney, to inform Napoleon that he had not yet occupied Quatre-Bras, in consequence of reports which made him apprehensive of being turned by the enemy; but that he would advance, if the emperor still required it. Napoleon blamed him for having lost eight hours, repeated the order, and added that, as soon as Ney had made good that position, he (Ney) was to send a detachment by the causeway of Namur and the village of Marchais, whence it should attack the heights of Bry in the Prussian rear. Ney received this order at 12 o'clock, noon; his detachment might reach Marchais by about 2 o'clock.

At this latter hour, therefore, the emperor having descended from the heights whence he had formed a correct view of his position, gave orders for an immediate attack by a change of the whole front, divided into several columns, on Fleurus. The attack extended all along the line of the enemy, and which would be enclosed between two fires on the arrival of the detachment from Ney's division in the rear of the Prussians. "The fate of the war," said Napoleon, in answer to a question from Count Gérard, "may be decided in three hours. If Ney executes his orders well, not a gun of the Prussian army will escape." The soldiers had hardly advanced a few paces, amid vociferous cries of *"Vive l'Empereur!"* when terrible ravages were made in their ranks by the chain-shot from the village and the balls from the batteries above. A single ball killed eight men in one of the columns. But the enthusiasm of the troops, all eager for battle, was too great to cause them to waver and they advanced almost without firing, drove the Prussians at the point of the bayonet from their positions in the gardens and orchards, and entered the village after a stout resistance, only to retire a short time later being unable to conquer the masses of infantry drawn up in a semi-circle on a slope which surmounted the hill of Bry.

The action at Ligny had commenced a little later but not less aggressively. As Gérard's three columns approached the village of Ligny they were received with such a volley that they were obliged to fall back. A large body of artillery was then thrown forward and riddled the village of Ligny and Gérard's columns again advanced, finally taking possession of the place. This was followed by a series of combats, exceedingly ferocious, as the French gave no quarter nor did they receive any from the Prussians.

Blücher now advanced at the head of his soldiers and made a vigorous attempt upon the three St. Amands; but with only partial success for a time. At length, by a series of skilful attacks and manoeuvres, the French became masters of these three points, but had not been able to cross the sinuous stream of Ligny. It was now 5:30 o'clock and Napoleon was directing the Imperial Guard upon Ligny in support of the advantages already gained by Count Gérard at the head of 5,000 men, at St. Amand, when he was informed that an army of 30,000 was advancing upon Fleurus. The emperor suspended the movement of his Guard in order to meet this new force; but the alarm was unfounded. It proved to be the first corps,—Count d'Erlon's,—which formed part of Ney's division, at last complying with Napoleon's repeated orders, and had come up to take the enemy in the rear:—their unexpected appearance had occasioned the loss of two hours.

The Old Guard now resumed its suspended movements upon Ligny: the ravine was passed by General Pecheux, at the head of his division, supported by the infantry, cavalry, artillery and Milhaud's *cuirassiers*. The reserves of the Prussians were driven back with the bayonet, and the centre of the line broken and routed. A bloody conflict ensued in which the French were victorious. The slaughter among the Prussians, was most remarkable. They, however, divided into two parts, effected a retreat, favoured by the night and by the failure of that attack in the rear which Ney had been so expressly ordered to make by a detachment from his force. Their loss amounted to the prodigious number of 18,000 men, killed, wounded or prisoners; forty pieces of cannon and eight stands of colours, while the French loss was between 8,000 and 9,000.

For five hours, two hundred pieces of ordnance deluged the field with slaughter, blood and death, during which period the French and Prussians, alternately vanquished and victors, disputed that ensanguined post hand to hand and foot to foot, so that no less than seven times in succession Ligny was taken and lost.

The emperor had repeatedly sent to Ney saying "that the destiny of France rested in his hands" but the veteran marshal failed to appreciate the importance of the orders and did not act promptly.

Many of the Prussian generals were killed or wounded; and Blücher himself was overthrown, man and horse, by a charge of cuirassiers, and galloped over by friends and foes. Night was coming on and the marshal, who was much battered and bruised, effected his escape. He joined a body of his troops, directed the retreat upon Wavres, and continued to mask his movements so skilfully, that Napoleon knew not until noon on the 17th what way he had taken.

The total loss of the French amounted to no more than nine thousand, killed or wounded—the extraordinary disproportion being occasioned by the more skilful disposition of the French troops, whereby all their shots took effect, while more than half of those of the enemy were wasted.

On the same day as the battle of Ligny,—June 16th,—was also fought the Battle of Quatre-Bras, and at about the same time. Ney, with 45,000 men, began an attack on the position of Wellington at Quatre-Bras. At this point the French were posted among growing corn as high as the tallest man's shoulder, and which enabled them to draw up a strong body of *cuirassiers* close to the English, and yet entirely out of their view. The 49th and 42nd regiments of Highlanders were thus taken by surprise, and the latter would have been destroyed but for the coming up of the former. The 42nd, formed into a square, was repeatedly broken, and as often recovered, though with terrible loss of life, for out of 800 that went into action, only ninety-six privates and four officers remained unhurt.

The pressing orders of Napoleon not allowing the marshal time for reflection, and doubtless anxious to repair the precious time lost in which he might have taken possession of Quatre-Bras, he did not sufficiently reconnoitre but entered into the contest without being wholly prepared. The first successful attack was soon suspended by the arrival of fresh reinforcements, led by the Duke of Wellington, and the shining bravery of the Scotch, Belgians and the Prince of Orange suspended the success of the French. They were repulsed by a shower of bullets from the British infantry added to a battery of two guns which strewed the causeway with men and horses.

Ney was desirous of making the first corps, which he had left in the rear, advance; but Napoleon had dispatched positive orders to Count d'Erlon, at the head of that body, to join him, for which purpose the latter had commenced his march. Ney, when made acquainted with this fact, was stationed amidst a cross-fire from the enemies' batteries. "Do you see those bullets?" cried the marshal, his brow clouded by despair; "would that they would all pass through my body!" and he instantly sent General Delcambre with all speed after Count d'Erlon, directing that whatsoever might have been his orders, although received from the emperor himself, he must return. This he did, but when he arrived in the evening, Ney, dispirited by the checks already received, and dissatisfied with himself and others, had discontinued the engagement. D'Erlon had spent the day in useless marches, his valour wasted by a fatality over which he had no control. Between 5 and 6 o'clock General Delcambre had overtaken the first corps on its march to Bry and brought it back towards Quatre-Bras!

Night found the English, after a severe and bloody day, in possession of Quatre-Bras, the French being obliged to retreat. The gallant Duke of Brunswick, fighting in front of the line, fell almost in the beginning of the battle. The killed and wounded on the side of the French was 4,000 and the Allies' loss was nearly 6,000, in consequence of their having scarcely any artillery. As at Ligny, little quarter was either asked or given, there being much hatred between the French and Prussians. The French were next driven out from the Bois de Bossu by the Belgians, and the English divisions of Alten, Halket, Maitland, Cooke, and Byng, successively arrived.

By neglecting to move the whole of his division upon Quatre-Bras early in the morning, Ney failed to cut off the means of junction between the Prussian and English Armies; and by not sending the detachment to attack the Prussians in the rear at Ligny, it now appears that the whole Prussian Army was saved from being destroyed, or made prisoners, before it could receive the full support which had been promised by the Duke of Wellington. The latter intended to advance on Quatre-Bras at 2 o'clock, and debouch on St. Amand at 4 p. m. Ney, however, did an important act in checking the advance of five or six divisions of the main army during the rest of the day while the battle of Ligny was decided, and in this repaired, in a measure, his various faults committed on the 16th.

The French bivouacked, on the night of the 16th, on the battlefield of Ligny, with the exception of Grouchy's division, which encamped at Sombref. The Duke of Wellington passed the night at Quatre-Bras,—his army gradually joining him till the morning of the 17th,—when they amounted to 50,000 men. The victory acquired by Napoleon at Ligny did not fulfil his expectations. The emperor said:

> If Marshal Ney had attacked the British with his united forces they must inevitably have been crushed; after which, he might have given the Prussians a conclusive blow; but, even if after neglecting that first step he had not committed a second, in impeding the movement of Count d' Erlon, the appearance of the first corps would have curtailed Blücher's resistance, and secured his overthrow without a possibility of doubt; then his entire army must have been captured or annihilated.

Ney was now ordered to advance on Quatre-Bras at daybreak, and attack the British rearguard, while Count Lobau was to proceed along the causeway of Namur, and take the British in flank. General Pajol, at daybreak, also went in pursuit of the Prussians under Blücher. He was supported by Grouchy, with Excelmans' cavalry, and the third and fourth corps of infantry, amounting in all to about 32,000 men. Grouchy was ordered by the emperor to "above all things, pursue the Prussians briskly, and keep up a communication with me to the left" so as to rejoin the main army whenever required.

Napoleon rode over the field of battle at Ligny, and directed every assistance be given to the wounded. He then hurried to the support of Ney's attack on Quatre-Bras. He learned that it was still held by the British, and that Ney had not made the attack. He reproached Ney on meeting him, and the marshal excused his delay by declaring he believed the whole British army was there. This, however, was not the case.

The Duke of Wellington, who intended a junction with the Prussians at Quatre-Bras,—but had been frustrated by their disastrous defeat at Ligny,—now ordered a retreat on Brussels, leaving the Earl of

Uxbridge, with his cavalry, as a rearguard. Napoleon directed Count Lobau's division to advance, and the British cavalry then began to retire in battle-array. The French army moved forward in pursuit, the emperor leading the way.

The weather was extremely bad, the rain falling in torrents, so that the roads were scarcely passable. The attack of cavalry on the British rearguard was, therefore, impracticable, but they were much discomfited by the French artillery. About 6 o'clock the air became extremely foggy, so that all further attack was relinquished for the night; but not until the emperor had ascertained that the whole English Army was encamped on the field of Waterloo, in front of the forest of Soignies.

Napoleon, having ascertained the retreat of Blücher on Wavres, and committed the pursuit of him to Marshal Grouchy, believed that the latter was close to the same place,—as he ought to have been; but was not. At 10 o'clock on the night of the 17th the emperor dispatched an officer to Wavres, to inform Grouchy that there would be a great battle next day; that the English and Belgian Armies were posted on the field of Waterloo, its left supported by the village of La Haye; and ordered him to detach seven thousand men, of all arms, and six pieces of cannon, before day break to St. Lambert, to be near to the right of the French Army, and co-operate with it; that as soon as Blücher evacuated Wavres, either towards Brussels, or in any other direction, he should instantly march with the rest of his force, and support the detachment sent to St. Lambert. About an hour after this dispatch was sent off, the emperor received a report from Grouchy, dated from Gembloux at 5 o'clock, stating that "he was still at this village, and had not learned what direction Blücher had taken!"

At 4 o'clock in the morning a second officer was sent to Grouchy to repeat the communication, and the orders which had been sent to Wavres at 10 o'clock. Another dispatch soon after arrived from Grouchy,—who had not at that time been found by either of the officers sent by the emperor, to state that, "he had learned that Blücher was in Wavres, and would follow him—in the morning!"

The emperor was now convinced that he had not an hour to spare. He saw the possibility of the duke's retreat with Blücher through the forest, their subsequent junction, while the great armies of Russia and Austria were about to cross the Rhine and advance on Paris. He now regretted more than ever that he had been unable to attack the English army before the night had intervened, and determined to follow and attack it now, if it commenced a retreat.

It was not until 6 o'clock on the 17th of June that the advance guard of the French army arrived on the plains of Waterloo,—a delay being occasioned by unfortunate occurrences upon the road,—otherwise the forces would have gained the spot by 3 o'clock in the day. The circumstance appeared to disconcert the emperor extremely, who, pointing to the sun, exclaimed with much emphasis, "What would I not give, to be this day possessed of the power of Joshua, and enabled to retard thy march for two hours!"

The Duke of Wellington, on being made aware of Blücher's march on Wavre, and in adherence to the common plan of campaign, had given orders for falling back from Quatre-Bras. He had before now been heard to say, that if it ever were his business to defend Brussels, he would choose to give battle on the field of Waterloo, in advance of the forest of Soignies; and he now retired thither, in the confidence of being joined there in the morning by Blücher. The English at last reached the destined field, over roads covered with deep mud, and in the face of considerable rain. The troops, although somewhat discouraged by the command to retreat, were enthusiastic when they heard of their leader's purpose, and having taken up their allotted stations, bivouacked for the night assured of a battle on the morrow—the 18th of June.

Arrangements having been effected early in the evening, Wellington now, it appears, according to Lockhart, although the statement is not fully substantiated, rode across the country to Blücher to inform him personally that he had thus far effected the plan agreed on, and to express his hope to be supported on the morrow by two Prussian divisions. Blücher replied that he would reserve a single corps to hold Grouchy at bay as well as they could, and march himself, with the rest of his army upon Waterloo. Wellington then returned to his post.

The cross-roads at Mont St. Jean were in an almost impassable condition and the rain continued to fall in torrents. Wellington was before the village of Mont St. Jean, about a mile and a half in advance of the small town of Waterloo, on a rising ground, having a gentle and regular declivity before it,—beyond this a plain of about a mile in breadth,—and then the opposite heights of La Belle Alliance, on which the French were expected to form their line. The duke had 76,700 men in all; of whom about 30,000 were English. He formed his first line of the troops on which he could most surely rely,—the greater part of the British infantry, with the troops of Brunswick and Nassau, and three corps of Hanoverians and Belgians. Behind this the

Napoleon on the Heights at Ligny

ground sinks and then rises again.

The second line, formed in the rear of the first, was composed of the troops whose spirit and discipline were more doubtful—or who had suffered most in the action at Quatre-Bras; and behind all these was placed the cavalry. The position crossed the two highways from Nivelles and Charleroi to Brussels, nearly where they unite. These roads gave every facility for movement from front to rear during the action; and two country roads running behind, and parallel with the first and second lines, favoured movements from wing to wing. The chateau and gardens of Hougomont, and the farmhouse and inclosures of La Haye Sainte, about 1,500 yards apart, on the slope of the declivity, were strongly occupied and formed the important outworks of defence.

The opening of the country road leading directly from Wavre to Mont St. Jean, through the wood of Ohain, was guarded by the British left, while those running further in advance might be expected to bring the first of the Prussians on the right flank of the French, during their expected attack. The British front extended in all over about a mile, with the strong outposts of Hougomont (situated near the centre of the right) and La Haye (which was in front of the centre) and in the rear the village of Mont St. Jean with the reserve force stationed there,—further back, the town of Waterloo (which has given its name to the battle because it was thence that the English general dated his dispatches)—and the forest of Soignies, as positions to retire upon, to make a stand or cover a retreat. A more advantageous ground for receiving an attack could not easily be obtained in any open country, not previously fortified. It was, therefore, sufficiently evident that the Duke of Wellington had availed himself of all these means of defence, by a circumspect and masterly disposition of his forces.

It was Wellington's design to hold Napoleon at bay until the Prussian advance should enable him to charge the French with superior numbers, while it was Napoleon's wish to beat the Anglo-Belgian army, or at least to divide it, as well as to cut off its communications, ere Blücher could arrive on the field.

Napoleon hoped to turn the left wing of the duke's army, it being the weakest, and divide it from the right wing because he should thus intercept its junction with the Prussians by the road from Wavre,— and because he was in constant expectation of being joined himself by Grouchy from that side. Having effected this separation of the wings, and made a vigorous attack on both wings to distract the attention, it was his design to fall suddenly on the centre, break it, and rout all its component parts in detail. The duke considered it his business to defeat, if possible, all these attempts; not to venture a general attack in return, but to hold his defensive position in the most cautious and determined manner until the arrival of Blücher.

The emperor had in the field 72,000 men, all French veterans—each of whom was, as he declared, worth one Englishman and two Prussians, Dutch or Belgians. Napoleon's forces, however, unlike those of Wellington's, had been on the march all through the tempestuous darkness, many of them had not had sufficient food, and the greater part of them did not reach the heights of La Belle Alliance until the morning of the 18th was considerably advanced. The duke's followers had by that time had refreshment and some hours of repose.

At 1 o'clock in the morning, the emperor having issued the necessary orders for the battle during the earlier part of the night, went out on foot, accompanied by his grand marshal, and visited the whole line of the main guards. The forest of Soignies, occupied by the British, appeared as one continued blaze, while the horizon between that spot and the farms of La Belle Alliance and La Haye Sainte, was brightened by the fires of numerous bivouacs; the most profound silence reigning. Sometime later the rain began to fall in torrents. Napoleon feared more than anything else that Wellington would continue his retreat on Brussels and Antwerp,—thus deferring the great battle until the Russians should approach the valley of the Rhine. The night of June 17-18, often called the "Vigil of Waterloo" was solemn, dark and without unusual incident during the early hours.

Several officers sent to reconnoitre, and others who returned to headquarters at half-past three, announced that the British had made no movement. At 4 o'clock the scouts brought in a peasant, who had served as a guide to a brigade of English cavalry which had proceeded to secure a position on the left at the village of Ohain. Two Belgian deserters, who had just quitted their regiments, also reported that their army was preparing for a battle; and that no retrograde movement had taken place; that Belgium prayed for the success of the emperor, as the English and Prussians were alike unpopular.

The French troops bivouacked amidst deep mud and the officers thought it impossible to give battle on the following day; the ground being so moistened that artillery and cavalry could not possibly manoeuvre, while it would require twelve hours of fine weather to dry the soil. On reaching the eminence of La Belle Alliance at sunrise, and beholding the enemy drawn up on the opposite side and in battle array, the emperor exclaimed, with evident joy, "At last! at last, then, I have these English in my grasp!" And yet, at this time, his exertions had been most phenomenal, and he was far from being in the physical condition necessary for such a contest as he had every reason to expect. He had been eighteen hours in the saddle on June 15th, and had slept but three hours before the Battle of Ligny. On the 16th he was again for eighteen hours on horseback. On the 17th he rose at five in the morning and that night was almost continually astir.

The emperor's breakfast was served at 8 o'clock and many officers of distinction were present. "The enemy's army" said Napoleon, "is superior to ours by nearly a fourth; there are, nevertheless, ninety chances in our favour, to ten against us." The emperor now mounted his horse, and rode forward to reconnoitre the English lines; after which he remained thoughtful for a few moments, and then dictated the order of battle. It was written down by two generals seated on the ground, after which two *aides-de-camp* promptly distributed it among the different corps. The army moved forward in eleven columns, and as they descended from the heights of La Belle Alliance the trumpets played "To the Field!" and the bands alternately struck up airs which recalled the memories of many victories.

The French line of battle was formed in front of Planchenois, having the heights of La Belle Alliance in the rear of its centre. The forces were drawn up in six lines, on each side of the causeway of Charleroi. The first and second lines were of infantry, having the light cavalry at each of its wings, so as to unite them with the six lines of the main force. The artillery was placed in the intervals between the brigades. All the troops were in their stations by about 10:30 o'clock.

Amidst this mass of men there was an almost painful silence until the emperor rode through the ranks when he was received with the utmost enthusiasm; then, giving his last orders, he galloped to the heights of Rossome, which commanded a complete view of both armies below, with a considerable range on each side beyond.

While Napoleon's design for making his grand attack from the centre, on La Haye Sainte,—which was directly in front of the enemy's centre,—was preparing, he gave orders for the commencement of the battle.

The grand attack on the centre of the Anglo-Belgian Army was to be made by Marshal Ney. The marshal had sent word to Napoleon that everything was ready, and he only awaited the order to begin.

Before giving it Napoleon looked over the field of battle and the surrounding country,—the last he was ever to contest. He then perceived a dark mass at a distance in the direction of St. Lambert, where he had ordered Grouchy to send a detachment. The glasses of all the officers were instantly turned towards the object. Some thought it only a mass of dark trees. To remove all doubts the emperor dispatched General Daumont, with a body of three thousand light cavalry, to form a junction with them if they were the troops of Grouchy, or to keep them in check if they were hostile. Through a Prussian hussar, who was brought in a prisoner, it was learned that the dark mass was the advanced guard of Bülow, who was coming up with thirty thousand fresh men; that Blücher was at Wavres with his army, and that Grouchy had not appeared there.

A messenger was immediately dispatched to Marshal Grouchy, to march on St. Lambert, without a moment's delay, and take Bülow's division in the rear. It was believed that Grouchy must be near at hand, whether he had received the various orders sent him or not, as he himself had sent word that he should leave Gembloux in the morning, and from this place to Wavres was only three leagues distance.

Napoleon had a high opinion of Grouchy and his punctuality, he being an officer of great experience; but the emperor was in a state of great suspense on account of his failure to hear from him. He now ordered Count Lobau to follow and support the cavalry of Daumont, and to take up a strong position, where, with ten thousand men, he might keep thirty thousand in check; also to redouble the attack directly he found that Grouchy had arrived on the rear of the Prussians. Napoleon thus early found himself deprived of the services of ten thousand men on this grand field of battle. These events caused some change in his first plans, being deprived of the men whom he was thus obliged to send against General Bülow.

Napoleon said to Soult:

> We had ninety chances for us in the morning, but the arrival of Bülow reduces them to thirty; we have still, however, sixty against forty; and if Grouchy repairs the horrible fault he has committed by amusing himself at Gembloux, victory will therefore be more decisive for the corps of Bülow must in that case be entirely lost.

It was now 11:30 o'clock and the emperor at once turned his attention to the main attack and sent word to Ney to begin his movement.

Instantly one hundred and twenty pieces of artillery were unmasked. Then the French opened their fire of musketry on the advanced post of Hougomont and Jerome Bonaparte, under cover of its fire, charged impetuously on the Nassau troops in the wood about the house. They were driven before the French, but a party of English guards instantly unmasked forty pieces of cannon and maintained themselves in the chateau and garden, despite the desperate character of many repeated assaults. Jerome, masking the post thus resolutely held, pushed on his cavalry and artillery against Wellington's right.

The English formed in squares to receive them and defied all their efforts. For some time both parties opposed each other here, without either gaining or losing a foot of ground. At length the English forced back the French, and the garrison of Hougomont was relieved and strengthened. There was great loss on the side of the British, owing to the suddenness of the attack, and the fixed position and dense array of the squares. The loss of the French was also considerable; and as the squares remained unbroken, no apparent advantage was gained by the assault.

The French, being again repelled, a communication was reopened with Hougomont and the small body of English guards, defending the chateau, received a reinforcement under Colonel Hepburn. The garrison of Hougomont now made a combined charge; and, after a furious struggle, in which the utmost valour, both individual and collective was displayed on either side, drove back the French once more out of the wood, and recovered the position. The French in their turn rallied,—returned with renewed vigour,—and the English were now dislodged and driven out with great slaughter. They rallied in turn and immediately returned, and again they recovered the position. The French charged again but the martial spirit of the English guards was now wrought up to the highest pitch, and all the attempts of the assailants to dislodge them proved unavailing. This contest lasted through the greater part of the day. The killed and wounded on both sides during the struggle for this single outpost has been estimated at upwards of four thousand.

The emperor, calmly observing the whole from the heights, praised the valour of the English guards highly. He now ordered Hougomont to be attacked by a battery of howitzers and shells. The roofs and barns then took fire, and the remnant of the English guards remaining were obliged to retreat before the flames, over the mingled heaps of dead and dying bodies of their comrades and assailants.

The first onslaught of the French made a series of dreadful gaps along the whole of the enemy's left and one of its divisions was completely swept away. The gaps were quickly filled by fresh men, however, as a column of French began to advance. Before it could be supported a grand charge of English cavalry was made, which broke the column of French infantry, routed it, and took two eagles and several pieces of cannon. While the English were wheeling off triumphantly, they were met by a brigade of Milhaud's *cuirassiers*. A desperate conflict ensued at sword's length, the combat lasting much beyond the usual time, the result of a meeting of two bodies of cavalry being generally determined in a few minutes.

A quartermaster of the lancers, named Urban, rushed into the thickest of the fight, and took prisoner the brave Ponsonby, commander of the 1,200 Scotch dragoons,—called the "Scotch Greys," from the colour of their horses. The Scotch sought to free their general but Urban struck him dead at his feet; he was then attacked by several dragoons, but instantly rushing at the holder of the standard of the 45th he unhorsed him with a blow of his lance, killed him with a second, seized the colours, killed another of the Scotch who pursued him close, and then, covered with blood, returned to his colonel with the trophy which had but a short time before been captured from Marcognet's division.

Desperate charges of infantry and cavalry now followed in rapid succession, the immediate object of the French being the occupation of the outpost of the Anglo-Belgian Army at the farm of La Haye Sainte, and thence to push on to the farm of Mont St. Jean. Some of the Scotch regiments made a gallant defence, but were overpowered; the 5th and 6th English divisions were nearly destroyed, and General Picton, who commanded the English left, was laid dead on the field.

The French eventually carried La Haye Sainte; a body of their infantry pushed forward beyond the farm, and overwhelmed and scattered several regiments; but were charged in their turn by two brigades of English foot and heavy cavalry and routed. In consequence of this the farm of La Haye Sainte was vigorously assaulted by the English; and with the assistance of cannon and shells, was recovered.

This important post was taken and retaken several times, with an energy that never relaxed on either side. An error in tactics, of which Ney and d'Erlon had been guilty, had left four or five columns of French infantry at the mercy of the enemy's cavalry, and cost them 3,000 men in dead, wounded and prisoners. The English had lost part of their dragoons, part of Kempt and Pack's cavalry, and Generals Picton and Ponsonby,—all amounting to about the same number as the French had lost; but the English had maintained their position and the whole operation was to be recommenced under the disadvantage of having foiled in the first attempt.

The French were still masters of a part of La Haye Sainte farm and were rallying again on the side of the valley which lay between them and the English. Napoleon joined them, and walked in front of their ranks midst bullets rebounding from one line to another, and howitzers resounding in the air, General Desvaux, commander of the artillery of the Guard being killed at his side.

During these assaults on the centre of the British line, the French *cuirassiers* had advanced to the charge in the face of a terrific fire from the artillery in front of the British infantry. The infantry awaited it, formed in a double line of squares, placed checkerwise, so that the sides of each square could fire a volley on the advancing cavalry, and protected in front by a battery of thirty field-pieces. The French *cuirassiers* rode up to the very mouths of the cannon, charged the artillerymen, drove them from their guns, and then rode fiercely on the squares behind. These remained steadfast, withholding their fire until the French were within a few yards of their bayonets, and then opened on them with deadly effect. The cavalry was all but broken, then rallied and renewed their charge. This they did several times, and always with the same result. Sometimes they even rode between the squares, and charged those of the second line. As the *cuirassiers* retired the artillerymen rushed from behind the squares, formed four deep, manned their guns, and fired grape-shot with terrible effect on the retreating body of gallant but ineffective cavalry.

At length protracted exposure to such a murderous fire completed the ruin of these fearless cavaliers, the far greater part being annihilated in this part of the battle.

When the relics of the *cuirassiers* at last withdrew, the French cannonade opened up furiously once more all along the line. It was vigorously returned, but the effect was far more devastating amidst the British ranks than in those of their assailants. The English were then commanded by Wellington to lie flat on the ground for some space, in order to diminish its effects. The duke had by this time lost 10,000 men and Napoleon possibly a few more.

It was now 4 o'clock and about this time the emperor received intelligence from Gembloux, that, notwithstanding his repeated orders,

Marshal Grouchy had not left his encampment at that place till after 10 o'clock in the morning, in consequence, it was said, of the state of the weather. The body of ten thousand men, under Count Lobau and General Daumont, were now in action with the Prussians under Bülow, near St. Lambeth. The cannonade continued for considerable time; the Prussian centre was then attacked and beaten back, but its wings advancing, Count Lobau was obliged to retire.

At this crisis Napoleon dispatched General Dufresne, with two brigades of infantry of the young guard, and twenty-four pieces of cannon, and the Prussian advance was checked. They still endeavoured to outflank the French right, when several battalions of the Old Guard, with sixteen pieces of cannon, were sent forward; the Prussian line was then outflanked, and Bülow driven back.

At about 5 o'clock Count d'Erlon had taken possession of the village of Ter-la-Haye; outflanking the English left and Bülow's right. It appears that Count Milhaud's *cuirassiers*—which Ney had so often led against the enemy, and who were behind d'Erlon—and the Chasseurs of the Guard, supported by an incessant fire from the infantry of General Lefebvre-Desnoettes, dashed across the plain beyond the farm of La Haye Sainte. The advance of eight regiments and four brigades of their formidable horsemen created a great sensation, as it was believed the final moment was come. As General Milhaud passed before Lefebvre-Desnoettes, he grasped his hand and said, "I am going to charge, support me!" The commander of the light cavalry of the Guard believed it was by order of the emperor he was desired to support the *cuirassiers*, and following their movement he took up a position behind them. It was Ney's belief, as he had said to Druot, that were he allowed to act he could, unaided, with such a body of noble cavalry at his disposal, now put an end to the English Army.

A fierce struggle ensued in which Ney had some advantage over the English, but not what had been expected. He now hastened towards Lefebvre-Desnoettes, made a signal to advance, and precipitated him on the Duke of Wellington's English and German cavalry. This charge allowed the somewhat disorganized *cuirassiers* time to form again, and they, with the chasseurs and lancers, fell again upon the English cavalry. Thousands of hand-to-hand conflicts now were in progress, ending in the enemy retreating behind the squares of the English infantry, thus stopping the onward progress of the French horsemen.

Ney had two horses killed under him, but he was still determined to fulfil his vow to break the English lines. Observing now, on the other side of the plateau, 3,000 *cuirassiers* and 2,000 mounted grenadiers of the Guard that had not been yet engaged, the Marshal asked that they be given him to complete the victory.

About 6 o'clock there was disorder in a great part of the Duke of Wellington's army. The ranks were thinned by the number killed, by those carried off wounded, and by desertions. Soldiers of various nations, Belgian, Hanoverian and English "crowded to the rear" and fled in a panic from this dreadful action. Captain Pringle says;

> A number of our own dismounted dragoons, together with a portion of our infantry, were glad to escape from the field. These thronged the road leading to Brussels, in a manner that none but an eye-witness could have believed.

Cries of "Victory!" now resounded from the French over different parts of the field. Napoleon on hearing this, observed,—"It is an hour too soon; but we must support what is done." He then sent an order for a grand charge of three thousand *cuirassiers* under Kellerman on the left, and who were to move forward briskly and support the cavalry on the low grounds.

A distant cannonade was now heard in the direction of Wavres. It announced the approach of Grouchy—or Blücher!

At 12:30 o'clock Grouchy was midway between Gembloux and Wavres. The tremendous cannonade of Waterloo resounded from the distance. General Excelmans rode up to the marshal, and told him that "he was convinced that the emperor must be in action with the Anglo-Belgian army; that so terrible a fire could not be an affair of outposts or skirmishing; and that they ought to march to the scene of action, which, by turning to the left, they might reach within two hours."

Grouchy paused awhile, and then reverted to his orders to follow Blücher, although he did not know where Blücher really was. Count Girard came up, and joined in the advice of General Excelmans. Still Grouchy remained doubtful, and as if stupefied. Hazlitt says:

> At one moment he appeared convinced; but just then a report came that the Prussians were at Wavres, and he set out once more after them, (instead of instantly hurrying off to join the emperor in his great battle.)

It was a rearguard which Blücher had left at Wavres; and the Prussian leader had gone to Waterloo, at the head of 30,000 men, having been advised, as previously stated, that the Duke of Wellington would hazard a battle on the morning of the 18th, if he could depend on the co-operation of the Prussians. The veteran marshal, at an early hour, had detached the corps of Bülow, with orders to march on St. Lambert, leaving Mielman with his corps at Wavres.

The duke had expected to be joined by Blücher as early as 11 o'clock; but the roads were in such a condition that the Prussians could not accomplish the march in any such time as had been calculated. Their advance was necessarily slow,—but it was in the right direction!

Meanwhile, the emperor on the battlefield of Waterloo, had reluctantly ordered the charge of Kellerman's three thousand *cuirassiers*, asked for by Ney, to sustain and follow up the advantage of the *cuirassiers* of Milhaud and the *chasseurs* of the Guard, on the plain below. The marshal's contest had been carefully watched by Napoleon who declared at once that Ney was too impatient, and had begun an hour too soon. "This man is always the same." said Marshal Soult. "He will compromise everything as he did at Jena and Eylau."

Kellerman was now all ready for action, but he condemned the desperate use which at this moment was to be made of the cavalry. Distrusting the result, he kept back one of his brigades, the *carbineers*, and most unwillingly sent the remainder to Ney, whom he accused of foolish zeal.

These twenty squadrons, led on by their generals and officers, now advanced at full gallop as if in pursuit of the English Army, shouting, "*Vive l'Empereur!*" and under the cannonade of the Prussians, for Bülow was still pressing upon the flank and rear. Other bodies of cavalry also advanced upon the centre of the Anglo-Belgian Army, making a spectacle which General Foy, an eyewitness, afterwards declared that during his long military career he had never been present at such a fearful scene as he then beheld.

While Napoleon was watching their several charges, General Guyot's division of heavy cavalry was seen following the *cuirassiers* of Kellerman. This latter movement was without the emperor's orders, and seems to have been the result of ungovernable excitement on the part of the officers and men, who thought they could finish the battle by a *coup de main*.

The emperor instantly sent Count Bertrand to recall them; but it was too late! The cavalry, once started, nothing could arrest its rush— they were in action before the order could reach them; and to recall

Preparations for the Advance of the Old Guard at Waterloo

them now would have been dangerous, even if possible. This division was the reserve, and ought by all means to have been held back. Thus was the emperor deprived of his reserve of cavalry as early as 5 o'clock.

It is said that during the preparation of this grand charge of 12,000 French cavalry,—the finest in the world,—the Duke of Wellington ran forward with his glass in front of the lines, amidst the hot fire which preceded the charge. He was reminded that he was exposing himself too much. "Yes," said the duke, "I know I am,—but I must see what they are doing." To an officer who asked for instructions in case he should be slain, he answered; "I have no instructions to give; there is only one thing to be done—to fight to the last man and the last moment!"

Some years later the duke said:

> I have never seen anything more admirable in war than those ten or twelve reiterated charges of the French *cuirassiers* upon our troops of all arms.

It was obvious to the English commander, as he viewed this splendid spectacle, that unless this last and decisive onset should drive him from the post which he had continued to hold during nearly seven hours of intermitting battle, his allies would come fully into the field and give him a vast superiority of numbers wherewith to close the work of the day. The duke now decided to sacrifice the remainder of his cavalry, and he moved them forward to meet the shock of the advancing foe.

The matchless body of French cavalry continued to dash forward towards the hostile lines, in successive masses, and with all the triumphant fury of a charge upon a retreating enemy. Breaking through many squares of infantry, overthrowing the opposing cavalry, and overwhelming the artillery in front of the lines, they were received by the squares of British infantry, first with a volley of musket-balls, and then upon the immovable array of bristling bayonets. Men and horses, struggling in the agonies of violent death, bestrewed the ground. In his extremity Wellington determined on employing Cumberland's one thousand hussars, who had not yet been engaged; but at sight of this scene of slaughter the hussars fell back in disorder.

The resistance of the duke was most stubborn but Ney still hoped to destroy the English Army at the point of the sword by keeping up a continued charge, having been reinforced by the heavy cavalry of the

Guard whose advance had been made apparently without orders.

Meanwhile Ney, seeing Kellerman's *carbineers* in reserve, hastened to where they were, asked what they were doing and then, despite Kellerman's resistance, led them to the front where they succeeded in making fresh breaches in the British infantry, but were unable to get beyond the second line.

For the eleventh time Ney led on his 10,000 horse to the attack. The *cuirassiers* wheeled about, reformed, and again charged with tremendous energy, and a valour that set at contemptuous defiance the tempest of grape-shot, and balls of the artillery and musketry which opposed their advance. Men rolled off, and horses fell plunging; even pistols were discharged in their faces, and swords thrust over their bayonets in vain. The British infantry, though shaken for a moment again closed their ranks, fell into line and continued to fire. About this time Ney was heard to say to General d'Erlon, "Be sure, my friend, that for you and me, if we do not die here under the English balls, nothing remains but to fall miserably under those of the *émigrés*." To his artillery a few moments before he had said, "It is here, my friends, that the fate of our country is about to be decided; it is here that we must conquer in order to secure our independence!"

The emperor, who was now suffering great bodily pain, scarcely able to sit upon his horse, and falling at times into a sort of lethargy, was much moved by this spectacle. He had never before commanded in person against the English soldiery; but he knew them now—when it was too late! He observed their wonderful self-command, and unflinching courage, and praised it;—but it was his ruin!

Again and again did the brilliant cavalry of the French rush forward to the charge with redoubled fury. They frequently passed between the squares of the first line amidst their united cross-fire from front and rear, and charged the squares of the second line whose fire they also received, but no general effect was produced, no real advantage gained beyond an occasional breaking of the squares in both lines, particularly the second. The baffled *cuirassiers* were always obliged to retire, receiving the terrible cross-fire of the squares as they passed between them and followed by a volley of musketry and often by the grape-shot of the artillery.

Four thousand of the French cavalry now strewed the ground, while 10,000 English, horse and foot had laid down their lives. Many were the deeds of individual gallantry performed by officers and men on both sides, among cavalry and infantry all over the field. During the conflict Colonel Heymes hastened to Napoleon to ask for the infantry of which Ney was in need. "Infantry!" cried the emperor, with considerable irritation, "where does he suppose I can get them? Does he expect me to make them? You can see the task before me, and you see what troops I have!" When the emperor's irritation had somewhat subsided he sent another message to Ney, more hopeful than the former. He made Colonel Heymes tell the marshal that if he were in a difficult position at Mont St. Jean, he was himself in still greater difficulties on the banks of the Lasne, where he was opposed by the entire Prussian Army, but when he had repelled, or even checked them, he, with the Guard, would hasten to complete the conquest of the English; until then the plateau was to be held at any cost for an hour when he might reckon on reinforcements.

The desperate assaults of the French cavalry ought to have been supported by strong bodies of infantry; they could not, however, be spared, being needed for the contest with Bülow, on the French right and to prevent his advance.

By 7 o'clock, Bülow's corps of 30,000 men was successfully repulsed, and Count Lobau, with 10,000 men, occupied the positions from which the Prussian general had been driven.

Still the French cavalry could do no more than maintain itself on the plateau from which the duke's 36,000 men had made a slight retrograde movement. A fresh cannonade was opened by the French along the British line, after the assaults of the *cuirassiers*, but no further advance was attempted by the former. As one authority truly says, the British were beaten to a stand-still—*but there they stood!* It was, in effect, a drawn battle up to this time.

There was not the least demonstration on the part of the Duke of Wellington to make any general advance during this almost interminable contest,—nor had there been all day,—and as little sign of his moving back. About twenty thousand men had already been killed, or otherwise lost, on each side.

It was now nearly 7 o'clock. The distant cannonade, which had been faintly heard in the direction of Wavres, opened nearer at hand. It was the announcement,—not of the arrival of Grouchy, in the rear of Bülow's division; but that of the two columns of Blücher, amounting to about 31,000 fresh troops!

The relative strength of the two armies, allowing twenty thousand as lost on both sides, was now considerably over two to one against the French,—the majority on the other side being chiefly composed of fresh men. Wellington was heard to say during the day, "Would to God that Blücher or night would come!" and now both were at hand.

The presence of mind of the emperor now became most alert, and it was never so clearly manifested as at this critical moment when everything hung in the balance.

The fresh army, advancing to the assistance of the Anglo-Belgian forces, was soon discovered by the French troops, who were in action on the field. The cavalry on the plain were waiting in constant expectation of the emperor's orders for the advance of his reserves of the infantry of the Guard. They were not alarmed when they saw the communication finally effected between Bülow and the English, but when they perceived the approach of the dense columns of Blücher, they were confounded, and several regiments began to fall back.

Napoleon now sent his *aides-de-camp* along the whole line to announce the arrival of succour, and that Blücher's advance was only a retreat before Grouchy, who was pressing on his rear. It was a clever ruse, and warranted by the situation in which he now found himself, as it momentarily revived the spirits of the weary troops to a wonderful degree.

At the head of four battalions of the infantry of the Guard, the emperor now advanced on the left in front of La Haye Sainte. He ordered General Reille to concentrate the whole of his corps near Hougomont and make an attack. He then sent General Friant to support the cavalry on the plain with four battalions of the middle guard. If, by sudden charge, they could break and disorder the centre of the British line before the columns of Blücher could force their way into the plain, a last chance of success still remained. Blücher was hurrying on to La Haye; there was not a moment to lose!

The attack was made, the infantry drove back all that opposed them, and repeated charges of the French cavalry disordered the hostile ranks. Presently some battalions of the Old Guard came up. They too were going to the attack to retrieve the ground lost by the young guard who had fallen back, for, as Thiers says, "It is the privilege of the Old Guard to repair every disaster." The emperor ranged his veterans by brigades; two battalions being in line, and two in column. As he rode along in front of these battle-scarred battalions, he said, "My friends, the decisive moment is come; it will not do to fire; you must come hand to hand with the enemy, and drive them back at the point of the bayonet into the ravine whence they have issued to threaten the army, the empire and France."

General Friant was now carried by, wounded. He said that all was going well, but that the attack could not be successful till the balance of the Guard were employed. This movement could not be effected on the instant and in a few minutes it was too late, as the Prussians were coming up in great numbers. The British still stood on the defensive and Blücher had reached the village of La Haye. A violent struggle now ensued, but it was of brief duration; the overwhelming mass of fresh men soon bore down all opposition.

The Duke of Wellington now prepared,—for the first time during the day,—to advance his entire line. He was aware that the decisive moment was at hand and that his safety, as well as that of his gallant men, depended on this last effort.

A panic soon seized some of the French soldiers, exhausted and maddened by the terrible strain they had undergone during the day, and at the sudden appearance before them of the dark mass of fresh assailants, the cry of *"Sauve qui peut!"* (Every man for himself!) was raised. The disorder soon became general and the men fled as the columns of Prussians poured into the plain.

Napoleon instantly changed the front of the Guard so as to throw its left on La Haye Sainte and its right on La Belle Alliance; he then met the fugitives and led them back to their post. They at once faced the Prussians, whom they immediately charged. The fresh brigade of the English cavalry from Ohain arrived at this crisis and forced their way between General Reille's corps and the Guard, to their utter separation. The emperor now ordered his four reserve squadrons to charge the fresh brigade of English cavalry but their attack met with no success. As he was leading the four battalions destined to their place of attack on the Charleroi road he met Ney, who was greatly excited, and who declared that the cavalry would certainly give way if a large reinforcement of infantry did not immediately arrive. Napoleon gave him the battalions he was bringing up and promised to send six more.

The ranks of the French were now in general confusion all over the field. Napoleon had barely time to gallop into one of the squares of the Guard which still maintained its position; Ney, Jerome, Soult, Bertrand, Druot, Corbineau, de Flahaut, Labedoyere, Gourgaud and others drew their swords, became soldiers again and followed close to their chiefs heels. They entered the square of the last battalion of reserve,—the illustrious and unfortunate remains of the "granite column" of the fields of Marengo, who had remained unshaken amidst the tumultuous waves of the army. The old grenadiers, incapable of fear for themselves, were alarmed at the danger threatening the emperor, and appealed to him to withdraw. "Retire" said one of them, "You see that death shuns you!" The emperor resisted, and commanded them to fire.

The four battalions of the Guard, and the cavalry which had so long held the plains below in opposition to the whole Anglo-Belgian Army, were being rapidly depleted. Wellington had ordered Maitland's guards to fire on them at short range as they moved forward for the last time. The sudden shock did not cause the advancing soldiers to stop, but closing their ranks they continued to push on. They were soon beaten, however, by overwhelming numbers of cavalry, both English and Prussian, and were at last compelled to retire that they might not be cut off from the centre of the army, while the enemy continued to advance, preceded by their artillery, which poured forth a most destructive fire.

But one last effort to stem the torrent still remained. If the British centre could be broken, and their advance checked, some favourable chance was just possible. The emperor therefore ordered the advance of the reserve infantry of the Imperial Guard,—the flower of his army. He exhorted them, by a hasty personal appeal, and confided the direction of their efforts to "the bravest of the brave," who had had five horses killed under him and who now advanced on foot, sword in hand. The 2900 heroic stalwarts moved forward in two columns, headed by Ney, and supported by a heavy fire of artillery, while four battalions of the Old Guard, formed into squares, took post in their rear as a reserve and to protect the march of the columns.

Either wing of the English had by this time advanced in consequence of the repulses of the French and their line now presented a concave. They were formed in an unbroken array, four deep, and as the French advanced poured on them a shower which never intermitted, each man firing as often as he could reload. Wellington gave the order to advance in the familiar and brusque terms of, "Up guards and at them!" The English wings kept moving on all the while; and when the heads of the French columns, who continued to advance till within forty or fifty yards, approached to this point, they were met with such a storm of musketry in front, and on either flank, that they in vain endeavoured to deploy into line for the attack, under a terrific and unremitting fire. They stopped to make this attempt, reeled, lost order, and the 800 men who were left standing fled at last in one mass of confusion.

The Duke of Wellington now dismounted, placed himself at the head of his line and led his men against the remaining numbers of four battalions of the Old Guard—the only unbroken troops remaining behind, while Ney was striving to rally his fugitives. His cocked hat was gone, and his clothes were literally riddled with bullets, though he himself remained untouched. The intrepid marshal, at Wellington's approach, took part once more in the *mêlée*, sword in hand, and on foot. But nothing could withstand the impetuous assault of the victorious British.

Napoleon, who had watched this last terrible contest from the heights of La Belle Alliance suddenly exclaimed, "They are mingled together, all is lost for the present," and accompanied by but three or four officers, he gave the signal for retreat and hurried to the left of Planchenois, to a second position, where he had placed a regiment of the Guard, with two batteries in reserve.

The four battalions of the Old Guard, under General Cambronne, still remained to protect the retreat of the French Army. If they could succeed in holding the British in check, and prevent their advance during half an hour longer, darkness would enable the army to retreat in safety, and partially recover its disorder by morning. The Old Guard formed in square, flanked by a few pieces of artillery, and by a brigade of red lancers. "The Duke of Wellington" says Captain Pringle, "now ordered his whole line to advance and attack their position." They advanced to the charge in embattled array, condensed and tremendous, against the remnant of noble veterans of that old Imperial Guard, which, during twenty years of slaughterous wars, had never once been vanquished. Gathering round the standards of their former glory, they received the dreadful onset with souls prepared for death. Nothing could now withstand the vigour of the attack of the British soldiers who thus had an opportunity to relieve their breasts of the heavy burden they had borne all day when compelled, for hours, to stand the fierce attacks of the French, being frequently driven back, and never making an advance.

The Old Guard, as was to be expected, were beaten down,— slaughtered. Their general, Cambronne, was called upon to surrender by some British officers who seemed to revolt at the uneven contest. The only reply made by him was,—not the generally believed, but inaccurate declaration recorded by some historians, "The Old Guard dies, but does not surrender!" but was a single word of military jargon frequently used by French soldiers. Almost immediately afterwards he fell from his horse, cut down by a fragment of a shell striking him on the head; but he would not allow his men to leave their ranks to bear him away.

Once more these heroes, now reduced to but one hundred and fifty men, are commanded to surrender; "We will not yield!" they answer back, and discharging their muskets for the last time, rush on the cavalry and with their bayonets, kill many men and horses, and then sink to the earth exhausted or in death.

The Old Guard was destroyed,—not defeated! The advancing British troops rode over their prostrate bodies piled in ghastly heaps,—a monument to their valour and heroism, even in death. Ney, bareheaded, his clothes hanging in shreds, and with his broken sword in his hand, seeing a handful of his followers still remaining, ran forward to lead them against a Prussian column that was pursuing them. As the fearless marshal threw himself once more into the fray he exclaimed, "Come my friends; come see how a marshal of France can die!" But his time had not come: he was not destined to die upon the battlefield. His small band was soon overpowered and scarcely two hundred escaped death. Rulliere, who commanded the battalion, broke the flagstaff, hid the eagle beneath his coat, and followed Ney who had been unhorsed for the fifth time, but who was still unwounded. Under cover of the darkness they made their escape.

The emperor attempted to protect the retreat and rally the fugitives; but it was now fast growing dark. The soldiers could not see him or they might have rallied, while many believed the report that he had been killed. "He is wounded," said some, "He is dead" cried others. Nothing could be heard above the uproar and hideous confusion that everywhere prevailed. The Prussian cavalry, supported by some battalions of infantry, and the whole of Bülow's corps, now advanced by the right of Planchenois.

In a few minutes the emperor was almost surrounded by hostile forces. He had formed the regiment into a square, and was still lingering, when Marshal Soult seized the bridle of his horse, exclaimed that he would not be killed, but taken prisoner, and, pulling him away, the emperor at last yielded to his destiny! Behind him on the battlefield lay 60,000 French, English and Prussians, dead or wounded. The Battle of Waterloo was lost and this hitherto almost invincible warrior was obliged to gallop across the fields in the dark, amidst the whistling of the Prussian bullets, and detachments of their cavalry which were scouring the field in all directions.

Napoleon was so fatigued, on the road to Genappe, that he would no doubt have fallen from his horse, had he not been supported by General Gourgaud and two other persons, who remained his only attendants for some time.

Wellington and Blücher met about 10 o'clock, at the farm-house of La Belle Alliance, and after congratulating each other on the success of the day, the Prussian commander, whose men were still fresh, eagerly undertook to continue the pursuit during the night, while the English general halted to rest his weary men and care for the dead and wounded.

The English loss on this eventful day was 100 officers slain and 500 wounded; very many mortally. The duke who was himself exposed to great danger throughout the day, and one other person, were the only two among his numerous staff who escaped unhurt. The enemy, according to their own accounts, lost over thirty thousand men, including Hanoverians, Belgian troops of Nassau, Brunswick, etc.; those of the English Army alone amounted to 22,800; to which are to be added 8,000 to 10,000 Prussians. Of the 72,000 men whom Napoleon headed in this, his 85th pitched battle and greatest defeat, not more than 30,000 were ever again collected in arms. The remainder were either killed or wounded on the battlefield, or deserted and fled separately to their homes, or were murdered by the Prussians who followed hard on the miserable and defenceless fugitives, cutting down all they overtook without resistance or mercy.

Several French officers blew out their brains to escape their brutality and some of the veterans of the Imperial Guard, who lay wounded upon the battlefield, killed themselves when they heard the emperor had lost the battle, in order that they might not fall into the hands of the enemy, or through remorse at the downfall of their chief.

Napoleon made a brief halt at Genappe, at about 11 o'clock at night; but all his attempts to rally the frantic masses were in vain. He then continued his course towards Quatre-Bras, where he dismounted at a bivouac at about 1 o'clock in the morning. At Phillipville, he received news of Grouchy's movements, and sent him word of the loss of Mont St. Jean, (Waterloo).

At this point he caused orders to be dispatched to Generals Rapp, Lecourbe and Lamarque, to proceed by forced marches to Paris, and to commanders of fortified towns to defend themselves to the last extremity. He also dictated two letters to his brother Joseph, one to be communicated to the council of ministers relating imperfectly the fatal issue of the day, and the other for his private perusal giving a faithful account of the total rout of the army, and declaring that he would soon have an army of 300,000 troops with which to oppose the enemy. The Duke of Bassano (Maret) and Baron Fleury now came up and greeted the emperor who was much affected at meeting them, and was scarcely able to suppress his emotions. He then prepared to set off in a *calash*, accompanied by Bertrand. At Rocroi, where Napoleon stopped to take refreshments, his attendants appeared in a pitiable state; their clothes were covered with blood and dust, their looks were haggard, and their eyes were filled with tears. Napoleon continued his journey to Paris, *via* Laon, accompanied by two or three hundred fugitives, who had been collected to form an escort, arriving at the capital on the evening of the 20th of June.

17

Conclusion

The "military career" of Napoleon Bonaparte having ended at Waterloo, but little remains to be added here. Other writers, especially those noble self-sacrificing friends who shared with the exile his life at St. Helena, have told in detail of his weary hours on the rocks in the Atlantic Ocean, and a brief summary of the events which finally ended in Napoleon becoming a prisoner of England for life will only be recited.

The arrival of the emperor at Paris had been preceded by the news—received on June 19th, of the victories at Charleroi and Ligny, and one hundred cannon had been fired in honour of his successes. On the morning of the 21st it became known that the emperor had arrived the night before, at the Elysée. When he stopped at the flight of steps leading to the palace General Druot, who had accompanied him exclaimed, "All is lost!"

"Except honour," answered Napoleon quickly. He had not spoken before since leaving Laon.

Immediately on his arrival the emperor was received by Caulaincourt—his censor in prosperity and real friend in adversity. To him he said, with head bowed by grief and fatigue, "The army performed prodigies; a panic seized it, and all was lost. Ney conducted himself like a madman; he got my cavalry massacred. I can say no more—I must have two hours' rest, to enable me to prepare for business;" "I am choking here!" he exclaimed a moment later, laying his hand upon his heart. After ordering a bath, and a few moments silence he said: "My intention is to assemble the two Chambers in an imperial sitting and demand the means of saving the country."

He was then informed that the deputies appeared hostile towards him, and were little disposed to grant his requests. While he remained in his bath the ministers and great officers of state hastened towards the Elysée. When they arrived, his clothes were still covered with dust, as he had left the field of Waterloo; yet, exhausted by the fatigues of three battles, and the dreadful events of his flight and the hurry of his journey being still vivid in his mind, he gave a rapid but distinct view of the resources of the country, the strength already organized for resistance, and the far greater power still capable of development. Among his listeners were his brothers Joseph and Lucien.

While consulting with his ministers, presided over by Joseph, on the morning of the 21st, as to what manner he should inform the Chambers of his great misfortune, news was received that both assemblies had met on learning of his defeat and resolutions passed,—one of which declared the State to be in danger, and the other that their own sittings be made permanent. Thus the Chamber of Representatives overturned the new constitution, and put aside the authority of the emperor. These resolutions were also adopted by the Chamber of Peers. Lucien Bonaparte, and some of Napoleon's more intimate friends, wished him to instantly put himself at the head of 6,000 of the Imperial Guard, who were then in the capital, and dissolve the Senate, which was unfriendly to him. The emperor, however, was undecided; as Lucien said of him ever after that, "the smoke of Mont St. Jean had turned his brain."

Late in the evening of the 21st Napoleon held a council to which the presidents and vice presidents of both Chambers were admitted, but no decision was arrived at. Lafayette, the friend of Washington, declared that nothing could be done until "a great sacrifice could be made." The emperor heard all in silence and broke up the meeting without having come to any decision.

Napoleon said to Las Casas at St Helena:

> I have often asked myself, whether I have done for the French people all that they could expect of me—for that people did much for me. Will they ever know all that I suffered during the night that preceded my final decision? In that night of anguish and uncertainty, I had to choose between two great courses; the one was to save France by violence, and the other to yield to the general impulse.

He finally decided that abdication was the only step he could adopt, and his determination was taken.

Early next morning—the 22nd—the Chambers again met, and

Napoleon at Waterloo

the necessity of the emperor's abdication was discussed with vigour. It was demanded on all hands, and without any reservation or condition whatever. Finally, Lafayette instructed that word should be sent Napoleon that he would be given an hour in which to abdicate, and be told if he had not done so by that time he would be deposed. Between noon and 1 o'clock the abdication was signed and carried by Carnot to the Chamber of Peers, and by Fouché to the Chamber of Deputies.

When Fouché appeared, the deputies were about to declare the emperor deposed, and he saved them that trouble by producing the following proclamation, in the handwriting of Joseph Bonaparte, to whom it had been dictated, and addressed to the French people:

> Frenchmen! When I began war for the maintenance of the national independence, I relied upon the union of all efforts, all wills and all the national authorities. I had reason to hope for success, and I braved all the declarations of the powers against my person. Circumstances appear to be changed. I offer myself as a sacrifice to the hatred against France. May they prove sincere in their declarations, and to have aimed only at me! My political life is ended. I proclaim my son under the title of Napoleon II., Emperor of the French. The present ministers will provisionally form the council of the government. The interest which I take in my son induces me to recommend the Chambers should immediately enact a law for the organization of a Regency; unite together for the general safety, and to the end of securing your national independence.
> Done at the Palace of the Elysée, June the 22nd, 1815.
> —Napoleon.

The Chambers had awaited this reply in a state of the greatest impatience in both houses. In the Chamber of Peers, Carnot, having received some exaggerated accounts of the force and success of Grouchy, endeavoured to persuade the Assembly that the marshal must ere then have added 60,000 men at Laon to Soult, the relics of Waterloo, thus forming an army capable, under proper guidance, of yet effectually retrieving the affairs of France.

Ney, who had arrived in Paris the same morning, declared otherwise:

> Grouchy cannot have more than twenty, or at most, more than twenty-five thousand men; and as to Soult, I myself command-

ed the Guard in the last assault—I saw them all massacred before I left the field. Be assured there is but one course,—negotiate and recall the Bourbons. In their return I see nothing but the certainty of being shot as a deserter. I shall seek all I have henceforth to hope for in America. Take you the only course that remains for France.

Ney's prophecy was soon to be fulfilled, for on the return of the Bourbons to the throne he was shot as a traitor to France, although, as has been frequently said of him, he fought more than five hundred battles for his country and never raised arms against her!

A deputation from the Senate waited on the emperor at the Elysée, and in respectful terms thanked him for the sacrifice he had made, but he was unable to exact from them the avowal that his abdication necessarily carried with it the immediate proclamation of Napoleon II.

The emperor, for the last time clothed in imperial garb, and surrounded by his great officers of state, received the deputation with calmness and dignity:

> I thank you for the sentiments which you express, I desire that my abdication may produce the happiness of France; but I cannot hope it; the State is left by it without a chief, without a political existence. The time lost in overturning the Empire might have been employed in placing France in a position to crush the enemy. I recommend that the Chamber promptly reinforce the armies; whoever wishes for peace must be ready for war. Do not place this great nation at the mercy of strangers. Beware of being deceived in your hopes. This is the real danger. In whatever position I may be placed, I shall always be satisfied, if France is happy.

He perceived clearly that there was no hope for his son. Thus ended the second reign—the "Hundred Days" of Napoleon. His public career was ended. The council of ministers broke up, and the palace of the Elysée soon presented the appearance of being deserted. Napoleon, surrounded only by a few friends, had now become a private individual. When Caulaincourt advised him to seek safety from the Allies in flight to the United States, he replied; "What have I to fear? I have abdicated—it is the business of France to protect me!"

The repeated protestations of Napoleon and his friends, that unless Napoleon II. was recognized the abdication of his father was null, and that the country that could hesitate about such an act of justice was worthy of nothing but slavery, began to produce a powerful effect among the soldiery in Paris, and Napoleon was called upon to signify to the army that he no longer claimed any authority over them, to which he complied.

A provisional government was now proclaimed, consisting of Fouché, Carnot, Caulaincourt and Generals Grenier and Quinette, and installed in the Tuileries. Fouché declared that Napoleon's continued presence at the capital might produce disturbance, and Carnot was deputed to request him to withdraw to Malmaison, which he was compelled to do on the 25th. Arriving there he soon became aware of the fact that he was in effect a prisoner, for Fouché's police surrounded him on all sides—ostensibly "to protect his person." It was at Malmaison, in compliance with the suggestions of some members of the government, that Napoleon addressed his last proclamation to the army:

> Soldiers! When I yield to the necessity which forces me to separate myself from the brave French army, I take away with me the happy conviction that it will justify, by the eminent services which the country expects from it, the high character which our enemies themselves are not able to refuse to it. Soldiers! I shall follow your steps, though absent. I know all the corps, and not one among them will obtain a single advantage over the enemy that I shall not render homage to the courage which it will have shown. You, and I, have been calumniated. Men, incapable of appreciating your actions, have seen, in the marks of attachment which you have given me, a zeal of which I was the whole object; let your future success teach them that it was the country, above all, that you served in obeying me, and that if I have any part in your affection, I owe it to my ardent love of France, our common mother. Soldiers, some efforts more, and the coalition will be destroyed. Napoleon will know you by the blows that you will give to it. Save the honour, the independence of the French; be what I have known you for twenty years, and you will be invincible.

This address, however, although written at the instigation of the government, its representatives would not allow to be published in the *Moniteur*.

The relics of Waterloo, and Grouchy's division, were now marching towards Paris under Soult, followed closely by Wellington and

Blücher. The provisional government began to feel some anxiety concerning Napoleon, whom they feared might make his escape from Malmaison and place himself at the head of an armed force to take the field against the invaders, and in favour of Napoleon II.

General Becker, who had been appointed by Fouché to the unthankful office of guarding Napoleon, was prevailed upon to repair to Paris and convey a letter to the government, in which the ex-emperor offered to assume the command of the army and beat the enemy, not with an intention of seizing the sovereign power, but agreeing to pursue his journey as soon as victory should give a favourable turn to the negotiations. In this letter, which was addressed to the Committee of Government, Napoleon said:

> In abdicating the sovereign authority, I did not renounce the noblest right of a citizen, that of defending my country. The approach of the Allies upon the capital leaves no doubt of their intentions and bad faith. Under these weighty circumstances, I offer my service as general, still considering myself the first soldier of my country!

Fouché read the letter aloud, and then exclaimed, "Is he laughing at us? Come, this is going too far." His proposal was of course rejected, although Carnot was desirous that his prayer should be granted.

General Becker was instructed to carry back to Malmaison this response:

> The duties of the committee toward the country do not permit it to accept the proposition and the active assistance of the Emperor Napoleon.

He found the emperor in uniform, believing a favourable reply would be returned. When he had finished the missive Napoleon said: "These men are incapable of energy. Since that is the case, let us go into exile."

Fouché now urged his prisoner to consent to depart at once for some foreign port—naming the United States as a haven in which he might find relief from outside interference. If Napoleon had acted promptly, as he had all his life been accustomed to do, he might in all probability have made his escape to this country, as our vessels were in every French port—and he could have crossed the Atlantic; but he hesitated, and those golden moments, which meant so much to him, even liberty itself, were soon irretrievably lost. Fouché, who was extremely anxious to have the man who had made him all he was out of the way, did not hesitate to resort to questionable means of pressure to get Napoleon to leave France. One of these was the stimulating of the personal creditors of the dethroned emperor, and his family, who repaired incessantly to Malmaison to torment him with their demands.

Meanwhile Fouché sent to the Duke of Wellington announcing that Napoleon had declared his intention of departing for America, and requesting for him a safe conduct across the Atlantic. The duke replied that he had no authority to grant passports to Napoleon Bonaparte but the request, as Fouché hoped, had the effect of causing the English Admiralty to quicken their diligence and there was immediately stationed no less than thirty cruisers along the western coasts of France in order to intercept Napoleon should he attempt to depart. No one could be deceived as to the intention of this proceeding; it clearly denoted that the men, who, for the moment, possessed the government of France, had determined that the late emperor should not leave the country freely. The fear that he might return to the capital, and to his throne, had made them take a step which was certain to place him in the power of the English Government.

The next move was to inform Napoleon of the duke's reply and with it the declaration that two frigates, and some smaller vessels, awaited his orders at Rochefort. He was informed that "if he repaired thither on the instant" he would still be in time. For a moment he hesitated, wavering between hope and doubt. Baron Fleury then went to Paris and learned that the Prussians designed to carry off the emperor; that Blücher had said, "If I can catch Bonaparte, I will hang him up at the head of my army," but that Wellington had strenuously opposed such a cowardly design. At half past 3 o'clock in the morning Napoleon was informed that Wellington had refused him safe conduct, and he was ordered to depart immediately from Malmaison. Preparations were hurriedly made, and on the 29th of June, eleven days after the Battle of Waterloo, he left Malmaison, accompanied by Savary, Bertrand and Las Casas, and others of his attached servants, and attended by a guard of mounted men.

If one of his followers had not taken the precaution to have the bridges in front of Malmaison burned, Napoleon would have run a great risk of falling into the hands of the Allies, as three corps of Prussian cavalry appeared there in quest of him very soon after he started. They had arrived by a circuitous route, and must have been led by a guide well acquainted with the locality. Napoleon, however, had escaped this danger. He slept at Rambouillet the first night, at Tours on the 30th, and at Niort on the 1st of July. He was well received wherever he was recognized; but at the last named place the enthusiasm of the people and troops was extreme.

Rochefort was reached on the 3rd of July. Here Napoleon, who was joined by his brother Joseph, took up his residence in the prefect's house with the view of embarking immediately, but he was informed that a British line-of-battle ship, and some smaller vessels of war, were off the roads, watching the roadstead and harbour, and his departure was therefore impossible.

Meanwhile the French Army had once more retired from before the walls of Paris under a convention, and Blücher and Wellington were about to enter the capital and reseat Louis on the throne. The only alternative, therefore, was to open negotiations with Captain Maitland, who commanded the *Bellerophon*, an English man-of-war which had taken up its station at Rochefort two days before the arrival of the ex-emperor.

On being asked for a safe conduct to America the English commander replied that his orders were to make every effort to prevent "Bonaparte" from escaping, and if so fortunate as to obtain possession of his person, to sail at once with him for England. Savary and Las Casas, who conducted the negotiations, were unable to exact a definite promise from the captain, when they visited him on the 10th of July, or to learn from him if it was the intention of the British Government to throw any impediment in the way of his voyage to the United States. In the course of the conversation, Captain Maitland, according to his own statement, threw out the suggestion, "Why not seek an asylum in England?" to which various objections were urged by Savary, and thus the interview terminated.

The succeeding days were passed by Napoleon in discussing various plans devised for his escape, but they were all abandoned by him. He saw no possible chance of success, for, as he himself said: "Wherever wood can float, there is the flag of England. I will throw myself into her hands—a helpless foe." Then, too, Napoleon was weary of strife, and had the feelings of one who had done with action, and whose part it was to endure. He at last rejected all such proposals, and once more dispatched Las Casas, accompanied by Lallemand, to Capt. Maitland, on the 14th of July, with instructions to inquire again whether the intentions of the British Government were yet declared as to a passage to America, or if permission for Napoleon to pass in a neutral vessel could be obtained. The answer was in the negative; but Capt. Maitland again suggested his embarkation on board the *Bellerophon*, in which case he should be conveyed to England. The words of Captain Maitland, quoted by himself to Lord Keith were:

> If he chooses to come on board the ship I command, I think, under the orders I am acting with, I may venture to receive him, and carry him to England.

Upon this a negotiation took place, which terminated in Las Casas saying; "Under all circumstances, I have little doubt that you will see the emperor on board the *Bellerophon*."

Las Casas returned to the Isle of Aix after his interview with Captain Maitland on the 14th. The result of his mission appeared to be "that Captain Maitland had authorized him to tell the emperor if he decided upon going to England, he was authorized to receive him on board; and he accordingly placed his ship at his disposal." Napoleon then finally made up his mind to place himself on board the British vessel. On the same day Gourgaud delivered to Captain Maitland the following letter addressed to the Prince Regent of England:

> Royal Highness:—Exposed to the factions which divide my country, and to the hostility of the greatest powers of Europe, I have closed my political career. I come, like Themistocles to seek the hospitality of the English nation. I place myself under the protection of their laws, which I claim from your Royal Highness as the most powerful, and most constant, and the most generous of my enemies.
>
> Rochefort, July the 13th, 1815.
>
> Napoleon.

The letter was received by the royal commander and sent to England, but no answer was returned.

On the 15th Napoleon and his friends decided to board the *Bellerophon* and were transported thither by a barge sent by Captain Maitland. The parting scenes with those left behind were most affecting. The English commander received his charge in a respectful manner, but without salute or distinguished honours; Napoleon uncovered himself, on reaching the quarter-deck, and said in a firm tone of voice, "I come to place myself under the protection of your prince and laws!"

The captain then led him into the cabin, which was given up to his use, and afterwards, by his own request, presented all the officers to him. He visited every part of the ship during the morning, conversing with much freedom with those on board, about naval and other affairs. About noon the ship got under weigh and made sail for England.

On the 23rd of June the *Bellerophon* passed Ushant, and for the last time Napoleon gazed long and mournfully on his beloved country, but said nothing. At daybreak on the 24th they were close to Dartmouth, and when the ship was at anchor the captain was instantly admonished by the Lords of the Admiralty to permit no communication of any kind between his ship and the coast. On the 26th the commander was ordered to Plymouth Sound, where he was the object of great curiosity on the part of thousands of people who swarmed about the vessel in small boats, eager to behold the man who had had the attention of the world for so many years. Napoleon appeared on deck and was greeted with loud cheers, to which he bowed and smiled in return, and remarked to Captain Maitland: "The English appear to have a very large portion of curiosity." On one occasion the captain counted upwards of a thousand boats within view, each containing on an average eight people.

On the 31st of July Napoleon was visited by Sir Henry Bunbury, under-Secretary of State, and Lord Keith admiral of the channel fleet, who came on board and announced the final decision of the British Government respecting him, and which was that "General Bonaparte," their prisoner, should not be landed on the shores of England, but removed forthwith to St. Helena, as being the situation which, more than any other at their command, the government thought safe against a second escape, and the indulgence to himself of personal freedom and exercise, and which might be reconciled with the "indispensable precautions which it would be necessary to employ for the security of his person." Secondly, with the exception of Savary and Lallemand, he was to be permitted to take with him any three officers he chose, besides one surgeon and twelve domestics, none of whom were to be allowed, however, to quit the island without the sanction of the British Government.

Napoleon, on listening to the decree which sealed his fate for life, made no comment whatever until the reading of the decision had ended. He then solemnly protested against their cruel and arbitrary act. He protested, not only against the order, but against the right claimed by the English Government to dispose of him as a prisoner of war:

> I came into your ship as I would into one of your villages. If I had been told I was to be a prisoner I would not have come. I asked him if he was willing to receive me on board, and convey me to England. Captain Maitland said he was, having received, or telling me he had received, special orders of government concerning me. It was a snare then, that had been spread for me. As for the Island of St. Helena, it would be my sentence of death. I demand to be received as an English citizen.

He objected strenuously to the title given him, declared his right to be considered as a sovereign prince, that his father-in-law, or the *Czar*, would have treated him far differently, and concluded by expressing his belief that "if your government act thus, it will disgrace you in the eyes of Europe." "Even your own people will blame it," he added.

His protests were in vain, however, and at length, the interview having terminated, he was informed that Admiral Sir George Cockburn was ready to receive him on board the *Northumberland* to convey him to St. Helena. Napoleon then declared with animation:

> No, no, I will not go there; I am not a Hercules; but you shall not conduct me to St. Helena. I prefer death in this place. You found me free—send me back again; replace me in the condition in which I was, or permit me to go to America.

Still his protests were ignored and preparations were at last begun for departure. In a private conversation with Captain Maitland, Napoleon reverted to the painful subject in the following terms:

> The idea is a perfect horror to me. To be placed for life on an island within the tropics, at an immense distance from any land, cut off from all communication with the world, and everything I hold dear to it! It is worse than Tamerlane's iron cage. I would prefer being given up to the Bourbons.

Napoleon's suite, as finally arranged, consisted of Counts Bertrand, Montholon and Las Casas, General Gourgaud, and Dr. O'Meara, an Irish naval surgeon. Bertrand and Montholon were accompanied by their ladies and children, and twelve upper domestics of the late imperial household, who desired to share in the fortunes of their master. The money, diamonds and saleable effects Napoleon had with him he was deprived of. When the search of his belongings was in progress, Bertrand was invited to attend, but he was so indignant at the measure that he positively refused. Four thousand gold *napoleons* ($16,000) were taken from him; the rest of the money, amounting to about one thousand five hundred *napoleons*, were returned to enable the exile to pay such of is servants as were about to leave him.

The *Northumberland* sailed for St. Helena on the 8th of August. After a voyage of about seventy days, without unusual incident, on the 15th of October, 1815, Napoleon had his first view of his destined retreat. He was then forty-six years of age, enjoyed fairly good health, and but for the repeated denials of many necessary comforts to which he was now to be subjected might, in a measure, have enjoyed the remaining years of his life. Here he found himself immured for life in a small volcanic island, in the southern Atlantic, measuring ten miles in length and seven in breadth, at a distance of two thousand leagues from the scenes of his immortal exploits in arms, and separated from the two great continents of Africa and America by the unfathomable ocean.

The admiral landed about noon with a view of finding a fitting abode for Napoleon and his suite, returning in the evening. On the 16th the imperial prisoner landed, and as he left the Northumberland the officers all assembled on the quarter-deck with nearly the whole of the crew stationed in the gangways. Before he stepped into the small boat to be taken ashore he took leave of the captain and desired him to convey his thanks to his officers and men. He then made off for the shore to take up his residence at "the Briars,"[1] a small cottage about half a mile from Jamestown, during the interval which must elapse before other quarters could be provided for him. On the 10th of December he took possession of his newly appointed abode at Longwood, a villa about six miles distant from Jamestown.

At this latter place he died on the 5th of May 1821 at half past 5 o'clock in the evening, after an exile of nearly six years. His death was no doubt hastened by a succession of petty annoyances on the part of his "jailer," Sir Hudson Lowe, governor of the island, which began on his arrival, and were followed up during all the years of his exile, despite his repeated protestations. He had already lived much longer than he desired, and had completed all his preparations for death's coming, during his last year of bad health. In his final hours he was surrounded by Bertrand, Montholon and other devoted friends to whom he had given his final instructions.

Four days later, or on May 9th, with the cloak he had worn at

---

1. *Recollections of Napoleon at St. Helena, The Remarkable Story of a Fallen Emperor and a Teenage Girl* by Mrs. Abell (late Miss Elizabeth Balcombe) also published by Leonaur.

Marengo thrown over his feet, and clothed in the uniform of the Chasseurs of his Guard, he was buried with military honours, surrounded by the sorrowing friends who had shared his long confinement. The only inscription permitted on the tablet over his body was "General Bonaparte."

Nineteen years later, at the request of the French Government, England honoured a request for his ashes, and his body was disinterred and conveyed to France to rest once more "on the banks of the Seine, among the French people whom he had loved so well." On December 15th 1840, in the midst of the most imposing and magnificent ceremonies Paris had ever witnessed, the body of the emperor was borne to the Invalides where it lay for many days publicly exposed. On the 6th of February 1841 the coffin was taken from the imperial cenotaph and placed in the chapel of St. Jerome, in the church of the Invalides where it was to remain till the completion of the mausoleum some years later. Beneath the golden dome which crowns the Invalides, and towards which the faces of all visitors to Paris are most frequently turned, there still rests all that is mortal of this most wonderful warrior and statesman. His magic name continues to defy even time itself, and as the years roll on each generation inquires of its predecessors what they knew of this man who was so great that his name fills more pages in the world's solemn history than that of any other mortal.

ALSO FROM LEONAUR
AVAILABLE IN SOFTCOVER OR HARDCOVER WITH DUST JACKET

THE ART OF WAR by *Antoine Henri Jomini*—Strategy & Tactics From the Age of Horse & Musket

THE MILITARY RELIGIOUS ORDERS OF THE MIDDLE AGES by *F. C. Woodhouse*—The Knights Templar, Hospitaller and Others.

THE BENGAL NATIVE ARMY by *F. G. Cardew*—An Invaluable Reference Resource.

THE 7TH (QUEEN'S OWN) HUSSARS: Volume 4—1688-1914 by *C. R. B. Barrett*—Uniforms, Equipment, Weapons, Traditions, the Services of Notable Officers and Men & the Appendices to All Volumes—Volume 4: 1688-1914.

THE SWORD OF THE CROWN by *Eric W. Sheppard*—A History of the British Army to 1914.

THE 7TH (QUEEN'S OWN) HUSSARS: Volume 3—1818-1914 by *C. R. B. Barrett*—On Campaign During the Canadian Rebellion, the Indian Mutiny, the Sudan, Matabeleland, Mashonaland and the Boer War Volume 3: 1818-1914.

THE CAMPAIGN OF WATERLOO by *Antoine Henri Jomini*—A Political & Military History from the French perspective.

THE AUXILIA OF THE ROMAN IMPERIAL ARMY by *G. L. Cheeseman*.

CAVALRY IN THE FRANCO-PRUSSIAN WAR by *Jean Jacques Théophile Bonie & Otto August Johannes Kaehler*—Actions of French Cavalry 1870 by Jean Jacques Théophile Bonie and Cavalry at Vionville & Mars-la-Tour by Otto August Johannes Kaehler.

NAPOLEON'S MEN AND METHODS by *Alexander L. Kielland*—The Rise and Fall of the Emperor and His Men Who Fought by His Side.

THE WOMAN IN BATTLE by *Loreta Janeta Velazquez*—Soldier, Spy and Secret Service Agent for the Confederacy During the American Civil War.

THE MILITARY SYSTEM OF THE ROMANS by *Albert Harkness*.

THE BATTLE OF ORISKANY 1777 by *Ellis H. Roberts*—The Conflict for the Mowhawk Valley During the American War of Independenc.

PERSONAL RECOLLECTIONS OF JOAN OF ARC by *Mark Twain*.

AVAILABLE ONLINE AT **www.leonaur.com**
AND FROM ALL GOOD BOOK STORES

www.ingramcontent.com/pod-product-compliance
Lightning Source LLC
Chambersburg PA
CBHW021957160426
43197CB00007B/167